First World War
and Army of Occupation
War Diary
France, Belgium and Germany

59 DIVISION
Headquarters, Branches and Services
Commander Royal Engineers
9 January 1916 - 16 July 1919

WO95/3015/2

The Naval & Military Press Ltd
www.nmarchive.com
Published in association with The National Archives

Published by

The Naval & Military Press Ltd

Unit 10 Ridgewood Industrial Park,

Uckfield, East Sussex,

TN22 5QE England

Tel: +44 (0) 1825 749494

www.naval-military-press.com

www.nmarchive.com

This diary has been reprinted in facsimile from the original. Any imperfections are inevitably reproduced and the quality may fall short of modern type and cartographic standards.

© **Crown Copyright**
Images reproduced by permission of The National Archives, London, England, 2015.

Contents

Document type	Place/Title	Date From	Date To
Heading	WO 3015 59th Div Commander Royal Engineers 1916 Jan-1916 Feb 1917 Mar-1919 July		
Heading	59th Division C.R.A. Mar 1917-July 1919 1916 Jan-Feb		
Heading	59th (North Midland) Divisional RE (Head Quarters) From-1st January 1916 To:- 31st January 1916 (Volume 1)		
War Diary	Radlett	09/01/1916	29/01/1916
Heading	Head Quarters Of The 59th N.M Divisional R.E. From February 1st 1916 To February 29th 1916 (Volume 1)		
War Diary	Radlett	02/02/1916	29/02/1916
Heading	59th Divisional Royal Engineers From March 1st 1917 To March 31st 1917 Volume (2)		
War Diary	Mericourt	01/03/1917	01/03/1917
War Diary	St Martins Camp Foucaucourt	02/03/1917	07/03/1917
War Diary	P.C.Gabrielle	09/03/1917	28/03/1917
War Diary	Mons-En-Chaussee	30/03/1917	30/03/1917
War Diary	Larkhill	19/02/1917	19/02/1917
War Diary	Southampton	20/02/1917	21/02/1917
War Diary	Le Havre	23/02/1917	23/02/1917
War Diary	Longueau	24/02/1917	24/02/1917
War Diary	Glisy	24/02/1917	24/02/1917
War Diary	Hamel	25/02/1917	25/02/1917
War Diary	Morcourt	26/02/1917	28/02/1917
Heading	59th Divisional R.Engineers From 1st April 1917 To 30th April 1917 Volume III		
War Diary	Mons-En-Chaussee	01/04/1917	10/04/1917
War Diary	Bouvincourt	10/04/1917	30/04/1917
Heading	59th Div R.E. Vol IV May 1st 1917 To May 31st 1917 Vol 4		
War Diary	Bouvincourt	01/05/1917	27/05/1917
War Diary	Equancourt	28/05/1917	31/05/1917
Miscellaneous	Daily Work Report-May 13th.1917.	13/05/1917	13/05/1917
Miscellaneous	Water Supply 180th Co.R.E No.2 Section	14/05/1917	14/05/1917
Miscellaneous	Water Supply 180th Coy R.E No.2 Section		
Heading	59th Div. R.E. Volume V. 1st June 1917 To 30th June 1917 Vol 5		
War Diary	Equancourt	01/06/1917	30/06/1917
Miscellaneous	256th. Tunnelling Co. R.E. Daily Progress Work for 24 hours ending midnight 15.6.17. Appendix I	15/06/1917	15/06/1917
Miscellaneous	256th. Tunnelling Co. R.E. Daily Progress Work for 24 hours ending midnight 16th June 1917. Appendix II	16/06/1917	16/06/1917
Miscellaneous	256th. Tunnelling Co. R.E. Daily Progress Report for 24 hours ending midnight 18.6.17. Appendix III	18/06/1917	18/06/1917
Miscellaneous	256th. Tunnelling Co. R.E. Daily Progress Report for 24 hours ending midnight 19.6.17. Appendix IV	19/06/1917	19/06/1917
Miscellaneous	256th. Tunnelling Co. R.E. Daily Progress Work for 24 hours ending midnight 20.6.17. Appendix V	20/06/1917	20/06/1917
Miscellaneous	256th. Tunnelling Co. R.E. Daily Progress Report for 24 hours ending midnight 21.6.17. Appendix VI	21/06/1917	21/06/1917

Miscellaneous	256th. Tunnelling Co. R.E. Daily Progress Report for 24 hours ending midnight 22.6.17. Appendix VII	22/06/1917	22/06/1917
Miscellaneous	Daily Progress Report 256th. Tunnelling Coy. R.E. 24 hrs. ending midnight 23.6.17. Appendix VIII	23/06/1917	23/06/1917
Miscellaneous	256th. Tunnelling Co. R.E. Daily Progress Report for 24 hours ending midnight 24.6.17. Appendix IX	24/06/1917	24/06/1917
Miscellaneous	256th. Tunnelling Co. R.E. Daily Progress Report for 24 hours ending midnight 25.6.17. Appendix X	25/06/1917	25/06/1917
Miscellaneous	256th. Tunnelling Co. R.E. Daily Progress Report for 24 hours ending midnight 26.6.17. Appendix XI	26/06/1917	26/06/1917
Miscellaneous	256th. Tunnelling Co. R.E. Daily Progress Report for 24 hours ending midnight 27.6.17. Appendix XII	27/06/1917	27/06/1917
Miscellaneous	256th. Tunnelling Co. R.E. Daily Progress Report for 24 hours ending midnight 28.6.17. Appendix XIII	28/06/1917	28/06/1917
Miscellaneous	256th. Tunnelling Co. R.E. Daily Progress Report for 24 hours ending midnight 29.6.17. Appendix XIV	29/06/1917	29/06/1917
Miscellaneous	256th. Tunnelling Co. R.E. Daily Progress Report for 24 hours ending midnight 30.6.17. Appendix XV	30/06/1917	30/06/1917
Heading	Head Quarters 59th Divisional Royal Engineers Vol VI 1st July 1917 To 31st July 1917		
War Diary	Equancourt	01/07/1917	09/07/1917
War Diary	Barastre	10/07/1917	31/07/1917
Miscellaneous	256th. Tunnelling Coy. R.E. Daily Progress Report for 24 hours ending midnight 1.7.17. Appendix I	01/07/1917	01/07/1917
Miscellaneous	256th. Tunnelling Co. R.E. Daily Progress Report for 24 hrs. ending midnight 2.7.17. Appendix II	02/07/1917	02/07/1917
Miscellaneous	256th. Tunnelling Co. R.E. Daily Progress Report for 24 hrs. ending midnight 3.7.17. Appendix III	03/07/1917	03/07/1917
Miscellaneous	256th. Tunnelling Co. R.E. Daily Progress Report for 24 hrs. ending midnight 4.7.17. Appendix IV	04/07/1917	04/07/1917
Miscellaneous	256th. Tunnelling Co. R.E. Daily Progress Report for 24 hrs. ending midnight 5.7.17. Appendix V.	05/07/1917	05/07/1917
Miscellaneous	256th. Tunnelling Co. R.E. Daily Progress Report for 24 hrs. ending midnight 6.7.17. Appendix VI.	06/07/1917	06/07/1917
Miscellaneous	256th. Tunnelling Co. R.E. Daily Progress Report for 24 hrs. ending midnight 7.7.17. Appendix VII.	07/07/1917	07/07/1917
Miscellaneous	256th. Tunnelling Co. R.E. Daily Progress Report for 24 hrs. ending midnight 8.7.17. Appendix VIII	08/07/1917	08/07/1917
Miscellaneous	256th. Tunnelling Co. R.E. Daily Progress Report for 24 hrs. ending midnight 9.7.17. Appendix IX.	09/07/1917	09/07/1917
Miscellaneous	467th Field Coy. R.E. (Training Programme For Fortnight Commencing)	09/07/1917	09/07/1917
Miscellaneous	467th Field Co.R.E (Training Programme))	23/07/1917	23/07/1917
Miscellaneous	469th Field Co.R.E.	14/07/1917	14/07/1917
Miscellaneous	469th Filed Co.R.E (Training Programme))	29/07/1917	29/07/1917
Miscellaneous	470th Field Co. R.E.	11/07/1917	11/07/1917
Miscellaneous	470th Field Co.R.E (Training Programme)	25/07/1917	25/07/1917
Heading	Head Quarters 59th Divisional R.E. Vol VII. 1st August 1917 To 31st August 1917 Vol 7		
War Diary	Barastre	01/08/1917	23/08/1917
War Diary	Acheux	24/08/1917	31/08/1917
Miscellaneous	Order By Lt. Col. G.B. Roberts R.E. C.R.E. 59th Division.	03/08/1917	03/08/1917
Miscellaneous	Order By Lieut. Colonel G.B. Roberts R.E. C.R.E 59th Division.	06/08/1917	06/08/1917

Miscellaneous	Order By Lieut Colonel G.B. Roberts R.E C.R.E 59th Division	06/08/1917	06/08/1917
Miscellaneous	Order By Lieut Colonel G.B. Roberts R.E C.R.E 59th Division	10/06/1917	10/06/1917
Miscellaneous	467 Field Coy. R.E. August 1st To August 7th.1917.	07/08/1917	07/08/1917
Miscellaneous	469th Field Co. R.E.	07/08/1917	07/08/1917
Miscellaneous	470th.Field Co. R.E.	08/08/1917	08/08/1917
Miscellaneous	467th Field Co. R.E.	08/08/1917	08/08/1917
Miscellaneous	469th Field Co. R.E.	08/08/1917	08/08/1917
Miscellaneous	470th Field Co. R.E.	09/08/1917	09/08/1917
Heading	Headquarters R.E 59th Division Vol.VIII 1st Sept 1917 To 30th Sep 1917		
War Diary	Winnezeele	05/09/1917	22/09/1917
War Diary	Ypres	22/09/1917	28/09/1917
War Diary	Ypres and Brandhoek	29/09/1917	30/09/1917
Miscellaneous	Minute 1. Appendix No.I.	03/09/1917	03/09/1917
Miscellaneous	C.R.E. 59th Division. Appendix II	13/09/1917	13/09/1917
Miscellaneous	O.C. 467th Field Co. R.E. Appendix III	19/09/1917	19/09/1917
Miscellaneous	O.C. 467th Field Co. R.E. Appendix IV.		
Miscellaneous	Orders By Lt. Col. G.B. Roberts., R.E. C.R.E. 59th. Division. Appendix No.5.	22/09/1917	22/09/1917
Miscellaneous	Orders By Lt. Col. G.B. Roberts., R.E. C.R.E. 59th. Division. Appendix 6.	22/09/1917	22/09/1917
Miscellaneous	Appendix VII	24/09/1917	24/09/1917
Miscellaneous	Operation Order No.1 By Lieut. Colonel. G.B. Roberts, R.E. C.R.E. 59th Division. Appendix VIII.	24/09/1917	24/09/1917
Miscellaneous	O.C. 9th Seaforths. Appendix IX.	25/09/1917	25/09/1917
Miscellaneous	O.C. 9th Seaforths. (Pioneers). Appendix X	26/09/1917	26/09/1917
Miscellaneous	O.C. 9th Seaforths. (Pioneers). Appendix XI.	27/09/1917	27/09/1917
Miscellaneous	O.C. 9th Seaforths Pioneers. Appendix XII.	28/09/1917	28/09/1917
Heading	Headquarters R.Engineers. 59th Division Vol. IX 1st October 1917 To 31st October 1917 Vol 9		
War Diary	Mersey Camp Vlamertinghe No 1 Area	01/10/1917	01/10/1917
War Diary	Watou	02/10/1917	02/10/1917
War Diary	Stafford Camp	03/10/1917	04/10/1917
War Diary	Steenbecque	05/10/1917	06/10/1917
War Diary	Bomy	07/10/1917	13/10/1917
War Diary	Chateau De La Haie	14/10/1917	16/10/1917
War Diary	Ytres	17/10/1917	22/10/1917
War Diary	Le Cauroy	23/10/1917	25/10/1917
War Diary	Chateau De La Haie	16/10/1917	31/10/1917
Miscellaneous	C.R.E. 59th Division. Appendix I.	01/10/1917	01/10/1917
Miscellaneous	II Anzac Corps. 59th Division (for information). Appendix II.	01/10/1917	01/10/1917
Miscellaneous	C.R.E. 59th Division. Appendix III.	03/10/1917	03/10/1917
Miscellaneous	C.R.E. 176th Inf. Bde. D.M.G.O. Appendix IV.	04/10/1917	04/10/1917
Miscellaneous	Orders No.4 by Lieut. Colonel. G.B. Roberts. C.R.E. 59th Division. Appendix No.5.	10/10/1917	10/10/1917
Miscellaneous	59th Division. G. Appendix No.6.	16/10/1917	16/10/1917
Miscellaneous	470th. Field Co. R.E. Appendix VII	16/10/1917	16/10/1917
Miscellaneous	469th Field Co.RE Progress Reports	17/10/1917	17/10/1917
Miscellaneous	467th Field Co.RE Progress Report	17/10/1917	17/10/1917
Miscellaneous	470th. Field Co. R.E. Appendix VIII	17/10/1917	17/10/1917
Miscellaneous	469 Field C.R.E Progress Report	18/10/1917	18/10/1917
Miscellaneous	467 Field company R6 Progress Report		
Miscellaneous	470th Field Co.RE Progress Report 181017	18/10/1917	18/10/1917

Miscellaneous	Daily Progress Report. Appendix IX.	18/10/1917	18/10/1917
Miscellaneous	469th Field Co R.E Progress report	18/10/1917	18/10/1917
Miscellaneous	Th. Field Co. R.E. Appendix X	19/10/1917	19/10/1917
Miscellaneous	Th. Field Co. R.E. Appendix XI	20/10/1917	20/10/1917
Miscellaneous	Th. Field Co. R.E. Appendix XII	21/10/1917	21/10/1917
Miscellaneous	Th. Field Co. R.E. Appendix XIII	22/10/1917	22/10/1917
Miscellaneous	Th. Field Co. R.E. Appendix XIV	23/10/1917	23/10/1917
Miscellaneous	Th. Field Co. R.E. Appendix XV.	24/10/1917	24/10/1917
Miscellaneous	467th. Field Co. R.E. Appendix XVI	25/10/1917	25/10/1917
Miscellaneous	467th. Field Co. R.E. Appendix XVII	26/10/1917	26/10/1917
Miscellaneous	467th. Field Co. R.E. Appendix XVIII	27/10/1917	27/10/1917
Miscellaneous	467th. Field Co. R.E. App XIX	28/10/1917	28/10/1917
Miscellaneous	467th. Field Co. R.E. Appendix XX	29/10/1917	29/10/1917
Miscellaneous	467th. Field Co. R.E. Appendix XXI	30/10/1917	30/10/1917
Miscellaneous	C.R.E. 59th Division Order No.3 by Lieut. Col. G.B. Roberts. R.E. Appendix XIV	30/09/1917	30/09/1917
Operation(al) Order(s)	C.R.E 59th Division Order No. 2	29/09/1917	29/09/1917
Miscellaneous	Orders By Lt Col. G.B. Roberts R.E. C.R.E. 59th Division. Appendix B	24/11/1917	24/11/1917
Miscellaneous	470th. Field Co. R.E. Appendix I	01/11/1917	01/11/1917
Miscellaneous	467th. Field Co. R.E. Appendix II.	02/11/1917	02/11/1917
Miscellaneous	467th. Field Co. R.E. Appendix III.	03/11/1917	03/11/1917
Miscellaneous	467th. Field Co. R.E. Appendix IV.	05/11/1917	05/11/1917
Miscellaneous	469th. Field Co. R.E. Appendix IV.	05/11/1917	05/11/1917
Miscellaneous	467th. Field Co. R.E. Appendix IV.	05/11/1917	05/11/1917
Miscellaneous	467th. Field Co. R.E. Appendix V.	06/11/1917	06/11/1917
Miscellaneous	469th. Field Co. R.E. Appendix V.	06/11/1917	06/11/1917
Miscellaneous	467th. Field Co. R.E. Appendix V.	06/11/1917	06/11/1917
Miscellaneous	467th. Field Co. R.E. Appendix VI.	06/11/1917	06/11/1917
Miscellaneous	470th. Field Co. R.E. Appendix VII.	08/11/1917	08/11/1917
Miscellaneous	469th. Field Co. R.E. Appendix VII.	08/11/1917	08/11/1917
Miscellaneous	467th. Field Co. R.E. Appendix VII.	08/11/1917	08/11/1917
Miscellaneous	467th. Field Co. R.E. Appendix VIII	09/11/1917	09/11/1917
Miscellaneous	469th. Field Co. R.E. Appendix VIII.	09/11/1917	09/11/1917
Miscellaneous	467th. Field Co. R.E. Appendix VIII	09/11/1917	09/11/1917
Miscellaneous	467th. Field Co. R.E. Appendix IX.	10/11/1917	10/11/1917
Miscellaneous	469th. Field Co. R.E. Appendix IX.	10/11/1917	10/11/1917
Miscellaneous	467th. Field Co. R.E. Appendix IX.	10/11/1917	10/11/1917
Miscellaneous	470th. Field Co. R.E. Appendix X.	11/11/1917	11/11/1917
Miscellaneous	469th. Field Co. R.E. Appendix X.	11/11/1917	11/11/1917
Miscellaneous	467th. Field Co. R.E. Appendix X.	11/11/1917	11/11/1917
Operation(al) Order(s)	59th Divisional R.E Order No. 4	12/11/1917	12/11/1917
Miscellaneous	59th Divisional R.E. Movement Table		
Miscellaneous	467th. Field Co. R.E. Appendix XI	11/11/1917	11/11/1917
Miscellaneous	467th. Field Co. R.E. Appendix XII	12/11/1917	12/11/1917
Miscellaneous	467th. Field Co. R.E. Appendix XIII	13/11/1917	13/11/1917
Miscellaneous	467th. Field Co. R.E. Appendix XIV	14/11/1917	14/11/1917
Miscellaneous	467th. Field Co. R.E. Appendix XV	15/11/1917	15/11/1917
Heading	Headquarters R.Engineers 59th Division Volume X From 1st Nov 1917 To 30th Nov 1917 Vol 10		
War Diary	Chateau De La Haie	01/11/1917	17/11/1917
War Diary	Hermaville	17/11/1917	19/11/1917
War Diary	Basseux	21/11/1917	21/11/1917
Heading	Headquarters R.Engineers 59th Division Volume XI From 1st Dec 1917 To 31st Dec 1917 Vol 11		
War Diary	Trescault	01/12/1917	05/12/1917

War Diary	Little Wood	05/12/1917	16/12/1917
War Diary	Ytres	16/12/1917	16/12/1917
War Diary	Le Cauroy	26/12/1917	31/12/1917
War Diary	Addendum Ytres	21/12/1917	21/12/1917
Miscellaneous	Order By Lieut. Col. G.B. Roberts, R.E. C.R.E. 59th. Div. (Appendix 1)	08/12/1917	08/12/1917
Miscellaneous	Orders by Lieut. Col. G.B. Roberts. R.E. C.R.E. 59th Div. Appendix II	08/12/1917	08/12/1917
Miscellaneous	Daily Progress Report. Appendix III	12/12/1917	12/12/1917
Miscellaneous	Daily Progress Report. Appendix IV	13/12/1917	13/12/1917
Miscellaneous	Daily Progress Report. Appendix V	14/12/1917	14/12/1917
Miscellaneous	Daily Progress Report. Appendix VI	15/12/1917	15/12/1917
Miscellaneous	Daily Progress Report. Appendix VII	16/12/1917	16/12/1917
Miscellaneous	Daily Progress Report. Appendix VIII	17/12/1917	17/12/1917
Miscellaneous	Daily Progress Report. Appendix IX	18/12/1917	18/12/1917
Miscellaneous	Daily Progress Report. Appendix X	19/12/1917	19/12/1917
Miscellaneous	Daily Progress Report. Appendix XI	20/12/1917	20/12/1917
Miscellaneous	Special Orders By Lieut. Colonel.G.B. Roberts.R.E.C.R.E.59th Division	20/12/1917	20/12/1917
Miscellaneous	Daily Progress Report. Appendix XIII	21/12/1917	21/12/1917
Miscellaneous	470th Field Co. R.E. Appendix XIV	22/12/1917	22/12/1917
War Diary	Achiet-Le-Petit	22/11/1917	22/11/1917
War Diary	Etricourt	23/11/1917	28/11/1917
War Diary	Trescault	29/11/1917	30/11/1917
Heading	Headquarters R.Engineers 59th Division Volume XI From 1st Jan 1918 To 31st Jan 1918		
War Diary	Le Cauroy Billet	01/01/1918	31/01/1918
Miscellaneous	467th Field Coy. R.E. Programme of Work. Appendix I.	06/01/1918	06/01/1918
Miscellaneous	470th Field Co. R.E Programme Of Training	31/12/1917	31/12/1917
Miscellaneous	467th Field Co.RE CRE 59th Division	15/01/1918	15/01/1918
Miscellaneous	470th Field Co. R.E. Appendix II	27/01/1918	27/01/1918
Miscellaneous	470th Field Co. R.E. Appendix III	30/01/1918	30/01/1918
Miscellaneous	C.R.E. 59th Division. Appendix IV	27/01/1918	27/01/1918
War Diary	Le Cauroy	01/02/1918	10/02/1918
War Diary	Gomiecourt	10/02/1918	12/02/1918
War Diary	Behagnies	13/02/1918	28/02/1918
Miscellaneous	O.C. 467th. Field. Co. R.E. Appendix I	03/02/1918	03/02/1918
Miscellaneous	Herewith Progress Report of work carried out on this Divisional Front. Appendix II	19/02/1918	19/02/1918
Miscellaneous	Schedule Of Work		
Miscellaneous	Progress Report of work carried out on this Divisional Front herewith. Appendix III	26/02/1918	26/02/1918
Miscellaneous	Chief Engineer VI Corps Hd. Qtrs G.59th Division Schedule Of Work		
Operation(al) Order(s)	Operation Order 74-2 by Lieut. Col. O.C. Reward M.C. C.R.E. 59th Division	27/02/1918	27/02/1918
Heading	War Diary Of Headquarters R.E. 59th Division Volume XIII From 1st July 1918 To 28th July 1918 Vol 13		
Heading	59th Divisional Engineers C.R.E. 59th Division March 1918		
Heading	War Diary Of Head Quarters R.Engineers 59th Division Volume XIV 1st March 1918 To 31st March 1918 Vol 14		
War Diary	Behagnies	01/03/1918	22/03/1918
War Diary	Bucquoy	22/03/1918	23/03/1918

Type	Description	Start	End
War Diary	Bouzincourt	25/03/1918	25/03/1918
War Diary	Comtay Fienvillers	26/03/1918	26/03/1918
War Diary	Villers Chatel Area	28/03/1918	30/03/1918
War Diary	Lillers Area	31/03/1918	31/03/1918
Miscellaneous	Chief Engineer, VI. Corps. Appendix I	05/03/1918	05/03/1918
Miscellaneous	Schedule of Work	05/03/1918	05/03/1918
Operation(al) Order(s)	Operation Orders No.3. by C.R.E. 59th Division	09/03/1918	09/03/1918
Miscellaneous	Chief Engineer, VI. Corps. Appendix III	12/03/1918	12/03/1918
Miscellaneous	Schedule Of Work	12/03/1918	12/03/1918
Operation(al) Order(s)	Operation Order No. 4. by C.R.E. 59th Division	17/03/1918	17/03/1918
Miscellaneous	Chief Engineer, VI. Corps. Appendix V	19/03/1918	19/03/1918
Miscellaneous	Schedule Of Work	19/03/1918	19/03/1918
Miscellaneous	Headquarter G. 59th Division. Appendix VI	04/04/1918	04/04/1918
Operation(al) Order(s)	Operation Order No. 5. by C.R.E. 59th Division	27/03/1918	27/03/1918
Operation(al) Order(s)	Operation Order No. 9. by C.R.E. 59th Division	30/03/1918	30/03/1918
Heading	59th Divisional Engineers C.R.E 59th Division April 1918.		
War Diary	Couthove Chateau	01/04/1918	04/04/1918
War Diary	Ypres	05/04/1918	13/04/1918
War Diary	Abeele Westoutre	14/04/1918	14/04/1918
War Diary	Westoutre	15/04/1918	17/04/1918
War Diary	Boeschepe	17/04/1918	19/04/1918
War Diary	Couthove Chateau	19/04/1918	21/04/1918
War Diary	Convent F22 D Sheet 27	21/04/1918	23/04/1918
War Diary	Bombecque	24/04/1918	27/04/1918
War Diary	Convent F22d Sheet 27	28/04/1918	30/04/1918
Operation(al) Order(s)	Operation Order No. 10 by C.R.E. 59th Division	03/04/1918	03/04/1918
Operation(al) Order(s)	Order No. 11. by C.R.E. 59th Division	20/04/1918	20/04/1918
Miscellaneous	Order By C.R.E 59th Division.	27/04/1918	27/04/1918
Heading	War Diary Of Head Qrs R.E 59th Division Vol XVI From 1st May To 31st May 1918 Vol 16		
War Diary	Convent F22 d	01/05/1918	03/05/1918
War Diary	Vogelje Camp F22d.58	04/05/1918	05/05/1918
War Diary	Shrine Camp Houtkerque	06/05/1918	06/05/1918
War Diary	St. Omer	07/05/1918	09/05/1918
War Diary	Hestrus	10/05/1918	15/05/1918
War Diary	Therouanne	17/05/1918	28/05/1918
Miscellaneous	Work on 'B.B' Line. Appendix II	11/05/1918	11/05/1918
Operation(al) Order(s)	Order No. 13. by C.R.E. 59th Division	05/05/1918	05/05/1918
Heading	War Diary Of Head Quarters R.E 59th Division Vol XVII From 1st June To 30th June 1918 Vol 17		
War Diary	Therouanne	01/06/1918	24/06/1918
War Diary	Bomy	24/06/1918	30/06/1918
Heading	War Diary Of Head Quarters R. Engineers 59th Division Vol XVIII 1st July 1918 To 31st July 1918 Vol 18		
War Diary	Bomy	01/07/1918	07/07/1918
War Diary	Monchy Cayeux	11/07/1918	24/07/1918
War Diary	Grosville	26/07/1918	31/07/1918
Operation(al) Order(s)	Order No 20 by Lieut Colonel L.J. Coussmaker M.C. R.E. C.R.E. 59th Division	07/07/1918	07/07/1918
Heading	War Diary Of Headquarters R Engineers 59th Division Vol XVII 1st August 1918 To 31st August 1918 Vol 19		
War Diary	Grosville	01/08/1918	23/08/1918
War Diary	Bavincourt	23/08/1918	24/08/1918
War Diary	Norrent Fontes	24/08/1918	24/08/1918

War Diary	Busnes P 26 C.15.00	27/08/1918	29/08/1918
War Diary	Busnes	29/08/1918	31/08/1918
Miscellaneous	Headquarter G. 59th Division. Appendix I	26/08/1918	26/08/1918
Miscellaneous	O.C. 467th Field Co.R.E. Appendix II	30/08/1918	30/08/1918
Miscellaneous	Notice Board O.C 467th Field Co.R.E	31/08/1918	31/08/1918
Heading	Hd Qtrs R.E 59th Div Vol XVIII 1st September 1918 To 30th September 1918 Vol 20		
War Diary	Busnes	01/09/1918	06/09/1918
War Diary	R13d45.70	07/09/1918	17/09/1918
War Diary	R 14 C2.9	17/09/1918	25/09/1918
Miscellaneous	Reference 59th Division Operation Policy No.4 Appendix I	29/09/1918	29/09/1918
Heading	Headquarters R.E 59th Divn Volume XXI 1st To 31st October 1918 Vol 21		
War Diary	R14c2.9 Sheet 36 A	01/10/1919	03/10/1919
War Diary	Rill Works	03/10/1919	04/10/1919
War Diary	La Gorgue	04/10/1918	04/10/1918
War Diary	G24d30.25	15/10/1918	15/10/1918
War Diary	Lavesee	16/10/1918	17/10/1918
War Diary	St. Andre	18/10/1918	18/10/1918
War Diary	Hem	19/10/1918	30/10/1918
War Diary	Sailly-Lez-Lannoy	31/10/1918	31/10/1918
Operation(al) Order(s)	59th Division Order No. 170.	02/10/1918	02/10/1918
Miscellaneous	C.R.E. Orders for Advance of 59th Division. Appendix II	14/10/1918	14/10/1918
Miscellaneous	Orders for Bridging the Escaut River. Appendix III		
Heading	Headquarters R.E 59th Division Vol XXII 1st Nov 1918 To 30th Nov 1918 Vol 22		
War Diary	Sailly-Lez Lannoy	01/11/1918	08/11/1918
War Diary	Ramegnies Chin	09/11/1918	15/11/1918
War Diary	Wattignies	16/11/1918	30/11/1918
Miscellaneous	O.C. 467th Field Co. R.E. Appendix I	06/11/1918	06/11/1918
Heading	HQ War Diary Of 59th Division R.E For Month Of December 1918 Vol 23		
War Diary	Wattignies	01/12/1918	06/12/1918
War Diary	Verquin	06/12/1918	31/12/1918
Heading	War Diary Of Headquarters 59th Division R.E To For January, 1919 Vol 24		
War Diary	Verquin K.5.a.6.8	01/01/1919	27/01/1919
War Diary	Vaudricourt K.4.b.2.6	28/01/1919	31/01/1919
War Diary	Vaudricourt (k.4.b)	01/02/1919	06/03/1919
War Diary	Beaumarais 1.e.9.3	07/03/1919	13/06/1919
War Diary	Dunkirk G.6.b.5.7.	14/06/1919	16/07/1919

WO
3015
59th Div
Commander Royal
Engineers
1916 Jan – 1916 Feb
1917 Mar – 1919 July

59TH DIVISION

C. R. E.
MAR 1917 - ~~DEC 1918~~
JULY, 1919

(1916 JAN & FEB)

Confidential

War Diary

of

59th (North Midland) Divisional R.E. (Head Quarters.)

From:- 1st January 1916.   To:- 31st January 1916.

(Volume)

(61)

Army Form C. 2118.

WAR DIARY
or
INTELLIGENCE SUMMARY.
(Erase heading not required.)

Instructions regarding War Diaries and Intelligence Summaries are contained in F. S. Regs., Part II and the Staff Manual respectively. Title pages will be prepared in manuscript.

Place	Date	Hour	Summary of Events and Information	Remarks and references to Appendices
RADLETT	9.1.16		Instructional parties sent to each of the three Infantry Brigades	Appx
"	12.1.16		Operation maps received for the 1/3rd N.M. Field Coy and checked	Appx
"	19.1.16		Scout duty party under Lt E.S.C. CHIVERS proceeded on duty	Appx
	25.1.16		Special duty party of 33 men under 2 Lieut H. TAYLOR proceeded to MARKYATE	Appx
	29.1.16		Instructional party on duty with the 178 Brigade returned	Appx

K. Moulton hoo
Lt and Adj.
31/1/16

Confidential.

War Diary

of

Head Quarters of the 59th N.M. Divisional R.E.

From February 1st 1916 to February 29th 1916.

(Volume 1)

WAR DIARY
or
INTELLIGENCE SUMMARY.

HEAD QUARTERS 59TH N.M. Div. Army Form C. 2118.
R.E.

(Erase heading not required.)

Hour, Date, Place		Summary of Events and Information	Remarks and references to Appendices
2.2.16	RADLETT	Ainsworth Route March and inspection by Lt. Gen. A.E. Codrington GOC 3rd Army	Khm
3.2.16	"	Front Billy party under Lt. E.S.C. Chivers returned	Khm
7.2.16	"	Individual party under 1st Lt. G.L. Bronsden proceed to Watford (178th Brigade)	Khm
10.2.16	"	Inspection of R.E. work on 1st Engineering field by Col. Grant CE 3rd Army	Khm
15.2.16	"	First Supervisors check of record office rolls	Khm
17.2.16	"	2nd " " " " " " by independent officer	Khm
18.2.16	"	Inspection of R.E. took by Major Gen A.E. Sandbach GOC Division	Khm
19.2.16	"	Each company received 50 rifles on loan from the 3 Infantry Brigade	Khm
23.2.16	"	W.E. Part VIII now applicable to the Division D.O. 332	Khm
27.2.16	"	1/3 NM Field Coy proceeded to Brightlingsea for a pontooning and bridging course	Khm
29.2.16	"	2nd practice of emergency scheme (Table B) put into operation	Khm

R. Keith Moss Surveyor
Lieut. & Adj.
for CRE 59 NM.

Confidential

Vol II

War Diary
of
59th Divisional Royal Engineers

From March 1st 1917 to March 31st 1917.

Volume (2).

Army Form C. 2118.

WAR DIARY
or
INTELLIGENCE SUMMARY.
(Erase heading not required.)

HEAD QUARTERS.
59 DIVISIONAL
ROYAL ENGINEERS.

Instructions regarding War Diaries and Intelligence Summaries are contained in F. S. Regs., Part II. and the Staff Manual respectively. Title pages will be prepared in manuscript.

Place	Date	Hour	Summary of Events and Information	Remarks and references to Appendices
MERICOURT.	1.3.17	9 am	O.R.E. and Adjutant proceeded to O/C R.E. 50th Divn with a view to taking over from O/C R.E. 50th Divn	C.R.E.
-"-	"	7.30 pm	Divisional Order No. 1 received, including orders for the relief of Field Coys R.E. of the 50th Divn by Field Coys R.E. of the 59th Divn	khin
ST MARTINS CAMP FOUCAUCOURT	2.3.17	11.15 am	O.R.E. moved his Old Office to St Martins Camp, Foucaucourt	khin
-"-	7.3.17		Adjutant takes over Divl. R.E. Park from 50th Divl. R.E.	khin
H.C. GRABRIELLE	9.3.17	9 am	O.R.E. takes over from O/C R.E. 50th Divn and moves his Old Office to H.C. Gabrielle	khin
-"-	10.3.17		399 frs worth of R.E. stores purchased.	khin
-"-	12.3.17		138 frs -"- -"- -"- -"-	khin
-"-	13.3.17	5 pm	Divisional Order No. 3 received.	khin
-"-	16.3.17		C.R.E. attends Conference at III Corps O/C R.E.	khin
-"-	-"-		Divisional Order No. 4 with Amendment, received.	khin
-"-	17.3.17	7.20 pm	Divisional Order No. 5 received.	khin
-"-	-"-		Sappers from Field Coys ordered to accompany Infantry Patrols (moving forward) in order to assist in discovery of hidden mines etc.	khin

Army Form C. 2118.

WAR DIARY
INTELLIGENCE SUMMARY.
(Erase heading not required.)

Instructions regarding War Diaries and Intelligence Summaries are contained in F.S. Regs., Part II. and the Staff Manual respectively. Title pages will be prepared in manuscript.

Place	Date	Hour	Summary of Events and Information	Remarks and references to Appendices
P.C. GABRIELLE	17.3.17		2 Sections of 469th Fd. Co. R.E. ordered to assist 176th Bde. with support of bridges BERRY-FRESNES-MAFANCOURT.	
			2 " " 467th Fd. Co. R.E. " " " " " 177th Bde. " " " " ESTREES-VILLERS-CARBONNEL	
			10 Rb. with remaining R.E. responsible for other road work from N.27.c.7.5. & N.28.a.2.5. thence to HORGNY.	
	18.3.17		10 Rb. ordered to construct foot bridges across R. Somme opposite BERRY-ESTREES & main AMIEN road as far as N.27.a.7.5. St CHRIST and LIZANCOURT.	
	19.3.17		Aeroplane reconnoitre R. Somme near St CHRIST.	
	19.3.17 & 20.3.17		10 R.E. supervises Bridging Operations over R. Somme.	
	19.3.17		Devised Order to be received.	
			10 R.E. carries important stores to the field loco on water-supply work in forward area.	
	20.3.17		469th and 476th Studer loco R.E. ordered to move to St CHRIST 21st.	
			467th Studer Loco R.E. ordered to move to ESTREES 21st.	
	23.3.17		Ob., 469th Studer R.E. ordered to pursue active normal communication between St CHRIST and BRIE, and extend bridges from R. DORIGNON N. of St CHRIST.	

Army Form C. 2118.

WAR DIARY
or
INTELLIGENCE SUMMARY.

(Erase heading not required.)

Continued.

Place	Date	Hour	Summary of Events and Information	Remarks and references to Appendices
P.C. GABRIELLE	24.3.17		469 Field Coy. R.E. ordered to move to BRIE on 26th and to be employed on water supply at VILLERS-CARBONNEL, BRIE and ETERPIGNY and road repairs N. of the main Villers-Carbonnel - Rochies-en-Chaussee road.	Khan
			No. 479 L. Fd. Coy. R.E. to be employed on water supply at FRESNES and MISERY and for road repairs S. of Villers-Carbonnel – Rochies-en-Chaussee Road and to make arrangements for watering horses at Villers-Carbonnel and Marcy.	Khan
"	25.3.17	8pm	Divisional Order No 7 received.	Khan
"	26.3.17	9pm	Divisional Order No 8 received.	Khan
"	27.3.17	8pm	Divisional Order No 9 received. 606 R.E. to attack & restore N.B.15 head side in front line.	Khan
"	28.3.17		606 R.E. moved his Adv. Hq. to MONS-EN-CHAUSSEE.	Khan
MONS-EN-CHAUSSEE	30.3.17		Divl Orders No 10 and 11 received	Khan

M Griffith how Cpt and Adjutant
for C.R.E. 59 Division

Army Form C. 2118.

WAR DIARY OF HEAD QUARTERS 59 DIVISIONAL

INTELLIGENCE SUMMARY

(Erase heading not required.)

Feb. 1917

Instructions regarding War Diaries and Intelligence Summaries are contained in F. S. Regs., Part II. and the Staff Manual respectively. Title Pages will be prepared in manuscript.

Place	Date	Hour	Summary of Events and Information	Remarks and references to Appendices
LARKHILL	19.2.17	9.25	Left AMESBURY Station for SOUTHAMPTON arriving there at 11-20 am and proceeded to rest camp	Khm
SOUTHAMPTON	20.2.17		Remained in SOUTHAMPTON for day and night	Khm
"	21.2.17	3 pm	Embarked on the ARCHIMEDES and sailed at 4 p.m.	Khm
LE HAVRE	23.2.17	7 am	Disembarked at LE HAVRE at 7 am and proceeded to GARE des MARCHANDISES entraining at 9 am. R.S.M. TIDMAN was sent to Hospital with slight injury	Khm
"				Khm
LONGUEAU	24.2.17	Noon	Detrained at NOON Arrived and went into billets for night	Khm
GLISY	"	17.0	Arrived and went into billets for the night	Khm
HAMEL	25.2.17	15.0	Arrived and went into billets for the night	Khm
MORCOURT	26.2.17	12.0	Arrived and went into billets for the night	Khm
MERICOURT	27.2.17	11.0	Arrived and went into our temporary Head Quarters	Khm
"	28.2.17		CRE and ADJUTANT visited 467 and 469 FIELD Coys MAPS were distributed to OC 467, 469 and 470 FIELD Coys by Special messenger	Khm

W. Bradbury? Lieut
Capt & Adjt 59 Division
for CRE

2449 Wt. W14957/M90 750,000 1/16 J.B.C. & A. Forms/C.2118/12.

ORIGINAL.

Confidential

War Diary of
59th Divisional R. Engineers

From 1st April 1917 to 30th April 1917.

Volume III

ORIGINAL

Army Form C. 2118.

WAR DIARY OF HEAD QUARTERS
INTELLIGENCE SUMMARY. 59th DIVISIONAL R.E.
(Erase heading not required.)

Instructions regarding War Diaries and Intelligence Summaries are contained in F.S. Regs., Part II. and the Staff Manual respectively. Title pages will be prepared in manuscript.

Place	Date	Hour	Summary of Events and Information	Remarks and references to Appendices
MONS-EN-CHAUSSEE	1.4.17		Two sections of the 467th FIELD Co RE attached to 178th INFANTRY BDE engaged upon work in the line	
			Two Sections " " " 469th " " " 177th do	
			A party of men of 467th FIELD Co RE employed erecting 9 Nissen Huts at DHQ	NISSEN HUTS
			" " " " " " " prisoners camp	
			" " " " " " " filling in mine craters at PRUSLE and MONS-EN-CHAUSSEE and making diversions round them.	Sheet 62 C
			A party of men of 467th FIELD Co RE. Engaged upon repairs to Church at MONS-EN-CHAUSSEE " " " " " " " filling in subsidence on main road West of PRUSLE "	
			Two Sections of 469th Field Coy RE Engaged upon construction of LAMIRE Bridge Q15 a and b	
			" " " 470th " " " " " " " " "	
			Two Sections " " " " " approaches to bridges at ST CHRIST	
	4.30 pm		Received 59 Division warning order No 13	Uhm
do	2.4.17		Two sections of 467 and 469 FIELD Coys at work with 178th and 177th Infantry Bns respectively	
			One Section of 467 FIELD Coy erecting 9 NISSEN HUTS at D.H.Q	Ref Sheet 62 C
			" " " " " " " working on roads	
			Two " " 469 " " " " working on road crater at P8 a.55.	
			470 FIELD Coy (complete) infantry employed upon LAMIRE BRIDGE O15 and	
	8 am		59 Division Order No 14 received	Uhm

WAR DIARY / INTELLIGENCE SUMMARY

Army Form C. 2118. *Continued*

Place	Date	Hour	Summary of Events and Information	Remarks and references to Appendices
MONS-EN-CHAUSSEE	3.4.17		Two Sections of 467 and One Section of 469 Field Coys were engaged upon work in the line under 178th and 177th Infantry Bdes respectively. The 467th Field Coy R.E. carried out the following additional work:— (a) Work on ESTREES-EN-CHAUSSEE crater (b) " MONS-EN-CHAUSSEE and HANCOURT craters and road from HANCOURT north to point 114 (c) " Wells in MONS-EN-CHAUSSEE. (d) " Huts at D.H.Q. The 469th Field Coy R.E. carried out the following additional work (a) One section employed on BAUMETZ crater P.12.b.5.5. (b) " " CATELET crater P.8.a.5.5. The 470th Field Coy were engaged upon construction of LAMIRE BRIDGE	heep 24/4 to G.2.C. 1/4.9.000
		8 p.m.	DIVISIONAL ORDER No 15 and No 16 received.	Kerr
do.	4.4.17		Two Sections of 467 and two Sections of 469 Field Coys were engaged upon work in the line under 178th and 177th INFANTRY BDES respectively. 467th FIELD Coy carried out the following additional work:— Work on ESTREES-EN-CHAUSSEE mine crater " " MONS-EN-CHAUSSEE " " " HANCOURT — ROISEL main road and mine crater at point 114 " " HANCOURT — ROISEL " 469th FIELD Coy R.E. carried out the following additional work:— Repairing the mine craters at the following points J24.d.6.1, P12.b.4.5, P8.a.5.5. 470th FIELD Coy R.S. were engaged upon construction of LAMIRE BRIDGE over River SOMME 3 Sept. DIVISIONAL ORDER No 17 Received	Kerr

Army Form C. 2118.

WAR DIARY
or
INTELLIGENCE SUMMARY. *Continued.*

(Erase heading not required.)

Instructions regarding War Diaries and Intelligence Summaries are contained in F. S. Regs. Part II and the Staff Manual respectively. Title pages will be prepared in manuscript.

Place	Date	Hour	Summary of Events and Information	Remarks and references to Appendices
MONS-EN-CHAUSSÉE	5/4/17		Two Sections of 467th and two Sections of the 469 FIELD Coys engaged with 178th and 177th INFANTRY BDES in work in the front line	Map referred to Sheet 62 c 1/40,000
			467 FIELD Co RE was engaged upon the additional works falling in cratere at HANCOURT and point 114. K33 a.8.3. and improving HANCOURT – ROISEL main road making road diversions round the following craters at ESTREES-EN-CHAUSSÉE, and PRUSLE, Point K33 a.8.3. and HANCOURT	
			469th FIELD Coy RE was engaged upon the additional works of making road diversions round crater at P12 b.6.5. and ESTREES-EN-CHAUSSÉE	
			470th FIELD Coy RE LAMIRE BRIDGE provided with cross roads at O12 c.7.1 repaired	Khm
	6pm		DIVISIONAL ORDER No 19 received	
	6/4/17		Two Sections of 467th and two Sections of the 469 FIELD Coys engaged with 178th and 177th INFANTRY BDES respectively for work in the front line	
			467 FIELD Coy RE continued work on main crater at ESTREES-EN-CHAUSSÉE and HANCOURT	
			469 " " " " " " " " crater at BOUCLY J24 a.6.1.	
			470 " " " " " " " " " P8 a.55"	Khm
	9pm		DIVISIONAL ORDER No 20 received	
	7/4/17		Two Sections of 467th and two Sections of 469. FIELD Coys continue to work with their Bdes.	
			467 FIELD Coy RE continued work on main craters at ESTREES and MONS-EN-CHAUSSÉE	
			469 " " " " " " " " BOUCLY J24 a.6.1.	
			470 " " " " " " " " PEA 55", P12 b.45, Q8 a.6.9	
	7.30AM		No 2 and No 4 SECTIONS of 180 TUNNELLING Coy attached to assist with water supply and work on roads	
			DIVISIONAL ORDER No 21 received	
	7.30pm		" " " " postponed until further orders by G F04.	Yhm

Army Form C. 2118.

WAR DIARY
~~INTELLIGENCE SUMMARY~~ continued
(Erase heading not required.)

Instructions regarding War Diaries and Intelligence Summaries are contained in F.S. Regs., Part II. and the Staff Manual respectively. Title pages will be prepared in manuscript.

Place	Date	Hour	Summary of Events and Information	Remarks and references to Appendices
MONCHY-CHAUSSEE	8/4/17		Two sections of 467th and 469th FIELD COY attached to 178 and 177 BRIGADES	Map reference Sheet 62 C 2/40,000
			467 FIELD COY RE at work on ESTREES-EN-CHAUSSEE crater and on BERNES-MONTIGNY road	
			469 " " " making diversion of road round craters at ROISEL (K22 a 2.9) and BOUCLY cross roads (J24 d.6.1)	
			470 " " " at work on HANCOURT, CATELET and BEAUMETZ craters also HANCOURT-ROISEL and PERONNE roads	
			No. 2 Section 180 TUNNELLING COY at work filling up dugouts under road at O.29.a.5.5. and draining main road	
			No. 4 " 180 TUNNELLING COY RE at work on wells at RAPERIE Q.13 d 8.9 SUCERIE K.36 c 8.8, HANCOURT Q.8 d 3.6 and SUCERIE at Q.4.a.O.6.	
		11am	DIVISIONAL ORDER No. 22 issued	JKerr
		11.30pm	" " No. 23 " (a section RE and detailed fifth work with 176th and 177 Bden.)	
"	9/4/17		Two sections of 467th and 469th FIELD COY attached to 178th and 177 BRIGADES.	
			467 FIELD COY RE at work on PRUSLE crater and road diversion round MONS crater	
			469 " " " making road diversions round craters at K22 a 2.9 and J24 d.6.1	
			470 " " " road repairs on BOUVINCOURT-VRAIGNES and HANCOURT-ROISEL road also collecting material for causeway round crater at K33 a 5.2	
			No. 2 Section 180 tunnelling Coys. — clearing wells and draining road between MONSEN-CHAUSSEE and ESTREES-EN-CHAUSSEE	
			No. 4 " " " — work on wells at RAPERIE Q.13 d 8.9 SUCERIE K.36.c.88 HANCOURT Q.8 d.3.6. SUCERIE Q.4 a.0.6. VENDELLES R.1.c.7.6.	
		6.30 pm	DIVISIONAL ORDER No. 24 issued	JKerr

WAR DIARY or INTELLIGENCE SUMMARY — continued

Army Form C. 2118.

Place	Date	Hour	Summary of Events and Information	Remarks and references to Appendices
MONS-EN-CHAUSSEE	10/4/17		Moved our Headquarters from MONS-EN-CHAUSSEE to BOUVINCOURT	Ref map 62 C 1/40000
BOUVINCOURT	10/4/17	4 pm	Opened our new Headquarters at BOUVINCOURT. Two sections of 467 and 469 Field Coy RE. at work with 178 and 177 Brigades. 467 Field Coy RE moved from ESTREES-EN-CHAUSSEE to BERNES at work on roads in HANCOURT and BERNES	
			469 " moved from BOUCLY to ROISEL. at work upon division of roads round craters at ROISEL and BOUCLY	
			470 " One section with 176 Bde for consolidation purposes. ½ " at work at D.H.Q. and ½ section on water supply and road drainage at BOUVINCOURT. 2 Sections engaged repairing roads BOUVINCOURT – VRAIGNES and HANCOURT – ROISEL and on crater at POINT 116.	
			180 Tunnelling Coy RE (2 sections) at work in water supply at BOUVINCOURT, HANCOURT, VENDELLES, BERNES, FLECHIN and ESTREES-EN-CHAUSSEE.	/Knm
"	11/4/17		Two sections of 467 and 469 Field Coy RE at work with 178 and 177 Bdes. 467 FIELD COY RE at work on roads in BERNES and taking up old German track at MONTIGNY FARM for corduroy purposes.	
			469 " " " making road diversions round craters at ROISEL. HERVILLY and MONTIGNY.	
			470 " " " at work on HANCOURT – BERNES, & VRAIGNES – BOUVINCOURT roads and improving road diversion round crater at K 33 a 8.2	
			180 TONNELLING Coy RE spent work as for TL 10 K.	
		12.30	G.907 received	
		4.30 pm	Divisional Order No. 25 received	/Knm

Army Form C. 2118.

WAR DIARY
or
INTELLIGENCE SUMMARY.
(Erase heading not required.)

Instructions regarding War Diaries and Intelligence Summaries are contained in F. S. Regs., Part II. and the Staff Manual respectively. Title pages will be prepared in manuscript.

continued

Place	Date	Hour	Summary of Events and Information	Remarks and references to Appendices
BOUVINCOURT	12/4/17		Two sections of 467 and 469 FIELD Coy. at work with 178 and 177 INFANTRY BDES.	Ref. MAP 62 c 1/40,000
			467 FIELD Coy RE making road diversions round craters at VENDELLES and JEANCOURT.	
			469 " " " " MONTIGNY FARM and HERVILLY	
			470 " " " " HANCOURT. Clearing and drawing	
			HANCOURT – BERNES, – HANCOURT – VRAIGNES and BERNES	
			2 Sections 180 TUNNELLING Coy engaged upon work in BOUVINCOURT, HANCOURT, VENDELLES and BERNES	
"	13/4/17		Two sections of 467 and 469 FIELD Coy at work with 178 and 177 Bdes.	
		7 p.m.	Our " 467 FIELD Coy RE order to report to CC 2/6 NORTH STAFFS for consolidation of line after the attack.	
			The infantry in consolidation of line after the attack.	
			467 FIELD Coy RE at work on JEANCOURT crater and roads in its vicinity	
			469 " " " making road diversions round craters at K 22 a.38, K 36 a.2.7) and HERVILLY	
			470 " " " " HANCOURT and at K 33 a 5.2	
			" " also repairing and drawing BERNES – HANCOURT – BOUVINCOURT – VRAIGNES road	
			2 Sections 180 TUNNELLING Coy. RE engaged upon work at BOUVINCOURT, NOBES COURT FARM, VENDELLES	
			BERNES, AIX FARM and on road with return VRAIGNES and P 30 d	
"	14/4/17		Two sections each of 467 and 469 FIELD Coy RE at work with 178 and 177 Bdes.	
			One " of 467 FIELD Coy RE returned from 6 NORTH STAFFS to the company.	
			467 FIELD Coy RE at work on JEANCOURT crater	
			469 " " " " making diversion of road craters at K 36 a.2.7 and K 12, d.1.S. also HERVILLY crater. Demolishing dangerous houses in ROISEL	
			470 " " " Continuing road diversion at crater at P114 (HANCOURT – ROISEL ROAD)	
			Draining and repairing BERNES – HANCOURT ROAD, BOUVINCOURT – VRAIGNES and HANCOURT – ROISEL Roads	
			2 Sections 180 TUNNELLING Coy RE engage upon work in BOUVINCOURT, BERNES, HERVILLY, HANCOURT, AIX FARM, VENDELLES and NOBES COURT FARM, also repairing return VRAIGNES and P 30 d.	

Army Form C. 2118.

WAR DIARY
INTELLIGENCE SUMMARY.
(Erase heading not required.)

Continued

Instructions regarding War Diaries and Intelligence Summaries are contained in F. S. Regs., Part II. and the Staff Manual respectively. Title pages will be prepared in manuscript.

Place	Date	Hour	Summary of Events and Information	Remarks and references to Appendices
BOUVINCOURT	15/4/17	—	Two sections of 469 FIELD COY attached to 177 BDE	Ref: map G2 1/40,000
			" " " 467 " " " returned to the company from 178 BDE	
			One section of 470 " " " attached to 176 INFANTRY BDE.	
			467 Field Coy RE at work on road Louveau Craters at JEANCOURT	
			469 " " " MONTIGNY and filling in crater at MONTIGNY and HERVILLY road. Erecting Adrian shed in HERVILLY. Look on MONTIGNY - HERVILLY road. Erecting bridge damaged by motor transport. HAMELET and repairing bridge damaged	
			470 FIELD COY RE Draining and repairing HANCOURT - BERNES, BOUVINCOURT - VRAIGNES BOUVINCOURT - HANCOURT, HANCOURT - ROISEL ROADS. Looping road, dinner round crater at POINT 114 filling crater and clearing HANCOURT - FLECHIN ROAD	
			2 SECTIONS 180 TUNNELLING COY RE look on walls in BERNES, AIX FARM, HANCOURT, FLECHIN, BOUVINCOURT, HESBECOURT and JEANCOURT.	Khm
	16/4/17	—	Two sections of 469 FIELD COY RE attached to 177 INFANTRY BDE"	
			" " " 467 " " " 178 " "	
			" " " 470 " " " having return the junction of roads about Q17.c.2.2	
			467 FIELD COY RE clearing draining and filling in of the roads BERNES - MONTIGNY FARM and JEANCOURT- VENDELLES also Erecting of Adrian sheds, repair of huts, construction of baths and repair of wells etc in BERNES.	
			469 " " " at work on orders at MONTIGNY and HERVILLY craters	
			470 " " " draining and clearing roads HANCOURT - BERNES, HANCOURT - CARTIGNY, VRAIGNES - HANCOURT, HANCOURT - ROISEL ROAD work on orders at Q.9.C.III and at P.114 HANCOURT - HERVILLY, HESBECOURT,	
			2 Sections 180 TUNNELLING COY RE at work on walls in BOUVINCOURT, HERVILLY, HESBECOURT, JEANCOURT and BERNES.	
		2 p.m.	DIVISIONAL ORDER No 27 received	
		6 p.m.	HeadQuarters G.27 and G.29 amendments to D.O. Order No 27.	Khm

WAR DIARY
INTELLIGENCE SUMMARY
(Erase heading not required.)

Army Form C. 2118.

Continued:—

Instructions regarding War Diaries and Intelligence Summaries are contained in F.S. Regs. Part II and the Staff Manual respectively. Title pages will be prepared in manuscript.

Place	Date	Hour	Summary of Events and Information	Remarks and references to Appendices
Bouvincourt	17/4/17	7.30 a.m.	DIVISIONAL ORDER No 28 received. 2nd Section of 469 FIELD Coy RE, and one section of 470 FIELD Coy employed as yesterday. 467 FIELD Coy RE. Same as yesterday. 469 " . Filling up crater at K24 c.9.7 and clearing main roads through HERVILLY. Erecting Adrian Hut at HAMELET and demolishing dangerous buildings in ROISEL. 470 " . Same as yesterday. 2 Section 180 TUNNELLING Coy R.E. at work on wells as detailed in work for yesterday.	Ref. map 62 c 1/40,000. Khan
"	18/4/17	10 a.m.	DIVISIONAL ORDER No 29 received. 2nd Section of 469, one section of 467 and one Section of 470 FIELD Coys RE employed as detailed on 16/4/17. 467 FIELD Coy RE. Work on BERNES–MONTIGNY road and crater at Q4 c.6.1. Erecting Adrian Hut and constructing road diversion round crater at VENDELLES. 469 " . Work on roads between MONTIGNY and HERVILLY and in ROISEL. Pulling down dangerous buildings. 470 " . Same as for the 16th inst. 2 Sections of 180 TUNNELLING Co RE at work on wells in BOUVINCOURT, HERVILLY, HESBECOURT, JEANCOURT, LE VERGUIER, FLECHIN and SUCRERIE at MONTIGNY FARM	Khan
"	19/4/17		As detail of work for all concerned is the same as yesterday, 18th inst.	Khan
"	20/4/17		2nd Section of 469, one section of 467 and one section of 470 FIELD Coys RE employed as detailed on 18/4/17. 467 FIELD Coy RE. Construction of road diversions round crater at VENDELLES. Erection of ADRIAN Huts and Repair of billets in BERNES. Erecting of NISSEN Hut at DH.Q. 469 " . Erecting Adrian Hut at HAMELET, opening culvert to liberate flood water, clearing roads in ROISEL, erecting shelters for Artillery and screens Huts for Regmt. 470 FIELD Coy RE Repairing road diversion at BEAUMETZ crater and clearing BEAUMETZ – BOUVINCOURT Road – VRAIGNES – HANCOURT, BOUVINCOURT–VRAIGNES and HANCOURT FLECHIN roads – Laying down nissen hut at FOUCACOURT. 2 Section 180 Tunnelling Coy R.E. at work on wells in BOUVINCOURT, HERVILLY, HESBECOURT, JEANCOURT, TEMPLEUX-LE-GUERARD, FLECHIN, MONTIGNY–CARP	Khan

WAR DIARY
Continued
INTELLIGENCE SUMMARY.
(Erase heading not required.)

Army Form C. 2118.

Place	Date	Hour	Summary of Events and Information	Remarks and references to Appendices
BOUVINCOURT	21/4/17		(1) Divn Section of 469 Field Coy, one Section of 467 and one Section of 470 Field Coy R.E. working as detailed on 16/4/17.	Ref 62 & 11/4/17
			(2) 467 Field Coy R.E. - continuation of road diversion round crater at VENDELLES - Erection of Aerrian Hut and repair of huts in BERNES.	
			(3) 469 " Superising infantry working parties, erecting Aerrian Hut at HAMELET, opening culverts to evacuate flood water in ROISEL, erecting frozen Hut for R.F.M.E. and clearing roads in ROISEL.	
			(4) 470 Field Coy R.E. Repairing HANCOURT-FLECHIN Road and completing road over crater at 9 9 b 0.2. Clearing, draining and repairing HANCOURT-VRAIGNEL, HANCOURT-ROISEL, BOUVINCOURT-VRAIGNES and BOUVINCOURT-BEAUMETZ Roads.	
			(5) 180 Tunnelling Coy R.E. Same work as for 20th.	
do.	22/4/17		(1) Same as yesterday.	Kuhn
			(2) 467 Field Coy R.E. completion of road diversion round crater at VENDELLES clearing MONTIGNY-VENDELLES Road, and erecting Aerrian Hut at la RAPERIE in HANCOURT. VRAIGNES Road and laying floor for hut in BERNES	
			(3) 469 Field Coy R.E. Same as yesterday.	
			(4) 470 " " " "	
			(5) 180 Tunnelling Coy R.E. " on 20/4/17.	
		4.30 p.m.	DIVISIONAL ORDER No. 30 received	
do.	23/4/17		(1) Same as detailed on 21st	Kuhn
			(2) 467 " yesterday	
			(3) 469 " detailed on 21st.	
			(4) 470 Field Coy R.E. Same as detailed on 21st with the following additional work. Making Road metal at BRIE, making manure incinerator in BOUVINCOURT, erecting Aerrian Hut, more huts in HANCOURT.	
			(5) 2 Sections 180 Tunnelling Coy R.E. at work on wells in BOUVINCOURT, HERVILLY, HESBECOURT, TEMPLEUX-LE-GERARD, LEVERGUIER.	

Army Form C. 2118.

WAR DIARY of — Continued

INTELLIGENCE SUMMARY.

(Erase heading not required.)

Instructions regarding War Diaries and Intelligence Summaries are contained in F. S. Regs., Part II. and the Staff Manual respectively. Title pages will be prepared in manuscript.

Place	Date	Hour	Summary of Events and Information	Remarks and references to Appendices
Bouvincourt	24/4/17	1 a.m.	DIVISIONAL ORDER No. 32 received	Appx ref 62 c 1/copy
		5-30 p.m.	" " " 33	
			Two sections of 469 Field Coy and two sections of 470 Field Coy with Brigade in front line.	
			467 Field Coy R.E. improving and deepening trenches in Corps line.	
			Clearing road at MONTIGNY FARM and erecting Adrian and Nissen Huts	
			469 FIELD COY R.E. working on intermediate line and wiring ROISEL and ROISEL HAMLET.	
			Erecting Adrian Huts in ROISEL and erecting Adrian Huts	
			Repairing Roads and erecting Adrian Huts	
			470 " 180 TUNNELLING Coy at work on wells in forward area	Khan
			2 Sections "	
do	25/4/17		The 3 FIELD COYS and 180 TUNNELLING Coy same as for yesterday.	Khan
do	26/4/17	10 a.m.	G 32/2 received which gave zero hour in connection with Divisional order No. 32.	
			Two sections of 469 FIELD Coy and two sections of 470 FIELD Coy with Brigade in forward area.	
			467 FIELD COY R.E. improving wire and digging new posts in Corps Line	
			Clearing roads at MONTIGNY FARM and erecting Adrian and Nissen Huts	
			469 " " working on intermediate line and wiring ROISEL — also making	
			communication post & G.S. at TEMPLEUX-LE-GUERARD (RUELLES WOODS)	
			Erecting Adrian Huts in ROISEL and HAMLET.	
			470 " " Repairing Roads and constructing dug-outs	
			Erecting Huts.	
			2 Sections 180 TUNNELLING Coy R.E. at work upon wells in divisional area.	Khan
do	27/4/17	10-10 a.m.	G 124 received. Correction to Divisional Order No. 33 re- midups.	
			The detail of work for the three field companies and 180 TUNNELLING Coy 129 is the same as for yesterday.	Khan

ORIGINAL.

Army Form C. 2118.

Continued

WAR DIARY
or
INTELLIGENCE SUMMARY.
(Erase heading not required.)

Place	Date	Hour	Summary of Events and Information	Remarks and references to Appendices
BOUVINCOURT	28/4/17	7 am	G 126 received - detailed Afternoon policy of the Division. Two Sections of 469 and 2 Sections of 470 FIELD Coy attached to Brigades in forward area 467 FIELD Coy RE working on corps line - wiring and digging new posts. Erecting Adrian Huts in HANCOURT and BERNES. Continued storage protection pits and shelter in ROELLES TROOPS. Kin 469 " Erecting Adrian Huts in ROISEL and HAMELET 470 " filling in HANCOURT and BEAUMETZ craters - work on roads and Erection of Adrian Huts at HANCOURT. 2 Sections 180 TUNNELLING Coy RE at work on wells in the Divisional area	Kh-n
do	29/4/19	10 am	G 2/1 - giving attachment to Brigade boundaries Two sections of 469 and 2 Sections of 470 FIELD Coy attached to Brigades in forward area. 467 FIELD Coy RE wiring and digging new posts in corps line - erecting Adrian Huts 469 " - filling in craters near ROISEL Station - erecting Adrian Huts 470 " - Erecting and breaking Adrian Huts - making dugout at JEANCOURT 2 Sections 180 TUNNELLING Coy RE at work on wells in Divisional area	Kh-n
do	30/4/17		Two sections of 469 and 2 Sections of 470 FIELD Coy attached to Brigades in forward area. 467 FIELD Coy RE wiring the corps line and completion of posts. Erecting Adrian Huts 469 " Erecting Huts and repairing culverts in ROISEL 470 " filling in BEAUMETZ and HANCOURT craters Erecting and breaking Adrian Huts 2 Sections 180 TUNNELLING Coy RE at work on wells in HESBECOURT, JEANCOURT, LE VERGUIER, TEMPLEUX-LE-GUERARD, HARGICOURT, ROISEL and FLECHIN.	

K Meinhehoo
Capt RE
59 Div

WAR DIARY

FRANKIN HOLMES LIEUT.

WAR DIARY

of

HEAD QUARTERS, 59th DIV. R.E.

VOL. IV.

May 1st 1917   to   May 31st 1917.

ORIGINAL

Army Form C. 2118.

WAR DIARY
— or —
INTELLIGENCE SUMMARY.
(Erase heading not required.)

HEAD QUARTERS 59 DIVISIONAL R.E.

Instructions regarding War Diaries and Intelligence Summaries are contained in F.S. Regs. Part II. and the Staff Manual respectively. Title pages will be prepared in manuscript.

Place	Date	Hour	Summary of Events and Information	Remarks and references to Appendices
BOUVINCOURT	1.5.17		Two sections of 469 and two sections of 470 FIELD Coys RE with Brigades in the forward area.	Sheet 62ᵃ 1/40,000
			467 FIELD Coy RE - Working on Corps line - wiring and constructing posts. Erecting Adrian Huts.	
			469 " " - bringing the main line of resistance and filling in craters at MONTIGNY and TEMPLEUX	
			470 " " - filling in crater at Pt 114 (HANCOURT-ROISEL ROAD) and erection of Adrian Huts	Khr
			2 Sections 180 TUNNELLING Coy RE at work on walls at HERVILLY, HESBECOURT, JEANCOURT, LE VERGUIER, TEMPLEUX-LE-GUÉRARD, ROISEL, FLÉCHIN and BERNES and HARGICOURT.	Khr
do.	2.5.17	6 pm	370/8/C.G. received. Corps and Divisional defense policy for the immediate future.	
			The detail of work of units is the same as for yesterday.	
		4.30 pm	Divisional Order No 34 received.	
do.	3.5.17		2 Sections of 469 and two sections of 470 FIELD Coys RE with 178 and 177 Brigades respectively.	
			467 FIELD Coy RE - Erecting Adrian Huts in BERNES and SUCRERIE at Q4.a.22 - Clearing Road to SUCRERIE.	
			469 " " - Erecting and Banking Adrian Huts. Filling in craters at K36.a.2.7 and K12 & 4.2.	Khr
			470 " " - Erecting and Banking Adrian Huts. Filling in craters at HANCOURT and NOBESCOURT FARM.	Khr
			2 Sections 180 TUNNELLING Coy RE. proceeding with work as detailed in diary for May 1ˢᵗ.	
		5 pm	Divisional Order No 35 received.	
do.	4.5.17		The detail of work of units is the same as for yesterday.	Khr
		2.55 pm	Divisional Order No 36 received.	
	5.5.17	7.50 pm	" " " Cancelled	
			Two sections of 469 and two sections of 470 FIELD Coys RE with Brigades in the forward area.	
			Detail of work for all units to the same as that shewn for the 3ʳᵈ unit except	
			that the 469 FIELD Coy RE was also engaged upon spoil-locking trenches at three posts.	Khr
			E.L.A.G. cutter, buck nagrate + attachment to W467 rail Cy.	
			Divisional order No 37 received.	
do.	6.5.17	5 pm	2 Sections of 469 and two sections of 470 FIELD Coy RE attached to 178 and 177 Brigades respectively.	
			467 FIELD Coy RE. Sighting and putting out points in the intermediate line. Also erecting Huts	
			469 " " . Spoil-locking trenches at post L.9.6. Filling in craters at K12 a 5.5. Completing	
			roadway over filled in craters (Between TEMPLEUX and HARGICOURT - also erecting Adrian Huts	Khr

WAR DIARY continued
INTELLIGENCE SUMMARY.
(Erase heading not required.)

Army Form C. 2118.

Place	Date	Hour	Summary of Events and Information	Remarks and references to Appendices
BOUVINCOURT	6.5.17		Continued	
			470 FIELD Coy RE. Filling and bricking over HANCOURT craters and NOBESCOURT craters. Bricking over completing section of Adrian huts.	Khan
			2 Sections 180 TUNNELLING Coy. RE. at work upon wells in HERVILLY, HESBECOURT, ROISEL, TEMPLEUX-LE-GUERARD, HARGICOURT, JEANCOURT, LEVERGIER, FLECHIN, BERNES and stations at L 23 a 5.2.	
do.	7.5.17		Owing to the relief of 178 Bde by the 176th Bde, the two Sections of the 469 Field Coy RE are now with the 176 Bde in the forward area. Two Sections of the 470 FIELD Coy with 177 INFANTRY BDE in forward area.	
			467 FIELD Coy RE. working on intermediate line and erecting Adrian huts.	
			469 " . Filling in craters at K 12 a 3.5, making road diversion round craters at L 4 c 2.4	
			470 " . Filling in craters at NOBESCOURT and HANCOURT and bricking Adrian huts.	
			2 Sections of 180 TUNNELLING Coy RE. at work upon wells in the villages mentioned in diary for 6th inst.	Khan
		5 pm	59 Divisional Warning Order No. 38 Copy No. 5 received	
do.	8.5.17	12.15 pm	Addendum to Divisional Order No. 37 received – two hour given	
			Two Sections 470 FIELD Coy RE and 2 Sections with 469 Coy RE attached to 177 and 176 Brigades respectively	
			467 FIELD Coy RE at work on Adrian huts and clearing road JEANCOURT to HARGICOURT	
			469 " . making road diversion round TEMPLEUX-HARGICOURT crater. completed 4 Adrian huts at ROISEL, 5th and 6th huts commenced.	
			470 " . Bricking over craters at BEAUMETZ HANCOURT and NOBESCOURT craters. Opening walls at K 34 c 4.3, putting bunks in 4 and 5th Adrian huts at HANCOURT. work in Camp, making bath house, preparing cellar for trying gas helmets.	
			2 Sections 180 TUNNELLING Coy RE. – propping up well of VRAIGNES Church and working on the same wells as detailed in diary for the 6th inst.	Khan
do.	9.5.17	12.45 pm	G 134 Cancelling 59 Div training Order No. 38 and para 1 (a) of G 126 dated 28/4/17 received.	
			The work done by units here in continuation of the work detailed hereinbefore the 8th inst.	Khan

Army Form C. 2118.

WAR DIARY
of
INTELLIGENCE SUMMARY. Continued
(Erase heading not required.)

Instructions regarding War Diaries and Intelligence Summaries are contained in F.S. Regs., Part II. and the Staff Manual respectively. Title pages will be prepared in manuscript.

Place	Date	Hour	Summary of Events and Information	Remarks and references to Appendices
BOUVINCOURT.	10/5/17	5 p.m.	59 DIVISIONAL WARNING ORDER No 39 re the relief of the 8th Division by the 3rd Cavalry division, received. Two Sections of 469 Field Coy RE and 2 Sections of 470 Field Coy RE at work with 176 and 177 INFANTRY Bdes respectively.	Appx. Ref 62 & 1/10000
			467 FIELD Coy R.E. Filling craters and repairing JEANCOURT-HARGICOURT ROAD, erecting huts and a petrol pump at the SUCRERIE in BERNES.	
			469 " " Repairing road round TEMPLEUX-HARGICOURT, repairing MONTIGNY-HERVILLY road. Filling in craters at L2 b.35. Erecting Adrian huts.	
			470 " " Bricking in HARGICOURT, BEAUMETZ and NOBESCOURT craters. Distributing scrim on roads. Pumping and erecting Adrian Huts. Clearing and draining HARGICOURT-BERNES ROAD. Making bell tents in BOUVINCOURT. Opening up wall at K34 c 43.	
			2 Sections 180 TUNNELLING Coy. RE at work on walls on ROISEL, HERVILLY, HESBECOURT, TEMPLEUX-LE-GUERARD HARGICOURT, BERNES, FLEEVIN, LEVERGUIER, CHATEAU at L2 3 a.5.2. BEAUMETZ and wood on HARGICOURT, BOUCLY Road.	Khun Khun
do.	11/5/17	5.30	Conducted experiments with mobile charges upon dugouts and trenches. Detail of work of units is the same as that detailed for the 10th inst.	
do	12/5/17	1 pm.	59 DIVISIONAL ORDER No 40 Copy No 9 received. Two Sections of 469 Field Coy RE and Two Sections of 470 FIELD COY RE at work with 176 and 177 INFANTRY BDES respectively.	
			467 FIELD Coy RE. Filling in craters and cleaning JEANCOURT-HARGICOURT ROAD. Repairing BERNES-MONTIGNY road. Erecting power pump at SUCRERIE BERNES. Works on Adrian Huts in BERNES, ESTREES-EN-CHAUSSEE HAMELET.	
			469 FIELD Coy RE Filling in craters at HARGICOURT L12 a.45, and craters at TEMPLEUX L2 b.35. Constructing an O.P at L4 a.97 and constructing support and intermediate line at L9 b.2.8 and L9 a.8.2.	
			470 FIELD Coy RE. Filling in NOBESCOURT, HANCOURT and BEAUMETZ craters and repairing HANCOURT-ROISEL and HANCOURT-BEAUMETZ roads. Bombing Huts in HAM COURT.	
			No 2 Section 180 TUNNELLING Coy RE. Working on following wells in ROISEL, K16 d.45, K16 d.27, K16 d.45, HERVILLY L3 b.1.0. to. K24 c.4.45. HESBECOURT L13 c.60, L13 c.1.74. TEMPLEUX-LE-GUERARD L2 d 19, L2 d ½.71. HARGICOURT L10 A 6.16, L5 C 826. L2 C 29, Q 17 C 29, K31 d 81, K31 c 81, L26 c 7.9, L26 c 92, L26 d 1.2, L26 c 54, L26 d 2.3, L33, b.98, L3a a.71.	Ref Sheet 62c N.E. 1/20000
			No 4 Section in Excavating and making tunnel shelters, pump shelters at L3 c 9.8. Working on wells at See paper attached for details.	Jehn

A 5534 Wt. W4973 M687 750,000 8/16 D. D. & L. Ltd. Forms/C.2118/13.

WAR DIARY or INTELLIGENCE SUMMARY

Army Form C. 2118. — Continued

Place	Date	Hour	Summary of Events and Information	Remarks and references to Appendices
BOUVINCOURT	13/5/17		Two sections of 469 Field Coy RE and 2 Sections of 470 Field Coy RE attached to 176 and 177 Infantry Bdes. respectively.	62c NE (2) SE 1/12 0,000
			467 Field Coy RE Filling in craters and clearing of Hancourt–Hargicourt Road, Repairing Bernes–Montigny Road. Working on Aerian Huts in Bernes, Estrées, Roisel and Hamelet. Erecting pump at Sucrerie Bernes. Continuing work on O.P. at L4 a.97; working on intermediate line at L9 a.P.2, and entrenching at Brosse Woods at L21 d.1.9. Filling in craters at L10 a. & 84.	
			469 " " L2 b.3.5. (TEMPLEUX). Breaking Hancourt – Nobescourt, Hancourt – Beaumetz and Hancourt (Village) roads, also road at K21 a.90. Repairing roofs to Adrian huts in Hancourt. Fixing up pump and windlass gear at well at K34 c 4.3 and erecting bath house in Bouvincourt.	
			470 " "	
			2 Sections 180 Tunnelling Coy RE – working on wells as detailed on attached works report	Khin
do	14/5/17	6.30am	59 Divisional order No. 41 received which cancelled Div Order No. 40	
		3 pm	59 " Administrative order Instructions No. 2 received copy No. 4.	
		10 pm	III Corps Administrative Instructions No. 32 dated 14/5/17 received	Khin
			Work of units in the same as that detailed in report yesterday. Wells report attached.	
do	15/5/17		Two sections of the 467 Field Coy RE and 2 Sections 470 Field Coy RE attached to 176 Infantry Bde and Secunderabad Cavalry B.de. respectively. The Secunderabad Cavalry Bde having relieved the 177 Infantry B.de.	
			467 Field Coy RE – Work on Aerian Huts in Bernes, Estrées–En–Chaussée, Roisel and Hamelet. Erecting pump at Sucrerie Bernes. Repairing Bernes – Hancourt road. Entrenching and wiring on support line at	
			469 " " Working on O.P. at Hargicourt L4a.9.7. Hancourt crater L10 a.84. Filling in Hancourt craters completely (picked men out partly metalled)	
			470 " " Beaumetz and Hancourt. Repairing roads Beaumetz–Hancourt, Hancourt–Bernes, Hancourt–Roisel and Nobescourt. Fixing up well & windlass supply of K 34 c 4.3. Repairing roofs of Adrian huts.	
		2 pm	2 Sections 180 Tunnelling Coy RE. working on wells as detailed on attached works report	
			Handed over 59 Divisional RE Park to 5th Field Squadron of the 5th Cavalry Division	Khin
do	16/5/17	9 am	CRE 59 Division hands over to OC 5th Field Squadron RE who assumes the position of C.R.E. 5th Cavalry Division.	
			2 Sections 180 Tunnelling Coy RE handed over to OC 5th Field Squadron RE. Detail of work of 467, 469, and 470 Field Coys is the same as that of yesterday	Khin

Army Form C. 2118.

WAR DIARY
INTELLIGENCE SUMMARY. Continued.—
(Erase heading not required.)

Instructions regarding War Diaries and Intelligence Summaries are contained in F.S. Regs., Part II. and the Staff Manual respectively. Title pages will be prepared in manuscript.

Place	Date	Hour	Summary of Events and Information	Remarks and references to Appendices
BOUVINCOURT	17.5.17		Two sections 469 FIELD Coy RE and two sections 470 FIELD Coy RE attached to 176 INFANTRY BDE and SECUNDERABAD Cavalry Brigade respectively.	Map Refs Sheets 62c NE 62c SE 1/20,000
			467 FIELD Coy RE constructing shelters at HERVILLY, working on Adrian Huts in BERNES, ESTREES-EN-CHAUSSEE and ROISEL, making engine bed for pump at SUCRERIE BERNES.	
			469 " working on O.P. at L4.a.9.7, spitlocking trenches at L15.c, metalling filled in crater at K12.d.4.8, making shelters for grenades at K12.N.4.1.	Khun
			470 " Repairing BEAUMETZ-HANCOURT and HANCOURT-ROISEL roads. Renewing up stone at ROISEL. Repairing roofs of Adrian Huts at HANCOURT.	Khun
"	18.5.17		Detail of work of units is the same as that for yesterday	
	19.5.17		Two sections of 469 and 470 FIELD Coys RE working as detailed in diary for 17th.	
			467 FIELD Coy RE working upon Adrian Huts at BERNES and erecting wooden hut at ESTREES-EN-CHAUSSEE, also Adrian Hut at HERVILLY and shelters.	Khun Khun
"			469 " continuing work on OP at L4 a.9.7 and grenade shelters at K12.d.4.1.	
			470 " loading stones at ROISEL and dumping it on BERNES-VENDELLES ROAD. Erecting Adrian Hut at D.H.Q., tarring roofs of Adrian Huts in HANCOURT.	
"	20.5.17		Detail of work of units is the same as that for yesterday.	Khun Khun
"	21.5.17		Detail of work of units is the same as that of yesterday except that the 469 FIELD Coy RE have completed the OP at L4 a.9.7 assisted in the erection of a double apron wire fence in front of roads at COLOGNE FARM	
		9 p.m.	Two sections of 467 FIELD Coy RE ordered to proceed to EQUANCOURT tomorrow morning 22nd inst.	
		11 p.m.	59th DIVISION WARNING ORDER No 42 copy No 9 received	Khun
	22.5.17		Two sections 469 and 470 FIELD Coys RE attached to Brigades in the forward area 467 FIELD Coy RE Erecting Adrian Huts and shelters in BERNES all HERVILLY and wooden hut in ESTREES. Digging trenches on main line of resistance at L22.c.6.7. and at L4.c. 469 " loading stones at ROISEL for BERNES-VENDELLES ROAD. Finishing Adrian hut at H.H.Q. 470 " Special work in camp for baths and cycle shelters	Khun

WAR DIARY
INTELLIGENCE SUMMARY. *Continued:—*

(Erase heading not required.)

Army Form C. 2118.

Place	Date	Hour	Summary of Events and Information	Remarks and references to Appendices
BOUVINCOURT	23/5/17	1.30 pm	59 DIVISIONAL ORDER No. 43 - Copy No 9 received. Two sections of the 469 and 470 FIELD Coys, with the Infantry Brigade in the forward area. 467 FIELD Coy RE - Two Section preparing D.H.Q. Camp at EQUANCOURT XV CORPS AREA. Erecting Aaron huts and constructing shelters at HERVILLY.	Map Reference Sheet 62C NE SE 1/20,000
			469 " " Wiring round B² post at L17 & 94; wiring No 8 post at L12 c 57 and widening and deepening trenches in main line of resistance. Repairing Aaron huts and making bunks for same at ROISEL. Punching hut at D.H.Q. & waterproofing huts at HANCOURT - repairing BERNES—	Khin.
			470 " " VENDELLE'S ROAD	Khin.
	24/5/17		Detail of work as per yesterday.	
	25/5/17		Detail of work as per the 23rd inst. except that the 2 Section returned from the 176 Bde. and reported back to their company.	Khin.
	26/5/17	5 pm	59 DIVISION ORDER No 44 - copy No 9 received. 2 Sections and Headquarters 467 FIELD Coy RE proceeded by route march to join the other two Sections at EQUANCOURT in the XV Corps area.	
		5 am	469 FIELD Coy RE putting in bunks in huts at ROISEL.	
			470 " " Two Sections with SECUNDERABAD Cavalry Brigade in the forward area. Two " " Waterproofing huts at HANCOURT. Repairing BERNES - VENDELLES Road	Khin. Khin.
	27/5/17		Detail of work if the same as that shewn for 26 "inst.	
EQUANCOURT	28/5/17	5 am	Head Quarters RE moved from BOUVINCOURT to EQUANCOURT. Two sections of 470 FIELD Coy RE returned from SECUNDERABAD CAVALRY Bde to their company stationed in BOUVINCOURT.	Map Reference Sheet 57c S.E. 1/20,000
			467 FIELD Coy RE constructing New Camp for D.H.Q. at EQUANCOURT.	
			469 } FIELD Coys, Clearing up work and making preparation to move early tomorrow.	Khin.

Army Form C. 2118.

WAR DIARY
INTELLIGENCE SUMMARY. — Continued
(Erase heading not required.)

Place	Date	Hour	Summary of Events and Information	Remarks and references to Appendices
EQUANCOURT	29/5/17	11.30 am	59. DIVISIONAL ORDER Nº 45 received (Copy Nº 9).	Map Ref Sheet 57d S.E Scale 1/20,000
		5 am	469 } FIELD Coys R.E. proceeded by route march to NEUVILLE and METZEN-COUTURE 470 } respectively	
	30.5.17		467 FIELD Coy R.E. constructing A.H.Q. Camp at EQUANCOURT. 2 Sections of 467 FIELD Coy attached to 177 INFANTRY BDE } in the forward area 2 Sections of 470 " " " 178 " 467 FIELD Coy R.E. constructing new H.Q. Camp 469 " Filling in crater at road junction V4 b.21.25 470 " making strong shelters in METZEN-COUTURE, putting up shelters at horse lines, marking out C.T.ˢ Nº 3 and 4	Km
	31.5.17		2 Sections each of 467 and 470 FIELD Coys attached to INFANTRY BDES in forward area 467 FIELD Coy R.E. constructing new H.Q. Camp Spillocking out digging new C.T.ˢ Nº 1 and 2. and spillocking the southern portion of TRESCAULT SWITCH 469 " Constructing shelters and camp services at NEUVILLE Siting and Spillocking Strong point at QUEENS CROSS Q.28 d.3.3 Q.27.a " " Filling in mine crater at V4 b.21.25 470 " making out and spillocking 1100 yards of C.T. number Nº 3 and 4 Putting up shelters at horselines and making shelters in METZEN-COUTURE	Km

KM Hilhoss
Capt and adjutant R.E.
59 Divisional R.E.

DAILY WORK REPORT - May 13th. 1917.

WATER SUPPLY.   Ref. Sheet 62c N.E. 1/20000.

180th. Tunnelling Co. R.E.

No.2 Section.

ROISEL.
  K.16.c.6½.8½. Put new delivery pipe and new handle on pump also new bucket - now in working order.
  K.16.a.6½.7½. Pumping water to purify it. Water very muddy.
  K.16.b.6.1.   60' to timber. Removing timber from well. The well is to be used for ablution.

HERVILLY.
  K.24.c.4.4½.   Winding water to purify.

HESBECOURT.
  No.4.L.13.c.6.0.   Clearing debris from well. 84' down.
  No.5.L.13.c.1.7½. Digging down to make solid foundation for brickwork

TEMPLEUX-LE-GUERARD.
  L.2.d.0½.7. No.17. Removing debris from well. 91' down.
  L.2.c.8.6.   No.18. Fixing windlass and staging. Removing debris 83' down.
  L.2.d.1.9.   No.11. Grappling for machinery below water and repairing gas-engine.

HARGICOURT.
  L.10.a.6½.6. No.2. Removed iron girder built in sides of well.
  L.5.a.8½.6.   No.8. Built up top of well, fixed staging and windlass and graded top. Removing debris.

No.4 Section.

BERNES.
  Q.4.c.5.2.   Building up brickwork at top of well. Baling water after chlorinating.

FLECHIN.
  Q.17.c.8.9. Bricking up top of well.
  Q.17.c.2.9. Baling water and repairing defective brickwork.

WOOD on HANCOURT-BOUCLY Road.
  K.31.c.8.2. Timbering.
  K.31.d.8.2. Filling in crater on top.

JEANCOURT.
  L.32.a.6.6. Placing brickwork at surface.
  L.26.d.1.2. Baling and clearing bottom of well.
  L.26.c.9.4. Clearing debris. Present dpeth 45 ft. No water yet.
  L.26.d.2.3. Bricking upper 10' and sinking.

LE VERGUIER.
  L.34.a.7.1. Defective brickwork being repaired and building up above surface level.

WATER SUPPLY.

180th.Co.R.E.
No.2 Section.

(Ref. Sheet 62c.N.E. 1/20000).

ROISEL.
K.16.b.6.1.   Clearing debris from well. Depth 65'.

HERVILLY.
No.7.K.24.c.4.4½. Winding water to purify it and opening out
                   old drain near to it.

HESBECOURT.
No.4.L.13.c.6.0.   Clearing debris from well. Depth 88'.
No.5.L.13.c.1.7½. Digging down side of well for foundation
                   for brickwork - 13' down.

TEMPLEUX.
No.11.L.2.d.6.5½. Repairing gas engine.
No.17.L.2.d.0½.7. Removing debris from well. 98' down.
No.18.L.2.c.8.6.   Removing debris from well - chiefly manure.
                   86' down.
No.8.L.2.d.5½.4.   Cleared top and erected windlass. Depth 50'.

HARGICOURT.
No.2.L.10.a.6½.6. (in works) Removing pump pipes from well.
No.8.L.5.c.8.3.   Removing debris below water, chiefly large
                   stones which have probably formed coping for
                   top of well. These have been got out for 4'6"
                   below water, but this is the limit until the
                   pumps are available for pumping well dry.
                   In the meantime windlass and bucket fixed
                   ready for use. Requires 1 measure chlorination
                   Depth to water 88'. Depth of water 4'6".

No.4 Section.

BERNES.
Q.4.c.5.2.   Finished brickwork on top of well. Fixed dustproof
                   cover. Baling water and clearing refuse.

FLECHIN.
Q.17.c.8.9.   Finished bricking top. Put on dustproof cover.
                   Erected windlass. Baling water.
Q.17.c.2.9.   Bricking and repairing top of well.

WOOD on the HANCOURT-BOUCLY Road.
K.31.c.8.2.   Timbering.
K.31.d.8.2.   Filling in crater on top.

JEANCOURT.
L.32.a.5.6.   Fixing brickwork on surface.
L.26.d.1.2.   Clearing well. Present depth 48'. Depth of water 2'
L.32.a.9.7.   Fixed new rope and bucket.
L.26.c.9.4.   Clearing debris. Present depth 49'.
L.26.d.2.3.   Bricking up to surface.

LE VERGUIER.
L.34.a.7.1.   Brickwork on top finished.
L.33.b.9.8.   Clearing timber below water level and baling.

14/5/17.

WATER SUPPLY. (Ref. Sheet 62c.N.E. 1/20000).

180th.Coy.R.E.

No.2 Section.

ROISEL.
K.16.b.6.1.   Made platform and erected windlass.
                42' to water. 20' of water.   (by.
                This well is to be used for the baths close
K.16.c.6½.8½. Made platform round. Put pump in working order.
                Concreted top of well.
K.16.d.2.8.   Made concrete platform round well.

HESBECOURT.
No.4. L.13.c.6.0. Removing debris from well. 91' down.
No.5. L.13.c.1.7½. Digging down sides of well for foundation
                   to depth of 14'. Building up stones and
                   bricks from bottom upwards. 4' completed.

HARGICOURT.
No.2. L.10.a.6½.6. In works. Removing suction pipes of pump
                   from below water.
No.14. L.4.d.10.8. Removing fallen debris (brickwork) from
                   round top and digging down to get solid
                   brickwork. (Top badly blown by charge).

TEMPLEUX-LE-GUERARD.
No.1. L.2.d.6.5½. Repairing gas engine.
No.6. L.2.b.9.1½. Winding water to purify it.
No.17. L.2.d.0½.7. Removing debris. Depth 103'.
No.18. L.2.c.8.6. Removing debris. Depth 91'.
No.10. L.2.b.6.5½. Repairing damage done to top by shell fire.

No.4 Section.

BERNES.
Q.4.c.5.2.   Chlorinating and baling water.
Q.4.d.5.3.   Bricking and repairing top of well. Erecting
                frame.

FLECHIN.
Q.17.c.8.9.   Chlorinating and baling water.
Q.17.c.2.9.   Bricking and repairing top of well.

WOOD on HANCOURT-BOUCLY Road.
K.31.c.8.2.   Timbering.
K.31.d.8.2.   Filling in crater on top and timbering.

JEANCOURT.
L.32.a.6.6.   Bricking top of well.
L.26.c.9.4.   Clearing debris, tree trunks, etc. Present
                depth 51'.
L.26.d.2.3.   Bricked up to surface. Present depth 17'.

LE VERGUIER.
L.33.b.9.8.   Baling water - still very thick.
L.34.a.7.1.   Bricked and ready for frame.

15.5.17.

- 2 -

WATER SUPPLY.

180th. Tunnelling Co. R.E.
(Ref: Sheet 62c N.E. 1/20000)

No.2 Section.

ROISEL.
- K.16.d.4.5.   Putting concrete top 4' x 4', also concrete drain. In use - requires 1 measure.
- K.16.d.2.8.   Removed portion of house from round top. Repaired pump and cut drain. Concreted top.
- K.16.d.4.4.   Replaced broken windlass by new one. In use - requires 1 measure.

HERVILLY.
- No.7. K.24.c.4.4½. Removed manure heap from close to top of well. Winding water to purify it. 6' of water.

HESBECOURT.
- No.4. L.13.c.6.0. Removed debris from well. Depth 82'. Progress here slow owing to debris being packed tight and large diameter of well (5'0").
- No.5. L.13.c.1.7½. Digging down to make solid foundation for brickwork damaged by charge.

TEMPLEUX-LE-GUERARD.
- No.11. L.2.d.1.9. Trying to get up heavy gear (?) 7' below water.
- No.17. L.2.d.0½.7. Removing debris from well. 82'0".

HARGICOURT.
- L.10.a.6½.6.   Removing pipes, bearers, etc. from well. 78' to water. Measuring down the suction pipe of old pump there is 41' of water.
- L.5.c.8½.6.   Digging round top of well for foundation to repair damage done by charge.

No.4 Section.

BERNES.
- Q.4.c.5.2.   Baling water. Removed a few branches and pieces of wood. Depth to water 99'. Depth of water 20'. Now being treated with chloride of lime to improve quality, which has not yet been passed fit for drinking.

FLECHIN.
- Q.17.c.8.9.   Clearing top. Repaired defective brickwork and bricking up above surface level.
- Q.17.c.2.9.   Well cleared as far as possible of debris. Depth to water 109'. Depth of water 18'. Baling water.

WOOD on HANCOURT-BOUCLY Road.
- K.31.c.8.2.   Timbering.
- K.31.d.8.2.   Filling crater on top.

JEANCOURT.
- L.26.c.7.4.   Windlass repaired and put in new rope.
- L.26.c.9.2.   Cleared well and put new rope.
- L.26.d.1.2.   Baling.
- L.26.c.9.4.   Clearing debris, fir branches, etc.
- L.26.d.2.3.   Sinking.

LE VERGUIER.
- L.33.b.9.8.   Well cleared.
- L.34.a.7.1.   Surface cleared and being bricked up above surface level. Defective brickwork repaired.

12.5.17.

Captain & Adjutant
for C.R.E. 59th. Division.

ORIGINAL.

SECRET.

WAR DIARY

of

HEADQUARTERS 59th DIVN. R.E.

VOLUME V.

1st June 1917.   to   30th June 1917.

Vol 5

ORIGINAL

Army Form C. 2118.

WAR DIARY
~~INTELLIGENCE SUMMARY~~

HEAD QUARTERS
59TH DIVISIONAL R.E.

(Erase heading not required.)

Instructions regarding War Diaries and Intelligence Summaries are contained in F.S. Regs., Part II. and the Staff Manual respectively. Title pages will be prepared in manuscript.

Place	Date JUNE	Hour	Summary of Events and Information	Remarks and references to Appendices
EQUANCOURT	1.6.17		2 Sections of 467 FIELD Coy RE attached to 177 INFANTRY BDE on the forward area until further orders	Sheet 57c S.E. 1/20,000
			2 " " " " 178 " " " " " "	
			467 FIELD Coy RE working on CT's No 1 and 2	
		469	Digging communication trenches in Q27b. Siting, spitlocking and digging strong point in Q27a. Looking for craters at V4 b.25.25. Entrenching and erecting Adrian Hut at V8.b.3.0. Wiring German Trenches at LE MESNIL.	
		470	working on CT No.4 570 yds from Q15 b.9.3. to Q10 c.92. - 1st Task Completed. Wiring out and clearing site of CT No 5 in HAVRINCOURT WOOD in Q15 b and Q15 a. Clearing roads in METZ and Wiring workshops site in camp.	Khun
do	2.6.17	467 FIELD Coy RE	CT No 1 worked to a depth of 8ft for a distance of 70 yards from origin and to 4ft for a further 400 yds.	
		469	Digging strong point at Cemetery SE of METZ Q27.a. One section attached to 467 FIELD Coy for work on communication trenches	
			Filling in craters at V4 b.3.2 and Q29.c.24. Erecting and taking down Adrian Hut at V8 b.88.	
		470	Wiring out and clearing Site of CT No 4 in HAVRINCOURT WOOD and clearing CT from TRESCAULT-GOUZEAUCOURT Road about 600 st of first task completed. Clearing roads in METZ-EN-COUTURE, making workshops and Camplaters.	Khun
do	3.6.17	467 FIELD Coy RE	CT No 1 50 yards completed commencing from Q29 a.4.7. - Excavated to 6' deep up to Q29 a.5.9, Excavated to 4' deep to Q23.C.6.2.	
		469	One Section attached to 467 FIELD Coy RE for work on CT No.1. Working on strong point at Q27.a. on dugouts at Q26 b.30. OP at Q5 c. Working over craters at V4 b.3.2. Sitting in crater at P29.c.2.u. Erecting Adrian Hut at V10 a.3.7. Taking down 2 Nissen huts at V2 b.3.2.	
		470	Digging front line trenches, making shelters in support line. Siting No 3 CT Working at CT No 4, widening and deepening CT 4 for 160 yards, and digging 30 yards in new ground.	
			2 Sections 256 TUNNELLING Co RE attached to Division for work on dugouts	

WAR DIARY / INTELLIGENCE SUMMARY

Army Form C. 2118. — continued.

Place	Date	Hour	Summary of Events and Information	Remarks and references to Appendices
EQUANCOURT	4/6/17		Detail of work of the 2/1st Companies in a continuation of the work of the previous day. 2 Sections of 256 TUNNELLING Coy RE at work on night Battalion Head Quarters at Q.15.c.7.5 and on Brigade Head Quarters at Q.15.c.7.5.	Sheet 57°S.E. 1/20,000 *Kerr*
do	5/6/17		467 FIELD Coy RE Continuing work on CT No 1. One section attached to 467 FIELD Coy RE. for work on Communication Trenches. 469 Working on strong point at Q.27.a, an O.P. at Q.25.a, and on dugout at P.29.c.24. Completing craters at V.6.1-32 and filling in craters at P.29.c.24. Erecting huts and Nissen huts at V.10.a.8.6.	
			470 — Digging trenches on front line, making shelters in support line, marking out CT No 4 "Hindenl' CT No 4 for 150 yards from Q.15.b.8.60 and completed excavation for further 200 yards (2 sects) making dugouts under Bank at Road at LONE TREE at Point Q.16.a.85.55. Clearing new site for entanglements line in HAVRINCOURT WOOD.	
			2 Sections 256 T.Coy RE Constructing dug outs at Q.17.b.55, Q.15.c.75, Q.34.a.9 Q.11.a.8.9, Q.11.d.74, Q.26.b.68.	*Kerr*
do	6/6/17		467 FIELD Coy RE Continuing work on CT No 1. 469 — One section attached to 467 FIELD Coy RE for work on Communication Trenches. Strong point at Q.27.a completed. Filling in crater at P.29.c.24. Erecting huts in EQUANCOURT - Instructing infantry in construction of wire entanglements.	
			470 — Improving front line trench in night Sub sector. Completing 2 shelters in support line in right Grenade Coy. Man. Continuing work on CT No 4, 750 yards from support line intermediate line in wood. Revetting night and left battalion site for entanglements. Head quarters and evening elephant shelters.	
			2 Sections 256 TUNNELLING Coy RE Continuing work detailed in yesterday's report together with dugout at R.13.a.4.8 and O.P. dugout at Q.5.c.6.3.	*Kerr*

WAR DIARY / INTELLIGENCE SUMMARY

Army Form C. 2118. — Continued

Place	Date	Hour	Summary of Events and Information	Remarks and references to Appendices
EQUANCOURT	7.6.17		Detail of work of units is a continuation of that for yesterday	Map Ref Sheet 57c SE 1/20,000
	8.6.17	8.30pm	DIVISIONAL ORDER No 46 Copy No 9 received. 467 FIELD Coy RE - working on CT N°1 (ONE) 469 " " Our section attached to 467 Field Coy RE to work on CT N° ONE. Filling in craters at P27.c.2.4, keeping in water to Brigade Camp at EQUANCOURT Constructing stables at Brigade finished dump. Extending infantry in the completion of new entanglements.	
	4.90 "		Improving front line trench in left Brigade sector, making shelters in M.G. and TM'B in Support line. Digging CT N°3 from Support line to BEAUCAMP AILLIEM Road and toward present line and making it out. Breastwork in CT N°4 across valley (near to 4") digging 270 yd of O.T. joining up with CT N°4 from about Q.10.d.6.7 to the German trench at Q.60.a.8.6. Revetting firesteps in front line. Laying duck boards in CT N°4. Excavating up CT N°4 trench unaltered LONE TREE road at Q.16.a.1.5. Enchelt, elephant shelters to Brigade H.Q. in wood at Q.15.c.7.3. Looking on Brigade baths at METZ-EN-COUTURE.	Khin
			2. Section 256 TUNNELLING Coy RE Continuing work on dug-out tunnel.	
	9.6.17		467 FIELD Coy RE. 200 yards of CT N°1 completed - tunning searching 469 " " Our section attached to 467 FIELD Coy RE to work on CT N°1. Filling in craters at P27.c.2.4. Construction of water scheme for 178 Inf Bde at EQUANCOURT. Laying unfinished pipe line by Femmes. Construction of water scheme to CT N°3, 1,500 yards from present line to FRESCAULT-GOUZEAUCOURT road.	
	4.90 "		Digging 14 track on CT N°3, 2,500 yards from present line to FRESCAULT-GOUZEAUCOURT road at about Q.110.a.1. Completing unfinished tasks of preceding night in CT N°3 from present to Support line banking out CT N°3 between TRESCAULT-GOUZEAUCOURT road and extension to line and improving front line. Completing shelters in Support line. Raising parapet where necessary out improving CT N°4. Joining up CT N°4 a bank mound at Q.16.a.15. Breaching and laying duck-boards in CT N°4. Making elephant shelters for Left Bde H.Q. Q.15.c.7.5. Jogging dug-outs at the following places Q.15.c.23, Q.34.a.19, Q.11.a.Fig, Q.26.c.28, R.13.a.6.2, Q.5.c.24, Q.5.c.63, Q.17.a.14.	Khin
			2. Section 256 TUNNELLING Co. RE	

WAR DIARY or INTELLIGENCE SUMMARY

Army Form C. 2118.

Place	Date	Hour	Summary of Events and Information	Remarks and references to Appendices
EQUANCOURT	10.6.17		467 FIELD Coy RE Continuing work upon CT No 1. One section attached to 467 Field Coy RE for work on CT No 1.	Map Reference Sheet 57 c. 1/20,000
			469 " Construction of Spray baths and ablution benches at V10.d.7.9. filling in craters at P29.c.2.4 and constructing sprag line in left Bde Sector.	
			470 " Repairing and improving front line in left Bde Sector, making shelters in sunken lane, making CT 3 South. Digging 600 yds of CT 3 from TRESCAULT-GOUZEAUCOURT road to Q16.c.8.1. Clearing CT4 and digging sunk roads. Erecting elephant shelters for BHQ working on Brigade baths at METZ-en-COUTURE.	Khan
			2 Sections 256 T. Coy RE at work on the following dugouts. Q15.c.7.5 Q30.a.19 Q11.a.5.9 Q11.a.7.4 Q26.b.7.? Q15.c.6.3 Q5.c.8.6 Q5.c.5.3 Q12.a.6.3 Q17.a.1.4, Q15.c.8.3 Q11.a.7.7 R13.a./A.F.	
do	11.6.17	8 pm	Cotton No 554/10/16.G received.	
			467 FIELD Coy RE Continuing work upon CT No 1 assisted by a section from 469 FIELD Coy RE	
			469 " Constructing spray baths and ablution benches at V10.a.7.9. Vg.a.2.5.Vg.2.5/V16.6. filling in craters at P29.c.2.4. Repairing well in EQUAN COURT and erecting sunken Inf Bn bivouac gutters.	
			490 " Digging CT3 540 yds of ? trench from Q.15.a/c.to Q.16.B.2.6.7 and marking out a further length. Improving front line in Right Bde Area. Erecting shelters in support line. Clearing CT No 4. Erecting elephant shelters for Brigade HQ at Q.15.a.7.7 Repairing roof of the setting Stone at Brigade Baths in METZ en COUTURE	Khan
			2 Sections of 256 T. Coy RE. Dugout at Q.15.c.7.5 finished, continuing work on others as detailed in yesterday report and commencing work upon the following new dugouts at Q.33.a.8.9 and Harden gun dugouts making road tunnel at Q.11.c.a.a.d.	
do	12.6.17	8.30 pm	DIVISIONAL ORDER No 47 continuing this work detailed in yesterday report. All units continuing the work detailed in yesterday report.	
		6 pm	G 521/11.G received. Inf Bn burying buried cable schemes.	
do	13.6.17		467 FIELD Coy RE continuing work upon CT N:1 assisted by a section from 469 FIELD Coy RE	
			469 " Construction of Spray baths & ablution benches at V10.d.7.9. Vg.a.2.5. and V16.b.2.3. Construction of gunrale shelters at Q.25.a.11. Making road in craters at P29.c.2.a. Working upon Youlo in EQUANCOURT.	
			470 " Digging CT3 1100 yds new trench on 1st task and marking out. Improving front line constructing shelters in outpost line. Repairing and strengthening CTH.C. in left Sub Sector of Right Brigade Sector. Issuing out kit to four up the 3 advanced posts in Left Sub Sector of Right	

Army Form C. 2118.

WAR DIARY
or
INTELLIGENCE SUMMARY.
(Erase heading not required)

Instructions regarding War Diaries and Intelligence Summaries are contained in F.S. Regs., Part II and the Staff Manual respectively. Title pages will be prepared in manuscript.

continued:-

Place	Date	Hour	Summary of Events and Information	Remarks and references to Appendices
EQUANCOURT	13.6.17		Continued:— 256 TUNNELLING Coy RE. 2 Sections continuing work upon the following dugouts :- Q.34.a.9, Q.11.a.89, Q.11.a.74, Q.26.b.88, R.13.a.1.9, Q.5.c.24, Q.12.c.63, Q.15.c.73. Q.25.c.97, Q.20.a.9, Q.20.a.66, Q.20.b.33, Q.21.c.67, Q.21.a.25, Q.29.c.25 and CT4 following OPs Q.5.c.63, Q.5.c.53, Q.17.a.14, Q.11.a.77, Q.5.c.41, Q.5.c.75.	Map Sheet 57 C S.E. 1/2 0000 Khm Khm
do	14.6.17		Units continuing work as detailed in yesterday's report	
	15.6.17		467 FIELD Coy RE. continuing work upon CT N°1. Coorah by our Section of 467 Field Coy RE. 469 " " hacking road over culvert at P.9.c.29. Drawing of iron cage at Q.25.b.37. Grenade Shelter at Q.25.a. Construction Spur belts at V.10.d.79, V.9.a.95, V.16.b.23. 470 " " hacking out line journey of outposts in right sub-sector. Left Brigade Motor also Left sub sector. Digging 2nd task on CT3. 520 yds forward from about Q.16.d.2.0, but making bridge over wind at Q.16.c.51. Digging 1st task on CT3 150 yds back from Q.16.c.20. Drawing and duckboarding CT4. Locating Boxes wired trunway from METZ to TRESCAULT and underconstruction RE. dumps. Erection of Elephant Shelters for Left 2dr Sec BEAUCAMP. Work on divisional RE. dumps.	Khm
			2 Sections 256 TUNNELLING Co RE. working on dugouts and observation posts as detailed on attached Appendix N° I.	
do	16.6.17		Detail of work is a continuation of that of yesterday. for work of 2 Sections 256 TUNNELLING Coy RE See appendix II	Khm
do	17.6.17		467 FIELD Coy RE. continuing work upon CT N°1 awarded by our section of 469 FIELD Coy RE. Constructing Spur belts and situation tunnels at V.10.d.79, V.11.a.88, V.9.d.23. Erection of 469 " " war cage Q.25.b.37. Grenade Shelter at Q.25.a. Erecting Horse trough and fencing at V.9.a.PF. Our Section employed upon buried Cable Salient. 470 " " improving front line. hacking out line of wire to outpost line. Digging second task on CT3 450 yds forward from about Q.16.c.30. Finishing unfinished task and laying duckboards in CT3. Drawing windsay & duckboarding CT4 in Q.co.6. Drawing silo & repairing buildings in METZ. Erecting elephant shelters in Q.15.c.	
			2 Sections 256 TUNNELLING Co RE. working on dugouts etc as detailed on attached Appendix N° III	Khm

WAR DIARY
INTELLIGENCE SUMMARY.
continued

Army Form C. 2118.

(Erase heading not required.)

Instructions regarding War Diaries and Intelligence Summaries are contained in F.S. Regs., Part II. and the Staff Manual respectively. Title pages will be prepared in manuscript.

Place	Date	Hour	Summary of Events and Information	Remarks and references to Appendices
EQUANCOURT	18.6.17	9 am	H.Quarter W.D. S.S. 4/18/19 G. detailing 59 Division Defence Scheme.	Map Sheet 57c S.E. 1/20,000
		8.45 pm	59 DIVISION ORDER Nº 48 Copy Nº 9 received.	
			467 FIELD Coy RE Continuing work upon CT Nº1 assisted by one Section of 469 FIELD Coy RE.	
			469 " Working on ablution trenches and spray baths at V10A79, V16623 and P23C27. Constructing means of water cap Q25f3.7. Horse standings at V6d27. One Section employed burying cable scheme.	
			470 " " Improving old front line. Japing out CT5 to advanced posts and digging them. Constructing RAP in sunken road at BEAUCAMP. Digging in CT3 and making steps to tunnel and CT3 at Q11c24. Also making tram between Q10b and Q11a. Clearing sites for new camp in METZ. Erecting elephant shelters for Brigade H.Q. in Q15c. Emergency ride to BEAUCAMP.	
			2 Section 256 TUNNELLING Coy RE continuing work detailed on attached appendix III.	Known
do.	19.6.17		Work of units a continuation of the work detailed in yesterday's report. 2 Section 256 TUNNELLING Coy RE continuing work detailed on attached appendix IV.	Known
do.	20.6.17		467 FIELD Coy RE Continuing work upon CT Nº1 and enlarging new Camp in METZEN COUTURE. 469 " the section working upon cable branch and one section assisting the 467 FIELD Coy RE. Constructing premises of new camp at Q25f3.7 and making horse standings around water trough at V6d77 and V6a.	
			470 " Working in front of front line. Japing out front line stepping up stations in new front line. Making shelters in forward support line. Making steps to tunnel in CT3 under road Q11C51 and draining and duck-boarding CT3. Clearing new CT in Q11a and carrying up trench bonds. Also clearing between Q10b and Q10d making RAP in sunken road BEAUCAMP. Preparing site for new camp in METZ.	Known
			2 Section 256 TUNNELLING Coy RE continuing work as detailed on attached appendix V.	Known

A5834 Wt. W4973/M687 750,000 8/16 D.D. & L. Ltd. Forms/C.2118/13.

WAR DIARY

INTELLIGENCE SUMMARY. — continued.

Army Form C. 2118.

Place	Date	Hour	Summary of Events and Information	Remarks and references to Appendices
EQUANCOURT	21:6:17		467 FIELD Coy R.E. at work upon C.T. N°1 assisted by one section 469 FIELD Coy R.E.	MAP REF. Sheet 57C S.E. 1/20,000
			469 " one section employed upon buried cable scheme. Constructing prisoners of war cage at Q.25.b.37. Repairing wall at P.22.a.2.6. Making standings round horse troughs at V.6.d.7.7. and V.8.a. Erecting shower baths at NEUVILLE P.23.c.5.3.	
			470 " " Making shelters in forward support line. Wiring and duckboarding C.T.3 at Q.16.c and C.T.4 in Q.11.a. also making berm on C.T.4. Pumping out tunnel under road at Q.11.C.5.1. and completing steps to tunnel. Erecting elephant shelters for Brigade Headquarters in Q.15.c. 1 shelter completed. Second 6" in progress as detailed in attached appendix III	
do	22:6:17		2 Sections 256 TUNNELLING Co R.E. at work as along with one section of 469th FIELD Coy. R.E.	Above
			467 Field Coy. R.E. at work upon C.T. No 1 assisted by one section of 469 Field Coy. R.E.	MAP. REF. SHEET 57C. S.E. 1/20,000
			469 " " " one section employed on buried cable scheme. Constructing Prisoners of war cage at Q.25.b.3.7. Making standing round horse troughs at V.6.d.7.7. & V.8.a. Wiring near Erecting shower baths at NEUVILLE P.23.c.5.3. Constructing shelters at Ammunition Dump P.29.c.6.1.	
			470 " " " R.E. Improving frontline. Work on tunnel for C.T.3 at Q.11.4.2. Taping out line for new front line. Constructing shelters for M.O. at R.A.P. in fort Gratia to BEAUCAMP. Wiring & duckboarding C.T.4. Q.11.a. Wiring near frontline. Work on near Bapaume H.Q. in Q.15.C.	31. F.
do	23.6.17		2 Sections 256 TUNNELLING Coy. R.E. at work on day-outs etc as detailed attached appendix VII.	
			467 Field Coy R.E. at work upon C.T. No 1 assisted by one section 469 Field Coy. R.E. Constructing prisoners of war cage at Q.25.b. 3.7. One section employed on buried cable scheme. Constructing prisoners of war Cage at NEUVILLE. Making standings round horse troughs at V.6.d.7.7. & V.8.a. Erecting shower baths at P.23. c.5.3. Constructing shelters at ammunition dump P.19.c.6.1.	
			470 " " R.E. Constructing shelters in forward support line. Driving tunnel for C.T. 3 at Q.11.C.5.2. Training & duckboarding C.T.4 & Q.11.a. Erecting Elephant Shelters for Brigade H.Q in Q.15.C. C.T.5 in Q.16.C. Making frames for R.A. O.P.	
			2 Sections 256 Tunnelling Coy. R.E. at work on day-outs etc. as detailed in attached appendix VIII	W.E.

Army Form C. 2118.

WAR DIARY
or
INTELLIGENCE SUMMARY.
(Erase heading not required.)

Instructions regarding War Diaries and Intelligence Summaries are contained in F.S. Regs., Part II. and the Staff Manual respectively. Title pages will be prepared in manuscript.

Place	Date	Hour	Summary of Events and Information	Remarks and references to Appendices
EQUANCOURT	24.6.17		467 FIELD Coy R.E. at work upon C.T. No.1 assisted by one section 469 FIELD Coy R.E.	MAP REF: Sheet 57c S.E./24000
			469 " " One Section employed upon Armoured Cable delivery. Constructing Bivouacs at War Cage at Q.27.d.1.2.7. Making planking round horse Trough at V.6.d.7.7. V.6.a. Burying Armoured Cable at NEUVILLE at P.23.c.5.3. Constructing Shelters on ammunition dump P.29.c.6.1. Construction of new Transport lines at EQUANCOURT.	
			470 " " Laying dumps in C.T.3. Training & dust-sprinkling C.T.4. Making Shelter Frames. Constructing Shelters & Shelters for Brigade H.Q. in Q.15.c.	N.T.
do.	25.6.17		2 Sections 256 Tunnelling Coy. R.E. on dug-outs etc. as detail in appendix IX. 467 FIELD Coy R.E. at work upon C.T. No.1 & 2 assisted by one Section of 469 FIELD Coy R.E.	
			469 " " One Section employed upon Buried Cable Scheme. Constructing Prisoners Wire Cage at Q.15 & 3.7. Building French Shelters at Q.25.a. (Stanleyfield). Making Standings round Horse Troughs at V.6.d.7.7. & V.6.a. Burying Armoured Cable at NEUVILLE P.23.C.5.3. Constructing Shelters on Ammunition dump. Constructing new Transport lines at EQUANCOURT.	
			470 " " Dusting Shelters & improved support lines. Training & track Grading. Making Dump in C.T.3 at about Q.11.c. & d. Pumping out water from C.T.3 in Q.11.6 + c. making Shelter Frames, Frames & duck-boarding C.T.4 in Q.11.a. Making Screens on Beaucamp Valley at Q.16.c.o.5. (Cardin) Replacement Shelter for Brigade H.Q. in Q.15.C. (Division Order No 49 received 5:30 p.m.)	N.T.
do:	26.6.17		2 Sections of 256 Tunnelling Coy. R.E. on dug-outs etc. as detail in appendix X (attached) 467 FIELD Coy R.E. at work upon C.T. the 1 & 2 Assisted by one Section of 469 FIELD Coy R.E.	
			469 " " One Section employed upon Burying Cable scheme. Making out Sites for Camps. Making Standings round Horse Troughs to V.6.d.7.7. Constructing Ground Sheeters Q.15.d. (Ramoy) attack at. on ETRICOURT, V.P.a. Repairing Road V.10.6.1.2. Burying Armoured Cable at NEUVILLE at P.23.c.5.3. Constructing new Transport lines at EQUANCOURT.	
			470 " " Making Shelters, Shelter frames, making dumps for C.T.3 at Q.11.c. & d. Making Screen on C.T.3 in Q.11.a. Pumping, Training & Shelter framing C.T.4 in Q.11.a. Shelter framing H.Q. in Q.15.c. Making terms on C.T.3 in Q.11. d. Dusting C.T. Shelter framing etc. on details in attached appendices XI.	N.T.

2 Sections 256 Tunnelling Coy. R.E.

A5834 Wt.W4973 M687 750,000 8/16 D.D.&L. Ltd. Forms/C.2118/13.

Army Form C. 2118.

WAR DIARY
or
INTELLIGENCE SUMMARY.
(Erase heading not required.)

Instructions regarding War Diaries and Intelligence Summaries are contained in F.S. Regs., Part II. and the Staff Manual respectively. Title pages will be prepared in manuscript.

Place	Date	Hour	Summary of Events and Information	Remarks and references to Appendices
EQUANCOURT	27.6.17		467 FIELD COY R.E. at work upon C.T's No.1 & No.2 assisted by one section of 469 FIELD COY. R.E. one section employed upon Aerial Cable Scheme. Making cut jointing boxes of Camps. Making Standards. Draining Camps at V.6.a.7.7. V.6.a.2.6. Repairing roads at V.10. 2.2. L. & V.10.a.2.75. & V.4.g.2.2. (EQUANCOURT) (Work complete).	Auth: Rep: Sheet 57c. S.E. 1/20,000
	"		469 " " " Lines at EQUANCOURT. Stores Shown. Battn at NEUVILLE. P.23.C.5.3. Constructing Ammunition Dump.	
	"		470 " " " Lines at EQUANCOURT. Erecting Pill Boxes. Erecting Huts in Dressing Stations. Sheets & Framing C.T.3 at Q.11.c.4.1. Wiring in front of front line. Making shelters frames & mounts & sheets under C.T. 4 in Q.11.a. Cleaning Ben on C.T. & in Q.11.a. Maintaining electric light for Bathhouse. Training & Work. (complete) C.T. 2. Completed Shelters & Shelters for Batt H.Q. in Q.15.c. (complete). Communication Trenches from O. NETZ - TRESSAULT road. Trenches in proof at Rile.	X.F.
	28.6.17		2 Sections 256 TUNNELLING COY. R.E. employed as sketched at apendix XII. 467 FIELD COY. R.E. at work upon C.T's No.1 & No.2 assisted by one section of 469 Field Coy. R.E. 469 " " " Making out Aerie [?] new Camps. Making Standing Posts for Shoe Thompos at V.6.a.7.7. V.8.a.5.6 & (P.33.c.a.3). Constructing Funnels Skidded at Q.25.a. Ammunition Transport (P.24.c.5.6).	
	"		470 " " " Lines at EQUANCOURT. Erecting new Camp near Ammunition Dump P.29.C.1.6. Constructing Pill boxes in Dressing Station. P24.C.1.6. Erecting Pill Boxes in Dressing Station. Pill Strips. 200 yds C.T.3 & making Dumps of Rolling down old Dump & lining up Switched by Battery of NETZ. Cleaning & making Tressault Rd. Sealed O.P. for R.F.A. at Billhim Dam. Draining & 130 yds (3rd Task) New Switch Road. 1 C.T. No.4. attached to Infantry Partieu C.T.4. 4 [?] 4 C.T. returning from line.	X.F.
	29.6.17		1 Section 256 TUNNELLING COY R.E. on duty nite in details in attack of junction of 469 FIELD COY. R.E. 467 FIELD COY R.E. at work upon C.T's No. 142 assisted by remainder of 469 Field Coy R.E. Making out Aerial new Camps. Making branching & making Shoe Thompos & wide Points at P.3.3.c.L.3. P.22.c.5.6. V.6.a.7.7. V.8.a.2.6. Making Gun Transport Lines at EQUANCOURT. Constructing Funnels Skidded at Q.25.a. Erecting Dump. Shower Baths at NEUVILLE. at P.21.c.3.4.5. Constructing Platform Ammunition Dump at P.29.c.1.6. Work commenced on Strong Point at Queens Cross at Q.2.d.4.3.	X.F.

A5834 Wt. W4073/M687 750,000 8/16 D.D. & L. Ltd. Forms/C.2118/13.

Army Form C. 2118.

WAR DIARY
or
INTELLIGENCE SUMMARY.
(Erase heading not required.)

Instructions regarding War Diaries and Intelligence Summaries are contained in F. S. Regs., Part II. and the Staff Manual respectively. Title pages will be prepared in manuscript.

Place	Date	Hour	Summary of Events and Information	Remarks and references to Appendices
EQUANCOURT	29-6-17		*Continued*.	map Ref. Sheet 57 c S.E. 1/20,000.
			470th FIELD COY R.E. Erecting shelters in front line system. Draining forward part of C.T.3. Revetting front bay in front system. Widening & draining slight trench. C.T.4 in Q.11.a. Widening front line left sub-station. Cleaning away old pump tilting pound well at BEE FACTORY METZ Q.25.b.5.9. Sinking O.P. for R.A. near BILLEM FARM Q.25.c.9.2. Cleaning & deepening C.T.3 in Q.17.a. Refixing METZ-TRESCAULT Road assisted by our Platoon of 150th Labour Coy. 3 M.T. lorries & 15 tons of stone drawn from siding.	N.T.
			2 Sections 256 TUNNELLING COY R.E. on duty as detailed in appendix XIV.	
			467th FIELD COY R.E. at work upon C.T. no 1	
	30-6-17		469th " " " Making new site for new Canteen. Making standings of new round horse troughs at V.6.d.7.7. P.33.c. P.28.c.5.6 & V.F.a.5.6 Making tunnel & shelters at Q.15.a. Making new transport lines at EQUANCOURT. Erecting stove & flag. Baths at NEUVILLE at P.23.c.3.5. Making dump point at QUEEN'S CROSS at Q.15.d.4.3.	
			470th " " " Pumping out C.T.3 in Q.11.c. Revetting forward line in front line system. Support trench to C.T.3 90 yds in Q.16.d. towards right battalion H.Q. Signal. 190 yds (with flares) in Q.11.d. Carrying out duck boards for C.T.3. Draining & duck boarding C.T.4 in Q.11.a. Widening front line. Cleaning out C.T.3 & duck boarding. Timbering pump at about Q.16.c. 6.9.4. Cleaning machine & pump well head in Best Factory METZ at Q.25.b.5.6. Work on O.P. K.6. at 8.5.C. 3. Mending shelter frames to. Refixing METZ-TRESCAULT Road assisted by one platoon of 150th Labour Coy; 2 M.T. lorries & 18 tons of stone drawn from siding at P.24 b.5.6.	W.T.
			2 Sections of 256th TUNNELLING COY 12 F.E. on duty out as detailed in appendix XV.	

A. Taylor Lieut:
for C.R.E. 59th Division.

1/7/17

APPENDIX I.

256th. Tunnelling Co.R.E.

DAILY PROGRESS REPORT for 24 hrs. ending midnight 15.6.17.

Index No.	Designation and Locality of working.		Progress.	Total length.	Percentage of total work cmpltd.	Remarks.
20.	Bde.H.Q.	Q.34.a.1.9.	6'9" 4'6"	57'9" 61'6"	88%	No.3 Chamber.Stretchers " 2 " and facing.
21.	Batt.H.Q.	Q.11.a.8.9.	3'0" 4'6"	15'0" 10'6"	44%	No.1 Chamber. " 2 "
22.	Batt.H.Q.	Q.11.d.7.4.	32'3"	166'6"	89%	Chambering.
23.	RAMC Dugout.	Q.26.b.8.8.	24'0"	76'6"	40%	Chambering.
26.	Bde.Battle H.Q.	Q.18.b.8.9.	14'3" 11'0"	263'3" 26'6"	80%	Chambering. Entrance.
27.	R.A.O.P.	Q.5.c.6.3.	3'5"	36'2"	55%	Entrance level.
30.	M.G.D.	Q.5.c.8.4.	3'4" 2'3"	27'4" 27'9"	55%	No.1 Entrance. " 2 "
31.	M.G.D.	Q.12.a.6.3.	2'6" 2'3"	28'6" 25'9"	55%	No.1 Entrance. " 2 "
32.	Bde.O.P.	Q.5.c.5.3.	3'7"	25'11"	42%	Entrance.
33.	Bde.O.P.	Q.17.a.1.4.	2'6"	26'4"	42%	Entrance.
34.	Arty.dugout.	Q.15.c.8.3.	2'0" 1'7"	23'0" 18'7"	27%	No.1 Entrance. " 2 "
36.	Arty.O.P.	Q.11.a.7.7.	4'6"	4'6"	58%	Chambering.
40.	GOUZEAUCOURT Wood well.	Q.28.c.1.7.	2'9" 6'8"	61'9" --	--	Found water at 60 ft. Deepening trench round well.
41.	Divl.Battle H.Q.	Q.25.c.9.7.	6'9" 4'0" 5'0" 4'0"	41'3" 4'0" 39'6" 4'0"	9%	No.1 Entrance. " 1 " lateral. No.2 " " 2 " "
42.	Bde.R.A.O.P.	Q.5.c.4.2.	3'0" 3'0"	13'9" 13'6"	27%	No.1 Entrance. " 2 "
43.	M.G.D.	Q.20.a.1.9.	4'0"	20'0"	33%	Entrance.
44.	M.G.D.	Q.20.a.6.6.	4'0"	20'0"	33%	"
45.	M.G.D.	Q.20.b.3.3.	4'0"	20'0"	33%	"
46.	Bde.R.A.O.P.	Q.5.c.7.5.	2'6"	11'0"	19%	"
47.	M.G.D.	Q.21.c.6.7.	4'0"	16'0"	27%	"
48.	M.G.D.	Q.21.d.2.5.	3'6"	15'6"	27%	"
49.	M.G.D.	Q.29.c.4.2.	4'0"	16'0"	27%	"
56.	Right Batt H.Q.	Q.23.c.6.3.	8'0" 8'0"	8'0" 8'0"	1%	No.1 Entrance. " 2 "

APPENDIX II.

256th. Tunnelling Co. R.E.

DAILY PROGRESS REPORT for 24 hours ending midnight 16th. June 1917.

Index No.	Designation and Locality of working.		Progress.	Total Length.	Percentage of total work completed.	Remarks.
20.	Bde H.Q.	Q.34.a.1.9.	--	--	100%	Clearing up. Finished.
21.	Batt H.Q.	Q.11.a.8.9.	3'0" 3'0"	18'0" 13'6"	45%	No.1 Chamber. " 2 "
22.	Batt.H.Q.	Q.11.d.7.4.	21'0"	187'6"	100%	Chambering. Finished
23.	RAMC Dugout.	Q.26.b.8.8.	15'0"	91'6"	45%	Chambering.
26.	Bde.Battle H.Q. 	Q.18.b.8.9.	18'0" 16'0"	281'3" 16'0"	85%	Chambering. Dump trench.
27.	R.A.O.P.	Q.5.c.6.3.	2'7" 3'3"	38'9" 3'3"	60%	Entrance Chambering.
30.	M.G.D.	Q.5.c.8.4.	3'3" 3'0"	30'7" 30'9"	60%	No.1 Entrance level. " 2 " "
31.	M.G.D.	Q.12.a.6.3.	2'6" 2'0"	31'0" 27'9"	60%	" 1 " " " 2 " "
32.	Bde O.P.	Q.5.c.5.3.	3'4"	29'3"	47%	Entrance.
33.	Bde O.P.	Q.17.a.1.4.	3'6"	29'10"	47%	Entrance going level.
34.	Artillery dugout. 	Q.15.c.8.3.	4'0" 3'0"	27'0" 21'7"	29%	No.1 Entrance. " 2 "
36.	Artillery O.P. 	Q.11.a.7.7.	3'0"	7'6"	65%	Chambering.
40.	GOUZEAUCOURT Wd.well. 	Q.28.c.9.7.	10'9"	14'9"	12%	~~Ne~~ Jumping a 7' hole and blasting it.
41.	Divl.battle H.Q. 	Q.25.c.9.7.	10'9" 8'10"	14'9" 12'10"	12%	No.1 Entrance lateral. " 2 " "
42.	Bde R.A.O.P.	Q.5.c.4.2.	3'0" 3'0"	16'9" 16'6"	35%	No.1 Entrance. " 2 "
43.	M.G.D.	Q.20.a.1.9.	5'6"	25'6"	42%	Entrance.
44.	M.G.D.	Q.20.a.6.6.	4'0"	24'0"	40%	"
45.	M.G.D.	Q.20.b.3.3.	4'0"	24'0"	40%	"
46.	Bde.R.A.O.P.	Q.5.c.7.5.	3'0"	14'0"	24%	"
47.	M.G.D.	Q.21½c.7.5 6.7.	4'0"	20'0"	33%	"
48.	M.G.D.	Q.21.d.2.5.	3'6"	19'0"	31%	"
49.	M.G.D.	Q.29.c.4.2.	4'0"	20'0"	33%	"
56.	Right Bde.H.Q. 	Q.23.c.6.3.	8'0" 8'0"	16'0" 16'0"	4%	No.1 Entrance. " 2 "
57.	"	Q.12.d.5.4.	8'0" 4'0"	8'0" 4'0"	1%	No.1 Entrance. " 3 "

APPENDIX III.

256th. Tunnelling Co. R.E.

DAILY PROGRESS REPORT for 24 hours ending midnight 18.6.17.

Index No.	Designation and locality of working.	Progress.	Total Length	Percent of total work compltd.	Remarks.
21.	Batt H.Q. Q.11.a.8.9.	4'6"	42'0"	47%	Chambering.
23.	RAMC Dugout. Q.26.b.8.8.	21'0"	127'6"	53%	"
26.	Bde battle H.Q. Q.18.b.8.9.	18'0"	317'3"	95%	"
27.	R.A.O.P. Q.5.c.6.3.	1'9" 3'6"	6'9" 9'9"	85%	Shaft, Chambering.
30.	M.G.D. Q.5.c.8.4.	3'3" 3'3"	33'10" 4'3"	79%	No.1 Entrance. " 2 " lateral.
31.	M.G.D. Q.12.a.6.3.	6'6" 1'9"	8'0" 31'6"	79%	No.1 Entrance. " 2 "
32.	Bde. O.P. Q.5.c.5.3.	5'9"	39'0"	58%	Entrance going level.
33.	Bde O.P. Q.17.a.1.4.	2'6" 3'0"	35'10" 3'0"	59%	Entrance. Shaft.
36.	Arty.OP. Q.11.a.7.7.	4'6"	15'0"	88%	Chambering.
34,	Arty.dugout. Q.15.c.8.3.	3'6" 3'9"	33'6" 28'9"	33%	No.1 Entrance. " 2 "
40.	GOUZEAUCOURT Wd.well. Q.28.c.1.7.	1'3"	61'9"	--	Fixing winch. Baling water.
41.	Divl.battle H.Q. Q.25.c.9.7.	9'9" 9'9" 2'0" 3'0"	35'9" 32'6" 2'0" 3'0"	16%	No.1 Entrance lateral. " 2 " " " 1 Chamber. " 10 "
42.	Bde. R.A.O.P. Q.5.c.4.2.	3'0" 2'9"	22'9" 22'3"	48%	No.1 Entrance. " 2 "
46.	Bde R.A.O.P. Q.5.c.7.5.	3'0"	20'0"	31%	Entrance.
56.	Right Bde.H.Q. Q.23.c.6.3.	4'0" 4'6" 5'0"	28'0" 4'6" 5'0"	21%	No.1 Entrance. " 1 " lateral. " 2 "
57.	Right Bde H.Q. Q.12.d.5.2.	5'0" 4'6" 8'0" 5'6"	25'6" 4'6" 25'6" 5'6"	18%	No.1 Entrance. " 2 " 80 c.ft.of dump trench cut.
62.	Dugout for "A" Batty, Q.28.b.4.4.	13'0"	32'0"	12%	Entrance.

APPENDIX IV.

256th. Tunnelling Co.R.E.

DAILY PROGRESS REPORT for 24 hours ending midnight 19.6.17.

Index No.	Designation and Locality of working.	Progress.	Total length.	Percent of total work compltd.	Remarks.
21.	Batt H.Q. Q.11.a.8.9.	4'6" 4'6"	24'6" 24'6"	48%	No.1 Chamber. " 2 "
23.	RAMC Dugout. Q.26.b.8.8.	3'9" 12'0"	87'9" 55'6"	55%	" 1 " " 2 "
26.	Bde battle.H.Q. Q.18.b.8.9.	18'9"	336'0"	100%	Chambering. Finished.
27.	R.A.O.P. Q.5.c.6.3.	5'3" 6'0"	12'0" 15'9"	87%	Shaft. Chambering.
30.	M.G.D. Q.5.c.8.4.	2'0" -	35'10" 4'3"	81%	No.1 Entrance. " 2 " (lateral)flooded
31.	M.G.D. Q.12.a.6.3.	2'0" 4'0"	2'0" 4'0"	83%	No.1 " chambering. " 2 " lateral.
32.	Bde.O.P. Q.5.c.5.3.	-	39'0"	58%	Flooded 1'6" of water No work.
33.	Bde.O.P. Q.17.a.1.4.	4'8" 4'6"	7'8" 4'6"	80%	Shaft. Chambering.
34.	Arty.Dugout. Q.15.c.8.3.	3'6" 3'7"	37'0" 31'2"	35%	No.1 Entrance. " 2 "
36.	Arty.OP. Q.11.a.7.7.	3'0"	18'0"	90%	Chambering.
40.	GOUZEAUCOURT Wd. well. Q.28.c.1.7.	1'0"	62'9"	-	Sinking.
41.	Divl.battle H.Q. Q.25.c.9.7.	10'0" 11'3" 5'0" 5'0"	45'9" 43'9" 7'0" 8'0"	17%	No.1 Entrance lateral. " 2 " (Holeing to impve air No.1 Chamber. " 10 "
42.	Bde. R.A.O.P. Q.5.c.4.2.	1'0" 2'0"	23'9" 24'3"	52%	No.1 Entrance. " 2 "
46.	Bde.R.A.O.P. Q.5.c.7.5.	-	20'0"	33%	Clearing water.
56.	Right Bde.H.Q. Q.23.c.6.3.	10'6" 9'0"	15'0" 14'0"	27%	No.1 lateral. " 2 "
57.	Right Bde.H.Q. Q.12.d.5.2.	5'6" 4'6" 3'0" 9'0"	31'0" 106'6" 28'0" 9'0"	23%	No.1 Entrance. " 2 " " 3 " " 3 " Chambering.
62.	Dugout for "A" Battery, Q.28.b.4.8.	27'0"	27'0"	18%	Chambering.

APPENDIX V.

256th. Tunnelling Co. R.E.

DAILY PROGRESS WORK for 24 hours ending midnight 20.6.17.

Index No.	Designation and Locality of working.	Progress.	Total length.	Percentage of total work completed.	Remarks.
21.	Batt.H.Q. Q.11.a.8.9.	- 6'0"	- 31'6"	49%	No.1 Chamber. 2 girders set " 2 "
23.	RAMC Dugout. Q.26.b.8.8.	15'0" 1'6"	70'6" 1'6"	57%	No.2 Chamber. (V.bad gr'nd No.1 " Clearing fall " 2 "
27.	R.A.O.P. Q.5.c.6.3.	6'0" 3'0"	18'0" 18'9"	89%	Shaft. Put small hole to Chambering. surface.
30.	M.G.D. Q.5.c.8.4.	3'6"	3'6"	85%	Chambering.
31.	M.G.D. Q.12.a.6.3.	3'0"	3'0"	87%	Chambering.
32.	Bde.O.P. Q.5.c.5.3.	3'0" 3'6"	3'0" 3'6"	70%	Shaft. Chambering.
33.	Bde.O.P. Q.17.a.1.4.	5'6" 3'0"	13'2" 7'6"	82%	Shaft. Chambering.
34.	Arty.dugout. Q.15.c.8.3.	3'6" 3'1"	40'6" 34'3"	39%	Lateral. "
36.	Arty.O.P. Q.11.a.7.7.	3'0"	21'0"	94%	Chambering.
40.	GOUZEAUCOURT Wd. well. Q.28.c.1.7.	3"	63'0"	-	Pumping water.
41.	Divl.Battle Hd.Qtrs. Q.25.c.9.7.	10'3" 7'0" 8'0" 5'6" 3'0" 3'0"	100'0" 14'0" 16'0" 5'6" 3'0" 3'0"	21%	Lateral. No.1 Chamber. " 10 " " 7 " " 2 " " 3 "
42.	Bde.R.A.O.P. Q.5.c.4.2.	2'9" 2'9"	26'6" 27'0"	59%	No.1 entrance. " 2 "
46.	Bde.R.A.O.P. Q.5.c.7.5.	-	20'0"	33%	Still a lot of water in this dugout and could not be worked.
56.	Right Bde.H.Q. Q.23.c.6.3.	4'0" 3'6" 6'6" 6'0" 4'6"	19'0" 17'6" 6'6" 6'0" 4'6"	34%	No.1 lateral. " 2 " " 1 chamber. " 2 " " 2 entrance level.
57.	Right Bde.H.Q. Q.12.d.5.2.	9'0" 8'6" 10'6"	9'0" 18'6" 19'6"	33%	No.1 Chamber. " 2 Entrance. " 3 Chamber. 8' of dump trench cut.
62.	Dugout for "A" Batty, Q.28.b.4.8.	22'6"	49'6"	29%	Chambering.

APPENDIX VI

256th. Tunnelling Co. R.E.

DAILY PROGRESS REPORT.
24 hours ending midnight 21.6.1917.

Index No.	Designation and Locality of working.	Progress.	Total length.	Percentage of total work completed	Remarks.
21.	Batt. H.Q. Q.11.a.8.9.	3'0" 3'0"	28'6" 34'6"	50%	No.1 Chamber. " 2 "
23.	RAMC Dugout. Q.26.b.8.8.	- 13'6"	- 84'0"	60%	No.1 Chamber. Clearing fall " 2 "
27.	R.A.O.P. Q.5.c.6.3.	4'0" 4'6"	22'0" 23'3"	91%	Shaft. Chambering.
30.	M.G.D. Q.5.c.8.4.	3'4" 1'6"	7'10" 5'9"	87%	No.1 Entrance. Chambering " 2 " Lateral.
31.	M.G.D. Q.12.a.6.3.	2'0" 3'0"	4'0" 6'0"	88%	No.1 Entrance. Chambering. " 2 " "
32.	Bde O.P. Q.5.c.5.3.	5'6" 3'0"	8'6" 6'6"	74%	Shaft. Chambering.
33.	Bde O.P. Q.17.a.1.4.	6'0" 3'0"	19'2" 16'6"	84%	Shaft. Chambering.
34.	Arty. dugout. Q.15.c.8.3.	2'7" 1'0"	37'3" 41'6"	40%	No.1 Entrance. " 2 "
36.	Arty. O.P. Q.11.a.7.7.	3'0"	21'0"	95%	Chambering.
40.	GOUZEAUCOURT Wd.Well. Q.28.c.1.7.	-	63'0"	-	Pumpg but could not lower water suff. to deepen well any further. 4' of water.
41.	Divl. battle H.Q. Q.25.c.9.7.	9'6" 9'0" 9'0" 9'3" 10'3"	23'6" 12'0" 12'0" 9'3" 26'3"	24%	No.1 Chamber. " 2 " " 3 " " 4 " "10 "
42.	Bde R.A.O.P. Q.5.c.6.2.	2'6" 2'3"	29'0" 29'3"	63%	No.1 Entrance. Level. " 2 Entrance. Level.
46.	Bde R.A.O.P. Q.5.c.7.5.	-	--	33%	Baling water out. Block'g up & straightening sets.
56.	Right Bde H.Q. Q.23.c.6.3.	16'0" 12'0" 2'2"	19'6" 18'0" 21'2"	40%	No.1 Chamber. " 2 Chamber. " 1 Lateral.
57.	Right Bde H.Q. Q.12.d.5.2.	15'0" 5'6" 15'0"	24'0" 24'0" 34'6"	44%	No.1 Chamber. " 2 Entrance. " 3 Chamber.
62.	Dugout for "A" Battery, Q.28.b.4.8.	16'6"	66'0"	40%	Chambering.

APPENDIX VII.

256th. Tunnelling Co. R.E.

DAILY PROGRESS REPORT
24 hours ending midnight 22.6.1917.

Index No.	Designation and locality of working.	Progress.	Total length.	Percentage of total work xmpltd.	Remarks.
21.	Batt.H.Q. Q.11.a.8.9.	3'0" 3'0"	31'6" 37'6"	51%	No.1 Chamber. " 2 "
23.	RAMC Dugout. Q.26.b.8.8.	13'6" 3'0"	97'6" 90'9"	68%	No.2 " " 1 "
27.	R.A.O.P. Q.5.c.6.3.	4'6"	27'6"	93%	Chambering.
30.	M.G.D. Q.5.c.8.4.	3'0" 3'0"	10'10" 3'0"	88%	No.1 Entrance.Lateral. No.2 " Chambering.
31.	M.G.D. Q.12.a.6.3.	1'6" 1'6"	5'6" 7'6"	88%	No.1 " " No.2 " "
32.	Bde.O.P. Q.5.c.5.3.	4'6" 1'0"	13'0" 7'6"	78%	Shaft. Chambering.
33.	Bde O.P. Q.17.a.1.4.	3'10" 3'6"	23'0" 14'0"	87%	Shaft. Chambering.
34.	Arty.Dugout. Q.15.c.8.3.	2'3" 3'0"	39'6" 44'6"	43%	No.1 Entrance level. " 2 " "
36.	Arty.O.P. Q.11.a.7.7.	3'0"	24'0"	96%	Chambering.
40.	GOUZEAUCOURT Wd.Well. Q.28.c.7.7.	1'6"	64'6"	-	FINISHED. Dismantled staging etc. Depth to water 61 ft. Depth of water 3'6" Total depth. 64'6"
41.	Div.Battle H.Q. Q.25.c. 9.7.	11'3" 12'6" 12'9" 3'6" 4'6" 5'0"	34'9" 24'6" 24'9" 12'9" 80'9" 5'0"	31%	No.1 Chamber " 2 " No.3 " " 4 " " 10 " Finished. " 5 "
42.	Bde R.A.O.P. Q.5.c.4.2.	3'0" 2'6"	3'0" 2'6"	66%	No.1 Entrance lateral. " 2 " "
46.	Bde R.A.O.P. Q.5.c.7.5.	-	20'0"	33%	Cleared out to bottom of chamber.
56.	Right Bde H.Q. Q.23.c.6.3.	9'11" 4'6"	31'1" 22'6"	50%	No.1 lateral. " 2 chamber.
57.	Right Bde H.Q. Q.12.d.5.2.	15'9" 15'9" 4'0" 10'0"	39'9" 50'6" 28'0" -	50%	No.1 " " 3 " " 2 entrance chamber Dump trench.
62½	Dugout for "A" battery, Q.28.b.4.8.	12'9"	78'9"	52%	Chambering.

APPENDIX VIII.

DAILY PROGRESS REPORT
256th. Tunnelling Coy. R.E.

24 hrs. ending midnight 23.6.17

Index No.	Designation and locality of working.		Progress	Total Length	Percentage of total work cmpd.	Remarks
21.	Batt.H.Q.	Q.11.a.8.9.	3'0"	34'6"	52%	No.1 Chamber.
23.	RAMC Dugout.	Q.26.b.8.8.	9'0" -	106'6" -	70%	No.2 Chamber. (etc.) No.1 " struttg, lagging
27.	R.A.O.P.	Q.5.c.6.3.	6'0"	33'6"	100%	Chambering. Finished.
30.	M.G.D.	Q.5.c.8.4.	- 3'0"	10'10" 6'0"	90%	No.1 Entrance. Chamber'g " 2 " "
31.	M.G.D.	Q.12.a.6.3.	3'6" -	9'0" 7'6"	90%	No.1 " " " 2 " "
32.	Bde.O.P.	Q.5.c.5.3.	5'0" 5'6"	18'0" 13'0"	82%	Shaft. Chambering.
33.	Bde.O.P.	Q.17.a.1.4.	1'0" 3'6"	24'0" 17'6"	89%	Shaft. Chambering.
34.	Arty.dugout.	Q.15.c.8.3.	7'6" 4'6"	16'6" 15'0"	48%	No.1 Chamber. " 2 "
36.	Arty.O.P.	Q.11.a.7.7.	3'0"	27'0"	97%	Chambering.
41.	Divl.battle H.Q. 	Q.25.c.9.7.	9'6" 10'3" 10'6" 11'0" 10'9"	44'3" 34'9" 35'3" 23'0" 15'9"	36%	No.1 Chamber. " 2 " " 3 " " 4 " " 5 "
42.	Bde.R.A.O.P. -	Q.5.c.4.2.	3'0" 3'0"	3'0" 3'0"	69%	No.1 Entrance lateral. " 2 " "
46.	Bde.R.A.O.P. -	Q.5.c.7.5.	2'0"	22'0"	34%	Entrance.
56.	Right Bde.H.Q.	Q.23.c.6.3.	4'2"	35'3"	51%	No.1 lateral.
57.	Right Bde.H.Q. 	Q.12.d.5.2.	19'9" 18'0" 4'6"	59'6" 68'3" 4'6"	55%	No.1 Chamber. " 3 " " 2 "
62.	Dugout for "A" Battery,	Q.28.b.4.8.	17'3"	96'0"	56%	Chambering.
75.	Signal dugout.	Q.18.a.8.5.	4'0"	4'0"	4%	Entrance.
76.	Signal dugout.	R.19.b.7.7.	4'0"	4'0"	4%	Entrance.

APPENDIX IX.

256th. Tunnelling Co. R.E.

DAILY PROGRESS REPORT for 24 hours ending midnight 24.6.17.

Index No.	Designation and Locality of working.	Progress.	Total length.	Percentage of total work cmpltd.	Remarks.
21.	Batt. H.Q. Q.11.a.8.9.	3'0" 3'0"	37'6" 40'6"	54%	No.1 Chamber. " 2 "
23.	RAMC Dugout. Q.26.b.8.8.	3'9" 3'0"	94'6" 109'6"	78%	No.1 Chamber. " 2 " lagging etc.
30.	M.G.D. Q.5.c.8.8.	3'0"	9'0"	92%	Chambering.
31.	M.G.D. Q.12.a.6.3.	3'0"	10'6"	92%	"
32.	Bde O.P. Q.5.c.5.3.	(2'0" (5'4"	20'0") 18'9")	86%	Shaft. Chambering.
33.	Bde O.P. Q.17.a.1.4.	5'0"	22'6"	92%	Chambering. Timber'g shaft
34.	Arty. dugout. Q.15.c.8.3.	6'0" 4'6"	22'6" 19'6"	52%	Left chamber. Right "
36.	Arty. O.P. Q.11.a.7.7.	-	-	98%	Setting girders & lagging
41.	Div. battle H.Q. Q.25.c.9.7.	9'9" 10'6" 9'9" 10'0" 11'3" 1'6" 1'6"	54'0" 45'0" 45'0" 33'0" 27'0" 1'6" 1'6"	50%	No.1 Chamber. Finished " 2 " " " 3 " " " 4 " " 5 " " 6 " " 8 "
42.	Bde R.A.O.P. Q.5.c.4.2.	3'0" 3'0"	6'0" 6'0"	72%	No.1 entrance lateral. " 2 " "
46.	Bde R.A.O.P. Q.5.c.7.5.	3'0"	25'0"	35%	Entrance.
56.	Right Bde H.Q. Q.23.c.6.3.	7'9" 10'6"	43'0" 33'0"	56%	No.1 lateral. " 2 chamber.
57.	Right Bde H.Q. Q.12.d.5.2.	17'6" 9'0" 16'9"	77'0" 13'6" 85'0"	70%	No.1 Chamber. " 2 " " 3 "
62.	Dugout for "A" Battery Q.28.b.4.8.	6'0"	102'0"	57%	Chambering. (Shelling delayed work).
75.	Signal dugout. Q.18.a.8.5.	6'0"	10'0"	8%	Entrance.
76.	Signal dugout. R.19.b.7.7.	1'6"	5'6"	5%	"
27.	R.A.O.P. Q.5.c.6.3.	-	-	-	Timbering.

APPENDIX X.

256th. Tunnelling Coy. R.E.

DAILY PROGRESS REPORT for 24 hours ending midnight 25.6.17.

Index No.	Designation and locality of working.	Progress	Total length	Percentage of total work comptd.	Remarks.
21.	Batt.H.Q. Q.11.a.8.9.	3'0"	40'6"	55%	No.1 Chamber.
23.	RAMC Dugout. Q.26.b.8.8.	10'6"	105'0"	82%	No.1 Chamber.
30.	M.G.D. Q.5.c.8.4.	5'0"	14'0"	93%	Chambering.
31.	M.G.D. Q.12.a.6.3.	3'0"	13'6"	93%	Chambering.
32.	Bde.O.P. Q.5.a.5.3.	3'6" 5'8"	23'6" 24'0"	95%	Shaft. Chamber.
33.	Bde.O.P. Q.17.a.1.4.	3'6"	26'0"	100%	Chambering. Finished.
34.	Arty.O.P. dugout. Q.15.c.8.3.	3'0" 3'0"	25'6" 22'6"	58%	Chamber. "
36.	Arty.O.P. Q.11.a.7.7.	-	-	99%	Lagging.
41.	Divl.Battle H.Q. Q.25.c.9.7.	8'3" 10'0" 9'3" 9'6" 8'0" 1'6" -	41'3" 37'0" 10'9" 15'0" 9'6" 1'6" -	60%	No.4 Chamber.Finished. " 5 " " 6 " " 7 " " 8 " " 9 " " 3 " lagging.
42.	Bde.R.A.O.P. Q.5.c.4.2.	4'0" 4'0"	10'0" 10'0"	75%	No.1 entrance lateral. " 2 " "
46.	Bde.R.A.O.P. Q.5.c.7.5.	2'6"	27'6"	39%	Entrance.
56.	Right Bde.H.Q. Q.23.c.6.3.	4'0" 8'6" 3'0" 3'0"	47'0" 26'0" 36'0" 25'6"	62%	No.1 lateral. " 2 " " 2 chamber. " 1 "
57.	Right Bde.H.Q. Q.12.d.5.2.	13'9" 9'9" 12'0"	90'9" 23'3" 97'0"	80%	No.1 Chamber. " 2 " " 3 "
62.	Dugout for "A" Battery. Q.28.b.4.8.	15'0"	117'0"	61%	Chamber.
75.	Signal Dugout. Q.18.a.8.5.	2'6"	12'6"	11%	Entrance.
76.	Signal dugout. R.19.b.7.7.	2'6"	3'0"	6%	Entrance.

APPENDIX XI.

256th. Tunnelling Co. R.E.

DAILY PROGRESS REPORT for 24 hrs. ending midnight 26.6.17.

Index No.	Designation and Locality of working.	Progress.	Total Length.	Percent -age of total work compltd.	Remarks.
21.	Batt.H.Q. Q.11.a.8.9.	3'0"	43'6"	56%	Chambering.
23.	RAMC Dugout.Q.26.b.8.8.	9'0"	114'0"	84%	Chambering.
30.	M.G.D. Q.5.c.8.4.	5'9"	19'9"	94%	Chambering.
31.	M.G.D. Q.12.a.6.3.	6'0"	19'6"	94%	Chambering.
32.	Bde O.P. Q.5.c.5.3.	-	-	98%	Timbering shaft.
34.	Arty.dugout.Q.15.c.8.3.	6'0" 6'0"	31'6" 28'6"	60%	Left hand chamber. Right " "
36.	Arty.O.P. Q.11.a.7.7.	-	-	100%	Lagging.
41.	Div.battle H.Q. Q.25.c.9.7.	9'6" 10'0" 13'0" 13'9" 11'0"	46'6" 20'9" 28'0" 23'3" 12'6"	68%	No.5 Chamber. Finished. " 6 " " 7 " " 8 " " 9 "
42.	Bde.R.A.O.P. Q.5.c.4.2.	4'0"	4'0"	79%	Chambering.
46.	Bde.R.A.O.P. Q.5.c.7.5.	3'0"	30'6"	40%	Entrance.
56.	Right Bde H.Q. Q.23.c.6.3.	16'6" 13'6"	42'0" 49'6"	66%	No.1 Chamber. " 2 "
57.	Right Bde H.Q. Q.12.d.5.2.	11'3" 7'6"	34'6" 98'3"	83%	No.2 " Lagging. " 3 "
62.	Dugout for "A" Battery, Q.28.b.4.8.	11'3" 12'0"	34'6" 129'0"	83% 70%	Chambering.
75.	Signal dugout.Q.18.a.8.5.	-	-	11%	No work.
76.	Signal dugout.R.19.b.7.7.	8'6"	17'0"	10%	Entrance.

256th. Tunnelling Co. R.E.

Appendix XII

DAILY PROGRESS REPORT for 24 hours ending midnight 27.6.17.

Index No.	Designation and Locality of working.	Progress	Total length.	Percentage of total work compltd.	Remarks.
21.	Batt. H.Q. Q.11.a.8.9.	3'0"	46'6"	58%	Timbering and lagging.
23.	RAMC Dugout. Q.26.b.8.8.	13'6"	127'6"	88%	Chambering.
30.	M.G.D. Q.5.c.8.4.	6'0"	25'9"	95%	Chambering.
31.	M.G.D. Q.12.a.6.3.	6'0"	25'6"	95%	Chambering.
32.	Bde O.P. Q.5.c.5.3.	-	-	100%	Fixing sets and clearing up chamber. FINISHED.
34.	Arty. dugout. Q.15.c.8.3.	6'0"	34'6"	62%	Right chamber.
36.	Arty. O.P. Q.11.a.7.7.	2'0"	2'0"	101%	Gallery to shaft.
41.	Div. battle H.Q. Q.25.c.9.1.	11'6" 11'0" 8'3" 8'6" 6'3"	32'3" 35'3" 31'6" 21'0" 6'3"	70%	No.6 Chamber. " 7 " " 8 " Finshd " 9 " " 1 Shaft
42.	Bde. R.A.O.P. Q.5.c.4.2.	3'6"	7'6"	81%	Chambering.
46.	Bde R.A.O.P. Q.5.c.7.5.	3'0"	33'6"	44%	Chambering.
56.	Right Bde H.Q. Q.23.c.6.3	7'6" 15'0" 15'0"	49'6" 15'0" 15'0"	70%	No.1 Chamber right. " 1 " left. " 2 " left.
57.	Right Bde H.Q. Q.12.d.5.2.	1'6" 13'3"	36'0" 111'9"	86%	No.2 Chamber - v. bad ground. " 3 "
62.	Dugout for "A" Battery, Q.28.b.4.8.	15'0"	144'0"	75%	Chambering.
75.	Signal dugout. Q.18.a.8.5.	5'6"	18'0"	13%	Entrance.
76.	Signal dugout. R.19.b.7.7.	9'0"	26'0"	20%	Entrance.

*Infantry fatigues withdrawn from 4 p.m. to midnight.

Appendix XIII

256th. Tunnelling Co. R.E.

DAILY PROGRESS REPORT for 24 hrs. ending 28.6.17.

Index No.	Designation and Locality of working.	Progress.	Total length.	Percentage of total work cmplted.	Remarks.
21.	Batt.H.Q. Q.11.a.8.9.	3'0"	46'6"	60%	No.2 Chamber.
23.	RAMC dugout. Q.26.b.8.8.	9'0"	136'6"	90%	No.1 chamber. Setting elephant shelters and lagging.
30.	M.G.D. Q.5.c.8.4.4.	6'3"	32'0"	96%	Chambering.
31.	M.G.D. Q.12.a.6.3.	5'3"	30'9"	96%	Chambering.
34.	Arty.dugout. Q.15.c.8.3.	6'0"	40'6"	65%	Chambering.
36.	Arty.OP. Q.11.a.7.7.	2'0"	4'0"	102%	Shaft.
41.	Div.battle H.Q. Q.25.c.9.7.	12'9" 6'9" 11'3" 6'0"	45'0" 45'9" 32'3" 15'6"	75%	No.6 Chamber. " 7 " Finished. " 9 " " 1 Shaft.
33.	Field Survey Co.O.P. Q.17.a.1.4.	5'0"	5'0"	15%	Shaft.
42.	Bde.R.A.O.P. Q.5.c.4.2.	2'6"	10'0"	85%	Chambering.
46.	Bde.R.A.O.P. Q.5.c.7.5.	3'6"	37'0"	47%	Entrance.
56.	Right Bde H.Q. Q.23.c.6.3.	13'6" 13'6" 7'0"	28'6" 28'6" 7'0"	75%	No.1 left. " 2 left " 2 right.
57.	Right Bde H.Q. Q.12.d.5.2.	15'0" 3'0"	126'9" 100'0"	88%	No.3 Chamber. " 1 "
62.	Dugout for "A" Battery. Q.28.b.4.8.	3'0" 3'6"	147'0" 3'6"	80%	Chamber. No.2 entrance.
75.	Signal dugout. Q.18.a.8.5.	-	18'0"	13%	Stopped by C.R.E's order 27.6.17.
76.	Signal dugout. R.19.b.7.7.	-	26'0"	20%	-do-

Appendix XIV

256th. Tunnelling Co. R.E.

DAILY PROGRESS REPORT for 24 hrs. ending midnight 29.6.17.

Index No.	Designation and Locality of workings.	Progress.	Total Length.	Percentage of total work completed.	Remarks.
21.	Batt.H.Q. Q.11.a.8.9.	3'0"	46'6"	62%	No.1 Chamber.
23.	RAMC Dugout. Q.26.b.8.8.	10'6"	147'0"	92%	No.1 Chamber.
30.	M.G.D. Q.5.c.8.4.	5'0"	37'0"	100%	Chambering and lagging FINISHED.
31.	M.G.D. Q.12.a.6.3.	3'3"	34'0"	100%	-do-
33.	Fld.Survey Co.O.P. Q.17.a.1.4.	7'3"	12'3"	36%	Shaft.
34.	Arty.dugout. Q.15.c.8.3.	4'6" 1'6"	33'0" 42'0"	67%	Left chamber. Right "
36.	Arty.O.P. Q.11.a.7.7.	-	-	102%	Lagging.
41.	Divl.battle H.Q. Q.25.c.9.7.	1'6" 15'0" 14'0"	86'6" 47'3" 29'6"	79%	No.6 Chamber. Finished " 9 " " 1 Shaft. 246' of lagging.
42.	Bde.R.A.O.P. Q.5.c.4.2.	2'9"	12'9"	88%	Chambering.
46.	Bde.R.A.O.P. Q.5.c.7.5.	4'0"	41'0"	50%	Entrance.
56.	Right Bde.H.Q. Q.23.c.6.3.	17'9"	26'9"	80%	No.2 Right chamber. entran. lagging.
57.	Right.Bde.H.Q. Q.12.d.5.2.	9'0" 9'0"	109'0" 135'9"	90%	No.1, Chamber. " 3 " Lagging.
62.	Dugout for "A" Batty. Q.28.b.4.8.	12'6"	16'0"	90%	No.2 Entrance.
	Raperie, BEAUCAMP, Q.12.c.1½.2.	-	-	-	Repairing top of well

APPENDIX XV.

256th. Tunnelling Coy. R.E.

DAILY PROGRESS REPORT for 24 hours ending midnight 30.6.17.

Index No.	Designation and Locality of working.	Progress.	Total length.	Percentage of total work compltd.	Remarks.
21.	Batt.H.Q. Q.11.a.8.9.	3'0"	49'6"	64%	No.2 Chamber.
23.	RAMC dugout. Q.26.b.8.8.	12'0"	159'0"	93%	No.1 Chamber.
33.	Field Survey O.P. Q.17.a.1.4.	6'6"	15'6"	38%	Shaft.
34.	Artillery dugout, Q.15.c.8.3.	6'0" 4'6"	39'0" 46'6"	69%	Left chamber. Right "
36.	Artillery O.P. Q.11.a.7.7.	-	-	-	No. work.
41.	Div.battle H.Q. Q.25.c.9.7.	9'0" 14'3"	9'0" 61'6"	80%	No.6 Chamber extension. " 9 " 60 ft.lagged. Clearing fall occasioned by dest'n of German explosives.
42.	Bde.R.A.O.P. Q.5.c.4.2.	2'0"¾	14'9"	90%	Chambering.
46.	Bde.R.A.O.P. Q.5.c.7.5.	4'0" 2'0"	4'0" 46'3"	55%	Shaft. Chambering.
56.	Right Bde.H.Q. Q.23.c.6.3.	16'9" 4'6"	40'6" 4'6"	85%	No.2 right.Lagging & No.1 entrance(clearing up
57.	Right Bde.H.Q. Q.12.d.5.2.	9'0" 3'0"	118'0" 138'9"	92%	No.1 Chamber. " 3 " timbering.
62.	Dugout for "A" Batty. Q.28.b.4.8.	8'0"	24'0"	92%	No.2 Entrance.
	Raperie, BEAUCAMP, Q.12.c.1½.2.	-	-	-	Repairing top of well.

ORIGINAL

Vol 6

WAR DIARY

of

HEADQUARTERS

59th DIVISIONAL ROYAL ENGINEERS

VOL. VI.

1st July 1917 to 31st July 1917

WAR DIARY

Army Form C. 2118.

HEADQUARTERS 59th DIVL. R.E.

INTELLIGENCE SUMMARY.
(Erase heading not required.)

Instructions regarding War Diaries and Intelligence Summaries are contained in F.S. Regs. Part II. and the Staff Manual respectively. Title pages will be prepared in manuscript.

Place	Date 1917 July	Hour	Summary of Events and Information	Remarks and references to Appendices
EQUANCOURT	1/7/17		467th FIELD COY R.E. augmented system C.T. No 1. Erecting Cabins on site of proposed Camp at NEUVILLE. Improving cart track of proposed Camp (completed). Bathing and slaughter point at QUEEN'S CROSS Q.16.d.4.3. Making Horse Standings, repairing ponies, water Transport at P.23.c. P.16.c. S.6. Constructing Summer Shelters at Q.15.a. Erecting Shelter & Marquee. Also at	MAP REF: 57c. S.E. 1/20,000.
	" "		469th " " " "	
	" "		470th " " NEUVILLE. 1P.23.c.3. 5. (completed) Constructing Road-being system. Dugouts at EQUANCOURT P.16.c. C.T.3 in Q.11.c. Revetting Truck bridges in C.T.3 Q.16.d. Dying Road C.T.3. Q.16.d. 100g/ds. Repairing 10 ton in BEAUCAMP VALLEY Q.11.d. Clearing Old Phosphate C.T.3. Erecting Camouflage Screens at BEETFACTORY METZ Q.5.b work. on O.P. in Q.6.c. 7.3. Repairing METZ-TRESCAULT Road. 3 bridges in Transport carts in road metal. (Division Order No 50 received 5.30pm No I. received 9 pm Coy R.E. on day outs no particular approaches No I.	H.L
"	2/7/17		2 Sections 251st TUNNELLING	
"	"		467th FIELD COY. R.E. engaged upon C.T. No 1. Erecting Cabins at site of Proposed Camp at NEUVILLE, work upon Stony Point at QUEEN'S CROSS Q.16.d.4.3. Making Horse Standings & repairing Near Transport at P.23.c. P.16.c. S.6. Work upon site of new Camp at P.23.c. Erecting Shelters for P.E.B. e.1.a. work upon new Transport lines up at RE at EQUANCOURT	
"	"		469th " " "	
	"		470th " " Improving front line system. Dying out C.T. 3 in Q.11.c. and in C.T. in BEAUCAMP VALLEY Q.11.d. Dying out taken O.T. 3 in Q.11.d. Erecting & Intrenching CT 4 in Q.11.a. Zinkhole in C.T.4. in Q.16.a. Erecting duckboard in CT3 in Q.11.c. Repairing METZ-TRESCAULT ROAD 3 M.T. lorries carting to The Road Metal. Backing pump apparatus at Beet Factory. In METZ Q.5-16. c.6. Coal & Lime for being forwarded.	H.T
	3/7/17		2 Sections 251st TUNNELLING COY. R.E. on day outs, no pre attached appendices No II.	MAP REF: 57c. S.E. 1/20,000
	"		467th FIELD COY. R.E. engaged upon O.T. No 1.	
			469th " " Erecting Cabins on site of proposed Camp at NEUVILLE. Work upon Stony Point at QUEEN'S CROSS Q.16.d.4.3. Making Horse Standings, repairing Near Transport at P.16.c. & P.26.c. S.6. Work on site of New Camp at P.23.c. Constructing Shelter Shelters at Q.15.a. Erecting Summer Transport at P.29.c. 1.6. Work upon new Transport lines for that R.E. at EQUANCOURT.	H.T

WAR DIARY or INTELLIGENCE SUMMARY

Army Form C. 2118. Continued

Place	Date	Hour	Summary of Events and Information	Remarks and references to Appendices
EQUANCOURT	3.7.17		470th FIELD COY. R.E. Shifting dumps in C.T.3. in Q.11.b. Improving front line Mr. Bates. drain from intermediate line into crater Q.17.a. Shifting branch C.T.3 from C.T.3, through crater Q.17.a. Junction work in C.T.3. Shifting dumps in C.T.3 at Q.11 to repairing METZ-TRESCAULT Road (Infantry working party) 3 M.T.Z. Loop. Stamped metal. Trimming & straightening C.T.2. Installing Pumps in BEET FACTORY: METZ. Re-excavating portions, frames, shuttering etc. C.T.4. Q.11.b. Sheet 17. C. 916 & 3rd Tank at C.T.4 in Q.10.c. Clearing bottom on C.T.4. in Q.11.b. Metal C.T.4 in Q.11.a.	MAP REF. 57c. S.E. 1/20,000 H.T.
"	4.7.17		2 SECTIONS 256 TUNNELLING COY. R.E. Engaged on C.T. No.1. 467th FIELD COY. R.E. 469th " " " See appendix No. III. Shifting returns on New Camp NEUVILLE. Parking and removing round Camps in quick. Clean making, over Horse Lines at EQUANCOURT for Hd.E. RE. Shelter Roof Standings. Fixing Nominal Horse Trough by at P.33.C.Y.P.T.R.E.S.G. Work ups in Group Point at QUEENS CROSS at Q.28.d.4.3. Erecting shelter. Benches at P.23.C.C.S.S.	MAP REF. 57c S.E. 1/20,000
"	"		470th " " Improving old panna trench at Q.10.d. Deepening & widening C.T.3. forward and Q.11.b. Trying dumps in C.T.3. Laying drain interconnecting lines to crater. Repairing METZ TRESCAULT Road. Road party at METZ Beet Factory. Running shelters No.4. C.T. betting out R.A.P. Hq.C.T.4 drawing Duckboards etc. layout of C.T. No.1.	H.T.
			2 SECTIONS 256 TUNNELLING R.E. on days see also for appendix No. IV.
"	5.7.17		467th FIELD COY. R.E. Shifting between cables of Mons Camp P.12 (central). Work upon stray bomb at Rheads Cross Q.18.d.4.3. Constructing funnels shelters at Q.5a. Making standings at Manor Camp Park. Brand huts through P.33.C.+ P.33.C.I.5.6. Erecting latrines & incinerator on new Camp Park at EQUANCOURT. P.33.a. Erecting latrines & incinerator at P.33.C.3.5.1. Making New Forming at EQUANCOURT. 469 " " " Shifting Dumps for C.T.3. in Q.11.b. & d. Removing & drawing CT.4. making small R.A. Post Q.10.A.5.8. Making shelters in ground. Authorities (two shifts per relay) too 2 SECTION scouts to Repairing METZ-TRESCAULT Road (Parties withdrawn at 11.30 last day). ROCQUIGNY.) Facing Pumps & laying maintenance at METZ Beet Factory.	H.T.
			2 SECTIONS 256 TUNNELLING COY R.E. on days and see for detailed appendix No.V.

WAR DIARY — continued
INTELLIGENCE SUMMARY

Army Form C. 2118.

Place	Date	Hour	Summary of Events and Information	Remarks and references to Appendices
EQUANCOURT	6.7.17		467 FIELD COY. R.E. Engaged upon C.T. No. 1. Y Sap, Point 44 Cemetery, S.E. of METZ. Construction of French Shelters in Q.15.a (completed). Shelters Q.9.a.a. Standings & framework Pt 8.C.P.5.C.6 & P.5.3.C. both completed. Sifting Latrines on new Camp at P.17. Central. Dwelling Latrines & incinerators on new Camp Site P.17.a. 2 Sections moved to BARASTRE.	MAP REF 57c. S.E. 57b. S.E. 1/20000
			469 " " One Section engaged on water on C.T. No. 1. (P.17.) Rail-Camp O.16.b on engineering work. Completing trench/rails for D.H.Q. BARASTRE. Section dug in on C.T.3. Improved Communication line between C.T.3 & crater at Q.17.d. 0.7. Special dug-outs for C.T.3. Improved North end of C.T.3. in front of C.T. in Trench. Dug out 3rd M.G. Emplacement & drainage C.T.4. New BEHIND WELL dug-out from Central bench to Coy. H.Q. Framework for R.A.P. Fixing pump flooring water mains for detachment at METZ. Bath & Laundry. One Section reconnoitred camp-site for 175th Pole Corps at O.35.	H.P.
	7.7.17		2. Sections 256 TONNELLING COY. R.E. engaged upon C.T.I. No. 1 Listening Point & cemetery S.E. of METZ. One Section moved to BARASTRE also. 467 FIELD COY. R.E. Gathering Pole Candles (saps) at O.9. Shelter Camps for 175th Brigade at BARASTRE. D.H.Q. at BARASTRE in O.16. Section D.H.Q. at BARASTRE also.	
			469 " " Construction Baths at BARASTRE. Employ Miners work for BARASTRE (D.H.Q.) Construction Latrines & Incinerators on new camp site on Q.15.A. Shelting Shed for Ammunition	
			470 " " Encamp in P. 29.c. Reconnoitred terrain for Camps & ditches drains of paste (bonds) and shelters. Work on various barracks/sheds of prefab long with Division Shelters buildings/dugout, drainage & similar; at C.T.4. etc between R.A.B. at O.10.d.7. and T.4. Reading, water tanks C.T.4 etc. for C.T.4 at Q.15.d. G.S. Work on Baths at our camp in O.35 for 175th Brigade.	
	8.7.17		2. Sections 256 TONNELLING COY. R.E. } Work on Main work in METZ Bath Laundry at Q.2.c.b. R.E. Repairs. 467th FIELD COY. R.E. 469th " " } On Duty & also on fire attached/appendix No VIII BARASTRE. Switch Back at BARASTRE (H.Q. 175th Section)	(15 DH 9 at O.9. a cemetery detail.)
			469 " " Working in various of Camps for 175th Bde. in D.16 Also constructing front line trench in short pieces from between C.T.3 & Crater, fixing Woods 60 yds strips. Well & Tank. Digging trench (Uhlan) between C.T.5 & Crater. Sentry boxes at Dug-outs in C.T.5. Improvement to top of dugouts, H.Q. C.T.5 a & b. Installing Pump & Laying mains for detachment at Q.25.E.5.a. Filling sandbags along C.T.A. Broken Blockhouse C.T.14.	
			470 " " Laying out tapes for new Camp in R.29. All day work as per attached appendix No VIII.	
			2. Sections 256 TONNELLING COY. R.E. on day outs as per attached appendix No VIII.	A.T.

WAR DIARY

INTELLIGENCE SUMMARY.

(Erase heading not required.)

Army Form C. 2118.
continued

Place	Date	Hour	Summary of Events and Information	Remarks and references to Appendices
EQUANCOURT	9.7.17		467th Field Coy; R.E. assisting in erection of (D.H.Q. of BARASTRE; also 176th Brigade group Camp; Field Ambulance Camp; in O.Q.	Map Ref: 57.c.S.E. 1/20,000.
			466th " " " assisting in erection of (D.H.Q) at BARASTRE (CAMP)	in O.16. meeting 17th.
			Bdgs Hqrs. at BARASTRE. Erecting Camp for M.G. Coy. in O.16.	" also 17th " " W.T.
			470th " " " moved to Brigade Group Camp in O.35.	
BARASTRE	10.7.17		2 Sections 256 TUNNELLING Coy; R.E. on duty - ards as per attached. Probable for Bde/coyn Transfer to IX Corps	
			467th Field Coy; R.E. assisting in erection of D.H.Q Camp at BARASTRE, also 176 Brigade Group Camp +	
			Field Ambulance Camp in O.9.	
			466th " " " moved to Brigade Group Camp in O.16. Hqrs, Section (remainder). Moving in erection	
			of D.H.Q. Camp at BARASTRE. also erecting Brigade Group Camp in O.16. Erecting Battn.	
			in BARASTRE.	
			470th " " " on section to erect Battn. for Brigade Group in O.35, assisting in erection	
		4 pm	at Brigade Group Camp in O.35.	
	11.7.17		Head Quarters R.E. moved into new Headquarters at BARASTRE	
			467 FIELD Coy R.E. Our Section taking down wooden huts at MONTAUBAN	
			" " " " " wiring with work upon Staff Camp	
			" " " " " erecting wooden huts in Brigade Group Camp	
			Ambulance - Remainder doing general Camp work.	
			469 " " " Training and doing general Camp work. Section on erection of	
			Brigade R.H.Q. incineration, wooden huts, bayonet and trenching courses, etc	
			470 " " " Erecting Huts, Baths, Latrines, etc. in Brigade Camp	
	12.7.17		467 FIELD Coy RE. One Section engaged upon Special drill, physical exercises and musketry	
			Another Section on wiring drill	
			3 Sections engaged upon work in Brigade Camp	
			469 " " Erecting wooden huts, baths, latrines, cook shelters etc, for D.H.Q. Camp	
			and 177 Brigade	
			470 " " Physical exercises, arm drill, bayonet exercises and musketry	
			Also general camp work for the Brigade.	

Army Form C. 2118.

WAR DIARY or INTELLIGENCE SUMMARY.

Continued

(Erase heading not required.)

Instructions regarding War Diaries and Intelligence Summaries are contained in F.S. Regs., Part II. and the Staff Manual respectively. Title pages will be prepared in manuscript.

Place	Date	Hour	Summary of Events and Information	Remarks and references to Appendices
BARASTRE	13/7/19		467 Field Coy RE 2/3 Section was called, one Section on inspection of Roman Road at D.HQ, 1/4 Section employed in camp. Mounted Section on driving drill.	Sheet S.7.C. /100000
			469 " " Training and completing Brigade Camp	
			470 " " do	Khan
	14/7/19		Purvisional RE engaged in training - Coaching of physical drill, signals and Company drill, Bombing, Bayonet practice. 62 men of 469 Company were inoculated. 2/a Sections of 467 " "	Khan
	15/7/19		Each Field Company attended church parade with its own Brigade group. No other parades or work done	Khan Khan
	16/7/19		Sappers of each Field Coy continue their Special training course - Physical exercises, company drill, bayonet and bombing exercises, wirework of strong points, and wire entanglement drill. Mounted men driving drill under Company transport officer and R.S.Major.	Khan
do	17/7/19		Sappers on various Field Cely Cos continue their special training as detailed on training programmes for each Field Company, attached	Khan
	18/7/19		do do do	Khan
	19/7/19		do do do	Khan
				Khan

Army Form C. 2118.

WAR DIARY
~~or~~
INTELLIGENCE SUMMARY.

Continued

(Erase heading not required.)

Instructions regarding War Diaries and Intelligence Summaries are contained in F. S. Regs., Part II. and the Staff Manual respectively. Title pages will be prepared in manuscript.

Place	Date	Hour	Summary of Events and Information	Remarks and references to Appendices
BARASTRE	20.7.17	—	Field Companies continue their training in accordance with attached	Sheet 57 c
			General programme of East Field Coy.	Khun 1/40,000
		1 pm	59 Field Coy. observed General holiday after 11 am on account of Divisional Sports	Khun
	21.7.17		Field Companies attended church parade with their respective Brigade groups.	Khun
	22.7.17		Field Companies continue training in accordance with attached training programmes of each Field Coy	Khun
	23.7.17		59" Divisional Technical course N° 1 Corps R.E. instructions N° 3 received. Field Companies continued their training.	Khun
	24.7.17 noon	Field Companies continue training in accordance with attached having programmes of each Field Coy	Khun
	25.7.17		do	Khun
	26.7.17		do	Khun
	27.7.17		Divisional Tactical Exercise took place. Field Companies did work as follows —	
			One section per Field Coy attached to its respective Brigade to assist infantry in consolidating objectives gained 467 Field Coy. constructing strong points N° 4 and 5. 469 " " " N° 3 and a length of communication trench. 470 " " " constructing strong points N° 1 and 2 and no communication trench	Khun
		7pm	59 Divisional Technical Exercise N° 2 Copy N° F received	

Army Form C. 2118.

Crokeerro

WAR DIARY
INTELLIGENCE SUMMARY.
(Erase heading not required.)

Instructions regarding War Diaries and Intelligence Summaries are contained in F. S. Regs. Part II. and the Staff Manual respectively. Title pages will be prepared in manuscript.

Place	Date	Hour	Summary of Events and Information	Remarks and references to Appendices
BARASTEE	28.7.17		Field Company's training proceeding	Khug Sheet 57/c 1/40,000
	29.7.17		Field Companies attend church parade with their respective Brigade Groups.	Khun
	30.7.17		Field Companies continue training in accordance with Training Programme attached	Khun
	31.7.17		do	Khun

K Waithman
Capt & adjutant
2 Wessex & R.E.
S9
31/7/17

APPENDIX I.

256th. Tunnelling Coy. R.E.

Daily Progress Report for 24 hours ending 1.7.17.

NIL

The Company were holding their Sports and work was temporarily suspended.

APPENDIX II.

256th. Tunnelling Co. R.E.

DAILY PROGRESS REPORT for 24 hrs. ending midnight 2.7.17.

Index No.	Designation and locality of working.	Progress.	Total length.	Percentage of total work compltd.	Remarks.
21.	Batt.H.Q. Q.11.a.8.9.	3'0"	49'6"	66%	No.1 Chamber.
23.	RAMC Dugout. Q.26.b.8.8.	-	-	100%	Lagging, strutting, lagging and fixing stretchers. FINISHED.
33.	Field Survey Co.O.P. Q.17.a.1.4.	9'0"	24'3"	50%	Shaft.
34.	Artillery dugout, Q.15.c.8.3.	3'0" 3'6"	49'6" 3'6"	72%	Chambering. Lateral to left chambe
36.	Artillery O.P. Q.11.a.7.7.	2'0"	2'0"	102%	Shaft.
41.	Divl. battle H.Q. Q.25.c.9.7.	10'6" 1'6"	72'0" 10'6"	82%	No.9 Chamber. " 6 " extension (finished). 455 sq.ft. lagged.
42.	Bde.R.A.O.P. Q.5.c.4.2.	6'3"	21'0"	91%	Chambering.
46.	Bde.R.A.O.P. Q.5.c.7.5.	3'0" 3'0"	3'0" 3'0"	60%	Shaft. Chambering.
56.	Right Bde.H.Q. Q.23.c.6.3.	15'0"	49'6"	100%	No.2 right. Clearing up lagging. FINISHED.
57.	Right Bde.H.Q. Q.12.d.5.2.	12'6"	130'6"	93%	No.1 Chamber. Re-open'g No.3 Chamber.
62.	Dugout for "A" Batty. Q.28.b.4.8.	8'0"	32'0"	100%	No.2 Entrance. FINISHED.
32.	Bde.R.A.O.P. Q.5.c.5.3.	-	-	-	Four sets put in shaft
27.	R.A.O.P. Q.5.c.6.3.	-	-	-	Three sets put in shaft.
31.	M.G.D. Q.12.a.6.3.	-	-	-	320 sq.ft. of lagging. FINISHED.
	RAPERIE, BEAUCAMP, Q.12.c.1½.2	-	-	-	Opening well.

APPENDIX III.

256th. Tunnelling Co.R.E.

DAILY PROGRESS REPORT for 24 hrs. ending midnight 3.7.17.

Index No.	Designation and Locality or working.	Progress	Total length	Percentage of total work compltd.	Remarks.
21.	Batt.H.Q. Q.11.a.8.9.	5'0"	104'0"	68%	Chamber.
33.	Fld.Survey Co. O.P. Q.17.a.1.4.	4'6"	28'9"	100%	FINISHED.
34.	Artillery dugout. Q.15.c.8.3.	8'3" 1'6"	12'0" 51'0"	74%	Gallery. Chamber.
36.	Artillery O.P. Q.11.a.7.7.	3'6"	5'6"	105%	Shaft.
41.	Div.battle H.Q. Q.25.c.9.7.	16'6" 6'6"	88'6" 6'6"	85%	No.9 Chamber. " 6 " 545 s.ft.of lagging.
42.	Bde.R.A.O.P. Q.5.c.4.2.	2'0"	21'8"	92%	Chambering.Slight fall of roof due to shelling.
46.	Bde.R.A.O.P. Q.5.c.7.5.	3'0" 3'0"	6'0" 6'0"	63%	Shaft. Chambering.
57.	Right Bde.H.Q.Q.12.d.5.2.	11'3"	1418'9"	95%	No.1 Chamber.lagging, strutting and clearing up.
	Raperie,BEAUCAMP, Q.12.c.1½.2.	-	-	-	Opening well.
31.	M.G.D. Q.12.a.6.3.	-	-	-	80 s.ft.lagging.Finished.
87.	216th.Battery dugout, Q.14.d.3.5.	5'9" 4'0"	5'9" 4'0"	3%	No.1 Entrance. " 2 "

APPENDIX IV.

256th. Tunnelling Co. R.E.

DAILY PROGRESS REPORT for 24 hrs. ending midnight 4.7.17.

Index No.	Designation and locality of working.	Progress.	Total length.	Percentage of total work compltd.	Remarks.
21.	Batt.H.Q. Q.11.a.8.9.	8'9"	112'9"	70%	Chambering.
34.	Arty.dugout. Q.15.c.8.3.	9'0" 3'0"	45'0" 20'0"	76%	Chambering. Lateral gallery.
36.	Arty.O.P. Q.11.a.7.7.	2'0"	7'6"	107%	Shaft.
41.	Divl.battle H.Q. Q.25.c.9.7.	2'6" 4'4" 1'6"	91'0" 4'4" 9'0"	88%	No.9 Chamber. " " " shaft.875 s.ft " 6 " lagging.
42.	Bde.H.Q.R.A.O.P. Q.5.c.4.2.	8'3"	29'11"	95%	Chambering.
46.	Bde.R.A.O.P. Q.5.c.7.5.	2'0" 9"	8'0" 3'9"	68%	Shaft. Chambering.
57.	Right Bde H.Q.Q.12.d.5.2.	7'6"	149'3"	96%	No.1 Chamber. V.bad ground Strutt^g, Lacing and lagging in No.3 chamber.
87½	216th.Bty dugout.Q.14.d.3 .5.	5'11" 6'6"	11'5" 10'6"	8%	No.1 Entrance. " 2 "
	Raperie,BEAUCAMP,Q.12.c.1½ .2	-	-	-	Revetting sides and fixing platform at well.
40.	GOUZEAUCOURT Wd.Well. Q.28.c.1.7.	3'6"	3'6"	--	Pump chamber.

APPENDIX V.

256th. Tunnelling Co.R.E.

DAILY PROGRESS REPORT for 24 hrs. ending 5.7.17.

Index No.	Designation and locality of working.	Progress	Total length.	Percentage of total work compltd.	Remarks.
21.	Battn.H.Q. Q.11.a.8.9.	9'9"	122'6"	72%	Chambering.
34.	Art'y dugout. Q.15.c.8.3.	4'6"	49'6"	78%	Chambering.
36.	Art'y O.P. Q.11.a.7.7.	2'0"	9'6"	109%	Shaft.
41.	Div.battle H.Q. Q.25.c.9.7.	15'6"	19'10"	92%	No.9 Chamber.635 s.ft of lagging.
42.	Bde.R.A.O.P. Q.5.c.4.2.	9'0"	38'11"	96%	Chambering.
46.	Bde.R.A.O.P. Q.5.c.7.5.	4'0" 3'0"	12'0" 6'9"	72%	Shaft. Chambering.
57.	Right Bde O.P. Q.12.d.5.2.	-	-	97%	Retimbering fallen chamber
87.	216th.Bty.dugout. Q.14.d.3.5.	8'1" 7'6"	19'6" 18'6"	13%	No.1 entrance. " 2 "
40.	GOUZEAUCOURT Wd.Well. Q.28.c.1.7.	4'0"	7'6"	-	Pump chamber.
89.	Well at BEAUCAMP, Q.12.d.1½.2 (Corrected).	-	-	-	Platform fixed ready for sinking.
90.	Art'y O.P. R.7.b.3.1.	5'10"	5'10"	-	Trench for entrance.

APPENDIX VI.

256th. Tunnelling Co.R.E.

DAILY PROGRESS REPORT for 24 hrs. ending midnight 6.7.17.

Index No.	Designation and locality of working.	Progress.	Total length	Percentage of total work cmpltd.	Remarks.
2L.	Batt.H.Q. Q.11.a.8.9.	6'6"	129'0"	74%	Chambering.
34.	Arty.dugout.Q.15.c.8.3.	10'6"	63'0"	80%	Chambering.
36.	Arty.O.P. Q.11.a.7.7.	2'0"	11'6"	111%	Shaft.
41.	Divl.battle H.Q. Q.25.c.9.7.	8'2"	28'0"	95%	No.9 Chamber shaft.544'sq lagged. Fixing struts and girders.
42.	Bde.R.A.O.P.Q.5.c.4.2.	2'1" 4'0"	36'6" 4'0"	97%	Chambering. Lateral.
46.	Bde.R.A.O.P. Q.5.c.7.5.	4'0" 5'0"	16'0" 11'9"	75%	Shaft. Chambering.
57.	Right Bde.H.Q. Q.12.d.5.2.	-	-	98%	Strutting, lagging & fixing girders.
87.	216th.Battery dugout. Q.14.d.3.5.	5'11" 5'10"	25'3" 23'10"	16%	No.1 Entrance. " 2 "
89.	Well at BEAUCAMP, Q.12.d.3½.2.	-	-	-	Commenced clearing well.
90.	Artillery O.P. R.7.b.3.1.	10'9"	10'9"	2%	Open cut.
40.	GOUZEAUCOURT Wood well, Q.28.c.1.7.	4'6"¼	12'0"	-	Pump chamber. Fixing air pump.

APPENDIX VII.

256th. Tunnelling Co. R.E.

DAILY PROGRESS REPORT for 24 hrs. ending 7.7.17.

Index No.	Designation and locality of working.	Progress	Total length	Percentage of total work comptd.	Remarks.
21.	Batt.H.Q. Q.11.a.8.9.	13'6"	142'6"	100%	Chambering. FINISHED.
34.	Arty.dugout. Q.15.c.8.3.	18'0"	112'6"	100%	Chambering. FINISHED.
36.	Arty.O.P. Q.11.a.7.7.	5'0"	16'6"	112%	Shaft.
41.	Div.battle H.Q. Q.15.c.9.1.	-	-	97%	Clearing up, timbering &c 357 s.ft. of lagging.
42.	Bde.R.A.O.P. Q.5.c.4.2.	-	-	100%	Clearing up. FINISHED.
46.	Bde.R.A.O.P. Q.5.c.7.5.	5'0" 24'3"	21'0" 36'0"	88%	Shaft. Chambering.
57.	Right Bde.H.Q. Q.12.d.5.2.	-	-	100%	Setting girders, strutting and lagging. FINISHED.
87.	216th. Battery dugout. Q.14.d.3.5.	5'6" 5'2"	30'6" 29'0"	20%	Entrances.
89.	Well at BEAUCAMP, Q.12.d.3½.2.	-	-	-	No work.
90.	Arty.O.P. R.7.b.3.1.	3'6"	3'6"	3%	Entrance.
40.	GOUZEAUCOURT Wd.Well, Q.28.c.1.7.	1'0"	13'0"	-	Chamber finished, well cleared of loose chalk and ready for sinking again.

APPENDIX VIII

256th. Tunnelling Coy. R.E.

DAILY PROGRESS REPORT for 24 hrs. ending midnight 8.7.17.

Index No.	Designation and locality of working.	Progress.	Total length.	Percentage of total work comptd.	Remarks.
36.	Artillery O.P. Q.11.a.7.7.	7'6"	24'0"	100%	Shaft. Finished.
41.	Divl. battle H.Q. Q.25.d.9.7.	-	-	99%	All work finished below ground. Removing spoil from entrances, fixing ent. frames, clg up and revetting dump.
46.	Bde. RA. O.P. Q.5.c.7.5.	5'0"	26'0"	100%	Shaft. Finished.
87.	216th. Bty dugout. Q.14.d.3.5.	4'0" 4'6"	34'6" 33'0"	25%	No.1 ent'ce. Dugout stopd " 2 " bty moving.
90.	Artillery O.P. R.7.b.3.1.	-	-	-	No work.
89.	Well at BEAUCAMP. Q.12.d.3½.2.	4'8"	89'2"	-	Clearing well.
34.	Artillery dugout. Q.15.c.8.3.	-	-	-	Strutting and lagging chamber.

APPENDIX IX.

256th. Tunnelling Co.R.E.

DAILY PROGRESS REPORT for 24 hrs. ending midnight 9.7.17.

Index No.	Designation and locality of working.	Progress.	Total length.	Percentage of total work compltd.	Remarks.
41.	Divl. battle H.Q. Q.25.c.9.7.	-	-	100%	Cleaning and revetting dump. 150 ft. of revetting done. 6 sets put in lateral. Finished.
89.	Well at BEAUCAMP, Q.12.d.3½.2.	4'10"	94'0"	-	Clearing well.
34.	Artillery dugout. Q.15.c.8.3.	-	-	-	Putting in stretchers. Finished.

467th. Field Coy. R. E.

TRAINING PROGRAMME for fortnight commencing Monday, July 9th. 1917.

FIRST WEEK.

Day.	6.45 a.m. to 7.15 a.m.	8.45 a.m. to 12.15 p.m.	2 p.m. to 4 p.m.
Monday.	Squad Drill.	Work in connection with erection of camps.	
Tuesday.	Physical Exercises.	Work in connection with erection of camps.	
Wednesday.	Squad Drill.	Inspections, Physical exercises, Rifle exercises.	Recreational training.
Thursday.	Physical Exercises.	Inspections, Squad Drill with Arms. Gas Drill.	Musketry (Care of Arms). Bayonet Fighting.
Friday.	Squad Drill.	Physical Exercises. Rifle Exercises. Squad Drill with arms. Musketry (Firing positions).	Kit Inspection. Short Route March.
Saturday.	Physical Exercises.	Squad Drill with Arms. Gas Drill. Company Drill.	———

SECOND WEEK.

Day.			
~~Day.~~ Monday.	Squad Drill.	Squad Drill with Arms. Bayonet fighting. Musketry (loading & aiming).	Route March.
Tuesday.	do.	Ceremonial Inspection. Company Drill. Musketry (Trigger pressing).	Gas Drill. Wiring Drill.
Wednesday.	do.	Physical exercises. Squad Drill with arms. Musketry (Fire discipline and Fire Control).	Recreational training.
Thursday.	do.	Gas Drill. Physical exercises. Musketry (Miniature range).	Company Drill. Bayonet fighting.
Friday.	do.	Ceremonial Inspection. Company Drill. Musketry (Miniature range).	Kit Inspection. Short Route March.
Saturday.	do.	Physical Drill. Gas Drill. Musketry. (Miniature Range). Company Drill.	———

Note: Whenever possible the Company will co-operate with the Infantry in their schemes.

467th. Field Co. R.E.

TRAINING PROGRAMME - July 23rd. to 28th. 1917.

Day.	6.45 a.m. to 7.15 a.m.	8.45 a.m. to 12.15 p.m.	2 p.m. to 4 p.m.
Monday.	Squad drill.	Squad drill with arms. Bayonet fighting. Musketry (loading & aiming).	Route March.
Tuesday.	-do-	Ceremonial inspection. Company drill. Musketry (trigger pressing).	Gas Drill. Wiring drill.
Wednesday.	-do-	Physical exercises. Squad drill with arms. Musketry (Fire discipline and fire control)	Recreational training.
Thursday.	-do-	Gas drill. Physical exercises. Musketry (Miniature range).	Company drill. Bayonet fighting.
Friday.	-do-	Ceremonial inspection. Company drill. Musketry (Miniature range).	Kit inspection. Short route march.
Saturday.	-do-	Physical drill. Gas drill. Musketry (Miniature range). Company drill.	-----

469th. Field Co. R.E.

TRAINING PROGRAMME FOR FORTNIGHT COMMENCING SATURDAY, JULY 14th. 1917.

FIRST WEEK.

Day.	6.30 a.m. to 7.30 a.m.	9.0 a.m. to 12.30 p.m.	2.0 to 3.30 p.m.
Saturday.	Squad Drill and Physical Exercises.	Bayonet and rifle practice. Bombing. Wire entanglements.	Forming Strong points. Wire entanglements. Bombing. Rifle & bayonet practice.
Sunday.		Church Parade	
Monday.	do.	Forming strong points. Wire entanglements and squad drill. Bayonet practice and rifle drill.	Bombing. Rifle and bayonet practice. Wire entanglements.
Tuesday.	do.	Company Drill. Wire entanglements. Rifle practice. Bombing.	Forming strong point. Bombing. Wire entanglements.
Wednesday.	do.	Forming strong point and wiring mines. Bombing and bayonet fighting. Wire entanglements.	Electric wiring. Wire entanglements. Bombing. Bayonet practice.
Thursday.	do.	Forming strong point. Wire entanglements and drill. Rifle practice. Bayonet fighting.	Drill and bayonet practice. Bombing. Wire entanglements.
Friday.	do.	Bombing, Rifle Drill and bayonet practice. Wire entanglements.	Forming strong point. Electric wiring. Wire entanglements. Squad drill. Bombing.

Second week will be similar to the first.

469th. Field Co. R.E.

TRAINING PROGRAMME - July 29th. to Aug. 4th. 1917.

Date.	6.30 - 7.30 a.m.	9 a.m. to 12.30 p.m.	2 to 3.30 p.m.
July 29th.	Church Parades.		
July 30th.	Squad Drill and Physical exercise.	Forming Strong Point. Wire entanglements. Squad Drill & Box Respirator drill. Bayonet fighting. Rifle drill.	Bombing. Box respirator drill. Rifle & bayonet practice. Wire entanglements.
July 31st.	Squad Drill and Physical exercise.	Company Drill and Rifle practice. Wire entanglements. Bombing. Box respirator drill.	Forming Strong Point. Bombing. Wire entanglements. Box respirator drill.
Aug. 1st.	Squad drill and Physical exercise.	Forming Strong Point and wiring mines. Bombing. Bayonet fighting. Wire entanglements.	Electrical wiring. Wire entanglements. Bombing. Bayonet practice.
Aug. 2nd.	Squad drill and Physical exercise.	Forming strong point. Wire entanglements. Box respirator drill. Rifle practice. Bayonet fighting.	Bayonet practice. Box respirator drill. Bombing. Wire entanglements.
Aug. 3rd.	Squad drill and Physical exercises.	Bombing. Rifle drill. Bayonet practice. Squad drill. Wire entanglements.	Forming strong point and electrical wiring. Wire entanglements. Bombing.
Aug. 4th.	Squad Drill and Physical exercises.	Bayonet and rifle practice. Box respirator drill. Wire entanglements. Bombing.	Forming strong point. Rifle practice. Box respirator drill. Bayonet practice.

470th. Field Co. R.E.

TRAINING PROGRAMME for the fortnight commencing Wednesday, July 11th.1917.

FIRST WEEK.

Day.	6.45 a.m. to 7.15 a.m.	8.45 a.m. to 12.15 p.m.	2 p.m. tto 4 p.m.
Wednesday.	Squad Drill.	Physical drill. Drill with Arms. Bayonet exercises. Musketry Instruction. Driving drill.	Rifle range. Barbed wire drill. Extended order drill: advancing & retiring.
Thursday.	do.	do.	do.
Friday.	do.	~~Extended order drill. Rifle range. Barbed wire drill.~~ do.	do.
Saturday.	do.	Route March.	----
Monday.	do.	Physical drill. Drill with Arms. Extended order. Musketry instruction.	do.
Tuesday.	--	Route march.	do.

SECOND WEEK.

Day.			
Wednesday.	Squad drill.	Physical exercises. Bayonet exercises. Extended order.	Barbed wire drill. Rifle range. Siting and marking out trenches and strong points.
Thursday.	do.	do.	do.
Friday.	do.	Route March.	Barbed wire drill. Rifle range.
Saturday.	do.	Physical exercises. Bayonet drill. Extended order drill: advancing & retiring.	Rifle range. Barbed wire drill.
Monday.		Route March.	
Tuesday.		Pontooning.	
Wednesday.		Pontooning.	

470th. Field Co. R.E.

TRAINING PROGRAMME – July 25th. to 31st. 1917.

Date.	6 - 6.30 a.m.	8 - 11.30 a.m.	1.30 - 3.30 p.m.
25th.	Squad Drill.	Wire entanglements. Stables. Squad drill (Drivers).	Physical exercises. Bayonet fighting.
26th.	Squad Drill.	Consolidating large shell holes. Stables & squad drill (Drivers.	Rifle range. Bayonet exercises. Field Geometry. Knots and lashings.
27th.	Divisional Tactical Exercise.		
28th.	Squad Drill.	Company Drill. Kit and gas helmet inspectn etc. Squad Drill (Drivers).	Half-holiday.
29th.	Church Parades only.		
30th.	Squad Drill.	Russian Saps. Squad Drill (Drivers).	Bayonet exercises. Rifle range. Knots and lashings. Field Geometry.
31st.	Squad Drill.	Russian Saps. Squad Drill (Drivers).	Field Geometry. Knots and lashings. Rifle range. Bayonet exercises.

ORIGINAL S.67

WAR DIARY

of

HEADQUARTERS 59ᵗʰ DIVISIONAL R.E.

VOL. VII.

1st August 1917 to 31st August 1917.

WAR DIARY or INTELLIGENCE SUMMARY

Army Form C. 2118.

HEAD QUARTERS 59th DIVISIONAL R.E.

Place	Date	Hour	Summary of Events and Information	Remarks and references to Appendices
BARASTRE	1.8.19		467 Field Coy RE. Begun upon erection of Nissen huts, construction of divisional baths at BARASTRE, erection of permanent structures in Camp O.9, instruction of infantry in Army pattern of wiring.	Sheet 57c
			469 " Erection of Nissen huts in Camp O.16.A, O.16.B and O.16.D and wiring. Brick shelving in Horse lines in Camp O.16. Recce of Company's training in accordance with attached programme of training.	/57c/ Jugero
			470 " Training in accordance with attached programme of training and above work in the Brigade Camp O.35.d.	/Chier/
2.8.19			467 Field Coy RE. Engaged upon erection of Nissen huts, construction of baths, construction of permanent structures in Camp O.9 and drainage in the same camp. Instruction of infantry in wiring. Training in accordance with Training Programme attached.	
			469 Field Coy RE. Continuation of work as detailed in yesterday's entry – Making horse standings in R.E. Camp – Erecting French Baths for 178th Brigade in Camp O.35.d and cleaning.	
			470 " Repairing and clearing roads round Camp O.35.d and practising rapid wiring this Camp. Solving work and pickets and practising rapid wiring Training in accordance with training programme attached.	
	8pm		Divisional Field Day No 1. Copy No 8 – orders and Instruction No 1 for same attached.	/Cun./
3.8.19			467 Field Coy RE. Continuation of work as detailed in yesterday's entry, also erecting Nissen huts in Camp O.16.B and dining huts in same Camp.	
			469 " Erecting brick standings for horse lines in Camp O.16.D. Re-erecting latrines in Camp O.16.D and altering Sewage for cookhouses. Training in accordance with training programme attached.	

WAR DIARY

INTELLIGENCE SUMMARY: Continued:—

(Erase heading not required.)

Army Form C. 2118.

Place	Date	Hour	Summary of Events and Information	Remarks and references to Appendices
BARASTRE	3.8.17		Contd:— 470 Field Coy RE Continuation of work as detailed in yesterdays entry with the addition of the erection of church army hut.	Map Ref to 57C S.W. 1/20000 Khun.
		8 pm	Orders by CRE (copy attached) issued to Field Coys in respect to Divisional Field Day	
do	4.8.17		467 Field Coy RE Continuation of work as detailed in entry for the 2nd inst. Erection of dining and mess huts in camp O16.b. booking standings for horses in Camp O16.D. Erecting shelter in Camp O16.D.	
			469 " " Training in accordance with programme attached	
			447[?] " " Drawing RE Camp in O35.d. and making horse standings	Khun Khun
			470 " " Completing Brigade baths and wiring Training in accordance with programme attached.	
		1 pm	Divisional Field Day No 1. Instruction No 2. Copy 8 received The divisional RE attended church parades in the morning	
	5.8.17			
	6.8.17	8.20	Orders by CRE to Field Coys despatched - marked K. Copy attached Orders marked K. despatched to 467, 469, 470 Field Coys - 176, 177 and 178 Infantry Bdes. and 59 Division G. - copies attached	Khun
		8.40	All the Field Coys took part in the Divisional Field day as detailed in the above orders :— Operations ceased at midday	
	7.8.17	6.30 pm	59 Divisional Tactical Exercise No 3 - Warning Order Copy me received 467 Field Coy R.E. Erecting mess huts. Constructing stronged Baths in Barastre. Knocking of camp. Continuation of Infantry in wiring and training in accordance with programme Contd:—	

Army Form C. 2118.

WAR DIARY
Continued:—

INTELLIGENCE SUMMARY.
(Erase heading not required.)

Place	Date	Hour	Summary of Events and Information	Remarks and references to Appendices
BARASTRE	7.8.17		C in C :- 469 FIELD Coy R.E. Erecting dining sheds and nissen huts in Camp O.16.B. making brick horse standings in Camp O.16.D. Training in accordance with programme 470 FIELD Coy R.E. Repairing wagons in Camp. Making horse standings in R.E. Camp. Drawing divisional pack Camp at ROCQUIGNY. Sunday Brigade baths. Training in accordance with programme	Map reference to Sheet 57cSW 1/20000 attached K.M.
do	8.8.17	6pm	5D Div Exercise No 3 Instructions No 1 Copy 8 received Lt Col. G.B. ROBERTS R.E. CRE DIVISION. Inspected the 3 Field Companies in marching order, march past, and in column of route	K.M.
do	9.8.17		467 FIELD Coy R.E. Erection of nissen huts and dining sheds. Drainage of camp Training 469 " " Erecting nissen huts in Brigade Camp, making brick horse standings in Camp O.16.D. Erecting flags for Divisional Exercise N.3 Training 470 " " Making horse standings in RE Camp. Repairing and cleaning roads near Camp O.35.D. Drawing divisional pack Camp Training	K.M.
	10.8.17	8 pm 9.30	The 3 Field Coys R.E. continued the work detailed above 5D DIVISION OPERATION ORDER No 300 Copy No E received CRE order marked K3 issued - copy attached	K.M.

Army Form C. 2118.

WAR DIARY
INTELLIGENCE SUMMARY.
(Erase heading not required.)

continued.—

Instructions regarding War Diaries and Intelligence Summaries are contained in F. S. Regs., Part II. and the Staff Manual respectively. Title pages will be prepared in manuscript.

Place	Date	Hour	Summary of Events and Information	Remarks and references to Appendices
BAPAUME	11.8.17		59th Division No 3 — The Field Coys took part as detailed in C.R.E.s orders No 3 of yesterday. The remaining Sections in Divisional Reserve remained in Camp and carried on with the work detailed in dairy for the 9th.	MAP REF. to 57 C.S.W. 1/20,000 Khun Khun
do	12.8.17		Field Companies attended Church parade with their respective Brigade groups. The remainder of the day being regarded as a holiday.	Khun
	13.8.17		467 FIELD COY RE Company was engaged upon bayonet count for Brigade Sports. The day being a general holiday for the Brigade group.	
			469 " Erecting dining sheds and nissen huts and constructing drains in walls Camp — Erecting brick standings in R.E. Camp. Training.	
			470 " Erecting dining huts in 177 Bde Camp. Erecting horse standings in R.E. Camp. Cleaning and repairing roads round Camp and improving entrances to Camps. Training — especially in bayonet fighting, wiring and gas drill.	Khun
	14.8.17		467 FIELD COY RE Drawing Camp — Erecting nissen huts and dining sheds. Training.	
			469 " Erecting nissen huts in Camp O.16.B. and constructing drains. Erecting brick standings to horse lines in R.E. Camp. Training — especially bayonet drill, bayonet fighting, gas drill.	
			470 " Erecting nissen huts in 176 Infantry Bde Camp and dining sheds in 177 Bde Camp and dining sheds for 178 Bde. Laying wires and Preparing raid practice trenches making overhead wire entanglements.	Khun

Army Form C. 2118.

WAR DIARY
or
INTELLIGENCE SUMMARY.

(Erase heading not required.)

Continued

Instructions regarding War Diaries and Intelligence Summaries are contained in F.S. Regs., Part II. and the Staff Manual respectively. Title pages will be prepared in manuscript.

Place	Date	Hour	Summary of Events and Information	Remarks and references to Appendices
BARASTRE	15.8.17	11.30 a.m.	MAJOR GENERAL C.F. ROMER G.O.C. Division inspected the Divisional Royal Engineers in marching order and also in the trench kit in column of sections	MAP REFD TO 57c 1/20,000
		2.30	470 FIELD Coy ordered to present its hutted camp near H.24.c.2.3. in LE TRANSLOY and obtain accommodation there in order to be nearer their work when constructing IV Corps rifle range in O.31.c and d. Company Headquarters M.18.c.60-15	
			467 and 470 Field Coys continued work in camp during the afternoon	Khin
do	16.8.17		467 FIELD Coy RE was engaged in moving their camp from BARASTRE to BEAUENCOURT (N18)	
			469 " " Erecting nissen huts and setting anouu nrat them, also protecting down brick bricks an Camp O.16.R. Making brick hoar standings on RE Camp O.16.D. Erecting nissen huts in 175 R&R Camp	
			470 " " No1, No2 and half No.3 Section working on IV Corps rifle range at LE TRANSLOY. Half No.3 Section cleaning up in the old camp	Khin
			No 4 Section making hoar standings and repairing huts in new camp, hoar lines	
	17.8.17		467 FIELD Coy RE commencing construction of necessary buildings, hoar lines bath etc to Hutment Camp in N.18 BEAULENCOURT.	
			469 " " } continuing work detailed in yesterdays report above	Khin
			470 " " }	
	18.8.17		467 FIELD Coy RE Erection of nissen huts, construction of hoar standings and accessory buildings in camps N.18 and N.24.	
			469 " " Same work as detailed for the 16 & 17 inst at LE TRANSLOY	
			470 " " Working on rifle range at LE TRANSLOY making hoar standings and oven for cookhouse. Repairing punctures	Khin

Army Form C. 2118.

WAR DIARY
or
INTELLIGENCE SUMMARY

Continued

(Erase heading not required.)

Instructions regarding War Diaries and Intelligence Summaries are contained in F. S. Regs., Part II. and the Staff Manual respectively. Title Pages will be prepared in manuscript.

Place	Date	Hour	Summary of Events and Information	Remarks and references to Appendices
BARASTRE	19.8.17		467 FIELD Coy. RE – Erecting wooden huts and accessory buildings in Camp N18 C. Erecting shower bath at Sugar factory M26 d.19. Erecting wooden huts and bakery ovens round Stores in Camp O16.	MAP. REF.D TO 57 C S.W. 1/20,000
			469 " Erecting wooden huts and drawing in Camp O10 - 17.5 B.S.C CAMP forming brick standings & stoves bases in Camp O16. D.	
			470 " Working on IV corps rifle range at LE TRANSLOY. Making kettle range and oven for cookhouse in camp.	Khun
	20.8.17 11-30 a.m		59th DIVISION WARNING ORDER No 53 Copy No 9 received and copies sent to Field companies	Khun
			Work of Field companies is a continuation of the work detailed in yesterdays diary.	
	21.8.17 10 a.m		O.C. 467 FIELD Coy RE handed over all work, plans etc to a representative of IV Corps CRE	
			469 " Continues work as detailed in the 19th and strengthen up all work, stores etc for handing on. Reprepare.	
			470 " Continue work on IV corps rifle range. Repairing pontoons in camp.	Khun
	22.8.17		467 FIELD Coy RE Prepare to move camp	
		4.00 a.m	469 " Proceed by route march and motor bus to entraining area ALBERT. Taking up temporary headquarters in MILLENCOURT	ALBERT sheet 1/60,000
		10 a.m	1 " Handed over all work in winter camps to a representative of CRE IV Corps troops.	
			470 " Prepare to move. Packing vehicles etc	Khun

Army Form C. 2118.

WAR DIARY
~~INTELLIGENCE SUMMARY~~ Continued.
(Erase heading not required.)

Instructions regarding War Diaries and Intelligence Summaries are contained in F. S. Regs., Part II. and the Staff Manual respectively. Title Pages will be prepared in manuscript.

Place	Date	Hour	Summary of Events and Information	Remarks and references to Appendices
BARASTRE	23.8.17	8 am	467 FIELD Coy RE proceeded by route march and motor bus to the entraining area and occupied temporary billets in FORCEVILLE	ALBERT SHEET outlined 1/40,000
			468.9 " " " cleaning up the billet camp occupied by them in MILLENCOURT	
			470 " " " Preparing to move camp	Kum
ACHEUX		4 pm	HEAD QUARTERS RE proceeded by motor bus and by road to ACHEUX opening up Head Quarters there at 4 pm	
do	24/8/17		470 FIELD Coy RE marched into hutted camp at W15a.6.7. between BOUZINCOURT and AVELUY	
			CRE and Adjt visited all companies camps and made an inspection of billets, horse lines, cookhouses latrines and horses	Kum
			All field companies ordered to practice their men in putting on respectly his box respirator and helmet until the Brigade entrains	Kum
	25/8/17		Field Companies continue antigas drill as per instruction	Kum
	26/8/17		Church parade in the morning	Kum
	27.8.17		Field Companies continue antigas drill and route march	Kum
	28.8.17		do	Kum
	29.8.17	6 am	59 DIVISION ORDER No 55 Copy No 9 with Time Table of entrainment received. Addendum to 59 DIVISION ORDER No 55 Copy No 9 received	
			Field Companies continues antigas drill and prepare for moving	Kum
		9 pm	22/4/3 G. 59 Division postponing move for 24 hours received	
		9 pm	Addendum to 59 Division Order No 55 received	

2449 Wt. W14957/M90. 750,000 1/16 J.B.C. &A. Forms/C.2118/12.

Army Form C. 2118.

WAR DIARY
of
INTELLIGENCE SUMMARY.
(Erase heading not required.)

Instructions regarding War Diaries and Intelligence Summaries are contained in F. S. Regs., Part II. and the Staff Manual respectively. Title pages will be prepared in manuscript.

Continued:—

Place	Date	Hour	Summary of Events and Information	Remarks and references to Appendices
ACHEUX	30.8.17	4 pm	HEAD QUARTERS 59 Div. Units packed for move	ALBERT SHEET Continued 1/40,000
	31.8.17	11 pm	HEAD QUARTERS 59 DIVISION RE entrained at BEAUCOURT - 1 officer 37 OR and left for WINNEZEELE via GODEWAERSVELDE	
		10.11 pm	467 Field Coy RE entrained at AVELUY and proceeded via HOPOUTRE to encamp in the WINNEZEELE AREA	
			The 469 and 470 Field Coys RE entrain in the early morning of SEPT 1st for which please see unit months diary.	

Marshall
Capt & Adjt R.E.
59 Division R.E.

Orders by
Lt.Col. G.B.Roberts R.E. C.R.E.59th.Division.

Reference Divisional Field Day No.1 dated 6.8.17.

Map: Sheet 57c.S.W.   1:20,000.

1. Companies will receive March Orders from their Brigades.

2. O.Cs.Companies will detail a Liaison Officer to be attached to Brigade Headquarters.

3. Each Field Company will detail 2 cyclists who are acquainted with Field Company Headquarters to report to the C.R.E. at BARASTRE Schools (O.15.d.78.97) at 8 a.m. on August 6th. 1917.

4. Sections of Field Companies will march complete with cyclists, tool-carts and pack animals, no other vehicle being taken.

5. Acknowledge.

In the Field.
3.8.17.

Captain & Adjutant,
59th.Divisional R.E.

SECRET.   Orders marked K.

ORDERS BY

Lieut.Colonel.G.B.Roberts R.E. C.R.E.59th.Division.

---:@:@:@:@:@:---

Map Reference: Sheet 57c S.W. 1:20,000.

To:
   O.C. 467th.Field Co. R.E.

   The remaining two sections of your Company will proceed to the road junction O.13.b.3.2. and will site and construct in this vicinity a Strong Point having due regard to tactical considerations. If necessary your men should be engaged upon the repair of roads in area occupied by your Brigade. You should move your Company up to this position in rear of the Battalion in ~~ress~~ reserve (if existing).

   Repeated to 176th.Brigade and 59th.Division G.

                                              Captain & Adjutant,
6th August,1917.   59th.Divisional R.E.
Issued at 8.20 a.m. by Orderly.

SECRET.   Orders marked K.

ORDERS BY
Lieut.Colonel.G.B.Roberts R.E. C.R.E.59th.Division.

---:0:0:0:0:0:---

Map Reference: Sheet 57c S.W. 1:20,000.

To:
  O.C. 469th.Field Co. R.E.

The remaining two sections of your Company will proceed to the road junction O.14.d.02.92. and will site and construct in this vicinity a Strong Point having due regard to tactical considerations. If necessary your men should be engaged upon the repair of roads in area occupied by your Brigade. You should move your Company up to this position in rear of the Battalion in reserve (if existing).

Repeated to 177th.Brigade and 59th.Division G.

6th August,1917.   Captain & Adjutant,
Issued at 8.20 a.m. by Orderly.   59th.Divisional R.E.

SECRET. 　　　　　　　　　　　　　　　　Orders marked K.

ORDERS BY

Lieut.Colonel.G.B.Roberts R.E. C.R.E.59th.Division.

---:0:0:0:0:0:---

Map Reference: Sheet 57c S.W. 1:20,000.

To:
    O.C. 470th.Field Co. R.E.

The remaining two sections of your Company will proceed to the road junction O.15.d.50.15. and will site and construct in this vicinity a Strong Point having due regard to tactical considerations. If necessary your men should be engaged upon the repair of roads in area occupied by your Brigade. You should move your Company up to this position in rear of the Battalion in res= reserve (if existing).

Repeated to 178th.Brigade and 59th.Division G.

6th August,1917.　　　　　　　　　　　　　Captain & Adjutant,
Issued at 8.20 a.m. by Orderly.　　　　59th.Divisional R.E.

Orders marked K 1.

S E C R E T.

Orders by

Lieut.Colonel.G.B.Roberts R.E.   C.R.E. 59th.Division.

---:@:@:@:@:@:@:@:@:---

Ref.Map 1/20,000 Sheet 57c S.W.   August 6th.1917.

1. INFORMATION.   The enemy, strength about 6 battalions and a brigade of field artillery, is reported by our aeroplanes to be digging in north east of LE TRANSLOY, and to the north of the LE TRANSLOY - ROCQUIGNY road which passes through O.25.a & b. and O.26.a & b.

2. INTENTION.   The 59th.Division will attack the enemy.
   The 109th.Division is advancing on ROCQUIGNY.
   The dividing line between Divisions in the BARASTRE-ROCQUIGNY road (inclusive to 59th.Division) as far as its junction with SINBAD Trench in O.21.c.10.1. and thence the SINBAD Trench (inclusive to 109th.Division).

3. DETAIL.
   (a) 176th.Inf.Bde. will move under cover to VILLERS AU FLOS and attack, from behind the LUBDA COPSE, the north end of LE TRANSLOY with the object of turning the enemy's flank. The left of the 176th.Inf.Bde. will not go east of the road running through O.19.a. and c.

   (b) The 177th.Inf.Bde.(less 1 Batt.) will attack the enemy's centre from the road through O.19.a & c.(exclusive) to the eastern end of the old German trench running through O.25.a. and b.

   (c) The 178th.Inf.Bde. will attack the enemy's right from the eastern end of the old German trench running through O.25.a. and b. to SINBAD Trench (exclusive).

   (d) The leading lines of attack will cross the old German trench in O.13.b., 14.c & d. and 15.c & d. at 10.0. a.m.

   (e) Field Companies R.E.   Two sections of the Field Company R.E. are at the disposal of each G.O.C. Inf.Bde. The remainder of each Field Company will be under the orders of the C.R.E.

Captain & Adjutant,
59th.Divisional R.E.

Issued at 8.20 a.m. by Orderly.
 to 467th.Field Co.R.E.
    469th.Field Co.R.E.
    470th.Field Co.R.E.

SECRET.   Copy No. 3.

ORDERS BY

Lieut.Colonel.G.B.Roberts R.E.   C.R.E.59th.Division.

---:@:@:@:@:@:---

Ref: Map 57c.S.W. 1:20,000.

With reference to 59th.Division Operation Order No.300
    dated 10.8.17.

1.   Officers Commanding Field Companies will place
two sections at the disposal of the G.O.C. of their
Brigade Group.

2.   The Senior Officer of these two sections will
also act as R.E. Liaison Officer to the Brigade.

3.   The remainder of each Company will be in
Divisional Reserve.

4.   Acknowledge.

         In the Field.   Captain & Adjutant,
           10.6.17.   59th.Divisional R.E.

Issued at 9.30 p.m. 10.8.17.

        Copy No.1.   File.
              2.   Spare.
              3.   War Diary.
              4.   59th.Div. "Q".
              5.   G.O.C. 176th.Inf.Bde.
              6.   G.O.C. 177th.Inf.Bde.
              7.   G.O.C. 178th.Inf.Bde.
              8.   O.C. 467th.Field Co. R.E.
              9.   O.C. 469th.Field Co. R.E.
             10.   O.C. 470th.Field Co. R.E.

PROGRAMME OF WORK 467 FIELD Coy. RE

August 1st. to August 7th. 1917.

Day.	8.45 a.m. to 12.30 p.m.	2 p.m. to 5 p.m.
Wednesday.	Erection of Nissen Huts.	Construction of Divisional Baths. Drainage of Camp O.9.
Thursday.	do.	and Instruction of Infantry in Fourth Army Pattern Wiring.
Friday.	Ceremonial Parade.	Erection of Nissen Huts. Construction of Divl. Baths. Construction of Horse Standings.
Saturday.	Erection of Nissen Huts. Instruction Infantry in wiring, Construction of Divl. Baths. Construction of Horse Standings.	
Monday.	Erection of Nissen Huts. Instruction of Infantry in Wiring. Construction of Horse standings and floors for Cookhouses.	
Tuesday.	-do-	-do-

Note: If any men are not required on work during any day, they will be trained in Squad Drill, Rifle Exercises, Bayonet Fighting, etc.

469th. Field Co. R.E.

PROGRAMME OF TRAINING from 1.8.17 to 7.8.17.

Section	Hours of Training	WEDNESDAY	THURSDAY	FRIDAY	SATURDAY	SUNDAY	MONDAY	TUESDAY
No.1	6.30-7.30	Squad Drill and Physical Exercises. Forming Strong Pt. and wiring mines.	Squad Drill and Physical Exercises. Forming Strong point.	Squad Drill and Physical Exercises. Bombing. Rifle Drill. Bayonet Practice.	Squad Drill and Physical Exercises. Bayonet & Rifle Practice. Box Respirator Drill.	C H U R C H P A R A D E 10.30 a.m.	Squad Drill Physical Exercises Forming Strong Point.	Squad Drill. Physical Exer Coy. Drill and Rifle practice
	9.0-12.30							
	2.0-3.30.	Electrical wiring.	Drill, Bayonet practice. Box respirator drill.	Forming Strong Pt. & electrical wiring.	Forming Strong Point.		Bombing. Box Respirator Drill.	Forming Strong Point.
No.2	6.30-7.30	Squad Drill and Physical exercises.	Squad Drill and Physical exercises.	Squad Drill and Physical exercises.	Squad Drill and Physical exercises		Squad Drill and Physical exercises	Squad Drill & Physical exer
	9.0-12.30	Bombing. Bayonet fighting.	Wire entanglements. Drill and box Respirator Drill.	Bayonet practice. Rifle drill.	Wire entanglements. Bombing.		Wire entanglements. Squad Drill. Box respirator drill.	Coy. drill and Wire entanglements. Bombing.
	2.0-3.30.	Wire entanglements.	Bayonet Practice.	Wire entanglements	Rifle practice Box respirator drill.		Rifle & bayonet practice.	Bombing.
No.3	6.30-7.30	Squad Drill and Physical exercises.	Squad Drill and Physical exercises.	Squad Drill and Physical exercises.	Squad Drill and Physical exercises.		Squad Drill and Physical exercises.	Squad Drill. Physicl exer:
	9.0-12.30	Wire entanglements. Bayonet practice.	Rifle practice Wire entanglements.	Bayonet practice, Squad Drill.	Box respirator drill Bombing. Wire Entanglements.		Wire entanglements. Squad Drill.	Coy. drill and Bombing.
	2.0-3.30.	Bombing.	Box Respirator Drill. Bombing.	Wire entanglements	Bayonet practice.		Bayonet practice.	Wire entanglements. Box respirator drill.
No.4	6.30-7.30	Squad Drill and Physical exercises.	Squad Drill and Physical exercises.	Squad Drill and Physical exercises.	Squad Drill and Physical exercises.		Squad Drill and Physical exercises.	Squad Drill & Physical exer:
	9.0-12.30	Drill, and Wire entanglements.	Rifle Practice. Bayonet fighting. Box respirator drill.	Bayonet Practice. Wire entanglements.	Bayonet fighting. Wire entanglements.		Bayonet practice. Rifle Drill.	Coy. Drill. Rifle practice Box respirator drill
	2.0-3.30.	Bayonet practice.	Wire entanglements.	Bombing.	Box respirator Drill. Rifle practice.		Wire entanglements	Wire entanglements.

470th. Field Co. R.E.

TRAINING PROGRAMME - 2.8.17 to 8.8.17.

Hours.	Section.	Thursday.	Friday.	Saturday.	Sunday.	Monday.	Tuesday.	Wednesday.
6.0 to 6.30.	all.	Squad Drill.	Squad Drill.	Squad Drill March	Squad Drill.	Squad Drill March.	Squad Drill.	Squad Drill March.
	Drivers.	Stables.	Stables.	Stables.	Stables.	Stables.	Stables.	Stables.
8 a.m. to 12 noon.	1.	Russian Saps.	Wiring.	Company Drill. Kit Inspections	Church Parade.	Consolidation.	Russian Saps.	Company Drill.
	2.	Wiring.	Russian Saps.	-do-	-do-	-do-	Wiring.	-do-
	3.	Russian Saps.	Wiring.	-do-	-do-	-do-	Russian Saps.	-do-
	4.	Wiring.	Russian Saps.	-do-	-do-	-do-	Wiring.	-do-
	Drivers.	Stables and Squad Drill	Stables and Musketry.	Stables.	Stables.	Stables and Drill.	Stables and Arm Drill.	Stables and Musketry.
1.30 p.m. to 4 p.m.	1.	Rifle Range.	Musketry.	----	----	Bayonet fighting.	Arm Drill.	Bathing.
	2.	Musketry.	Rifle Range.	----	----	Arm Drill.	Bayonet fight'g.	-do-
	3.	Bayonet fight'g.	Arm Drill.	----	----	Rifle Range.	Musketry.	-do-
	4.	Arm Drill.	Bayonet fight'g.	----	----	Musketry.	Rifle Range.	-do-
	Drivers.	Stables.	Stables.	Stables.	Stables.	Stables.	Stables.	Stables and Rifle Range.
Recreations		Cinema.		Football.		Concert.		

467th. Field Co. R.E.

PROGRAMME OF WORK - Aug.8th./14th.1917.

Day.	8.45 a.m. to 12.30 p.m.	2 p.m. to 5 p.m.
Wednesday.	Inspection by the C.R.E.	Recreational Training.
Thursday.	Construction of Divisional Baths.	Erection of Nissen Huts and Messing Rooms, etc.
Friday.	-ditto-	-ditto-
Saturday.	Construction of Divisional Baths. Erection of Nissen Huts. and Messing Rooms etc.	
Monday.	Construction of Divisional Baths. Erection of Nissen Huts and Messing Rooms etc.	
Tuesday.	-ditto-	

469th. Field Co. R.E.

PROGRAMME OF TRAINING from 8.8.17 to 14.8.1917.

Section	Hours of Training	WEDNESDAY	THURSDAY	FRIDAY	SATURDAY	SUNDAY	MONDAY	TUESDAY
No.1.	6.30-7.30	Squad drill and Physical exercises.	Squad drill and Physical exercises.	Squad Drill and Physical exercises.	Squad Drill and Physical exercises.	Church Parades 10.30 a.m.	Squad Drill and Physical exercises.	Squad Drill & Physical exer:
	9.0-12.30.	Forming Strong Point and wiring mines.	Forming Strong Point.	Bombing. Rifle drill. Bayonet practice.	Bayonet exercises. Rifle Practice. Respirator Drill.		Forming strong Point.	Coy.Drill & Rifle Practice
	2.0-3.30.	Electrical wiring.	Drill. Bayonet practice, & box respirator drill.	Forming strong point. and electrical wiring.	Forming strong point.		Bombing. Box Respirator drill.	Forming strong point.
No.2.	6.30-7.30	Squad Drill and Physical exercises.	Squad Drill and Physical exercises.	Squad Drill and Physical exercises.	Squad Drill and Physical exercises.		Squad Drill and Physical exercises.	Squad Drill & Physical exer:
	9.0-12.30.	Bombing. Bayonet fighting.	Wire entanglements. Drill & Box respirator drill.	Wire entanglements. Bayonet practice. Rifle drill.	Wire entanglements. Bombing.		Wire entanglements. Squad Drill. Box respirator drill.	Coy.Drill & Wire entanglements.
	2.0-3.30.	Wire entanglements.	Bayonet practice.	Wire entanglements.	Rifle Practice. Box respirator drill.		Rifle & bayonet Practice.	Bombing.
No.3.	6.30-7.30	Squad Drill and Physical exercises.	Squad Drill and Physical exercises.	Squad drill and Physical exercises.	Squad drill and Physical exercises.		Squad drill and Physical exercises.	Squad drill & Physical exer:
	9.0-12.30.	Wire entanglements. Bayonet practice.	Rifle practice. Wire entanglements.	Bayonet practice. Squad drill.	Box respirator drill. Bombing. Wire entanglements.		Wire entanglements. Squad Drill.	Coy.drill and Bombing. Wire entanglements.
	2.0-3.30.	Bombing.	Box respirator drill. Bombing.	Wire entanglements.	Bayonet practice.		Bayonet practice.	Box respirator drill.
No.4.	6.30-7.30	Squad drill and Physical exercises.	Squad drill and Physical exercises.	Squad drill and Physical exercises.	Squad drill and Physical exercises.		Squad drill and Physical exercises.	Squad drill & Physical exer:
	9.0-12.30.	Drill and wire entanglements.	Rifle practice. Bayonet fighting. Box respirator drill.	Bayonet practice. Wire entanglements.	Bayonet practice. Wire entanglements.		Bayonet practice. Rifle drill.	Coy.Drill. Rifle practice. B.Resp'r drill
	2.0-3.30.	Bayonet practice.	Wire entanglements.	Bombing.	Box respirator drill. Rifle drill.		Wire entanglements.	Wire entanglements.

470th. Field Co. R.E.

TRAINING PROGRAMME - Aug.9th. to Aug.15th.1917.

Times.	Sections.	Thursday.	Friday.	Saturday.	Sunday.	Monday.	Tuesday.	Wednesday.
6.0 a.m. to 6.30 a.m.	All. Drivers.	Drill Stables.	Drill Management.	March. Bathing etc.	— Stables	Drill Stables.	Drill Stables	March. Management.
8 a.m. to 12.0 noon	1	Wiring.	Russian Saps.	Company Drill.	Church Parades	Sapping.	Knots & Lashings.	Demolitions.
	2	Russian Saps.	Wiring.	do.		Wiring.	Demolitions.	Consolidation.
	3	Musketry.	Musketry.	do.		Rifle Range.	Consolidation.	Bridging.
	4	Rifle Range.	Range.	do.		Musketry.	Bridging.	Knots & lashings.
1.30 p.m. to 4.0 p.m.	1	Russian Saps.	Company Drill.	—		Musketry.	Bridging.	Kit Inspection.
	2	Wiring.	do.	—		Range.	Consolidation.	do.
	3	Rifle Range.	do.	—		Wiring.	Demolitions.	do.
	4	Musketry.	do.	—		Sapping.	Knots & Lashings.	do.
Recreations.		Cricket.	Cricket.	Football.		Cricket.	Cricket.	

ORIGINAL

WAR DIARY

of

HEADQUARTERS. R.E. 59th DIVISION.

Vol. VIII.

1st Sept. 1917 to 30th Sept. 1917.

WAR DIARY of HEAD QUARTERS 59 DIVISIONAL R.E.

INTELLIGENCE SUMMARY. For SEPTEMBER 1917.

Army Form C. 2118.

Place	Date	Hour	Summary of Events and Information	Remarks and references to Appendices
WINNEZEELE	1.9.17	1.21 am	469 FIELD Coy R.E. entrained at ALBERT and proceeded with its Brigade (177th) to the Camping area at WINNEZEELE via PROVEN	MAP REF 1/100.000 HAZEBROUCK 5A
		3 am	470 " " Entrained at BEAUCOURT with 178 BRIGADE GROUP and proceeded via GODEWAERSVELDE to WINNEZEELE CAMPING AREA	
		11.30 am	HEAD QUARTERS R.E. arrived at GODEWAERSVELDE entrained, and marched into billets in WINNEZEELE arriving at 2.30 pm	
		12.15 pm	467 FIELD Coy R.E. arrived at HOPOUTRE detrained and marched into billets in No 1 area	Map Ref Sheet 27 1/40.000 K.M.m
		"	469 " " arrived at PROVEN detrained and marched into billets in No 2 area	
		1.30 pm	470 " " arrived at GODEWAERSVELDE detrained and marched into billets in No 3. area	
		1.30 pm	Head Quarters R.E. units as follows	
			HEAD QUARTERS R.E. Billet No 9 WINNEZEELE	
			467 FIELD Coy R.E. J 6 a 1.7	
			469 " J 3 c.33	
			470 " J 1 d 90.	
	2.9.17		The 3 Field companies spent the day in making cooking, washing and latrine arrangements for their men	K.m.m
	3.9.17		Orders received from 59 Div G. in letter 59/13/G of the 2/9/17 to send two Field Companies to the forward area per arrangement with reference to same attached hereto and marked Appendix I.	K.m.m
			467 and 469 " FIELD Coys. proceeded to YPRES and POPERINGHE respectively and take up their headquarters as follows	
			467 at I 7 d. 11 } Sheet 28 1/40.000	
	4.9.17		469 at G, 8 B 2 95. }	K.M.m

WAR DIARY or INTELLIGENCE SUMMARY

Army Form C. 2118

Place	Date	Hour	Summary of Events and Information	Remarks and references to Appendices
WINNEZEELE	5/9/17		467 FIELD Coy RE making shelters for accommodation of troops in YPRES under orders from CRE XIX Corps troops	
			469 " working under orders of CRE 42 DIVISION	Keen
			470 " doing gen. duties, physical exercises and general work in camp	Keen
6/9/17			Same as for yesterday. The 469 Field Coy was employed in making alterations includes, employing training tasks. Erecting poxy for cement slab manufactory. Making Trench boards etc in the Corps R.E. Park	
	7/9/17		467 FIELD Coy RE. One Section repairing company billets in YPRES. One " constructing two splinter proof shelters in YPRES. Two sections erecting elephant shelters in YPRES. Employed in Corps workshops - continuing the work detailed in yesterdays report.	
			469 " " "	Keen
			470 " " "	Keen
	8/9/17		Detail of work of the field companies as same as for yesterday	
	9/9/17		467 FIELD Coy RE. Employed upon following work - Blocking openings and vents and gas proofing tunnels in Ramparts. Cleaning YPRES water conduit. Erection of Elephant shelters in YPRES and constructing latrines and cook houses for each group of shelters.	
			469 " Employed in V Corps workshops under the following work - making cook houses, Alluten trenches, machine gun aiming posts. Gun platforms - cement stalls, paving slabs.	
			470 " Training	Keen

WAR DIARY
INTELLIGENCE SUMMARY

Army Form C. 2118 — Continued —

(Erase heading not required.)

Place	Date	Hour	Summary of Events and Information	Remarks and references to Appendices
WINNEZEELE	10.9.17		467 FIELD Coy RE continuing the work detailed in yesterdays report.	
			469 " " looking in V Corps RE Park upon making Cook houses, ablution benches, machine gun aiming posts - gun platforms, Cinerete stalls paving slabs and Decauville Tramway Trucks.	Kerr
			470 " " Training	
do.	11.9.17		467 FIELD Coy RE continuing the work detailed in yesterdays report.	
			469 " " continuing work detailed in yesterdays report.	
			470 " " Training - route marching and commencing the erection of a Decauville bath alongside the existing one. Was previewed for the 9" inst.	Kerr
do.	12.9.17		467 FIELD Coy RE continuing the work detailed in the report for the 9" inst.	
			469 " " making window frames for Batt Hours, Decauville trucks, gun platforms, machine gun aiming posts. Constructing Horse Standing.	
			470 " " Training and erecting additions to Divisional baths as has been so that detailed in yesterday.	Kerr
do.	13.9.17		The work of each Field Coy is the same as that detailed in yesterdays report.	
		4 pm	CE. V CORPS ordered 467 FIELD Coy from present billets in YPRES to H.12.a.O.6. YPRES. NORTH - the move to take place on the 14th inst - see copy. appendix II attached.	Kerr
	14.9.17		467 FIELD Coy RE moved in accordance with orders issued on the previous day	
			469 " " making windows frames for dramo erecting Pump and levelling ground to bath troughs. Making Horse Standings all under the direction of CRE V Corps Troops	
			470 " " Training and finishing additions to Divisional baths	Kerr

Army Form C. 2118

WAR DIARY
INTELLIGENCE SUMMARY
(Erase heading not required.)

continued:—

Place	Date	Hour	Summary of Events and Information	Remarks and references to Appendices
WINNEZEELE	15.9.17		467 FIELD Coy R.E. continued the erection of shelters in YPRES and insuring shelters and galleries in the ramparts proof against gas.	Sheets 27 and 28 1/20,000
			469 " making window frames in V Corps Marqe. loading up wagons and constructing Renommé Staging Camp. Wiring drill.	Khan
			470 " Training. Gas drill and wiring - and doing odd jobs in and about the Infantry Camps.	
do	16.9.17 1 pm		59 Division Order N° 9 received - it did not affect the Divisional R.E. Work of units is the same as that detailed in the report for yesterday.	Khan
do	17.9.17		467 FIELD Coy RE continues the erection of Elephant shelters making them shell proof - also improving and gas proofing the galleries and dugouts in the ramparts.	
			469 FIELD Coy RE - making cork houses and wiring cables in V Corps RE Park wiring drill. Making O.P. for Heavy Artillery. Constructing Renommé Staging Camp.	Khan
			470 " Training	
do	18.9.17		467 FIELD Coy R.E. } Continuing work as detailed in report for yesterday.
			469 " "
			470 " "
		8-30 pm	59 DIVISION INSTRUCTIONS for the OFFENSIVE Copies N° 5 received as below	
			INSTRUCTIONS N° 1 LIAISON
			N° 2 N° of Officers and other ranks remaining out of action
			N° 3 Fighting kit etc
		10 pm	Officers detailed under Para 3 Instruction N° 2 as per appendix N° 3	Khan

Army Form C. 2118

WAR DIARY or INTELLIGENCE SUMMARY Continued

(Erase heading not required.)

Instructions regarding War Diaries and Intelligence Summaries are contained in F.S. Regs., Part II, and the Staff Manual respectively. Title Pages will be prepared in manuscript.

Place	Date	Hour	Summary of Events and Information	Remarks and references to Appendices
WINHEEZEELE	19.9.17		467 FIELD Coy RE – one section in rest at Transport lines at VLAMERTINGHE the remainder of Company were employed in erecting Elephant shelters, constructing work benches, latrines and ablution benches. Clearing the YPRES water conduit and fitting door frames and gas curtains to elephant shelters.	Sheet 27 and 28 1/40,000
			469 FIELD Coy RE. Making OP's for V CORPS HEAVY ARTILLERY. Constructing Remount staging Camp. Gave a wiring demonstration for V Corps recalls of which are given in appendix IV attached.	Khm
			470 " " Training	
		8 pm	59 DIVISION ORDER N° 57 Copy N° 9 with most (6) attached received, and a copy sent to OC 470 FIELD Coy RE with orders to move as directed therein	Khm
do.	20.9.17		467 FIELD Coy RE continuation of work detailed in yesterday's report.	
			463 " Working at Remount staging camp	
			470 " moved in accordance with 59 DIVISION ORDER N° 57 and took up their Head quarters at L.7.b.0.4. Sheet 27	Khm
do.	21.9.17	8 am	59 DIVISION G.S. 212/6/2.9 dated 20/9/17 received and copies sent to field companies	
		1 am	CE V CORPS WIRE E 459/9/17 placing OC 467 and 469 FIELD Coy RE under orders of CRE after having been detached from this Division for a period of 17 days from 4/9/17.	
			Companies continue work as detailed in yesterday's report.	
		8 pm	Officers on leave ordered back to their units	
		8.30 pm	59 DIVISION ORDER N° 58 Copy N° 5 received	Khm

WAR DIARY
INTELLIGENCE SUMMARY Continued

Army Form C. 2118

Place	Date	Hour	Summary of Events and Information	Remarks and references to Appendices
WINNEZEELE	22.9.17	10 am	Orders sent to OC 470 FIELD Coy RE to move to YPRES Grainway. Copy marked app I attached	Sheet 27 a – 28
		1-30 p.m.	Addendum No. 1 59 DIVISION ORDER No. 58 Copy No. 5 received	1/40000.
do		2 pm	59 DIVISION Instructions to the Officers – Instructions No. 5 "Employment of machine Guns" Copy No. 5 received	
		2 p.m.	CRE held a conference of OC companies in POPERINGHE	
YPRES		4 pm	CRE opened up his formed Headquarters in Canal DUGOUTS I/6.B.4. YPRES	Sheet 28
		11-30 p.m.	59 DIVISION ORDER No. 59 Copy No. 5 with branch table attached received	
			59 DIVISION PRELIMINARY INSTRUCTIONS Copy No. 5 received	
		8 p.m.	Orders sent to OC 469 FIELD Coy to move to YPRES Tomorrow. copy marked appendix III attached	Khin
do	23.9.17.	9 am	467 FIELD Coy RE took over from 422 FIELD Coy RE at CANAL LOCK. I.6.#9.1.	
		11 am	469 " " " " " " " " " " "Dixmude Street" I8 a central	
		10 am	470 " " " " " " " " " " CANAL BANK DUGOUTS I.1.6.59	
			Addendum No. 1 to 59 DIVISION PRELIMINARY INSTRUCTIONS Copy No. 5 received	
		3 pm	59 DIVISION INSTRUCTIONS No. 4 "SIGNAL COMMUNICATIONS" Copy No. 5 received	
		"	59 " " No. 6 "PRISONERS OF WAR" " " "	
		"	59 " " No. 7 "ACTION OF TANKS" " " "	
		9.30 p.m.	59 DIVISION ORDER No. 60 Copy 5 received	
		6 pm	CRE held a conference of OC companies at his Headquarters at I.6.B.4.	
			Casualties to-morrow 2 O.R. KILLED 10 O.R. wounded	Khin

Army Form C. 2118

WAR DIARY or INTELLIGENCE SUMMARY continued

(Erase heading not required.)

Instructions regarding War Diaries and Intelligence Summaries are contained in F.S. Regs., Part II. and the Staff Manual respectively. Title Pages will be prepared in manuscript.

Place	Date	Hour	Summary of Events and Information	Remarks and references to Appendices
YPRES	24/9/17		59 Division Instructions - Addendum to Instructions No 7 Tanks Copy 5 received	28 NE
			" " No 8 Miscellaneous Copy 5 received	28 NW
			" " No 9 Machine Gun Orders Copy 5 received	1/20 000
		1.30 pm	G.S./728 Lunching 5.9 Division Order No 60 received	
			CRE Instructions K 3360 sent to all concerned an appendix VII attached	
		3 pm	CRE Order No 1 issued to all concerned " VIII "	
		5 pm	CRE " " to 9th Seaforths received per appendix IV	
			Addendum No 1 5.9 Division Order No 60 Copy 5 received	
		11.30 pm	467 Field Coy RE repairing WIELTJE - GRAVENSTAFEL Road East of STEENBEEK RIVER	
			469 " " " " Repairing and extending No 5 Track	
			470 " " " " No 6 "	
		10 am	Battalion 9th Seaforths attached to CRE until further orders	
			3 half companies worked at night continuing the work 467, 469 and 470 Field Coys	Khn
			respectively. Our company worked on day on M/G Track	
du	25/9/17	3 pm	Capt C.I.B. Davis of 470 Field Coy wounded by bomb splinter and evacuated	
			The 3 Field Coys carry on with the work detailed in yesterday report and	
			in addition clear dugouts at BANK FARM and POND FARM for the use of	Khn
			Brigade Headquarters tomorrow	
	26/9/17	5.50	5.9 Division attacks German front line in accordance with orders	
			During the days offensive the Field Coys were employed as follows:	
			Lt J.H.B. Dixon was detailed as liaison officer to the 177th Infantry Bde	Khn
			Lt F.C. Salmon " " " " 178 " "	

Army Form C. 2118

WAR DIARY
INTELLIGENCE SUMMARY
Continued.
(Erase heading not required.)

Place	Date	Hour	Summary of Events and Information	Remarks and references to Appendices
YPRES	26/9/17		Continued:-	SHEET 28 N.E. 28 N.W. 1/20,000
			467 Field Coy RE were employed in repairing the WIELTJE - GRAVENSTAFEL Road, east of the STEENBEEK RIVER, but owing to very heavy shelling of this road, the company were only able to work intermittently.	
			469 Field Coy RE. 2 Sections attached to 177 Inf. Bde for construction of strong points - these sections were caught by the enemy barrage in their forming up position - they lost fairly heavily, both section officers being knocked out, one killed the other wounded and 15 OR killed and wounded" trying to the envolved situation at the time their section was not obvious apparent. 2 Sections were employed on No.5 MULE TRACK which they kept in repair as far as possible but were unable to continue it beyond Hill 35 owing to very heavy shelling on its day.	GRAVENSTAFEL 1/10,000
			470 Field Coy RE. The OC was killed early on in the day 2 Sections were attached to 178 Inf. Bde for making strong points at D.14 b.4.4. D.14 d.2.8. which they did satisfactorily. 2 Sections employed on M.G. mule track - they were unable to contain it owing to very heavy shelling but kept crashing track in a good a condition as possible	
	6 pm		Orders sent by CRE to OC 9 SEAFORTHS PIONEERS see appendix X attached The following casualties occurred during this days operations MAJOR F. FISHER killed by a shell OC 470 Field Coy I LT. P.M. LABDON " " 469 FIELD Coy RE 2 O.R. Killed	continued

WAR DIARY or INTELLIGENCE SUMMARY *continued*

Army Form C. 2118

Place	Date	Hour	Summary of Events and Information	Remarks and references to Appendices
YPRES	26/9/17		continued.	SHEET 28 NE. 28 NW 1/20,000 Khen
			Lt. J.H.B. DIXON 467 FIELD Coy wounded by shrapnel shell	
			" Lt. B. ROYCE 469 " " " " "	
		5 pm	37 Oth. Rank. wounded.	
			59 Division G 263 received	
	27/9/17	11.20	59 Division order Nº 61 Copy Nº 5 received	
do		12 noon	CRE orders K 3399 issued to 9th SEAFORTH PIONEERS, detailing the work to be night and tomorrow among her appendix XI attached	
			467 FIELD Coy RE commenced work on the WIELTJE—GRAVENSTAFEL Road East of STEENBEEK RIVER, assisted by a company of pioneers	
			469 FIELD Coy RE Repairing and continuing Hº 5 TRACK beyond HILL 35	
			" " " Nº 6 " "	
			" " " " CAPRICORN KEEP D/8 d central A company of pioneers was employed during the day doubling Nº 6 track from C 28 C 28 and found fav Centaurs in dugouts at YPRES and WIELTJE	Khen
			1 O.R. KILLED 8 wounded during the night and day.	
do	28/9/17		467 FIELD Coy RE continued work at night on the WIELTJE—GRAVENSTAFEL road East of STEENBEEK RIVER, also made roof diversion over River to to enable traffic to proceed during the repair of the Bridge over the river—Work was delayed owing to heavy gas shelling	
			469 FIELD Coy RE Clearing ground for, carrying up and erecting 6 baby-elephant shelters at C 26 c 5.5. Duckboards repaired and laid up to HILL 35	
			continued:—	

Army Form C. 2118

WAR DIARY
or
INTELLIGENCE SUMMARY Continued:—

(Erase heading not required.)

Instructions regarding War Diaries and Intelligence Summaries are contained in F. S. Regs., Part II. and the Staff Manual respectively. Title Pages will be prepared in manuscript.

Place	Date	Hour	Summary of Events and Information	Remarks and references to Appendices
YPRES	28/9/17		Continued:— 470 FIELD Coy RE Sandbagging and strengthening concrete dugouts at CAPRICORN KEEP working upon No 6 MULE TRACK — repairs and extension. 9TH SEAFORTH PIONEERS. Repairing and widening MULE TRACK from SCHULER GALLERIES to KANSAS HOUSE. 170 yds of duckboards laid on this track. Widening track from SCHULER GALLERIES to OLIVE HOUSE. Erecting yards of Camouflage across valley from SCHULER FARM to OLIVE HOUSE and strengthening bridge across HANEBEEK. Working No 6 TRACK (duckboards) 400 yds laid — giving 900 reviets in dugouts in WIELTJE	FREZENBERG SHEET 1/10,000
		11 am	CRE orders K 2690 detailing work to PIONEERS for following day marked Copies Approved — Copies marked appendix XII attached.	Khun
		1 pm 8 pm	59 DIVISION ORDER No 63 Copy 5th received Addendum to above Casualties. 1 or wounded 8 gassed.	
do and BRANDHOEK	29/9/17	10 a.m.	CRE order No 2 detailing reliefs — issued to all concerned see appendix XIII attached. Work of 467, 469 and 470 FIELD Coy RE and of SEAFORTH PIONEERS is a continuation of that detailed for work in yesterdays report. Casualties 1/1 gassed 1 missing. 27 Horses killed and 15 wounded by bombs	Khun
do.	30/9/17	10 a.m.	CRE 59. hands over to CRE NEW ZEALAND DIVISION 467 FIELD Coy RE } hand over as directed in CRE order No 2 of yesterday and 469 " " } march into VLAMERTINGHE No 2 area 470 " " — head Qrs and hand into billets at HOP FACTORY H8a.59 continued	

WAR DIARY
INTELLIGENCE SUMMARY — Continued

Army Form C. 2118

Place	Date	Hour	Summary of Events and Information	Remarks and references to Appendices
BRANDHOEK	30/9/17		Continued	
			Transport of 467 FIELD Coy R.E. marched into WATOU N° 3 area	
			" 469 " " " WATOU N° 1 area	
			" 470 " " " WATOU N° 2	
		10.45 am	59 DIVISION WARNING ORDER N° 64 Copy N° 5 Received	
		3 pm	G 281 correction to Air order N° 64 Received	
		9.30 pm	C.R.E. 59 DIVISION ORDER N° 3 issued to all concerned see appendix XIV attached	Kw

J Weatherhead
Capt. adj.
59 D.W. R.E.

APPENDIX No.1.

Minute 1.

R.E.

57/13. G.

XIX Corps have rung up to say that 2 Field Cos. will be required to move up for work in the forward area on the 4th. instant.

Busses will be provided for personnel, transport to move by road.

Will you please say what numbers busses will be required for and at what points busses should report.

This information is required by 8.30 a.m. tomorrow.

2.9.17.   for G.S. 59th.Division.

Minute 2.

Headquarters G.
59th. Division.

Reference your 57/13 G. dated 2.9.17, sheet 27 L/40.000.
5 Busses and 1 Lorry to report Cross Roads, J.8.a.7.3. for the 469th.Field Co.R.E. at 9 a.m. 4th.instant.
5 Busses and 1 Lorry to report Cross Roads J.12.a.8.3. for the 467th.Field Co.R.E. at 9 a.m. on the 4th.instant.

                                            Captain & Adjutant for
3.9.17.   C.R.E. 59th.Division.

Headquarters Q.
O.C. 467th.Field Co.R.E.
O.C. 469th.Field Co.R.E.
O.C. 470th.Field Co.R.E.

The 467th. and 469th.Field Cos.R.E. will be ready to move up for work in the Forward Area on the 4th.instant.
Busses will be provided for personnel - transport to move by road.
XIX Corps have been asked to provide 5 busses and 1 lorry to report at Cross Roads J.8.a.7.3. for the 469th. Field Co.R.E. and 5 busses and 1 lorry at the cross Roads J.12.a.8.3. for the 467th.Field Co. R.E.
Probable times of starting - Transport 6 a.m.
                               Busses and lorries 9 a.m.

In the Field.   Captain & Adjutant,
3.9.17.   59th.Divisional R.E.

S E C R E T.   57/13 G.

C.R.E.

1. Two Field Companies R.E. will move from WINNEZEELE to POPERINGHE and YPRES respectively on 4th. Sept. for work under C.E. XIX Corps.

2. Personnel will move by bus via WATOU and ST. JANS TER BIEZEN.

3. Billets will be arranged by Town Majors POPERINGHE and YPRES.

4. Transport will move by road via WATOU, ST. JANS TER BIEZEN and Switch Road. Transport not to enter WATOU before 12 noon.

5. 5 busses and 1 lorry will report at cross roads J.8.a.7.3. for the 469th. Field Co.R.E. 9 a.m. Sept 4th., and 5 busses and 1 lorry at the same hour at d.12.a.8.3. for the 467th. Field Co..RE.

                                        (Sd) R.St.G.Gorton, Lieut.Col.
3.9.17.   G.S. 59th.Division.

O.C. 467th.Field Co. R.E.
     469th.Field Co. R.E.

The 467th.Field Co. R.E. will proceed to YPRES and the 469th.Field Co.R.E. will proceed to POPERINGHE.

Each Company will send as early as possible to-day and officer and 2 N.C.os. to report to the Town Major of their respective billeting areas in order to arrange billets for the whole Company.

Headquarters of Company to be wired to this Office as soon as known.   Code calls must be used by the Units when in the forward area.

Arrangements are being made to ration the Companies in YPRES and POPERINGHE.

                                        (sd) K.Neville Moss,
                                             Captain & Adjutant,
3.9.17.   59th.Divisional R.E.

Appendix II

C.R.E.59th.Div. K.3303.

Copy.

~~C.R.E.~~ ~~9th.Division~~.   R.154.
C.R.E. 59th.Division.

      Orders are being issued for the following movements;-

467th.Field Co.R.E. from present billets to H.12.a.0.6. YPRES NORTH.

64th.Field Co.R.E. from WATOU to present billets of 467th.Field Co.R.E. in YPRES.

The moves to take place on 14th.instant.

An officer from 467th.Field Co.R.E. should report this afternoon to Area Commandant YPRES NORTH at GOLDFISH CHATEAU H.11.a.9.2. and arrange details about taking over accommodation.

13.9.1917.   (signed) J.H.RICHARD. Capt.R.E.
                                       for C.E. V. Corps.

Appendix No.5.

ORDERS BY Lt.Col.G.B.ROBERTS, R.E.
C.R.E. 59th. Division.

To C.C. 470th.Field Co. R.E.

Your Company will move to YPRES tomorrow morning, the 23rd. inst. to take over from the 423 Field Coy. R.E. of the 55th.Division, situated in Canal Bank Dugouts, Nos.50 to 70.

Seven busses or lorries will report at your headquarters at 8 a.m. tomorrow morning.

Acknowledge to C.R.E. 59th.Division c/o C.R.E. 55th.Division.

(Sd) K.Neville Moss,
Captain & Adjutant,
22.9.17. 59th.Divisional R.E.

Appendix 6.

ORDERS by Lt.Col.G.B.ROBERTS, R.E.
C.R.E. 59th.Division.

To 469th.Field Co. R.E.

    Send officer to take over from 419 Co. at 11 a.m. tomorrow.

    Your Company to proceed to new quarters as early as possible tomorrow morning.

22.9.17.

(Sd) K.N.Moss,
Captain & Adjutant,
59th.Divisional R.E.

SECRET.

War Diary.

Appendix VII.

K.3360.

```
59th.Division.G.(for information)
176th.Inf.Bde.           "       "
177th.Inf.Bde.           "       "
178th.Inf.Bde.           "       "
467th.Field Co.R.E.
469th.Field Co.R.E.
470th.Field Co.R.E.
9th.Seaforths (Pioneers).
```

With reference to 59th.Division Preliminary Instructions which have been explained to Field Co. Commanders concerned,

1. Tracings are attached showing;-

    (a) The Boundaries etc. referred to in para.3. of the instructions.

    (b) The routes Nos.6 and 5 which will be continued from their present termini.

2. O.C.469th.Field Co.R.E. will place 2 sections at the disposal of the G.O.C. 177th.Inf.Bde. on "Y" day. O.C.470th.Field Co.R.E. will place 2 sections at the disposal of G.O.C. 178th.Inf.Bde. on "Y" day.

3. O.C.467th.Field Co.R.E. will detail Lieut.J.H.B. Dixon R.E. as Liaison Officer for the 177th.Inf.Bde. and O.C.470th.Field Co.R.E. will detail a Liaison officer for the 178th.Inf.Bde.

4. O.C.467th.Field Co.R.E. will be responsible for the repair of the portion of WIELTJE - GRAVENSTAFEL Road E. of the STEENBEEK River.

    O.C.469th.Field Co.R.E. will be responsible for the repair and continuation of Track No.5.

    O.C.470th.Field Co.R.E. will be responsible for the repair and continuation of Track No.6.

24.9.1917.   (signed) G.B.ROBERTS. Lieut.Col.R.E.
                                          C.R.E. 59th. Division.

SECRET.   Copy No. 11.

APPENDIX VIII.

OPERATION ORDER No.1

By

Lieut.Colonel. G.B.Roberts, R.E.   C.R.E. 59th.Division.

-----:@:@:@:@:@:@:@:-----

Ref. Map: Sheet 28 N.W.2. 1/10,000.

1.   With reference to 59th.Division Order No.60, dated
        23.9.17, para.11, the following will be the places where
        the detachments for work under the C.R.E. will be formed
        up at 4 a.m. on 'Z' day :-

        467th.Field Co. R.E. - In the Old British Trenches
                at C.28.b.8.8., i.e. where the trench
                joins the WIELTJE - GRAVENSTAFEL Road.

        469th.Field Co. R.E.(less 2 sections) - In the
                Old British Trenches at C.29.a.0.3., i.e.
                where the trenches join No.5 Track.

        470th.Field Co. R.E.(less 2 sections) - In the
                Old British Trenches at C.22.d.3.2., i.e.
                where the trenches join No.6 Track.

2.   These detachments will proceed with the repairs of
        the tracks and roads forward of their forming up place after
        zero hour under ~~hours~~ orders of their C.O's. but will not
        proceed beyond the forming up lines of Brigades without
        reference to the General Officer Commanding the Brigade
        in their Sector.

3.   Acknowledge.

                                            Captain & Adjutant,
Sept.24th.1917.   59th.Divisional R.E.

        Copy No.1.   Hd.Qtrs.G. 59th.Division.
             2.   "   176th.Infantry Brigade.
             3.   "   177th.Infantry Brigade.
             4.   "   178th.Infantry Brigade.
             5.   O.C. 467th.Field Co. R.E.
             6.   O.C. 469th.Field Co. R.E.
             7.   O.C. 470th.Field Co. R.E.
             8.   O.C. 9th. Seaforth Pioneers.
             9.   File.
            10.   War Diary.
            11.   "

APPENDIX IX.

C.R.E. 59th.Div.No.K.3366.

O.C. 9th.Seaforths.

With reference to the copies of Operation Orders forwarded yesterday will you please hold your Battalion in reserve at your present billets in readiness to proceed forward on receipt of orders.

Probably the Battalion will be required to take over for a shift the track and roadwork the R.E. detachments will be employed on. In this case it would help very much if the same Companies could be ready to take over from the same Field Companies whom they relieved last night.

I think,

"A" Company (Capt.Hetherington) worked on the WIELTJE-GRAVENSTAFEL Road and relieved the 467th Field Co. R.E. (Major Frew).

?"B" Company. ½ Company worked on No.6 Track and relieved the 470th.Field Co. R.E. last night. ½ Company working on the same track this morning.

?"C" Company. Worked on No.5 Track last night and relieved the 469th.Field Co. R.E. (Major James).

Will you please send an officer to my Headquarters, Canal Bank, at 6.30 p.m. and 8.30 p.m. tonight for the purpose of synchronizing watches.

25.9.17.

(Sd) G. B. Roberts,
Lieut.Colonel, R.E.
C.R.E. 59th.Division.

War Diary   Appendix X

O.C.9th.Seaforths (Pioneers)

Confirming the verbal instructions conveyed to you;-

Will you please arrange for,

(1) One Company to proceed at once with the repairs and continuation of No.5. Track taking over the work from the 469th.Field Co.R.E.

(2) One Company to proceed at once with the repairs of the WIELTJE - GRAVENSTAFEL Road East of the STEENBEEK River taking over the work from the O.C.467th.Field Co.R.E.

(3) One Company to proceed at once with the construction of a Mule-track from No.6.Track (D.13.a.9.9) towards SCHULER FARM (D.13.a.9.9) and OLIVE HOUSE D.8.c.0.85.

The Track will require screening from observation on the right-hand side - due to the high ground in the direction of ZONNEBEKE.

This screen should not be made parallel to the Track but ziz-zagged in and out on the right-hand side of the track.

The following material is available for the purpose of making this screen;-

At BILGE DUMP (C.28.a.8.2) 60 rolls of camouflage which is being taken forward to a new Dump on the main road where the STEENBEEK River crosses the main GRAVENSTAFEL Road where the following stores are also available;-
    100 8' pickets
    200 18" "   )for stay wires
      8 coils of strong wire)to pickets.
      1 cwt staples.

Captain Robinson of the 470th.Field Co.R.E. has been ordered to meet the Company you detail in order to put them on the work.

26th.Sept.1917.

Lieut.Colonel.R.E,
C.R.E. 59th.Division.

SECRET.

O.C. 9th.Seaforths (Pioneers).

Appendix XI

Will you please arrange for :-

1. One Company to take over the work on the No.5 Track from the 469th.Field Co.R.E. at 5 p.m. to-day, reporting to Captain M.A.Boswell R.E. at Headquarters, 469th.Field Co. R.E. at 4 p.m.

2. One Company to assist the 467th.Field Co.R.E. in the repair of the WIELTJE - GRAVENSTAFEL Road E. of the STEENBEEK River. The Company will report to Major D.B.Frew, O.C. 467th.Field Co.R.E. at the Bridge over the STEENBEEK River at 7.30 p.m. to-night.

3. One Company to take over at 5 p.m. to-day the continuation of No.6 Track from the 470th.Field Co.R.E. and also to commence the diversion to the left of the Track to SCHULER Farm and OLIVE HOUSE together with the screen as detailed in para.3. of my K.3379 of yesterday.

This Company will be assisted by 2 sections of the 470th.Field Co. R.E.

4. One Company to continue the doubling of No.6 Track from C.28.b.2.8. and the fixing of gas curtains as detailed in my K.3384 yesterday.

In the Field.
27th.Sept.1917. 12.10 p.m.

Captain & Adjutant,
59th.Divisional R.E.

WAR DIARY Appendix XII

K.2690.

O.C. 9th. Seaforths Pioneers.

O.C. 467th. Field Co. R.E. For information.
    469th. Field Co. R.E.   "
    470th. Field Co. R.E.   "

With reference to K.3389 of yesterday.

'A' Company will continue work on the WIELTJE-GRAVENSTAFEL Road in conjunction with the 467th. Field Coy. R.E. meeting the O.C. Company at the Bridge over the STEENBEEK River at 8.30 p.m. tonight.

'B' Company to continue work on No.5 Track, meeting the O.C. 469th. Field Coy. R.E. at his Headquarters, No.58 Dixmude Street, at 2 p.m. to-day.

'C' Company to continue the doubling of No.6 Track etc. as detailed in K.3389 of yesterday.

'D' Company to meet the 470th. Field Co. R.E. to continue work as detailed in K.3389 of yesterday, reporting to the O.C. Company at CAPRICORN KEEP at 8 p.m. tonight.

28.9.17.

Captain & Adjutant,
59th. Divisional R.E.

Original

Vol 9

War Diary

of

Headquarters R. Engineers.

59th Division.

Vol. IX.

1st October 1917 to 31st October 1917.

Army Form C. 2118

WAR DIARY
INTELLIGENCE SUMMARY
(Erase heading not required.)

HEADQUARTERS 59th DIVL R.E.

Instructions regarding War Diaries and Intelligence Summaries are contained in F.S. Regs., Part II. and the Staff Manual respectively. Title Pages will be prepared in manuscript.

Place	Date	Hour	Summary of Events and Information	Remarks and references to Appendices
MERIS CAMP VLAMERTINGHE 10 AREA	1/10/17		Headquarters R.E. moved to Little Squires WATOU	Sheet 27 1/40,000
			467th Field Coy. moved to WATOU AREA No. 3	
			469 " " " " " 1	M.T.
			470 " " " " " 2	
			Received Chief Engineer XIV Corps Letter E 1738 dated 1/10/17 (attached) Appendix I	Sheet 27 1/40,000
WATOU	2/10/17		9th Report Inflation British Pioneers moved to WATOU vicinity	
			Headquarters R.E. moved to Stafford Camp near ST. SIXTE. F.6.a.1.5.	XIV Corps Staying Letter No. 2.
			467th Field Coy. moved to " " " F.S.c.4.6	
			469 " " " " " F.S.c.4.6	
			470 " " " " " F.S.c.4.6	M.T.
STAFFORD CAMP	3/10/17		(XIV Corps Letter G.164/17 dated 1/10/17 Appendix II) Field Companies all undergoing Camp Sanitation, Tool Cart & Equipment.	
			The following Officers reported for duty:	Sheet 2
			Lieut. L. G. Kemp 470th Field Company	1/40,000
			" H.S. Comet-Johns 467th "	
			" F.R.B. Whitehouse 469th " (20-10-17)	
			" G.H. Pickering 467th "	
			Received 8pm. XIV Corps Order for move to 1st Army area G 127/48 dated 3/10/17 Appendix III	M.C.
			C.R.E. Order 46 dated 3/10/17 (attached)	
			H.Q.R.S. 43 Field Companies moved by Bus & Lorry to STEENBECQUE AREA	
STAFFORD CAMP	4/10/17		H.Q.N.R.E. STEENBECQUE	Sheet
			467th Coy. " THIENNES	HAZEBRUCK
			469 " " "	5A
			470 " " BOLEGHEM.	1/100,000
			All Transport halted for night at CAESTRE.	
			Received Divisional Order 65	M.T.

Army Form C. 2118

WAR DIARY
or
INTELLIGENCE SUMMARY
(Erase heading not required.)

Instructions regarding War Diaries and Intelligence Summaries are contained in F. S. Regs, Part II. and the Staff Manual respectively. Title Pages will be prepared in manuscript.

Continued

Place	Date	Hour	Summary of Events and Information	Remarks and references to Appendices
STEENBECQUE	5/10/17		467th Field Company overhauling Equipment	Sheet HAZEBROUCK 5A 1/100,000
			469th " " " "	
			470th " " moved with Transport to DELETTE	
			Transport of (HQrs. R.E. 467th & 469th Field Coys) required Units in Hazebrouck area	N.T. do:
STEENBECQUE	6/10/17		HQrs R.E. moved to BOMY 9 a.m.	
			467th Field Coy: moved to CUHEM	
			470th " " improving Camp reconnaissance	N.T.
			469th " " " "	
BOMY	7/10/17		467th " " moved to VERCHIN	SHEET HAZEBROUCK 5A 1/100,000
BOMY	8/10/17		467th " " Overhauling Equipment	
			469th " " General Training	
			470th " " " " and repairing Rifle Range at Q.24.a.4.6. THÉROUANNE SHEET 1/40,000	N.T.
			also training Horse Standing. completed reference	
BOMY	9/10/17		467th Field Coy: R.E. improving Camp	N.T. do:
			469th " " " " General Training	
BOMY	10/10/17		470 59th Division Order No.66 Received 9/10/17. & ADDENDUM to DIVISION ORDER No.66	
			467th Field Coy: R.E. moved to PERNES	
			469th " " " " DIEVAL-lez-PERNES	N.T. do:
			470th " " " " BAILLEUL-lez-PERNES	
BOMY	11/10/17		ADDENDUM No.2 to 59th DIVISION ORDER No.66 Received. ORDER No.4 C.R.E. dated 10/10/17. APPENDIX V	
			467th Field Coy R.E. moved to MAISNIL BOUCHÉ	
			469th " " " " MAISNIL-LES-RUITZ	N.T. Sheet LENS 11 1/100,000
			470th " " " " HESTRUS	
BOMY	12/10/17		467th " " " " ABLAIN ST. NAZAIRE. 59th Division Order No. 67 Copy No 5 Received 12/10/17	
			469th " " " " CHATEAU de la HAIE	N.T. do:
			470th " " " " BARLIN	

Army Form C. 2118

WAR DIARY
INTELLIGENCE SUMMARY

(Erase heading not required.)

Continued —

Place	Date	Hour	Summary of Events and Information	Remarks and references to Appendices
BOMY	13/10/17		467th Field Coy; R.E. relieved 1st Field Coy: Canadian Engineers (HQrs Coy X.4.b.2.t.)	Sheet 36B. 1/40,000
			468th " " " " " " (" " X.10.b.2.t.)	M.T.
			470th " " " " moved to CARENCY X.18.a.2.7.	
CHATEAU de la Haie.	14/10/17		HQRS R.E. moved to CHATEAU de la Haie (X.11.c.8.8.)	Sheet 36B. 1/40,000
			467th Field Coy; R.E. improving Trenches = Crocodile & Abraham Comm: Trenches	
				Columbia, Adept, Cleaver, Gloucester & Avion.
			468th " " " " " " " "	M.T.
			470th " " " Relieved 2nd Field Coy Canadian Engineers (HQrs Coy: X.16.a.2.7)
			467th " " " 2 Sections working on Crocodile & Abraham Communication Trenches
CHATEAU de la Haie.	15/10/17		467 FIELD Coy R.E. 70 yards of tunnel cleared and drained, 140 yards been found and 40 tunnel boards laid in CROCODILE C.T.
			ABSALOM C.T. 200 yards cleared and sides trimmed at M 26 d.6.6. The rear sections were employed clearing road to Camp X4 d 30 to X10 b.2525.
			469 FIELD Coy RE Repairing CYRIL CLUCAS COLUMBIA and BEAVER Trenches and relaying duckboards. Constructing dugouts at S 6 d.40.90.
			470 " " " Nº 2 Section Repairing CYRIL TRENCH between BEAVER and ADEPT Trenches Nº 3 " Repairing roads in SOUCHEZ
			Nº 4 " Repairing CLUCAS C.T. between SOUCHEZ and GIVENCHY Repairing roads in and about camp and approaches to Horse Standings
do	16/10/17		59 DIVISION ORDER Nº 68 Copy Nº 5 received	
			59 DIV Nº 361/14G Subject- DEFENCES received
			59 DIV Nº 379/5/3G received
			CRE order K 3467 issued to Field Cos, R.E and Brigades see appendix VI attached

Army Form C. 2118

WAR DIARY
or
INTELLIGENCE SUMMARY
(Erase heading not required.)

Continued:—

Place	Date	Hour	Summary of Events and Information	Remarks and references to Appendices
YTRES	17/10/17		Work of 467, 469 and 470 FIELD Coys RE is shown on appendix VIII attached. 2 Sections 258 TUNNELLING Coy RE. continue work on dugouts.	Sheet 57c 1/40,000 Ypres
do.	18/10/17		Work of 467, 469 and 470 FIELD Coys RE is shown on appendix IX attached.	Khun
do.	19/10/17		Work of 467, 469 and 470 FIELD Coys RE is shown on appendix X. 59 DIVISION ORDER No. 89 Copy 6 received, detailing move to next area.	Khun
do.	20/10/17	10.30pm	Work of 467, 469 and 470 FIELD Coys RE is shown on appendix XI attached. CRE Orders K3880 issued to all concerned for appendix XII attached	Khun
do.	21/10/17	11am	59 DIVISION ORDER (WARNING) No. 90 Copy No.6 received	Khun
		12.15 pm	Work of 467, 469, 470 FIELD Coys RE is shown on appendix XIII attached. 2 Sections 258 TUNNELLING Coy RE constructing dugouts at K24 a.15, K23.6.31, Q4.0.2.6, K24 a.8.3, K24.6.32 and Q.10.6.7.8.	
do.	22/10/17	11am	Subordination to 59 DIVISION ORDER No.89 Copy No.6 received XIV attached. Work of Field Coys is shown in appendix XIV attached. 467 Field Coy RE being relieved by 78 Field Coy RE on the line marches into camp at BARASTRE 469 " " " " ROCQUIGNY 470 " " " " " BEAUVENCOURT being relieved by 93 FIELD Coy RE	Khun
LE CAUROY	23/10/17	4 pm	CRE opened office at LE CAUROY F.3 Sheet LENS 1/100,000	Sheet 51c 1/40,000
	25/10/17		467 FIELD Coy RE entrained at BARAUME and proceeded by rail and road to DENIER Headquarters I.19 C.4.5 Sheet 51c 1/40,000. 469 FIELD Coy RE entrained at BARAUME and proceeded by rail and road to SARS-LEZ-BOIS H.18.C.5.9 Sheet 51c 1/40,000 470 FIELD Coy RE entrained at BAPAUME and proceeded by rail and road to MONCHEAUX B.25.C.4.1 Sheet 51c 1/40,000	Khun

Army Form C. 2118

WAR DIARY
or
INTELLIGENCE SUMMARY
(Erase heading not required.)

Continued

Instructions regarding War Diaries and Intelligence Summaries are contained in F.S. Regs., Part II. and the Staff Manual respectively. Title Pages will be prepared in manuscript.

Place	Date	Hour	Summary of Events and Information	Remarks and references to Appendices
CHATEAU DE LA HAIE	16/10/17		Continued:- 467 Field Coy RE Continuing work details in yesterdays report. 469 " " Continuing work detailed in " 470 " "	Short per appendix VII attached
do	17/10/17	2 pm	39 Division order No 69 Copy No 5 received. 467 Field Coy RE Continuing work as detailed in work reports 469 " " Appendix VIII attached 470 " "	Khan
do	18/10/17	2 pm	Addendum to 59 Division Order No 69 Copy 5 received. 467 Field Coy RE Continuing work as detailed in work reports as shown 469 " " in appendix IX attached 470 " "	Khan
do	19/10/17	2pm	Addendum to 59 Division Order No 68 Copy 5 received - defence scheme for winter.	
		6	59 Division G 361/14 G received. 467 Field Coy RE Continuing work as detailed in work reports an appendix X attached 469 " " 470 " "	Khan
do	20/10/17		Work reports of units attached marked appendix XI	Khan
do	21/10/17		Work reports of units attached marked appendix XII	Khan
do	22/10/17		Work reports of units marked appendix XIII attached	Khan
do	23/10/17	6 PM	G/C 611 Reference Div Order 68. "SHUT" until further orders.	
		2 PM	59 Division Order No 70 Copy 5 received. Work reports of units attached, marked appendix XIV	Khan

WAR DIARY / INTELLIGENCE SUMMARY

Continued.

(Erase heading not required.)

Army Form C. 2118

Place	Date	Hour	Summary of Events and Information	Remarks and references to Appendices
CHATEAU DE LA HAIE	24/10/17	—	467 FIELD Coy RE } working in accordance with work reports. appendix XV attached	Khm
do	25.10.17	—	469 " " } 470 " " } Work of units in accordance with work reports, appendix XVI attached	Khm
		9 am	2 LIEUT. G.L. BRONSDON, 2 LIEUT G.H. PICKERING and 1STAR proceed to 1st ARMY MINING SCHOOL at HOUCHIN	
		11 pm	59 DIVISION ORDER No 71. Copy No 5 received — Relief of 176 BDE by 177 BDE	
do	26.10.17		Work of units in accordance with work reports, see appendix XVII attached	Khm
do	27.10.17		Work of units " " " " " " XVIII "	Khm
do	28.10.17		Work of units in accordance with work reports, see appendix XIX attached	Khm
do	29.10.17	1 pm	59 DIVISION ORDER No 72. Copy No 5 received	
			Work of units in accordance with work reports, per appendix XX attached	Khm
do	30.10.17		Work of units in accordance with work reports, see appendix XXI "	Khm
do	31.10.17		Work of units in accordance with work reports - see appendix XXII	Khm

Middleton
Capt & Adjt
179 Coy RE

APPENDIX I.

<u>C.E. XIVth Corps No.E.1738.</u>

C.R.E.
59th. Division.

      Your Field Companies will not be required for work at present.

      On arrival in XIVth Corps Area, they can remain in rest and carry out training.

                                (Sd) P.K.Boulnois, Capt.R.E.
                                        S.O. R.E.
1st.Oct.1917.   for Chief Engineer, XIVth Corps

SECRET.

APPENDIX II.

G.S.XIVth.Corps No.G.164/4.

II Anzac Corps.
59th.Division (for information).

Reference your G.A.929.

Please order 3 Field Companies, 59th.Division, to move on October 2nd. from WATOU AREA to XIV Corps Staging Area No.2. (SEATON CAMP, F.5.b. Sheet 27).

Route via PROVEN. Head of column not to enter SEATON CAMP before 2 p.m. Usual intervals will be kept.

Advance parties to report to Area Commandant, Corps Staging Area, ST. SIXTE, on October 1st.

Units will be rationed by XIV Corps on October 3rd for consumption on 4th.

                                (Sd) F. Gathorne Hardy.
                                        Lieutenant - General.
1st.October 1917.   Commanding XIV Corps.

Copy to "Q"
          C.E.
          C.R.E. 59th.Division.
              (c/o Town Major, WATOU).

APPENDIX III.

SECRET.

XIV Corps No. G.127/48.

C.R.E.
59th. Division.

The three Field Companies R.E. 59th. Division at present in Corps Staging area, will move to First Army Area as follows:

(A) <u>Dismounted Personnel</u> on the 4th. inst. by bus or lorry to STEENBECQUE Area, under arrangements to be made by XIV Corps "Q".

(B) <u>Mounted Portion</u> on the 4th inst. to CAESTRE Area, reporting to Area Commandant, CAESTRE, for billets.

<u>Route</u> - PROVEN - WATOU - STEENVOORDE.

On the 5th. inst move to STEENBECQUE Area.

<u>No restrictions as to route.</u>

Intervals of 100 yards between Companies will be maintained.

ACKNOWLEDGE.

(Sd) F. Gathorne-Hardy,
Brigadier-General,
General Staff, XIV Corps.

3rd. October 1917.

Copies to "Q"
C.E.
Area Commandant, Corps Staging Area.
II Army.
59th. Division.
Area Commandant, CAESTRE.

Appendix IV

59th.Div.No.G.65/1.

S E C R E T.

C.R.E.
176th.Inf.Bde.
D.M.G.O.

With reference to Movement Table to accompany 59th. Division Order No.65, the C.R.E. will order the move of the 467th.Field Coy. R.E. and the D.M.G.O. the move of the 200th.M.G.Coy, after consultation with the A.A. & Q.M.G.

The 176th.Inf.Bde. will allot billets in 'A' area in both cases.

(Sd) A.A. Dorien-Smith, Major
G.S. 59th. Division.

4th.October, 1917.

59th. G.
59th. Q.
176th. Inf.Bde.
467th. Field Co. R.E.

C.R.E. No.K.2773.
6.10.17.

1. Reference D.O.65 dated 4.10.17 and letter G.65/1 of 4th.inst, the 467th.Field Co.R.E. will move from STEENBECQUE to 'A' Brigade Area at 10 a.m. on 7th.October.

2. Busses for 5 Officers and 90 Other ranks, and 1 lorry with be at STEENBECQUE Station where the railway crosses the HARBECQUE-ST.VENANT Road at 10 a.m. on the 7th.instant.

3. O.C. 467th.Field Co. R.E. will arrange direct with 176th.Inf.Bde. for billetting his Company in 'A' Brigade Area.

(Sd) Lt.R.E.
for C.R.E. 59th.Divn.

9 a.m.

War Diary.   Appendix No.5.

S E C R E T.   Copy No.2.

ORDERS No. 4

by

Lieut.Colonel. G.B. Roberts. C.R.E. 59th.Division.

Reference Map: 36b. 1:40,000.   10.10.17.

        With reference to Addendum to 59th.Division Order No.66 dated 9.10.17, the following will be the arrangements for the relief of the Field Companies R.E. :-

1.   467th.Field Co.R.E. will relieve 1st.Canadian Engineers.
            Map ref: X.4.b.2½.2½.(ABLAIN ST.NAZAIRE)

    469th.Field Co.R.E. will relieve 3rd.Canadian Engineers.
            Map ref: X.4.b.2½.2½.(ABLAIN ST.NAZAIRE)

    470th.Field Co.R.E. will relieve 2nd.Canadian Engineers.
            Map ref: X.18.a.2.7. (Near CARENCY).

2.   Details of reliefs will be arranged between the Officers Commanding Companies concerned.

        The reliefs to be carried out by the 467th. and 469th. Field Companies R.E. will be completed by 12 noon on the 13th.October; the relief to be carried out by the 470th.Field Company R.E. will be completed by 12 noon on the 14th.October.

3.   The following details from each Field Company will proceed on the 11th October to the Headquarters of the Units being relieved, for the purpose of taking over work, etc.

        O.C. Company.
        1 Officer.
        6 Other ranks.

4.   The 467th.Field Co.R.E. will proceed on the 11th. inst to MAISNIL BOUCHE.

        O.C. 467th.Field Co. R.E. will arrange with Town Major ESTREE-CAUCHIE for billets at MAISNIL BOUCHE.

In the Field.   (Sd) H.Taylor, Lieut.R.E.
10.10.17.   for C.R.E. 59th.Divn.

Verbally to O.Cs. 467th., 469th. and 470th.Field Co.R.E.
        on the march - 10.10.17.

Copy No.1.   File.
      2.)
      3.) War Diary.
      4. 59th.Division G.
      5. 59th.Division A.
      6. 176th.Inf.Brigade.
      7. 177th.Inf.Brigade.
      8. 178th.Inf.Brigade.
      9. C.R.E. 1st.Canadian Division.

War Diary.

APPENDIX No.6.

C.R.E. No. K.3467.

```
59th. Division.G.  )
176th. Inf.Bde.    )   for
177th. Inf.Bde.    )   information.
178th. Inf.Bde.    )
467th.Field Co. R.E.
469th.Field Co. R.E.
470th.Field Co. R.E.
```

        The 467th.Field Company R.E. will be affiliated to the 176th.Infantry Brigade for work forward of the RED LINE exclusive.

        The 469th.Field Co. R.E. will be affiliated to the 177th.Infantry Brigade for work forward of the RED Line exclusive.

        The 470th.Field Co. R.E. will be at the disposal of the C.R.E. for work on, and in rear of the RED Line.

In the Field.
16th.October, 1917.

(Sd) G. B. Roberts.
Lieut.Colonel, R.E.
C.R.E. 59th.Division.

Appendix VII

470th. Field Co. R. E.

DAILY PROGRESS REPORT from 6 a.m. 16.10.17 to 6 a.m. 17.10.1917.

O.	R. SECT.	O.	O.R.	Bde.	Site.	Work carried out.	Hrs.	Remarks.
1	3	1	30	178	S.7.d.65.95.	(New road over Hill from SOUCHEZ and GIVENCHY). Leading G.S. wagons at slag dump.	8	
	3	1	90	178	S.8.c.4.8.	Unloading G.S.wagons, spreading slag 70 yds. and cleaning road bed 250 yds.	8	
	4	1	80	178	CLUCAS C.T.	Clearing trench. 600 yds between SOUCHEZ and GIVENCHY.	8	
	4		30	MGC	X.16.d.1.4.	Making horse standings.	8	10 lds.stone.
	4		10	177	X.16.d.0.4.	do.	8	3 lds.slag.
	4			175	X.17.c.4.6.	Commenced horse standings. 4th.Leicesters.	8)	4 lds.slag.
	4				X.17.c.3.6.	do. 5th.Leicesters.	8)	
	4				X.18.a.2.7.	Work in Camp on horse lines.	8	10 lds.slag.
1	1				S.6.d.4.9.	(Excavated 450 c.ft. of chalk, filled in sandbags, fixed 3 frames.	6	
	1				do.	(including 72 sq.ft. head cover.	4	
	1				do.	(This work has advanced.	8	
	1				do.	(Headings 3 ft. 3 ft. and 2 ft. respectively.	4	
			10		do.	(Filling sandbags and clearing up.	8½	
			22		do.	(Hauling chalk to top of shafts and disposing and covering	6½	
			23			(same.	6½	
	3		4	178	Junc.of Victoria Rd and CYRIL Tr.	Instructing Offrs. & O.R. in revetting at R.E.Dump at LENS Junc. (between ABLAIN ST. NAZAIRE and SOUCHEZ).	8	
1	2		11			Employed in unloading duckboards, pickets, etc. and laying out stores ready for day sappers.	8	Infy.working party failed to report.
13	2				CYRIL Trench.	60 yds of duckboarding laid on pickets and transoms, completing single track as far as ADEPT Trench. Duckboards in CYRIL Trench repaired abd replaced for 300 yds from entrance. Block caused by fall of sandbags by Y.M.C.A. in CYRIL Trench cleared. Speps cut into entrance to CYRIL Trench.	8	

(Sd) L. Robinson, Major.
O.C. 470th.Fld.Co.R.E.

Appendix VI

469th. Field Co. R.E.

PROGRESS REPORT to 8 a.m. 17.10.1917.

R.E.		Working parties			Work carried out.	hrs.	Remarks.
O.R.	Sect.	O.	O.R.	Batt.			
(4	2	1	50	-	Carrying 50 Trenchboards to COLUMBIA Trench.	4	Night.
(8	2	1	20	4th.Leic	Clearing 60 yds.COLUMBIA Tr., and 30 yds Trenchboards, transomes	7	10 men.) Day work
					and pickets laid. Working forward.	4	10 men.)
					CLUCAS Tr. cleared forward of ADEPT Tr.		
(4	2	1	39	-	Carrying 39 Trenchboards to CLUCAS Tr.	4	Night.
(3	4	1	45	-	Carrying 45 Trenchboards to BEAVER Forward.	4	Night.
(4	2	1	50	4th.Leic	Nil - (Working party reported at 10.30 a.m. and O.i/c Working Party decided not to commence		
(4	2	1	65	-	Clearing 30 yds.CLUCAS Tr. forward of ADEPT Tr. and making Berm.)	3½	Night. Party (work.) withdrawn owing to shel -in
3					46.Yds. partly cleared.		
2	4	1	65	-	BEAVER Tr. 75 yds cleared and berm on each side)	4	Night.
					10 yds widened and deepened.)		
10	4	1	18	4th.Leic	150 yds.Trench cleared. 70 yds deepened. 70 yds of trenchboards	8	R.E.
					(single) laid.	4½	Inf.
2	4	1	65	-	45 yds.BEAVER Tr. re-cleared on either side. 42 yds further)	4	Night.
					berm cleared. 42 yds trench widened and to double.trenchboard)		
					width, and cleared out.)		
(21	3	-c	-	-	Detailed for unloading transomes and pickets, LA COULETTE.	6	Night. Material did not arrive. 15.10.17.
(14	1	-	-	-	Unloading trench boards at LA COULETTE.	6	Night.
(13	1-3	-	-	-	Cleaning and repairing road to R.E. Camp. X.10.b.8.2.	8	Day.

(Sd) K.G.Griffiths,
Lt.for O.C
469th.Field Co.
R.E

467th. Field Co. R.E.   Appendix VII

PROGRESS REPORT   -   6 a.m. 16th. to 6 a.m. 17th.
                October, 1917.

CROCODILE Trench.

        100 yards cleared and drained at M.23.b.5.5.
        200 yards berm formed.
        80 yards trenchboards have been laid on pickets and transomes.
        A cellar at M.24.c.1.1. has been cleared for use as Brigade Soup Kitchen.

ABSOLUM Trench.

        100 yards cleared and drained at M.24.d.6.6.
        250 yards berm formed, and 200 yards of trench deepened.

Rear Sections.

        Clearing road to camp, X.4.d.3.0. to X.10.b.2½.2½.

                          (sd) D. B. Frew,
                Major. O.C. 467th.Field Co.R.E.

17.10.17.

Appendix VIII

470th Field Co. R.E.

PROGRESS REPORT - 6 a.m. 17.10.17 to 6 a.m. 18.10.17.

R.E.		Working Parties			Situation	Work carried out.	Hrs.	Remarks.
O.R.	Sect	O.	O.R.	Bde.				
5	3	1	20	178th	S.8.d.0.4	Loading G.S. wagons at slag dump.	8	
7	3	1	70	"		Unloading G.S. wagons and spreading slag 70 lin.yds. and cleaning road beds.	8	
3	3		10	"		Laying timber for cord-road - 8 lin.yds.	8	Between SOUCHEZ & GIVENCHY
11	4	2	100	"	CLUCAS C.T	Clearing Trench - 400 linyds.	8	
3	4		30	M.G.C.	X.16.d.1.4	Approaches to Horse lines.	8	6 lds. slag.
3	4		10	175 B.	do.	do.	8	4 lds. slag.
3	4		8	176 B.	X.17c.0.4.6	do.	8	4 lds. slag.
	4		4	176 B.	do.	do.	8	
4	4		-	-	X.18.a.2.7.	Camp horse standings.	8	
8	2	2	83	177 Bde.	ADEPT Tr.	Cleared, deepened and parapet built for 250 yds. from junction of BEAVER Tr.	8	
	1	-			S.6.d.4.9.	(470 c.ft. of chalk excavated.	6	
						(1 frame placed in position.	8	
							2	
8	1	1	20	178th	"	Emptying and hauling bags of chalk.	4½	Working party arrived at 9.30 p.m. instead of 4 p.m. greatly hindering work.
8	1	1	20	"	"	do.	4½	
8	1	1	10	"	"	Filling sandbags in day time.	8	

Date. Octr. 18th. 1917.

(Sd) Fred. C. Salmon, Capt. for O.C. 470th. Field Co. R.E.

Appendix VII

469th Field C. R.E.
Progress Report for week ending 13.10.17.

R.E.		Working Parties		Party	Work carried out.	Hours	Remarks
O.	Sect	O.	O.R.	Bat.			
	2	-	4	1 L.S.C.	COLUMBIA TRENCH. Laying Trench Boards. Fixing Transomes, Pickets &c. Clearing out trench for 70 yds from Sarkatoon to Front Line.	9	Day
2	2	1	6	-	COLUMBIA TRENCH. Clearing out trench where fallen in. 100 yds between Adept & Saskatoon.	7	
3	2	-	10	-	CLUCAS TRENCH. Clearing out trench where fallen in. 150 yds between Adept & Avion.	8	Night
12	2	-	-	-	ADEPT TRENCH. Preparing for fire step.	4	
1	19	5	-	-	CLUCAS TRENCH. Clearing falls in trench from Red Line to Adept.	4½	
1	10	4	-	-	BEAVER & CYRIL TRENCHES. Clearing berm & falls.	6	
1	10	4	20	-	ADEPT TRENCH. Preparing for fire step &c.	6	Day
	1	2	-	-	Detailed as Guide upon train for R.E. Dump.		

M.B. Jawes
O.C. 469 Field Coy R.E.

Appendix 112

467 Field Company R.E.

Progress Report 6 - 6 am October 18th 1917.

R.E. WORKING PARTY				WORK CARRIED OUT.	HOURS	REMARKS.
O	OR	SECT.	O	OR	SECT.	
	18	1	1	69	—	CROCODILE C.T. 250ˣ of frame found on both sides of trench	11.30 to 3.30	M.23 c.5.5
	18	3						
	12	2	1	50	—	ABSOLOM C.T. 150ˣ of berm formed on both sides of trench 30ˣ of trench bottom cleared	do	M.24 c.9.6
	11	4						
	2	4	—	—	—	Reconnoitring billets for Co. H.Q. and for men.		N.19. c.9.2. ? (billets) N.19. d.5. 8½ (Co H.Q.)

October 18th 1917.

Issued - C. Burgess Capt.
.467 Field Co R.E.

470th. Field Co. R. E.

PROGRESS REPORT – 6 a.m. 18/10/17 to 6 a.m. 19/10/17.

R. E.		Working Parties		Situation	Work carried out.		Hrs.	Remarks.
O.C.	Sect.	O.	O.R.	Batt.				
1	8	1			S6d 40.90	2ft cut A of shaft excavated and Sand-Bagged	6	
						2 frames fitted	3	Ceased work at 3 pm to prepare to move off
		10	198	"	Filling Sand bags including 4ft sap Head cover	8	Handed work over to 2 Lt W Kitehouse at 6·0 pm
		1	14	"		– do –		
		1	20	"		– do –	2	

Date 19/10/17

[signature] Major
O.C. 470th. Field Co. R.E.

Date .... R.E.

Appendix IX
470 Field Coy. R.E.

DAILY PROGRESS REPORT
From 6 a.m. 18/10/17 to 6 a.m. 19/10/17

R.E.			WORKING PARTIES			SITE	WORK CARRIED OUT	HOURS	REMARKS
O.	O.R.	SEC.	O.	O.R.	BRIG.				
							No 3 SECTION		
1	5	3	1	20	148th	S.8.d.0.4.	Loading G.S. Wagons at slag dump.	8	
	7	3	1	40	"		Unloading — do — & spreading slag. 45 Lin.yds. and clearing road bed.	8	
	3	3		10	"		Laying timber for cord-road 15 Lin yds.	8	
	11	4		100		Clucas C.T.	Clearing C. Trench (Clucas) 400 Lin.yds.	8	
							No 4 Section		
	6	4					Instructing in Revetting	8	
	3	4					Superintending work on Clucas C. Trench.	8	
	5	4				x18.a.2.4.	Approaches to Horse Lines.	8	
							No 2. SECTION		
1	18	2	3	125	148th	CLUCAS. TRENCH.	Clucas Trench, cleared and drained from S.10.D.3.5 to Red Trench. S.5.D.8.4. MAP 36c S.W.	6	
			3	140		RED TRENCH	Red Trench. Sump pits and drains repaired from CYRIL Trench S.12.a.2.4. to S.5.b.4.4.	6	

Appendix IX

469th Field Co. R.E.

PROGRESS REPORT – 6 a.m. 18.10.17. to 6 a.m. 19.10.17.

R.E.		Working Parties			Situation	Work carried out	Hrs.	Remarks
O.	O.R.	Sect.	O.	O.R.	Batt.			
		4	1	2	87	5th Lincs	Cyril Trench	Clearing & making berm – 200 yds	6	Night
		3	1	2	75	"	Beaver Trench	Clearing berm and widening trench – 120 yds	6	"
		4	1	1	24	"	Junction Cyril & Beaver Tr.	Clearing trench & laying duck boards (300 yds forward)	6	Day
		3	1	1	26	"	Do. to Avion Supp.	Clearing trench	6	"
		2	2	1	25	"	Adept Trench	50 yds berm & 50 yds trench partly cleared, Clucas to Columbia Tr.	4	Night
		2	2	1	40	"	Columbia Tr.	30 yds trench cleared & widened. 50 yds berm on either side	4	"
1		2	2	1	10	"	La Coulotte	Unloading train at R.E. Dump.	4½	"
		2	2	1	50	5th Leic.	Adept Tr. & R.E. Dump	Loading wagons, & unloading & carrying 63 "A" Frames	4	"
		3	2	1	75	"	Clucas Trench	60 yds berm on either side, & trench cleared (forward of Adept)	4	"
1		2	2	-	4	"	Columbia Tr.	Clearing trench & laying trench boards for 64 yds. between Saskatoon Rd & Front line	6	Day
		2	2	1	8	"	Do.	200 yds trench cleared where fallen in between Adept Trench & Saskatoon Rd.	6	"
		2	2	1	6	"	Clucas Trench	Do. – 100 yds between Adept & Avion Tr.	6	"
		2	2	-	7	"	Do.	Clearing parts blown in by shells near Avion Junction	6	"
1		14	3	1	40	"	S.6.d.4.9	Constructing dug-out (excavating) (2–8 hour shifts)	8	Day & Night
		1	4	-	-	"	R.E. Dump	Guide for train		

Date 19th October 1917.

W. R. Lawes, Major
O.C. 469th Field Co. R.E.

Appendix IX

467th. Field Co. R.E.

PROGRESS REPORT – 6 a.m. 18th October to 6 a.m. Oct 19th 1917

I.E. O.R.	Sect.	Working Parties O.R.	Batt.	Situation	Work carried out.	Hrs.	Remarks.
5	1	10	2/6.S.S.	ABSALOM TRENCH	Clearing trench 10 yards.	4½	
5	1	20	2/5 N.S.	do.	Clearing trench and laying duckboards 16 yards	4½	
4	3	20	2/5 N.S.	CROCODILE TRENCH	Clearing trench and laying duckboards 26 yards	5	Trench had fallen in and this made extra work.
4	3	10	N.S.	do.	do. 30 yards	5	
1 15.	1 4	{ 2 2	9.11 2/5 N.S. 9.8 2/6.S.S.	ABSALOM TRENCH	Revm. stands. 300 yards near Ruckwick 150 yards	4	Each of these infantry parties gave 3 N.C.O.s. Services of 2/6.S.S. were used for carrying party.
1 16.	3 2	{ 2 2	9.6 2/6 N.S. 10.0 2/6.S.S.	CROCODILE TRENCH	Revm. stands. 310 yards. Ruckwick 120 yards	4	In party from 2/6 N.S. there 96 men with 3 orderlies. 10 N.C.O.s.

A. B. Jones, Lt/Col.
O.C. 467th. Field Co. R.E.

Appendix Y

467th. Field Co. R.E.

PROGRESS REPORT – 6 a.m. 19th Oct to 6 a.m. 20th Oct 1917.

R.E.		Working Parties			Situation	Work carried out.	Hrs	Remarks.
O.R.	Sect	O.	O.R.	Batt.				
4	1	1	20	2/6 S.S	ABSALOM TRENCH	Clearing and deepening Trench 52 yds / Laying Duckboards 22 yds	5	
5	1	1	18	2/6 S.S	Do	Clearing and deepening Trench 56 yds / Laying Duckboards 25 yds	4	
4	3	1	20	2/6 S.S	CROCODILE TRENCH	Clearing Trench Laying Duckboards 35 yds	5	
4	3	1	20	2/6 S.S	Do	Clearing Trench 20 yds / Laying Duckboards 18 yds	5	
2	1	1	—	—	Batt'n H.Q.	Fixing Wire Cradles and Brackets to roof of Chateau	6	This work is completed
12	1 & 4	2	96	2/6 S.S	ABSALOM TRENCH	Berm widened and sloped and widened for 250 yds. Revetting carried up to Duckboards	2	Train with party did not arrive until 1.15 a.m. owing to damage on line. 86 men of party were working
5	3	—	—	—	CELLARS AT APPROACH TR	Clearing and making light prof. 3 Cellars	8	
14	3 & 2	2	100	2/6 S.S	CROCODILE TRENCH	75 yds of berm on both sides cleared. Earth thrown up during day removed. 10 men worked on bottom clearing sludge. 50 Pickets and 60 Tramways carried up to trench	2	Same remarks as above. 90 men of these 100 were working

Date 20th Oct. 1917.

P. B. Few... Major
O.C. 467th. Field Co. R.E.

Appendix F

469th. Field Co. R.E.

PROGRESS REPORT - 6 a.m. 19.10.17 to 6 a.m. 20.10.17.

R.E. O.i.C.	Sect.	Working Parties O.	O.R.	Batt.	Situation	Work carried out.	Hrs.	Remarks.
12	1	1	50	15th Lincs.	Cyril Trench.	60 yds cleared & widened. 50 yds trench boards. Repairing bad places. 32 yds trench boards laid alongside existing boards & completing dowels row	R.E. 8 Inf. 4	Day.
					Beaver Trench	50 yds cleared & boards taken out & cleaned. 60 yds boards laid on transomes only.		"
3	1	1	60	"	Cyril Trench	300 yds cleared forward. 260 yds widened. 260 yds berm cleared.	4	Night.
3	1	1	50	"	Beaver Trench	60 yds widened & berm cleared.	4	"
1	1	1	50	"	Junc. Cyril & Beaver Tr.	70 duck boards carried from La Coulotte Dump.	4	"
2	2	-	11	15th Leic.	Clucas Trench	120 yds cleared out where fallen in between Adept & Ayion Tr.	8	Day.
1	2	2	10	"	Dº	Battering trench sides 55 yds. Forward of Adept Tr.	8	"
1	2	-	4	"	Dº	Taking up & clearing trench boards & making sumps 10 yds	8	"
2	2	1	21	"	Columbia Trench	Battering trench sides 60 yds forward of Adept.	8	"
2	2	-	4	"	Dº	Laying trench boards & clearing out 30 yds between Damatoon Rd. & Front line	8	"
2	2	1	47	"	Adept Trench	Clearing out & making berm 150 yds by Clucas Tr.	4	Night.
2	2	1	50	"	Dº	Dº 50 yds. Dº (Bad part of trench).	4	"
3	2	2	75	15th Lincs.	Clucas Tr.	Clearing trench & making berm. 60 yds berm reclaimed & 30 yds berm made forward of Adept.	4	"
2	2	2	50	"	Adept & Columbia Trs.	11 hurdles & 50 trench boards carried	4	"
21	3	2	55	-	S.6.d.4.9	Excavating earth, erecting pit prop supports & iron joists in dug out.	6	3 - 8 hour shifts.
21	4	-	-	-	X.10.b.8.2	Erecting stable for sick horses. R.E.Camp.	8	

Date. 20..10.17.

W. Couch Johns.. I Lieut.
for O.C. 469th.Field Co. R.E.

469th FIELD COMPANY
ROYAL ENGINEERS

Appendix X

440th. Field Co. R.E.

PROGRESS REPORT - 6 a.m. 19/10/14 to 6 a.m. 20/10/14.

R.E. Sect	Working Parties O.	Working Parties O.R.	Working Parties Batt.	Situation	Work carried out.	Hrs	Remarks.
1		21		LUCAS TRENCH, Kings Rd Post Givenchy	Old duck-boards taken up and replaced by new. 1/4 do	4	
1	1	51	1/8th	-do-	Cleared bottom of trench, dug drain under Duck-boards. Assisted Sappers to lay boards. 110 yds	6	
2	3	116	1/8th	RED TRENCH	Duck-boards taken up. Trench cleared and drains dug. Sump pits excavated at intervals. Area worked on S.S.d. 2.5 to S.12.a.3.5. Trench drains cleared and Duck-boards replaced from S.S.d. 4.4 to S.5.C.6.6	4	
1	1	40	1/7th	Between Souchez and Givenchy	Clearing road 400 lin. yds	6	
3	3	10	"		Laying timber for corrdl. road. 10 lin. yds	8	
3	2	85			Loading and unloading wagons of slag.	12	4 wagons loaded, 10 unloaded
1	1	50	1/5th	LUCAS TRENCH	Clearing out & duck-boarding Clucas trench from commencement to Givenchy.	6	
10	3	100			Making track from Kings Road to Clucas trench	8	
5	4				Instructing infantry in revetting	8	

Date 20/10/14

(signed) [illegible]
O.C. 440th. Field Co. R.E.

Appendix XI

470th. Field Co. R.E.

PROGRESS REPORT – 6 a.m. 20/10/14 to 6 a.m. 21/10/14.

R.E.		Working Parties		Situation	Work carried out.	Hrs	Remarks.
O.	O.R.	Sect	O.	O.R.	Batt.				
1	22	1				LUCAS TRENCH GIVENCHY Rd TO Rd TRENCH	Making transoms on which to lay trench boards. Replacing old with new trench boards.	4	
						– do –	Carrying trench boards, taking up and digging under trench boards.	6	
1	14	2	2	128	14F	Rd TRENCH	French deepened fire steps repaired, drains dug and duck boards repaired from S.6.a.99 to S.12.a.9.5	4	
			2	100	14F				
1	4	3	1	20	14/8	Between SOUCHEZ & GIVENCHY	Loading slag into G.S. Wagons	8	
	8	3		20			Unloading slag and spreading on road 50 LIN YDS	8	
	6	3		10			Laying 3rd. row of 1st Rn Yds.	8	
	3	3					Making Timber kerb along roads 15 LIN YDS	8	
	2	3	2	100	14/8		Loading trucks of slag at Foss x6	8½	10 trucks loaded
							Unloading trucks of slag at Ringo x		10 – do – Unloaded
1	8	4	1	60	14F	KINGS Rd	Working on track from Kingo Rd to commencement of Circus Trench	8	
	9	4		50		CIRCUS TRENCH	Reseating Berms and Duck boarding Circus trench from commencement to GIVENCHY	6	
	2	4					Visiting and setting out new work	6	

Date 21/10/14

L. Cahusac Major
O.C. 470th. Field Co. R.E.

Appendix X¹

469th. Field Co. R.E.

PROGRESS REPORT — 6 a.m. 20.10.17 to 6 a.m. 21.10.17.

R.E.			Working Parties			Situation	Work carried out.	Hrs	Remarks.
O.	O.R.	Sect	O.	O.R.	Batt.				
	12	1	1	45	5th Lincs	Beaver Trench	92 yds trench cleared, boards removed & cleared. 42 yds trench boards laid on transomes	6	Day
						Cyril Trench	520 yds cleared from Beaver to Balsom Trench 80 yds cleared & repaired forward of Red Trench 80 yds trench boards on double track. 55 yds trench cleared ready for boards at far end of trench 30 yds trench boards (single) at far end of trench	6	Day
	3	1	1	75	"	Cyril Trench	220 yds top & bottom berm cleared	4	Night
	3	1	1	36	"	Beaver Tr.	40 yds trench widened to double track, & berm cleared	4	"
	1	1	1	29	"	Cyril Trench	40 trench boards carried from La Coulotte	4	"
		2	-	7	5th Leic	Junction Cyril Columbia and Kingston Road	Laying Trench Boards, making sumps & boxes for same. 64 yds. — — 3 sumps.	6	Day
	2	2	1	10	"	Clucas Trench	Taking up, clearing underneath & relaying 30 yds trench boards. Making sumps & 130 boxes for same. (3 sumps)	6	"
	2	2	-	14	"	Do.	Clearing out 200 yds trench fallen in & damaged by shell fire forward of Adept.	6	"
	4	2	-	12	"	Adept Trench	Fixing 11 "A" frames & digging 23 holes for same. (Clucas end)	6	"
	2	2	1	50	"	Do.	73 yds cleared & 50 yds berm made on either side, between Clucas & Columbia	4	Night
	2	2	1	50	"	Do.	Do.	3½	"
	2	2	-	68	"	Clucas Trench	45 yds trench cleared & berm made on either side.	3½	"
	3	2	-	45	"	Adept Trench	75 yds cleared & berm made. 50 yds berm recleared forward of Adept	3½	"
	2	2	-	-	"		Carrying 84 trench boards.		"
1	21	3	1	47	"	S.6.d.4.9	Excavating earth, fixing pit props &c. in dug out.	8	Day × night (3 shifts)
1	21	4	-	-	"	X.10.b.8.2	Erecting stabling for sick horses. R.E. Camp	8	"

Date 21..10..17

[signature] Major
O.C. 469th. Field Co. R.E.

Appendix X.

461 tn. Field Co. R.E.

PROGRESS REPORT - 6 a.m. Oct 20/17 to 6 a.m. Oct 21/17.

R.E.		Working Parties			Situation	Work carried out.	hrs	Remarks.
O.	O.R.	Sect	O.	O.R. Batt.				
—	5	1	—	20 2/6 SS	ABSALOM TRENCH	Making paths to trench 122 yards.	5	
—	4	3	—	20 2/5 SS	CROCODILE TRENCH	Clearing trench, trimming sides of same and laying duckboards 30 yards	5	
—	5	1	—	20 2/6 SS	ABSALOM TRENCH	Cutting sides of trench to required width and laying duckboards 30 yards	4½	
—	4	3	—	20 1/6 SS	CROCODILE TRENCH	Clearing trench & duckboards to trench 40 yards, 22 yards	5	CROCODILE TRENCH. Length of trench complete 198 yds
—	2	1	—	—	BRIGADE H.Q.	1 Stove fitted and Gun Post Store	4	ABSALOM TRENCH Length of trench complete 9 yds
—	—	—	—	—	CELLARS AT ATTAQUE TRENCH	3 Cellars examined & cleaned, and windows blocked. Putting stoves &c. &c.	8	

Date Oct 21/17

_____ Major
O.C. 461 tn. Field Co. R.E.

Appendix XII

470th. Field Co. R.E.

PROGRESS REPORT – 6 a.m. 21.10.17 to 6 a.m. 22.10.17.

R.E.		Working Parties			Situation	Work carried out.	Hrs	Remarks.
O.i.	Sect	O.	O.R.	Batt.				
1	1		4		NEW BILLETS	Clearing away rubbish, constructing cook-house, making bunks	4	
1	1		18		ACROSS MARSH BETWEEN RED & RED TRENCH	Laying new duck boards in place of very bad ones. Making and fixing new frames. Digging drains under frames.	4	
1	2		23		RED TRENCH	Trench excavated and bridge completed over RED TRENCH at junction with VICTORIA ROAD. Prefabs 35cm T7 and 9.	4	
1	3		20		between SOUCHEZ & GIVENCHY	Loading slag onto L.S. Wagons	4	Day
	4		22			Unloading G.S. Wagons & spreading slag on road 85m yds	4	3 wagons loaded
	3+4		40			Unloading & loading Wagons of slag	8	4 unloaded. Night

Date 22.10.17

V. Colmer Lieut.
O.C. 470th. Field Co. R.E.

Appendix X a

469th. Field Co. R.E.

PROGRESS REPORT - 6 a.m. 21.10.17 to 6 a.m. 22.10.17.

R.E.			Working Parties			Situation	Work carried out.	Hrs	Remarks.
O.	O.R.	Sect	O.	O.R.	Batt.				
	7	1	1	30	15th Lincs	CYRIL TRENCH	Trench cleared of falls from Partridge to Balsam. Trench boards repaired from Red Trench to Lens - Arras Road. Cleared trench of falls between Adept & Avion trenches. 36 yds single trench boards, & 60 yds double trench boards laid, 30 yds cleared to receive single row of duck boards to Meagre trench. (Duck boards in Cyril Tr. to 300 yds off front line.)	5½	Day — Duck boards in Beaver Tr. to Avion Tr.
1	3	1	-	20	"	BEAVER TR.	60 yds single trench boards laid, between Cyril & Beaver Juns. & Adept. 40 yds cleared ready for double boards. between Dº & Dº	5½	Day
	8	1	-	-	"	CYRIL TRENCH	24 duck boards carried.	4	Night
	4	2	1	16	"	ADEPT TRENCH	Fixing 16 "A" frames & digging 17 holes for same. (Right of Clucas)	8	Day
	2	2	-	8	"	- Dº -	" 10 " (Left of Clucas)	8	Day
	2	2	-	9	"	CLUCAS TRENCH	Taking up & relaying trench boards. Clearing trench & fixing (32 yds trench boards) between Adept & Avion. 3 sumps.	8	"
1	2	2	-	11	"	- Dº -	Clearing 180 yds trench fallen in & damaged by shell fire forward of Avion	8	"
	2	2	-	7	"	COLUMBIA TR.	Laying trench boards & fixing sumps - 52 yds. 2 sumps. Between Junction Clucas - Columbia and Kingston Road.	8	"
	10	2	-	-	"	ADEPT TRENCH	40 yds cleared, & continuing trench where blocked under railway between Clucas & Columbia.	4	Night
	6	3	-	15	"	S.G.d.4.9	Excavating earth & fixing pit props &c, in chambers "B" & "C"	R.E.8, Inf. 4	Day
1	7	3	-	20	"	- Dº -	Dº - - - - in "C" "D" Erecting bunks in "B"	R.E.8, Inf.8	Day & Night.
	7	3	-	20	"	- Dº -	Dº - - - - "C" & "D"	8	Day
	21	4	-	-	"	X.10.b.8.2	On Wiring Drill &c.	8	Day
1	4	1-4	-	-	"	-	Employed as runners at Cº HQrs & Forward Area	-	

Date 22.10.17

W.M.Bowie Capt.
for O.C. 469th. Field Co. R.E.

Appendix X

467th Field Co. R.E.

PROGRESS REPORT - 6 a.m. 21st Oct. to 6 a.m. 22nd Oct. 1917.

R.E.		Working Parties		Situation	Work carried out.	Hrs	Remarks.
O.R.	Sect	O.	O.R. Batt				
5	1.	1	20. 2/6 SS	ABSALOM TRENCH	Duckboards laid 114 yards. Trench cleared and side tunnels 110 yards.	4½	
5	2.	1	18. 2/6 NS	Do.	Duckboards laid 45 yards. Trench ready for duckboarding 15 yards.	4½	
11	3 and 4.	2	40. 2/6 SS	CROCODILE TRENCH	Duckboards laid 15 yards. Trench cleared ready for duckboards 110 yards.	4½	
1	1.			Battn H.Q.	Drains broken to mill	4	
6	3.			Bridges M.21 d.75-15. M.21 d.75-15.	Fixing harrows on roads.	2	Total length of trench completed. ABSALOM. 150 yds. CROCODILE. 213

A. B. Jones Major
O.C. 467th Field Co. R.E.

Date 22nd Oct 1917

Appendix XIII

470th. Field Co. R.E.

PROGRESS REPORT – 6 a.m. 22/10/17 to 6 a.m. 23/10/17.

R.E.		Working Parties			Situation	Work carried out.	Hrs	Remarks.
O.R.	Sect	O.	O.R.	Batt				
15	1	–	–	–	CRUCAS TR. LIGHT RAILY GIVENCHY RD	Drain dug in bottoms of trench & towards road. Two yards of trench cleared where it had fallen in	7	94 lin. yds.
7	1	–	–	–	BILLETS	14 Bombs built & billets cleared out	7	
22	2	–	–	–	RED TRENCH	Unloading slag on New Road. Excavating & fixing A frames under bridge at RED TRENCH and VICTORIA RD. junction	8	
12	3	–	–	–	KING'S X	Spreading slag on roads 10 lin. yds.	2	
3	3	–	–	–	BETWEEN TOUCHEZ? & GIVENCHY	Timber kerbing along road 20 lin. yds	2	No night working party.
3	3	–	–	–	"	Corduroy road laid – two yds	2	
14	4	–	–	–	KING'S X	Loading slag into G.S. Wagons & unloading. Two wagons	2	No night work done.

Date 23.X.17.

....
O.C. 470th. Field Co. R.E.

Appendix XIV

469th. Field Co. R.E.

PROGRESS REPORT – 6 a.m. 22.10.17. to 6 a.m. 23.10.17.

R.E.		Working Parties		Situation	Work carried out.	Hrs	Remarks.
O.C.	Sect	O.	O.R. Batt.				
		2	6	17th S.Ford	Cyril Trench	Laid & carried 16 yds Trench boards, single track		
		2	6	"	"	Repairing broken trench boards between Lens-Arras Rd & Beaver Junc.		
	1	–	9	"	"	Clearing trench broken in by shell, near Adept Trench	8	Day
		2	3	"	"	100 yds trench widened for double track		
		3	22	"	Beaver Tr.	52 yds double track laid		
		–	2	"	"	Widening trench for double track & sump made. 164 yds completed		
		2	35	"	Do	Laid 28 yds of Single Board track		
		–	25	"	Do & Cyril Tr.	64 yds trench deepened, widened & berm cleared, forward of Avion		
	1	4		"	Cyril Trench	35 duckboards carried to Beaver Tr. 40 duckboards to Cyril Trench	6	Night
		2	33	"	Adept Trench	110 pickets & 50 transoms carried		
		–	12	"	Do	40 yds cleared, 54 yds berm made. Between Clucas & Columbia	6	
		2	22	"	Clucas Trench	22 yds cleared & berm made. Do	5	
		2	32	"	Adept Trench	30 yds berm re-cleared & 50 yds berm made. Forward of Adept	5	
	2	1	7	18th S.Ford	Columbia & Kingston Rd	Carrying 26 "A" Frames	–	
		4	15	"	Adept Trench	Forming steps & sump, laying trench boards & clearing trench	6	
		2	8	"	Do	Laying 16 yds trench boards in Columbia Trench	6	
		3	10	"	Do	Fixing 16 "A" Frames (96 yds) right of Clucas	6	
				"	Clucas Trench	5 (18) left		
						Clearing 180 yds trench fallen in & damaged by shell fire, forward of Avion		
	3	13	15		S.10.d.4.3	Excavating in chambers C. & D. Erecting bunks in "B" (completed)	8	Day
	3	6	20		Do –	" (Ready for bunks)	8	Night
	3	7	20		Do –	Cutting trench to entrance of dug-out, & covering chalk with soil.	8	Day & Night
	4	21	–		X.10.b.8.2	Wiring Drill, Physical exercises &c	8	Day
	1-4	4	–		–	Employed as runners at Co H.Q. & with forward sections.	–	

Date. 23..10..17.

[signature] 2. Lieut
for O.C. 469 th. Field Co. R.E.

Appendix XIII

467th. Field Co. R.E.

PROGRESS REPORT – 6 a.m. 22nd Oct. to 6 a.m. 23rd Oct. 1917.

R.E.		Working Parties					
O.	Sect	O.	O.R.	Batt	Situation	Work carried out.	hrs
	2	1	30	2/5 NS 2/5 SS	ABSALOM TRENCH	Length of duckboards laid 25 yds. Length of trench cleared ready for duckboards 70 yds.	5
5	4	1	20	2/5 SS	Do.	Length of duckboards laid 36 yds. Length of trench cleared ready for duckboards 45 yds.	5
	3	1	30	2/5 SS 2/5 NS	CROCODILE TRENCH	Length of duckboards laid 20 yds. Length of trench cleared ready for duckboards 20 yds.	5
	3	1	30	2/5 SS 2/5 NS	Do	Length of duckboards laid 26 yds. Length of trench cleared ready for duckboards 20 yds.	5
	4	4	154	2/5 S.S.	ABSALOM TRENCH	Length of bm cleared from duckboards forward. 250 yds. Length of bm cleared 100 yds. Additional and final length of bm cleared 80 yds.	4
	1"	1	11	2/5 S.S	Do	Carrying pickets, knife-rests and duckboards.	4
					Do		4
	13.	34	4	186	2/5 S.S	CROCODILE TRENCH	Length of bm cleared from duckboards forward 580 yds. Carrying Pickets, knife-rests and duckboards.	4
	10				ENTRANCE TO ABSALOM TR.	Clearing daylight breaks to ABSALOM TRENCH 200 yds.	4
	12						3½

TOTAL LENGTH OF TRENCH COMPLETED.	ABSALOM	211 yds
	CROCODILE	254 yds

Date Oct 23/17

A. B. King, Major.
O.C. 467th Field Co. R.E.

Appendix XIV

422th. Field Co. R.E.

PROGRESS REPORT - 6 a.m. 23/10/17 to 6 a.m. 24/10/17

R.E. Sect	Working Parties O.R.	Working Parties Batt.	Situation	Work carried out.	Hrs.	Remarks.
1	10	50	144	OLUGAS TRENCH	Deepened trench apx 100 yds. average 2 ft. by railway & on return 100 yds of Duck-boarding.	7	To spare, 1/2 man railway bridge
	13	1			Deepened old German trench for drainage purposes average 1 ft. for 20 yds. Drainage trench made near ANGRES R.P. for 20 yds	5	Night working parts did not turn up.
1	9	2	46 144	RED TRENCH	Cleaning and laying Duck-boards in RED TRENCH from 5.1.a.9.5. to 5.1.2.t.51.	4	
	18	2	100 144		Deepened and widening trench nearby for laying Duck-boards from LENS - ARRAS R.P. to junction of RED TRENCH and VICTORIA R.P.	5	
	14	3	24 144	NEW ROAD between CUCHY and GIVENCHY	Grading O.U.G. road & spreading slag on road 43 km. 460.	8	Dry
	6	3	10		Laying boundary road 14 km 465	8	
	1	3	6		Facing Rail at sides of road. 50 km 460	8	
	2	3	100		Loading and unloading Trucks of slag	8	6 loads of ballast unloaded.
1	25.	14	2	LIEVIN	Engaged in preparing billets.	8	Working party High

Date: 24-10-17.

V. Cohen Major
O.C. 422 th. Field Co. R.E.
422th. (North Midland) Field Co.

Appendix XIV

469th. Field Co. R.E.

PROGRESS REPORT - 6 a.m. 23.10.17. to 6 a.m. 24.10.17.

R.E.		Working Parties			Situation	Work carried out.	Hrs.	Remarks.
C.	Sec.	O.	O.R.	Batt.				
				8th & 5th S.Fors.				
2	1	1	4	17	Beaver Trench	40 yds single track laid at head of trench	8	Day
2			17			40 yds trench widened ready to receive double track		
2						44 yds boards laid on double track		
2			14			Cleaned out very bad portions of trench. Laid 8 yds trench boards on single track near to head of trench		
2					Cyril Trench	250 yds trench widened ready to receive double trench boards. This completes the widening up to junction with Adept Trench		
2		1	30			62 yds trench boards laid on double track		
2		1	30		Cyril Trench	Deepening, battering & clearing berm, 75 yds.	6	Night
2		1	28		Beaver Tr.	Do.		
2					Beaver Tr.	10 trench boards; 30 pickets & 15 transoms carried		
					Cyril Trench	37 8		
4		1	13	8th & 5th S.Fors.	Adept Trench	Fixing 18 "A" frames, 36 yds, Right of Clucas.	8	Day
-			7		Do.	14 Left		
2	2	1	10		Clucas Tr.	Clearing 130 yds trench broken in by shell fire. Forward of Avion		
2		1	4		Adept Tr.	Revetting with hurdles. 6 hurdles. 36 yds Left of Clucas.		
2		1	20		Kingston Rd	Forming 6 steps, 1 sump & laying 6 trench boards		
-			23		Adept Tr.	40 yds widened; deepened & berm cleared		
2		1	20		Do.	30 " "	6	Night
2		1	25		Clucas Tr.	50 yds berm cleared & 10 yds trench battered		
11	3	1	15		La Coulotte	240 trench boards; 30 "A" frames, 4 bridge frames & 40 hurdles unloaded		
3	3	1	19		56.d.49	Removing trolley rails from entrance X to dug out. Digging up chalk making good fall in passage & boarding walls. Making & erecting bunks by "C" or "D" (Chamber "D" completed to sweep 1'3 high)	8	Day
7	3	1	20		Do.	Clearing falls of earth in Irish Tr. near dug-out	8	Day & Night
3					Do.	Erecting bunks in chamber "C" of dug-out (½ completed)	8	Night
2		2	6		T.1.b.3.0	Widening & deepening Irish trench near dug-out for 100 yds.	7	Day & Night
2	4	1			X.10.b.82	Constructing M.G. emplacements.	8	Day
4	1-4				Do.	Wiring drill etc.		
						Employed as runners.		

Date. 24..10.17....

[signature]
Acting O.C. 469th. Field Co. R.E.

[signature]
Acting 469th. Field Co. R.E. ....Capt.

Appendix XIV

th. Field Co. R.E.

PROGRESS REPORT – 6 a.m. 23rd Oct. to 6 a.m. 24 Oct. 1917.

R.E.		Working Parties			Situation	Work carried out.		Remarks.
O.R.	Sect	O.	O.R.	Batt.			Hrs	
8	2	4	30	2/5.S.S. 2/5 N.S.	ABSALON TRENCH.	Length of duckboards laid. Length of trench cleared ready for duckboards.	54 yds. 140 yds.	5
8	4	1	20	2/5. S.S.	Do	Length of duckboards laid Length of trench cleared ready for duckboards.	60 yds. 43 yds.	5.
7	3	1	30	2/5 S.S. 2/5 N.S.	CROCODILE TRENCH.	Length of duckboards laid. Length of trench cleared ready for duckboards.	45 yds. 30 yds.	5.
7	3	1	30	2/5.S.S. 2/5 N.S.	Do.	Length of duckboards laid. Length of trench cleared ready for duckboards.	40 yds. 20 yds.	5.
4 18	1st A. 2nd A.	3. 1	12.5. (8 others) 16	2/5 S.S. Do	ABSALON TRENCH	New length of trench cleared. Recleaning Carrying:- 60 duckboards. 430 pickets. 63 frames	300 yds. 90 yds.	3½ Task Work Completed.
9 8 1	2nd 3	3	140 20 15.	2/5.S.S. Do Do	CROCODILE TRENCH	New length of trench cleared. Recleaning Carrying:- 60 duckboards. 120 pickets to Dumasmo	190 yds. 100 yds.	4
1	3.				Bde. H.Q.	Fixing another Canadian Stove.		1.
3					ENTRANCE to ABSALOM TR.	Daylight task. Sleeping hammer.		4
						TOTAL LENGTH OF TRENCH COMPLETE ABSALON CROCODILE	325 340 yds 394 yds	

Basil P. Macow. Capt. R/Major
O.C. th. Field Co. R.E.

Date Oct. 24/1917

Appendix XV

th. Field Co. R.E.

PROGRESS REPORT – 6 a.m. 24/10/14 to 6 a.m. 25/10/14.

R.E.		Working Parties			Situation	Work carried out.	Hrs	Remarks.
O.C.	Sect	O.	O.R.	Batt.				
1	1	1	15	144	CLUCAS TRENCH BY RAILWAY	Deepening trench average 2ft. (including removing buried duck boards) and digging drain, 20 yds.	4	To drain under railway
	1		35	144	OLDEEPANT S.10.d.5.9	Cleaning trench over 1'6" deep for 60 yds	4	To drain CLUCAS
	1	2	50	144	CLUCAS TRENCH S.10.d.2.4	Cutting drain leading from trench. Over 3ft. 4" Deep for 50 yds	4	Night Work
	1	1	25	144	CLUCAS S.5.d.1.0	do. Over 2ft. 9" Deep for 30	4	do
	1	1	25	144	CLUCAS TRED EMP't AT ANGRES R'd	do. Over 2'-7" Deep for 30	4	do
						do. Over 1'4" Deep for 20	4	do
	1	1	50	144	TRED TRENCH	Trench deepened and Duckboards laid from S.12.b.20.85 to S.12.b.89	6	Night Work
	2	2	100	144	do	Trench deepened and made ready for laying duckboards from junction of TRED arm't and VICTORIA 1st to T.4.b.1.9	6	
1	3	2	47	144	GIVENCHY BETWEEN SOUCHEZ & GIVENCHY	Loading and unloading G.S. Wagons and preparing road to burnish layers forming road 15 in. yds	8	
	3		6			loading ft't at place of road 50 in. yds	8	
	3		3			loading from Neuvrine to blueas trench	8	
	3		10			loading and unloading G.S. wag'ns & plas	8	6 wag'ns & loads Unloading Night Work
	3	2	10				8	
1	4		2	1 R.E. Co	M.29.b.8.5	Commenced work on M.G. Emplacement	4	
5	4		2	—	do	do	6	Night Work
11	4					Making billets. Making camouflage & setting out new work	4	
	1 M'g'rs	1	50	144	SOUCHEZ RIVER	Cleaning SOUCHEZ river from M.28.c.1.9. to M.24.b.8.6	6	

Date. 25.10.14......

[signature]
O.C. 4/o th. Field Co. R.E.

Appendix XV

469th. Field Co. R.E.

PROGRESS REPORT – 6 a.m. 24.10.17. to 6 a.m. 25.10.17.

R.E.		Working Parties			Situation	Work carried out.	Hrs.	Remarks.
O.C.	Sect	O.	O.R.	Batt.				
	3		8	7/A.S.Ford	Cyril Trench	36 yds trench cleared for double track. Laid 114 yds single track	8	Day
	3		6	"	"	Laid 12 yds double track. 146 yds single track laid.	6	Night
	3	1	10	"	Beaver Trench	15 yds trench cleared for double track. 40 yds single track laid.	6	
	2		35	"	Cyril Trench	105 yds trench deepened. Battered & berm cleared forward of existing single duck-board track.	6	
	2		23	"	Beaver Tr.	60 yds trench deepened. Battered & berm cleared forward of existing single duck-board track.	6	
	1			"	Cyril Trench	27 duck boards. 30 pickets. 15 transoms carried.	8	Day
	1			"	Beaver Tr.	27 " 15 " 15 " "	8	
	3		28	"	Adept Trench	Revetting behind "A" frames with 6' hurdles. 12 hurdles in position 12 yds each side. Left of Clucas.	6	
	11	4		" S.Ford	Clucas Trench	Taking up 2 layers of double trench boards. Clearing out trench & cutting central waterway in trench under dugouts. Duckboards temporarily relaid. 200yds. forward of Adept.	8	Day
	1		17	"	Adept Trench	40 yds widened, deepened, cleaned out & 135km cleared.	8	
	1		18	"	D°.	42 " " " " " "	6	
	1		20	"	Clucas Trench	40 yds berm cleared. 10 yds trench sides battered.		
	2		26	"	Adept Trench	30 "A" frames, 21 hurdles & 4 special frames carried from La Coulotte.		
	21	2			X.10.b.8.2	Drills. Bathing &c.	8	Day
	4	1.4				Runners for Sections & Co. HQ		
	6	3			S.6.d.4.9	Fixing up cook-house & store in dug-out (Complete)	8	Day
	6	3			D°.	Making latrines & repairing covered trench		
	12	3			D°.	Fixing stove in Officers' Mess	8	Night
	11	3			D°.	Widening Irish trench near Cyril. (Completely clear for 150 yds)	7	
	1		4	M.G.C.	U.6.3.9	Constructing M.G. emplacements		
	1				D°.	D°.		

Date 25..10..17....

M. Beaver Capt.
Act. O.C. 469 th. Field Co. R.E.

Appendix XV
Map 36c S.W.1.

467th Field Co. R.E.

PROGRESS REPORT - 6 a.m. 24th Oct. to 6 a.m. 25th Oct. 1917.

R.E. O.	R.E. Sect	Working Parties O.	Working Parties O.R.	Working Parties Batt.	Situation	Work carried out.	Hrs.	Remarks.
1	7	2	1	20 10	2/5 S.S. 2/5 N.S.	ABSALOM C.T.	Length of Buckboard laid. Length of Trench cleared ready for Buckboard.	50 yds 130 yds	Map ref: M.24.d.35~75
1	8	4	1	20	2/5 S.S.	do	Length of Buckboard laid Length of Trench effectively ready for Buckboard	65 yds 110 yds	" M.24.d.35~75.
1	7	3	1	19 15	2/5 S.S. 2/5 N.S.	CROCODILE C.T.	Length of Buckboard laid Length of Trench cleared ready for Buckboard. Re-cleaning trench	35 yds 20 ft 30 yds	
1	7	4	1	20 10	2/5 S.S. 2/5 N.S.	do	Length of Duck Board laid. Length of trench cleared ready for Buckboard. Widening trench	27 yds 20 yds 20 yds	Map ref: M.23.b.95.55.
1	7	4+4	2 1 1	60 15 16	2/5 S.S.	ABSALOM C.T.	New length of trench cleared. Length of Bn trench cleared Camouflage to dug-out.	150 yds 180 yds	
1	7	2+3	3	106	2/5 S.S.	CROCODILE C.T.	New length of trench cleaned. Length of Bn trench cleaned. Camouflage	235 yds 80 yds	
1	2	3	1	-	2/6 N.S. Coy H.Q.		Fixing cable + bucket to well (complete)	-	Map ref: N.22.d.9.1.
1	5	-	1	-	-	APPROACH TR: (Gehrat)	Clearing + remaking up culvert.	7	Map ref: N.17.a.27.

Total lengths of trench completed.
ABSALOM C.T. 440 yds
CROCODILE C.T. 406 "

Date 25th October, 1917.

Cyril C. Stacon Capt.
for O.C. 467th Field Co. R.E.

Appendix XII

th. Field Co. R.E.

PROGRESS REPORT – 6 a.m. 25.10.17 to 6 a.m. 26.10.17.

R.E.		Working Parties			Situation	Work carried out	Hrs	Remarks
O.	Sect	O.	O.R.	Batt.				
	1	1	15	177	Old C.O.PR 7th TR	Deepened trench over 1ff for 20yds and relaid duck boards	1	for drainage
	2	1	35	–	CWGHS 7	do – Aver 1ft for 60	1	to drain CWGHS 7
	1	1	50	–	CWGHS S to T 2.1	Deepened drain Aver 3ft to 6ft for 60yds	4	do do Night
	3	1	21	–	CWGHS	do Aver 3ft to 6.1.3 for 30yds	2½	do do Night
	2	1	21	–	OCRGS	do do	4	do do Night
	2	1	9	–	CWGHS 7	Digging trenches for Latrines	2	
1	2	1	50	147	WESTHOEK	Placing trench and laying Duckboards from ARRAS – LAY T. to VICTORIA ST. and THEODORE DEN Junction	6	
	15	2	41	–	do	Deepening trench from VICTORIA R.D. to T/1 & 5 Unloading and laying out Duckboards.	6	1 truck
1	11	2	50	147	WESTHOEK Blue Gauntlet Cottages	Finding fatigue party 45 Unginees and of dressing on road not made up	8	
	3	3	6	–	do	Unloading plage	8	
	2	3	4	–		Making firetraps	8	
	2	3	2	–		Laying decks on road	8	
	3	3	110	–		Making Duckboards	8	5 trucks taken interior
	2	4	50	–		Laying duckboards Hugebeck Bridge to CWGHS Trench	6	
	1	4	2	–	near M23 c3	Further Excavation of M.G. Emp and C.T.	6	
	2	4	2	–	do	do	6	
	1	5	4	–	CRAZY	Cleaning out existing trees	6	
	1	6	1	–	REDOUBT M23 c.80	Putting 16yds each baryette (app)	9	
	1	8	2	–		Putting up also in field (quote word) Making Generator flags	9½	

Date 26.10.17

Nede Palmer Capt RE
O.C. 440th. Field Co. R.E.

Appendix XVI

469th. Field Co. R.E.

PROGRESS REPORT – 6 a.m. 25.10.17. to 6 a.m. 26.10.17.

R.E.			Working Parties		Situation	Work carried out.	Hrs.	Remarks.
O.	O.R.	Sect	O.	O.R.	Batt.			
	5			7	1st S. Fors.	Cyril Trench	Laid 36 yds single track	8	Day
	1			3	"		Clearing & laying 22 yds double track		
	1			2	"		Laid 20 yds double track		
	1			4	"	Beaver Trench	Clearing trench for double track		
	2		1	1	"	Beaver Trench	Laid 25 yds double track		
	4		1	7	"	Adept Trench	Laid 30 yds single track		
					"		Clearing & laying 12 yds single track		
	2			30	"	Cyril Trench	20 yds widened, deepened & berm cleared	5*	*Hour short owing to Bde order N° 60 re Lobster.
	2			30	"	Beaver Trench	D° D°		
	1			30	"	Beaver Trench	Carrying 20 duck boards, 20 transoms & 40 pickets	5½	
						Cyril Trench	" 20 " 30 "		
	13			18	S. Fors.	Clucas Trench	Taking up 2 layers of double duck-boards, clearing out trench & battering sides, cutting central water channel under bearers & relaying duckboards. 250 yds.	8	Day
	2		1	34	"	Adept Trench forward of Adept	80 yds widened, deepened & cleared out 95 yds berm cleared.	4½	Night.
	2	4			"	Clucas Trench	Cleared way through Clucas Tr. in village (To be completed tomorrow)		No working party supplied.
	2		1	20	"	D°	60 yds berm cleared. 12 yds berm recleared.	4½	Night.
	2			20	"	Adept Trench	41 "A" frames loaded at Salvage Dump, Givenchy, & unloaded in Adept		"
	6		1			S.6.d.4.5.	Laying duck boards in Irish Trench from dug-out towards Cyril Trench		100 yds completed.
	3					D°	Making latrine for use of 2 sections	8	Excavation finished & frame work erected
	2	3	1			La Coulotte	Fixing 2 water tanks for Town Major, La Coulotte (Completed)	8	Day.
				4	M.G.C.	T.1.b.3.0.	Constructing M.G. emplacements. (Work from 11.0 pm to 8.0 am. postponed during easy of La Coulotte.)	6	Day & Night.
	1					Irish Trench	Widening & deepening Irish trench from dug-out towards Clucas trench 150 yds cleared & ready for duck-boards.	8	Night
	10								
	16					X.10.b.8.2.	Constructing road to transport lines in R.E. Camp	6	Day.
	1	2				~	Attached 3rd Field Ambulance R.A.M.C. for carpenter's work	10	
	4	4	4			X.10.b.6.2.	Repairing cycles	9	
							Runners for C°H.Q. & forward sections.		

Date. 26th Oct. 1917.

M. M. Connell .... Capt.
Actg. O.C. 469th. Field Co. R.E.

Appendix XIV

467th. Field Co. R.E.

PROGRESS REPORT - 6 a.m. 25th Oct to 6 a.m. 26th Oct., 1917.

R.E.		Working Parties			Situation	Work carried out.	Hrs	Remarks
O.C.	Sect	O.	O.R.	Batt.				
-	2	1	20 / 10	2/5 SS / 2/5 NS	ABSALOM C.T.	Length of Buckboard laid. Length of Trench cleared ready for Buckboard.	5	
-	4	1	8	2/5 SS	do	Length of Buckboard laid. Length of Trench cleared ready for Buckboards.	5	Map ref: M.24.d.6.5.8.5.
-	3	1	19 / 10	2/5 SS / 2/5 NS	CROCODILE C.T	Length of Trench Buckboarded laid. Length of Trench cleared ready for Buckboard. Relaying Trench.	5	
-	3	1	17 / 10	2/5 SS / 2/5 NS	do	Length of Buckboard laid. Length of Trench cleared ready for Buckboard.	5	Map ref: M.24.a.1.+5.
-	1+4	1 / 1 / 1	2 / 37 / 11	2/5 SS	ABSALOM C.T.	Drainage channels (6). Length of Berm recleared. Carrying 47 Buckboards.	3½	
-	2+3	1	44 / 10	2/5 SS	CROCODILE C.T.	New length of Berm cleared. Length of Berm recleared.	-	
-	-	1	-	-	ENTRANCE TO ABSALOM C.T.	Pulverin Pargolytnook to ABSALOM TRENCH	5	Map ref: M.24.c.6.6.
-	-	1	-	-	CELLARS & APPROACH TR.	Clearing and connecting up cellar.	7	Map ref: N.19°.9.7.

Total length of Trench completed
ABSALOM C.T. 546 yds
CROCODILE C.T. 512 yds

Date 26th October, 1917.

Ragil P. Kearns Capt. R.
O.C. 467th Field Co. R.E.

Appendix XVI

___th. Field Co. R.E.

PROGRESS REPORT — 6 a.m. 26.10.14 to 6 a.m. 27.10.14.

R.E.		Working Parties			Situation	Work carried out.	Hrs.	Remarks.
O.	Sect	O.	O.R.	Batt.				
1	1		14	194	OLVERS TRENCH	Digging trenches for and fitting hurdles and fascines upon do. Clearing away fallen wall of trench.	6½	
	2	1	36	-	-do-	Filling up advanced sump holes in trench. Clearing away of fitting rough strand for Double wire barricade.	6½	6 to do.
	6	1	21	-	R.D. TRENCH S.6 b 7 d	Sandbags. Shaping bails & sandpit and cutting away to own better hill of line.	4	1st (by 2nd) Night
	6	1	42	-	-do-	Digging trench for drainage SH West at top over old Dutch.	4	130 & 50 ft Walk
	1	2	50	191	R.D. TRENCH	Laying duck boards. Deepening R.D. Trench from T7.a.1 to T7.a.2.8	6	150 duck boards laid. Digging 110 ft.
	2	2	11	100	-do-	Deepening. Widening trench from T7.a.9.8. to T7.a.9.1	6	
	3	2	59	191	NEW ROAD ELUDINGHEM BOUCHEZ & GIVENCHY	Loading GS Wagons & repairing road	8	110 linear
	2	3	6	-		Laying Boundary road	8	12 do
	3	3	14	-		Laying kerb & sett spread	8	35 m
	2	3	10	-		Laying double duct tracks	8	110
	2	3	68	-		Making berm, draining and preparing new latrine boxes	8	
	2	3	50	-		Loading & unloading wagons of slag.	5	7 wagons loaded & unloaded.
1	14	1	-	-	CRAZY REDOUBT M23 B.Z.U	Clearing out trench	8	130 yds.
	6	4			M29 b 6 3	Re-sitting & covering M.G. Emplacements	9	

Date 27.10.14

L. .... Major
O.C. 470th Field Co. R.E.

Appendix XVII

469th Field Co. R.E.

PROGRESS REPORT – 6 a.m. 26.10.17 to 6 a.m. 27.10.17.

R.E.	O.R. Sect	Working Parties O.	O.R.	Batt.	Situation	Work carried out.	Hrs	Remarks.
4	1	–	6	1ᴿˢ·ᶠᵘˢ	Cyril Trench	Laid 40 yds single track (advance)	8	Day.
2	1	–	–	"	"	Laid 50 yds single track to complete double (rear)		
4	1	–	6	"	Beaver Trench	Laid 40 yds single track (advance) shifting boards to fit double track, and laying same (rear) 12 yds.		
8	1	–	4	"	"	Laid 25 yds double track.		
–	–	–	–	–	–	Clearing trench for double track.		
–	1	–	43	5ᵗʰ	Cyril Trench	117 yds deepened, widened & berm cleared		
–	1	–	55	"	Beaver Trench	130 yds trench deepened, widened & berm cleared	6	
–	1	–	59	7ᵗʰ	Dº	36 duckboards, 24 transoms, & 66 pickets carried		
3	1	–	30	"	Cyril & Beaver Tr	Digging Latrines. (Earth excavated for 3 latrines at S.12.a.58; T.2.d.18; T.2.a.53)		
–	1	–	51	6ᵗʰ	Adept Trench	32 duckboards, 44 transoms & 36 pickets carried		
4	1	–	–	"	Irish Trench S.6.d.4.9	Laying duckboards (120 yds) between S.6.d.4.9 towards Clucas Trench (completed)	8	Day.
2	1	–	–	"	Dº	Constructing covered latrine.	8	Night. 210 yds cleared, of which 120 yds are duckboarded.
15	1	–	–	"	Dº	Ablution Benches	6	
					Irish Trench	Deepening & widening between S.6.d.4.9 towards Clucas Tr. (60 yds)	7	Night.
10	3	–	4	M.G.C.	T.1.b.3.0	Constructing M.G. emplacements		
–	–	–	4	"	Dº	Dº	8	
1	–	–	10	1ᴿˢ·ᶠᵘˢ	Adept Trench	Fixing 38 "A" frames. 76 yds trench cleared & sides battered	5	Awaiting bridge
5	1	–	6	"	Dº	Revetting. 20 yds each side behind "A" frames	6	
4	1	–	4	"	Clucas Trench	Taking up double layer of boards, cutting water channel, clearing trench & relaying boards	5½	
1	4	–	16	"	La Coulotte Rd	Preparing to bridge road. Trench deepened & widened, & ready for opening up road for artillery bridge		
2	1	–	56	"	Adept Trench	220 yds. cleared, bottomed & battered		
2	1	–	33	"	Dº	220 yds berm cleared. Side trench cut to sump for drainage. 120 yds	6	
3	1	–	18	"	Clucas Trench	Cleared from point instructed to front line. Duckboards relaid.		
–	–	–	–	–	–	Nil. (Carrying party failed to arrive)		
–	–	–	–	–	–	Camouflage party		6
12	–	–	–	–	X.10.b.8.2	Constructing road for transport in R.E. Camp		
6	2	–	–	–	Carency	Attached 470ᵗʰ Field Cʸ R.E. for erecting Nissen Huts.		
2	2	–	–	–	–	Working at 3ʳᵈ Fd Amb. R.A.M.C. – constructing shed.		
1	–	–	–	–	–	At First Army Mine School		
4	4	–	–	–	Houchin	Runners for forward sections & Cº H.Q.		

Date 27ᵗʰ Oct. 1917.

M. C. Bousead. Capt.
Actᵍ O.C. 469ᵗʰ Field Co. R.E.

Appendix XVII

467th. Field Co. R.E.

PROGRESS REPORT – 6 a.m. 26th Oct. to 6 a.m. 27th Oct. 1917.

R.E.		Working Parties			Situation	Work carried out.		Hrs	Remarks.
O.C.	Sect	O.	O.R.	Batt.					
7	2	1	20 / 10	2/5 S.S. / 2/5 N.S.	ABSALOM C.T.	Length of Duckboards laid. Length of Trench cleared ready for duckboards.	42 yd. / 250 yd.	5	
8	4	1	20	2/5 S.S.	do	Length of Duckboards laid. Length of Trench left cleared ready for duckboards.	56 yd. / 220 yd.	5	Map ref: 24 d. 75. 9.
5	3	1	20 / 10	2/5 S.S. / 2/5 N.S.	CROCODILE C.T.	Length of Duckboards laid. Length of Trench cleared ready for duckboards. Retaining trench	50 yd. / 40 yd. / 10 yd.	5	
5	3	1	20 / 10	2/5 S.S. / 2/5 N.S.	do	Length of Duckboards laid. Length of Trench cleared ready for duckboards.	30 yd. / 40 yd.	5	Map ref: 24 a. 3. 5.
2 / 9	1+4 / 1+4	2 / –	33 / – / 16	2/5 S.S.	ABSALOM C.T. / ADROIT TR.	New length of Berms cleared. Length of Berms re-cleaned. Carrying party (54 Duckboards, pickets & strainers)	80 yd. / 10 yd. / 360 to front / 8 to right trench	3	
12	1,2,3	2	83	2/5 S.S.	CROCODILE C.T.	New length of Berms cleared. Length of Berms re-cleaned. Retaining party.	130 yd. / 380 yd.	4	
3	–	–	–	–	ENTRANCE TO ABSALOM C.T.	Salvaging dumps & track to ABSALOM C.T.		5	Map ref: M 24 c. 6.6.

Total length of Trenches completed:
ABSALOM C.T.   644 yd.
CROCODILE C.T.   592 yd.

Date 27th October 1917.

Basil C. Stacey, Capt. for
O.C. 467th Field Co. R.E.

Appendix XLVII

470th. Field Co. R.E.

PROGRESS REPORT - 6 a.m. 27-10-17 to 6 a.m. 28-10-17.

R.E. Sect.	O.	Working Parties O.R.	Batt.	Situation	Work carried out.	Hrs.	Remarks.
1	1	4	144	CLUCAS TRENCH	Resetting steps and laying duck-boards to 4 latrines	4	
6	1	46	-	do	Widening trench and digging drain near GIVENCHY RD	4	80yds
6	1	25	144	do	Laying double duck-boards from junction to GIVENCHY TP	4	16
6	1	36	-	TRENCH N. OF CLUCAS	Clearing firm 5ft wide near GIVENCHY TP	4	50 Night working party
6	1	20	-	do	Digging drainage trench 3ft wide from 3ft to 6ft deep (Approx)	4	Work 21 minutes at 180 OR
					Clearing away spoil and cutting away to change direction of 6 fire-bays	4	
1	2	50	144	TRED TRENCH	Building parapet, draining and filling up bully holes from T4a to T4a.?4	5	
10	2	100	144	CLUCAS TRENCH	Cutting berm on both sides of trench for a distance of 130 yards.	5	Night work
1	3	36	144	NEW RD BETWEEN BUSNES & GIVENCHY	Loading slag into GS wagons - spreading on road	8	40 linages
2	3	3	-	do	Making up dummy road	6	do
2	3	6	-	do	Fixing Kent at side of road	8	40 do
3	3	83	-	do	Laying duck-boards on track from KINGS RD to CLUCAS TRENCH	2	40 do
2	3	50	-	do	Clearing & draining CLUCAS TRENCH	6	
					Loading and unloading wagons of slag	6	6 wagon loads fetched
5	4	2	mess	M29.6.85	Covering MG Emplacement	9	Night work
12				M23.a.94	Clearing out Duck boarding CRAZY REDOUBT	8	
2				M29.6.55	Collecting material for M.G. Emp.	8	

Date 28-11-17

[signature]
Major
O.C. 470th. Field Co. R.E.

Appendix XLIII

469th. Field Co. R.E.

PROGRESS REPORT – 6 a.m. 27.10.17. to 6 a.m. 28.10.17.

R.E.		Working Parties			Situation	Work carried out.	Hrs.	Remarks.
O.	C.R.	Sect	O.	O.R.	Batt			
	6			7	7/95Foss	Cyril Trench	38 yds single track laid	8	Day
	2			4	"	"	Laying single track to complete double, 50 yds.		
	1			4	"	"	Making Latrine near Canteen		
	1			4	"	"	Making Latrine at Cyril & Adept Junction		
1	4			7	"	Beaver Tr.	42 yds single track laid		
	2			4	"	"	Laying & shifting boards to form double track, deepening trench as necessary 30 yds.	6	Night.
	1		1	39	"	"	Making latrine, Beaver & Adept Junction		
	1		1	56	"	Cyril Trench	Deepening & battering forward part of Cyril. 110 yds		
	1		1	60	"	Beaver Trench	140 yds trench cleared, widened & battered		
	1		2	14	"	Beaver Trench Cyril Trench	36 duck boards, 72 pickets, 32 transoms carried		
	1			11	"	Cyril Trench Beaver Trench	28 " 48 " " "		
	3					S.G.d.4.9	Excavating Latrines at S.12.a.5.8 ; T.2.d.5.8 ; T.2.d.2.9	8	Day
	10					Irish Trench	D°. " " T.2.a.5.3 ; T.2.b.1.9	8	Night
	6		5		M.G.C.	-D°-	Constructing Ablution Benches, & drainage from same.	8	
	1			4	"	-D°-	Revetting Sides with sand bags where trench has fallen in between point where trench runs under Decauville & Irish-Lloyd Junction. (Night)	6	100 yds between junction of Irish-Lloyd Trench south towards Decauville Line is now cleared
	1			4	"	T1.b.3.0.	Clearing berm on East side of trench. (Locality as above.)	6	
	2		1	58	2 Foss	Clucas Tr.	Constructing M.G. emplacements. (Night Work) D°	7	
	2		1	67	6"	Kingston Rd.	700 cleared & duckboards relaid. (Within 20 yds of Front Line.)	6	Night.
	1			20	88	La Coulotte	Road cut through to a depth of 6ft & Artillery Bridge placed in position Side trench & Sump completed 50 yds N of Road. 250 yds berm cleared	5	"
	2			53	"	Adept Trench Clucas & Partridge	50 yds trench cleared & battered	7½	"
	2					X.10.b.8.2	Trench cromnavigated. Bridge placed in position. Road cut to depth of 5 ft Carried 60 duck boards, 13 hurdles & 1 Artillery Bridge from La Coulotte	6	Day
	1						Fixing Camouflage		
	2					Caresnoy	Constructing 120 sy yds. Road for Transport in R.E. Camp		
	2					Houchin	Erecting Officers' Huts at 2/3" Fd Amb		
	10						Erecting Nissen Huts		
	6		2				First Army Mine School		
1	5	1-4					Runners for C° H.Q. & Forward Sections		

Date 28..10..17...

M.M. Bowell, Capt.
Act.g O.C. 469th. Field Co. R.E.

Appendix XVIII

447th. Field Co. R.E.

PROGRESS REPORT – 6 a.m. 27th 9ct to 6 a.m. 28th 9ct. 1917

R.E.		Working Parties				Situation	Work carried out.	hrs	Remarks.
O.R.	Sect	O.	O.R.	Batt.					
–	7	2	1	20	2/5 S.S.	ABSALOM C.T.	Length of Duckboard laid — 144 yds Right side cleaned ready for duckboard — 200 yds Length of trench widened — 150 yds	5	Map ref. M 24 d 9.5 9.5
–	8	4	1	10	2/6 N.S. 2/5 S.S.	do	Length of Duckboard tail — 58 yds	5	
–	8	3	1	20 10	2/5 S.S. 2/6 N.S.	CROCODILE C.T.	Length of trench left cleaned ready for duckboards — 180 yds Width of trench widened	5	
–	8	3	1	20 10	2/5 S.S. 2/6 N.S.	do	Length of trench revetted — 40 yds Width of trench widened — 20 yds Length of duckboard laid — 50 yds Length of trench left cleaned ready for duckboard — 35 yds Length of trench widened — 40 yds Length of trench re-cleaned — 20 yds	5	Map ref. M 24 c 5.4.5
–	10 1 1	14 4 1	– –	4/6 4/6 25	2/6 S.S.	ABSALOM C.T. (ADROIT TRENCH)	Drainage works New bays of trench cleared Length of trench revetted — 120 yds Revetting party employed — 140 yds	4	
–	12	2+3	3	125	2/5 S.S.	CROCODILE C.T.	New bays of trench cleared — 27 yds Length of Bm. revetment — 90 yds	4	
–	3	–	–	–	–	Bay-Light-Line to ABSALOM C.T.	Carrying & laying abutments of Bm. revet Length of brickwork — 50 yds Length of duckboards laid — 45 yds	5	Map ref. M 24 c 6.6
–	5	1	–	–	–	CELLARS AT APPROACH TO do	Clearing cellars & up & putting topsoil Searching props etc & c	7	Map ref. N 19 c 9.7

Total length of trench completed — ABSALOM C.T. 740 yds
CROCODILE C.T. 667 yds.

Date 28th October 1917.

[Signature]
O.C. 447th Field Co. R.E.

App XIX

470th. Field Co. R.E.

PROGRESS REPORT - 6 a.m. 27/10/14 to 6 a.m. 28/10/14.

R.E.		Working Parties		Situation	Work carried out.	hrs	Remarks.
O.	Sect	O.	O.R. Batt.				
	1	1	50 1/4	LUCAS TRENCH by GIVENCHY	Widening trench and abutres walls (Both sides)	4	60 yds
					Digging drain and laying Duck boards in traverses		10 yds
	1	1	44 1/4	RED TRENCH N of LUCAS	Clearing Berm top of S.H. cutting away to change direction of 6 footbrs	4	100 yds } Night Work
	1	1	25 1/4	do		4	
	5	1	25 1/4	-do-	Deepening drain 15yds long to 6ft	4	
	1	1	2 1/4	LUCAS	Unloading stores from drain	2	
	1	2	50 1/4	RED TRENCH	Preparing parapet and cutting drains from S.H. side 96	5	
	10	2	170 1/4	LUCAS TRENCH	Clearing trench and cutting berm on South side of trench	4 1/2	100yds to high water
	5	3	34 1/4	NEW ROAD SOUCHEZ GIVENCHY	Loading slag into GS Wagons & spreading on road	8	125 tons 400
	3	3	6 -		Facing Rent in road	6	40 "
	1	3	10		Laying front bricks in traction trench & LUCAS T	8	80 "
	3	3	85		Clearing & draining LUCAS TRENCH	8	
	2	3	1 50		Loading & Unloading GS Wagons 6/10/14	8	6 wagons
	5	4		M 29 b 8.5	Finishing M.G. Emplacement	6	Nightwork
	12	4		M 28 b 84	Dugout boarding & cleaning out CRAZY REDOUBT	8	
	1	4			Inspecting Dug outs in area	8	

Date 28/10/17

.... Major
O.C. 470th. Field Co. R.E.

App XIX

459th Field Co. R.E.

PROGRESS REPORT – 6 a.m. 22.10.17. to 6 a.m. 23.10.17.

R.E.		Working Parties			Situation	Work carried out	Hrs.	Remarks
O.C.	Sect.	O.	O.R.	Batt.				
			4	4/5 Fus.	Cav. Trench	Six 20' single track sand. Making sixty sleepers during long single track. To complete 200 sq. track. 4 working track sq. yds. Making lozenge. Chin & Adopt Junction Cyn & Balsan. Cyn Canteen.	8 Day	N.3.b. 55.5 to N.3.c.67.70. T.3.c.6.6.70.
			4		Beaver Tq.	68'x24 single track sand. Making lozenge. Chin's Adopt lozenge. Laying single track to rem. Making single track to complete double. 30'x0'. Deepening 25 yds trench.	8 Day	N.24.d. 77.85. T.3.c. 45.85.
		1	47 50		Avon Trench Sullivan Tq. Chit & Canel	120 yds cleared & drained. & drain finished. 30 yds cleaned & battered.		T.5.a.35.4 to T.3.a.0.7. N.21.d.90.30 to N.22.c.4.35.
			55 40 25		S.C. 4 + 12 D?	78 duckboards 72 trimmed. 18 headers. 5ft x 7ft. (Bending covers) cleaned. Lowered in Cyn D. (T.3.d.O. in trench itself) (Connected)	9 Day Night	Connected S.6.b.4.3 to S.6.b.4.78 [illegible]
				M.G.C.	S.C.5 T.I.T.2.O.	Constructing shelter began & drainage from same. Laying duck boards. S.6.b.4.3 to S.6.b.4.75. D? & draining & widening trench. S.6.b.4.0.35 to S.6.b.4.97.40. Cutting back west side of trench. S.c.6.b.5.2 to S.6.b.6.1.	7 Night	
			4	A.W. & Co	Adopt Trench	Construction. N.G. emplacements. D?	9 Night	N implaced
			4		D?	Filling in ye shell holes & repairing of same. Filling ye a.s. revers. 80 yds duckboards, carried to Adopt.	8	
			60			Slight shell clearance.	6	N.30.d.4.5.
					Cross Jones Pillbox	Painting 4 track. Put it over a Bomb & ponies put in to support tracks needed for Horace. (Being clear from Cyn to Columba R.5.c.4.4 to N.31.c.4.5.) Cleared to 7ft. x 26ft. thick 2ft.6. Altered pass near Adept.		N.31.d. 5.6
			80 80		Adopt Trench	Excavated for latrine at N.31.d. 5.6. Jump out to drain bad part of trench. Laying boards at N.3.d. 5.3. Carried 68 duck boards a 3ft handles.		N.31.d. 7.6.
		2	15		X.10.0.8.2.	(Loading party failed to arrive) Gosson's salvage damp.		
					Canning Footing	Constructing 130 sq. yds. of road for transport. Erecting officers huts at 3rd Fld. Amb. Erecting nissen huts. First Army Mine School. Runners Pigeon Co. H.Q. & Forward Station.		Day

W. Bennett Capt.
O.C. 459th Field Co. R.E.

Date 22.10.17.

App XIX

467th. Field Co. R.E.

PROGRESS REPORT – 6 a.m. 28th Oct. to 6 a.m. 29th Oct. 1917

R.E.		Working Parties			Situation	Work carried out	Hrs.	Remarks
O.	Sect	O.	O.R.	Batt.				
1	2	1	20 10	2/5 S.S. 2/5 N.S.	ABSALOM C.T.	Length of trench completed for Duckboards...	5	
1	4	1	20	2/5 S.S.	do	...	5	Map ref: N19c.2.95
1	3	1	20 10	2/5 S.S. 2/5 N.S.	CROCODILE C.T.	... Duckboards	5	
1	3	1	20 10	2/5 S.S. 2/5 N.S.	do	...	5	Map ref. M.24.6.4.
2	4 1 4	1 1 1	36 30 26	2/5 S.S.	ABSALOM C.T. (ADROIT C.T.)	...	3¾	
1	2 3	2	1/10	2/5 S.S.	CROCODILE C.T.	New length of tram...	4	
1	1	1	—	1	CELLARS at APPROACH TR	...	7	R(ef of N.96.97
—	3	1	30	1	do	Camps & proposed shelters	4	
1	—	1	—	1	Daylight Trench ABSALOM C.T.	Length of protection: { Brick Duckboards	5	Map ref. M.24.6.6.

Total length of trench complete:
ABSALOM C.T. 888 yds
CROCODILE C.T. 757"

Date 29th Oct. 1917

Basil C Hearn Capt.
for O.C. 467 th. Field Co. R.E.

Appendix IX

4/0th. Field Co. R.E.

PROGRESS REPORT - 6 a.m. 29-10-17 to 6 a.m. 30/10/17.

R.E.		Working Parties		Situation	Work carried out.	Hrs.	Remarks.
O.	Sect	O.R.	Batt.				
9	1	—	—	TED TRENCH N. of LUCAS	Revetting fire steps commenced	2½	Let m. off this got to clear falls in LUCAS T.
9	1	—	—	LUCAS T	Clearing away falls near TED TRENCH	4½	
1	1	—	—	do	do do and laying 6 Duck boards	4	Night Work
12	1	—	—	do	Clearing loam near TED TRENCH	2	
1	21	2	—	LUCAS TRENCH	Cutting berm on both sides of trench for a distance of 40 yds	6	Night work
1	24	2	—	NEW FORD between SOUCHEZ & GIVENCHY	Loading G.S. Wagons and spreading slag on road	8	
—	15	3	—		Clearing LUCAS trench	8	
—	2	3	—		Laying duck boards on track between NEW FORD & LUCAS trench	6	
—	15	4	—	M23 b 8.4.	Quick loading, clearing out CRAZY REDOUBT Inspecting Dug-outs	8	
1	2	4	—				

Date 30-10-17.

O.C. 4/0th. Field Co. R.E.

Appendix XX

469th Field Co. R.E.

PROGRESS REPORT - 6 a.m. 29.10.17 to 6 a.m. 30.10.17.

R.E. Sect	Working Parties O.	O.R.	Batt.	Situation	Work carried out.	Hrs.	Remarks.
4		10	17th S.Fors	Cyril Trench	42 yds single track laid. N.33.c.80.15	8	T.2.c.30.74
2		4	"	"	Laying single track to complete double 26 yds.	6 Inf	
2		7	"	"	Completing latrine near canteen 5.12.a.50.90	Day	
4		7	"	D°	Cyril & Balsam Junc".		
1	1	2	"	Beaver Trench	48 yds single track laid. N.32.d.80.87		
1		2	5th "	"	Making latrine Beaver & Adept Junc"		
1		53	"	Avion Trench	Deepening trench, 10 yds. T.2.d.35.15		
1		18	7th "	Mn.Beaver Junc	Clearing & battering 230 yds. N.32.d.75.12	6	Night.
3		26	"	Avion Cyril Junc	Excavating — (Down to trench level)		
				Cyril Trench	Completing excavation for latrine. (Ready for Box & Bearers)		
					Carried 43 D.Bs. 4 lengths of 5'x 2" and 4 of 9'x 1".		
1	3	18		Irish Trench	Clearing & widening. From S.6.b.6.1 to T.1.c.02.57	8	Night
1	3	4	M.G.C.	T.1.b.8.9	Constructing M.G. Emplacements.	6	
1	3	4	"	D°	D°	6	
3		3	S.Fors.	Adept Trench	Fixing 30 yds hurdles each side & backing up complete.	8	Day
4		6	"	"	Clearing further 40 yds for fitting hurdles behind "A" Frames. N.31.d.4.8		
1		1	"	"	Cutting 30 yds waterway & relaying duck boards complete. N.31.d.4.7		
3		2	"	"	Continuing excavation of latrine.		
3		3	"	"	65 yds duckboards laid temporarily. N.31.b.4.2		
1		20	5th "	Clucas Trench	Cleared trench to front line. 40 yds (This work is now complete)		
3	4	38	6th "	Adept Trench	From N.32.a.5.3 to N.26.d.9.1	6	Night
1		15	"		Reclearing 42 yds Berm each side. Completed excavation for latrine		
1		5	5th "	Clucas Trench	Making sump pit & completing bridge under Decauville N.31.d.7.6		
1		10	5th "	Adept Trench	Completing latrine excavation & sandbag revetting entrance. Completed sump excavation N.31.a.5.3		
1		36		D°—	Completing latrine excavation. N.31.a.5.3		
				D°—	30 "A" Frames from Givenchy		
					50 duck boards. 15 hurdles. 150 sandbags from La Coulotte		
1				X.10.b.8.2	Constructing 120 s.yds Road for Transport, R.E.Camp	6	
2	2			X.10.b.8.2	Erecting Officers' Huts at 3rd Fd. Amb.	6	
2				Carency	Repairing & whitewashing R.E. Stables		
5				Houchin	Erecting Nissen Huts.	6	
1	4				First Army Mine School		
					Runners		

Date 30..10..17.

A.M. Boswell Capt.
O.C. 469th Field Co. R.E.

Act.g O.C. 469th Field Co. R.E.

Appendix XX

467th. Field Co. R.E.

PROGRESS REPORT – 6 a.m. 29th Oct. to 6 a.m. 30th Oct. 1917.

R.E.		Working Parties			Situation	Work carried out.		Hrs.	Remarks.
O.	Sect	O.	O.R.	Batt.					
1	1	–	16	2/5 S.S.	ADROIT TR. (ABSALOM C.T.)	Length of Duckboards laid. Length of Trench left cleared for Duckboards. Length of Trench not cleared.	64 yds 85 yds – yds	4½	
1	2	1	20 8	2/5 S.S. 2/5 N.S. (ABSALOM C.T.)	ADROIT TR.	Length of Duckboards laid. Length of Trench left cleared for Duckboards. Length of Trench not cleared.	60 yds 85 yds – yds	4½	Map ref: N.19.a.4.0.
1	3	1	20 10		CROCODILE C.T.	Length of Duckboards laid. Length of Trench left cleared for Duckboards. Length of Trench not cleared.	56 yds 40 yds 20 yds	4½	
1	3	1	20 10		do	Length of Duckboards laid. Length of Trench left cleared for Duckboards. Length of Trench not cleared.	40 yds 20 yds – yds	4½	Map ref: M.24.a.7.5.
5	–	–	–	–	CELLARS at APPROACH TR.	Cleaning, connecting up & planting cellars.		7	Map ref: N.19.c.9.7.
3	3	–	–	–	DAYLIGHT TRACK to ABSALOM C.T.	Length of path laid; bricks.	22 yds		Map ref: N.12.d.6.6.

Total length of Trench cmp'd w.

ABSALOM C.T. 1012 yds.
CROCODILE C.T. 823 yds.

30th. October, 1917.

Basil C. Macara Capt.
for O.C. 467 th. Field Co. R.E.

Appendix XXI

4/10th. Field Co. R.E.

PROGRESS REPORT - 6 a.m. 30/10/17 to 6 a.m. 31/10/17.

R.E.		Working Parties			Situation	Work carried out.	Hrs.	Remarks.
O.	Sect	O.	O.R.	Batt.				
12	1				RED TRENCH N OF CLUCAS	Revetting firesteps 100 ft	7	} Nights work
2	1				- do -	Clearing out & draining where damaged by shell fire	6	
7	1	1	45	1/6	CLUCAS	Clearing dam Br. B 57 (Working from N.E.D.Trench away from front line)	6	230 yds
12	2	1	45	1/6	CLUCAS TRENCH	Cutting 5ft berm on both sides of C.T. for a distance of 100 ft	6	Nights Work.
14	3	1			CLUCAS TRENCH	Clearing Elucis Trench	4	
8	3				"	- do -	4	
3	3	1	45	1/6	NEW ROAD from Square K to GITTERSON	Clearing Berm	6	
3	3	1	50	1/6		Loading & Unloading Wagons w/slag	6	} 2 Wagons loaded & Unloaded
3	3		5	1/6		Laying Corduroy Road	6	maintenance wagon. Night W. or R.
11	4				M28 & 34	Duckboarding & cleaning out CRAZY REDOUBT	8	
7	4	1	50	1/6	M30 A.18	Commenced BEAUMONT REDOUBT 1st task or 100 yds	6	

Date 31.10.17

Fred B Salmon. Capt. for
O.C. 4/10th. Field Co. R.E.

Appendix XXI

469th Field Co. R.E.

PROGRESS REPORT – 6 a.m. 30.10.17. to 6 a.m. 31.10.17.

R.E.		Working Parties			Situation	Work carried out.	Hrs	Remarks.
O.	O.R.	Sect	O.	O.R.	Batt.			
1	4	1	1	4		Cyril Trench	Laying single track. Making transoms & pickets, 12 yds. N.33.c.80.18.	3	Day
1	4	1	–	2	5/S.Bdr		Laying single track to complete double. Widening trench 36 yds. T.2.c.99.80.	8	"
1	8	1	1	12		Beaver Tr.	Completing Latrine, Cyril & Adept Junc. Laying single track. Making transoms, 32 yds. N.32.d.80.50.	4	"
1	17	1	1	17		Irish Trench	Completing Latrine, Beaver & Adept Junc. Deepening trench where necessary. T.2.c.1.7 to T.2.a.3.2. Sawing up transoms for trench boards.	6	Night.
1	11	2	1	–		D°	Clearing berm 150 yds. Laid 100 yds trench boards.	5	"
1	–	–	1	4	M.G.C.	T.1.b.83	Widening, deepening & clearing 35 yds trench. Constructing M.G. emplacement.	6	"
1	4	3	1	50	7/A&D	Irish Trench	Laying duck boards. S.6.B.7.0 to S.6.d.75.90	4	"
1	–	–	1	53	"	Sullivan Tr.	Deepening & battering trench & clearing berm N.33.c.17 to N.32.c.28	6	(1) Half excavated
1	–	–	1	43	5th	Avion Trench	D° N.32.d. 15.25 to N.32.d.65.30	6	(2) Completely excavated
1	–	–	1	18	"	Sullivan to Cyril	Carrying trench boards, 32 to Sullivan (right of Beaver). 41 to Cyril (forward of Avion)	6	
1	–	–	1	10	"	Cyril Trench.	Excavating for latrines :- (1) N.32.d.9.9. (2) N.32.d.4.0. (3) T.2.c.2.8	8	
1	2	2	1	20	3rd	Adept Trench	Clearing 100 yds trench between T.2.b.65.0 & T.2.b.7.1.		
1	2	2	1	24	"	D°	Fixing 16 hurdles behind "A" frames. N.31.d.4.9	4½	N.31.d.4.4.
1	4	2	1	–		D°	24 "A" frames, & clearing 60 yds ready for hurdles	2	
1	–	–	1	6		Clucas Trench	Clearing trench bottom & temporarily laying 220 yds duckboards	2	
1	3	–	1	–		Adept Trench	Repairing trench & duckboards	6	N.31.d.7.6
1	–	–	1	35		Columbia Trench	Completing Latrine.	4	
1	2	–	1	29		Adept Trench	260 yds berm cleared, from M.36.d.8.4.	6	
1	2	–	1	10		Columbia Trench	Clearing berm & 120 yds trench bottom. Completed sump. Cleared shell-holes	6	
1	2	–	1	34		Clucas Trench	Clearing berm & falls, 100 yds to N.31.c.2.9.		
1	2	–	1	48		Clucas-Columbia	180 yds berm cleared. Falls cleared & trench lowered to sump. N.31.d.5.6.		
1	1	–	–	–		"	Detailed to carry material from Dump. None arrived.		
1	5	2	–	–		Houchin.	Infantry working party failed to arrive.		
1	6	2	–	–		Carency	First Army Mine School		
1	4	4	–	–			Erecting Nissen huts		
							Runners		

Date 31.-.10.-.17.

M.M.Bouvell.........Capt.
Act.g. O.C. 469th. Field Co. R.E.

Appendix XXI

467th. Field Co. R. E.

PROGRESS REPORT - 6 a.m. 30th Oct. to 6 a.m. 31st Oct. 1917

R.E.		Working Parties			Situation	Work carried out.		Hrs.	Remarks.
O.	C.R. Sect	O.	O.R.	Batt.					
-	8	2	-	-	-	ADROIT C.T. (ABSALOM C.T.)	Length of Buckboard laid. Length of trench & clearing for duckboards. Length of trench retained.	58 yd. 15 yd. - yd.	5
-	7	4	-	20	2/4 LINCOLN	Do	Length of Duckboard laid. Length of trench & clearing for duckboards. Length of trench retained.	30 yd. 50 yd. - yd.	5	Map ref. N19c 4.5.7.5
-	7	3	-	-	-	CROCODILE C.T.	Length of Duckboard laid. Length of trench & clearing for duckboards. Length of trench retained.	40 yd. 10 yd. 10 yd.	5
-	7	3	-	21	2/4 LEICS	Do	Length of Duckboard laid. Length of trench & clearing for duckboards. Length of trench retained.	15 yd. 20 yd. - yd.	5	Map ref. N24 a 8.5
-	12 1	-	21 23 25	2/4 LINC	ADROIT C.T. (ABSALOM C.T.)	New bays & Fire steps cleaned. Length of trench cleaned. Carrying party (Duckboards &c).	70 yd. 100 yd.	4
-	8	2 or 3	2	70	2/4 LEICS	CROCODILE C.T.	New length of Berm cleaned. Length of Berm cleaned.	80 yd. 200 yd.	4
-	3	3	-	-	-	DAYLIGHT TRACK to ABSALOM C.T.	Length of path laid.	yd.	4	Map ref. N24 c 6.6
-	5	-	-	-	-	CELLARS & APPROACH TRENCH.	Cleaning, mending up & starting cellars.		7	Map ref. N19c 9.7

Total length of trench completed:-
ABSALOM C.T. 1105 yds.
CROCODILE C.T. 908 yds.

Date 31st October 1917

C.C. 467th Field Co. R.E.

SECRET. Appendix XIV Copy.No. 10.

C.R.E. 59th.Division Order No.3.

by

LIEUT.COL.G.B.ROBERTS.R.E.

1. The 467th., 469th., and 470th.Field Cos.R.E. will move to the WATOU areas Nos.3, 1, and 2, respectively, to-morrow the 1st.October under arrangements to be made by O.C.Field Cos.R.E.

2. The 9th.Seaforth Highlanders (Pioneers) will move from their present Camp to WATOU area No.3. to-morrow under arrangements to be made by the O.C.

3. From the 2nd.October the Field Cos. of the 59th. Divisional R.E. will be rationed by the XIV.Corps under whose administration they will come from that date.

4. The 9th.Seaforth Highlanders (Pioneers) will be rationed from the 2nd.October by the XVIII.Corps under whose administration they come from that date.

5. Lorries for transport purposes will be supplied if possible; instructions regarding which will be issued later.

6. Acknowledge.

30.9.1917.
Issued at

Captain & Adjutant.
59th.Divisional R.E.

Copy No.1. XIV.Corps.A.   6. 469th.Field Co.R.E.
       2. XVIII.Corps.A.   7. 470th.Field Co.R.E.
       3. 59th.Division.G.   8. O.C.9th.Seaforth Pioneers.
       4. 59th.Division.A.   9. File.
       5. 467th.Field Co.R.E.   10.and 11 War Diary.

S E C R E T.   Appendix XIII   Copy No. 8

C.R.E. 59th. Division Order No.2. 29.9.17.

by

Lieut.Colonel. G.B.ROBERTS, R.E.

Sheet 28.N.W. 1/20,000.

1.   The 59th.Divisional R.E. together with the 9th.Seaforth Pioneers will be relieved by the New Zealand Divisional R.E. and their Pioneers on the morning of the 30th.September.

2.   Headquarters R.E.(including Divisional R.E.Dumps) will hand over to the relieving Headquarters R.E. at MERSEY CAMP and Divl. Main Dump (H.8.a.5.9) at 11 a.m. 30th.September.

3.   The Dismounted portion of the 467th.Field Co. R.E. situated in CANAL LOCK Dugouts I.1.b.9.1. will be relieved by the Dismounted portion of the 1st Field Co. N.Z.Divisional R.E. at 11 a.m. on the 30th.September.
      The Transport Lines situated in VLAMERTINGHE will be taken over under arrangements made by the O.C.s. concerned.

4.   The Dismounted portion of the 469th.Field Co.R.E.situated in DIXMUDE STREET I.8.a.cent. will be relieved by the Dismounted portion of the 4th.Field Co.R.E. of the N.Z.Divisional R.E. at 11 a.m. on the 30th.September.
      The Transport Lines with accommodation situated at H.2.c.1.7. will be handed over under arrangements to be made by O.C.s. concerned.

5.   The Dismounted portion of the 470th.Field Co.R.E. situate in CANAL BANK Dugouts Nos.50 to 70 (I.1.b.5.9) will be relieved by the 3rd.Field Co. of the N.Z. Divl.R.E. at 11a.m. on the 30th.Sept.
      The Transport Lines situated at H.2.c.1.7. will be handed over under arrangements to be made by the O.Cs. concerned.

6.   The 9th.Seaforth Pioneers situated at H.18.a.3.8. will hand over to the Pioneers of the N.Z.Divisional R.E. on the morning of the 30th.Sept. under arrangements to be made by the O.Cs.Pioneer Battalions concerned.

7.   Field Company Commanders will endeavour to assist the relieving Field Cos.as much as possible by handing over clear statements as to work on hand together with complete lists of Area Stores etc. held on charge by them.

8.   On relief the Field Cos.will proceed as follows :-
      The 467th.Field Co. and 469th.Field Co. will each send an Officer to take over the accommodation for their Company and Transport Lines from the Brigade Area Commandant H.9.d.0.6. VLAMERTINGHE.

      The 470th.Field Co.R.E. will be accommodated in the HOP FACTORY, Main Divl.R.E.Dump at H.8.a.5.9. their Transport and horses being picketed in the open at the back of the Divl.Dump.

      The 9th.Seaforth Pioneers upon relief will take over accommodation at H.9.d.8.6. from the Brigade Area Commandant at H.9.d.0.6.

9.   ACKNOWLEDGE.

      Issued at 10 a.m.   Captain & Adjutant.

      Copy No.1.   59th.Div. G.   Copy No.5. 469th.Field Co.R.E.
          No.2.   59th.Div.A.   Copy No.6. 9th.Seaforths.
          No.3.   467th.Field Co.R.E. Copy No.7. File.
          No.4.   469th.Field Co.R.E. Copy No.8.& 9. War Diary.
                  470

WAR DIARY.   Appendix B   Copy No 14

ORDERS by Lt Col G.B.ROBERTS, RE
CRE 59th Division

No 6

1. In accordance with III Corps telegram S.367 dated 23.11.17 the three Field Companies are placed at the disposal of CE III Corps.

2. The Field Companies are to be employed on the erection of shelters at GOUZEAUCOURT and BEAUCAMP. They will proceed as follows:-
467th Field Co RE on 25th inst to BEAUCAMP
469"   "   "   "   "   "   GOUZEAUCOURT
470"   "   "   "   "   "   — do —

3. The Field Companies will draw the hutting material for their own accommodation at FINS RE DUMP today.
Officers Commanding will immediately get into touch with the OC No 239 HT Coy GOUZEAUCOURT (at Water Point Q 36 a 10 9.) and arrange sites for their camps.
469th Coy should have a site near MILL CAMP and 470th Coy near FISH CAMP.

4. Pontoons and Trestles are to be stored near GOUZEAUCOURT in a site to be selected by OC 470th Field Co RE. Field Companies will arrange a suitable guard.

K. Middlemiss
Captain & Adjutant
for CRE 59 Div.

24.11.17

Copy No 1.   OC 467th Field Co RE
     2   OC 469th   -"-
     3   OC 470th   -"-
     4   59th Division G
     5   -"-   Q
     6   59th Divisional Train
     7   176th Inf Bde
     8   177th   "
     9   178th   "
    10   CE III Corps
    11   OC No 239 A T Coy
    12   File
    13   War Diary
    14   - do -

Appendix 1.

470th. Field Co. R.E.

PROGRESS REPORT - 6 a.m. 1-11-17 to 6 a.m. 2-11-17.

R.E.		Working Parties		Situation	Work carried out	Hrs	Remarks
O.	Sect	O.	O.R.	Batt.			
1	1	1	6	176	CLUCAS TRENCH Between AYGRES ROAD and RIVERSIDE	Clearing falls in trench	8	
1	1	1	42	176	CLUCAS T. W of REDT.	Clearing trench, Digging drain & taking up old duck boards & temporarily relaying	8	80 yds
10	1		2	176	RED TRENCH N of CLUCAS	Digging drain and relaying duck boards		
3	1			176	CLUCAS T. W of REDT.	Laying double duck boards on Traverses & Pickets	8	15 yds
2	1	1	45	176	CLUCAS. T. W of REDT	Upgrading storm-open drain Clearing berm back 5ft	3 6	120 yds } Nightwork
1	2		50	176	RED TRENCH	Deepening, draining, & laying Duck boards T4 a 88. to T4 b 19	8	
11	2				do S.sd. B 335	Constructing Fireways and relaying Duck-boards.	8	
1	2	1	60	176	RED-TRENCH	Deepening and widening trench T4 b.19 to T4 a 26.10	6	Nightwork
6	3	1	40	176	NEWFORD Between SOUCHEZ & CIVILLEMENT	Loading slag into GS Wagons & spreading on road	8	150 ln yds
2	3		3	176	do	Fixing Kent on side of road	8	40 ...
2	3		4	176	do	Laying trench boards on path between new rd. & CLUCAST	8	40 ,,
3	3	1	50	176	CLUCAST.	Clearing & draining trench	8	Nightwork
4	3		45	176	"	Clearing Berm back	6	do
1	3		5	176	NEWROAD	Making Roadway 4'6" A	6	134yds
1	4	1	50	176	17.23 c 5.4 M.30.a.1.2	Duck boarding & clearing out CRAZY REDOUBT 2nd task on 100 yds of BEAUMONT REDOUBT	8	Nightwork
3		1	50	176	REDMILL M27d.4.1	Clearing SOUCHEZ river	8	

Date 2-11-17 ....

....
O.C. 470th. Field Co., R.E.

Appendix 1

469th. Field Co. R.E.

PROGRESS REPORT - 6 a.m. 1.11.17. to 6 a.m. 2.11.17.

R.E.		Working Parties			Situation	Work carried out.	hrs	Remarks.
O.	O.R.	Sect	O.	O.R.	Batt.			
8	-	-	-	-	-	Irish Trench	Laying trench boards, & widening trench for same. Left of Cril. 180 yds	6	Night.
8	-	2	-	4	M.G.C.	"	Raising parapet to screen trench. Left of Cril. 150 yds	6	
1	-	-	-	4	"	Adept Trench	Constructing M.G. emplacements at N.31.d.5.3.	6	Day.
5	-	-	-	-	-	Houchin	First Army Mine School		
½	-	1	-	-	-	Carency	Erecting Nissen Huts		
10	-	1	-	-	-	X.10.6.8.2	Constructing 30 sq yds Road. Laying drainage channel. Laying bricks & painting stables		
1	-	-	-	-	-	-	Employed as Runners.		
4	-	1	-	4	-	-			RE Camp
6	26	1	1	5th N. & D.		Cyril Trench	Widening & double duck boarding trench, from T.2.c.45.60. To T.2.d.25.90.	8	
2	51	1	1	5th "		Avion Trench	Excavating 9 fire bays, 5 yds long × 1 yd wide N.32.d.55.45. to N.32.d.85.90 to N.32.d.93.87	8	
5	51	"	1	5th "		Sullivan Trench	5 "		
4	23	3	1	5th "		Victoria Road	Carrying - Duckboards, Pickets & Transoms. From Victoria Rd. to Cyril Tr. T.1.d.89 (Forward of Beaver) & to Sullivan-Beaver Junction.		
3	-	-	-	-	-	Cyril Trench	Excavating Latrine at Irish Tr. Junction. T.2.a.6.4 to T.2.a.65.45.	6	Working party failed to arrive.
2	8	-	-	15th N.2.D		Dº	Clearing berm forward of Adept.	-	
8	32	"	1	"		Adept Trench	Fixing 36 "A" Frames & cutting ∨ waterway	8	
1	4	"	-	"		Lucas Trench	Cutting ∨ waterway (72 yds)	-	
2	48	"	-	8th "		Columbia Trench	Repairing duck boards	8	
4	54	4	1	6th "		Avion Trench	114 yds berm cleared both sides (in all 228 yds). 1 Sump & side trench completed. 1 Sump & side trench partly excavated. Latrine almost completed.	6	
"	-	-	-	-	-	"	120 yds berm cleared both sides (in all 240 yds). 2 Fire bays excavated		
-	-	-	-	-	-	-	60 yds trench deepened	-	
2	60	6th	1	6th "		Adept Trench	(Infantry working party countermanded by Boe Major).		
2	-	-	-	-	-	Avion Trench	140 duck boards, 38 hurdles, 36 "A" Frames carried from La Comotte 400 sandbags carried		

Date: 2. Nov. 1917.

M.M.Bennard Capt.
Actg. O.C. 469 th. Field Co. R.E.

Opposite !

467th. Field Co. R.E.

PROGRESS REPORT – 6 a.m. 1st Nov. to 5 a.m. 2nd Nov. 1917.

A.E.		Working Parties			Situation	Work carried out.	Hrs	Remarks.
C.S.M.	Sect	O.	O.R.	Batt				
	8	1	13	2/4 Leic	ADROIT C.T. (ABSALOM C.T.)	Length of French trench cleared. Length of French left cleared for duckboards. Length of trench for duckboards.	65 yds 12 yds	
	7	1	13	2/4 Leic	Do	Length of Duckboards laid. Length of trench left cleared for duckboards. Length of place for trench.	30 yds 20 yds - yds	Map ref. N.19.c. 65.85
	6	1	12	2/4 Leic	CROCODILE C.T.	Length of Duckboards laid. Length of trench to be cleared for duckboards. Length of trench cleared.	40 yds 50 yds 20 yds	
	5	1	19	2/4 Leic	Do	Length of Duckboards laid. Length of trench to be cleared for duckboards. Length of trench cleared.	40 yds 60 yds - yds	Map ref. M.24.b.0.5.7
	6	2	13 25	2/4 Leic	ADROIT C.T. (ABSALOM C.T.)	New length of berm cleared. Length of Berm cleared. Length of parapet, making grips.	- yds 170 yds	
	3	1	30	2/4 Leic	CROCODILE C.T.	New length of berm cleared. Length of berm cleared.	110 yds 60 yds	
	1	3×2	47 18	2/4 Leic		Parties putting duck boards.	35	
	3	3	-	-	DUGOUT IN ABSALOM C.T.	Length of gallery lined – 70 m.m.	25 yds	Map ref. M.24.c. 6.6
	-	-	-	-	PELLARS at APPROACH.	Cleaning, connecting up rotating collar.	7	Map ref. N.19.c.9.7
	2	2	-	-	Do	Carrying props, &c, to miles.	4	
	-	1	-	-	WORK on SIDE LINE	Carrying and erecting trenches.	5	Sapper supervising party.

Total length of French completed:
ABSALOM – ADROIT C.T. 1228 yds
CROCODILE C.T. 1048 yds

Date: 2nd. Nov. 1917.

Basil E. Seacon, Capt R.E.
O.C. 467th Field Co. R.E.

Appendix II

470th. Field Co. R.E.

PROGRESS REPORT - 6 a.m. 2-11-17 to 6 a.m. 3-11-17.

R.E. O.C.	Sect	Working Parties O.	O.R.	Batt.	Situation	Work carried out.	Hrs.	Remarks.
1	1	1	50	1/6	CLUCAS TRENCH W of REDT	Taking up old duck boards, widening bottom of trench and digging drain. Temporarily relaying duck boards.	8	4/24 ns
1	1	12	-	-	do	do	8	28
2	1	1	62	1/6	do	Laying double duck boards on traverses + Pickets	4	24
2	1	1	-	-	-	Clearing back Berm SA	6	1.60 Night Work
1	2	1	50	1/6	RED TRENCH	Deepening and draining trench from T7 a 90.25 to T7 a 15.95	6	
1	2	14	-	-	S.5 d 85.55	Completing 3 firebays at S.5 d 85.55.	8	Night work.
2	2	1	62	1/6	RED TRENCH	Deepening and widening trench from T6.11 to T7 d 15.95	6	
1	3	1	50	1/6	CLUCAS TRENCH	Clearing trench + laying duck boards	8	40 In gas
2	3	1	5	1/6	"	Laying duck board track from new road to Clucas trench	8	50 on
2	3	1	5	1/6	NEW ROAD SOUCHEZ–GIVENCHY	Spring Kerb on side of road	6	12 on " Night Work
2	3	1	5	1/6	"	Laying bordures road	6	110 on
3	3	1	45	1/6	CLUCAS T.	Clearing Berm on trench	6	
2	3	1	40	1/6	NEW RD	Grading slag into G.S. Wagons + spreading on road.	6	5 trucks loaded + unloaded
2	3	1	50	1/6	"	Loading slag at FOSSE 6 + unloading trucks at KINES x	6	
1	4	1	-	-	M.23 6.9 M.	Duckboarding + clearing out CRAZY REDOUBT	8	Night Work
1	4	1	50	1/6	M.30 a 1-2	Putting up wire. Duckboarding 1st lack on 40 yds trench	6	
1	4	-	50	1/6	M.27 d 7.1	Clearing SOUCHEZ river from M.27 a.7.1 & M.33 a 88. and 11.28 a 60.15	8	

Date 3-11-17

Fred Palmer
O.C. 470th. Field Co. R.E.

Appendix B

469th Field Co. R.E.

PROGRESS REPORT - 6 a.m. 2.11.17. to 6 a.m. 3.11.17.

R.E.		Working Parties			Situation	Work carried out.	Hrs.	Remarks.
O.R.	Sect	O.	O.R.	Batt.				
-	-	-	16	-	La Coulotte Tr.	Cutting trench under Railway (Light). Preparing material & carrying on site.		N.31.c.
1	2	1	4	M.G.C.	Adept Trench	Constructing M.G. emplacement #.	6 Night	N.31.d.5.3.
3	"	1	51	5th N&D	Avion Trench	Deepening & clearing trench, from N.32.d.55.46 to N.32.d.50.46. Filling sandbags for revetting fire-bays. N.32.d.51.45.		
3	"	1	52	"	Sullivan Trench	Revetting 2 fire-bays. Clearing & deepening trench. N.32.d.85.30. N.33.c.0.25 to N.33.c.40.48		
3	3	1	14	5th	La Coulotte M.	Carrying materials to Avion & Sullivan Trench		
2	"	-	28	"	D°	Trench boards to Beaver & Cyril	6 Night	
4	"	-	-	"	T.I.C.1.6.	Excavating latrines (completed)		
					T.I.d.15.85	D° (½") (Completed)		
					T.I.d.92.62.			
6	-	1	27	1st	Beaver & Cyril Tr	Widening & clearing r&cm. Ready for double duck boards		T.2.d.25.95 - T.2.d.30.20.
4	-	-	8	16th	Adept Trench	Laying 50 hurdles behind "A" frames N.31.b.3.1.		
2	-	-	5	"	- D° -	Fixing 12 "A" frames & cutting trench back for revetting.		
2	-	1	44	"	Clucas Trench	Repairing duck boards in C.T.		
4	4	1	50	"	Avion Trench	80 yds trench cleared & 40 yds duck boards laid. Sandbagging 2 firesteps		N.32.c.35.50
2	"	1	31	"	Adept Trench	Clearing 35 yds trench & berm each side. Excavation for latrine completed.		
2	"	-	25	"	- D° -	80 yds trench cleared to junction of Columba. 250 yds duckboards temp'ly laid.		
-	"	-	-	"	- D° -	41 hurdles carried from Dump.		
5	1-4	-	-	-	Houchin.	First Army Mine School		
6	1	-	-	-	Carency.	Erecting Nissen Huts.		
13	"	-	-	-	X.10.b.8.2	Constructing oven. Laying 20 sq.yds Bricks, & repairing standings in Horse Lines. R.E. Camp.	6	
4	1-4	-	-	-	-	Runners.		

Date 3-11-17

[signature] 2nd Lieut.
For O.C. 469th Field Co. R.E.

Appendix II

467th. Field Co. R.E.

PROGRESS REPORT — 6 a.m. 2nd Nov. to 6 a.m. 3rd Nov. 1917.

A.P. Sect	Working Parties O.	O.R.	Batt.	Situation	Work carried out.		Hrs	Remarks.
4 1+2	1	17	2/4 Leic	ADROIT C.T.	Length of duckboards laid.	20 yds	5	
3	-	1	-	ABSALOM C.T.	Length of trench left cleared for duckboards. Length of trench to be re-cleared. Making sniper	30 yds - yds		
8 4	1	20	2/4 Leic	do	Length of duckboards laid. Length of trench left cleared for duckboards. Length of trench to be re-cleared.	30 yds 45 yds - yds	5	Map ref. N 19 c 7.8.5.
7 3	1	18	2/4 Leic	CROCODILE C.T.	Length of duckboards laid. Length of trench left cleared for duckboards. Length of trench to be re-cleared.	60 yds 50 yds 40 yds	5	
7 -	-	21	2/4 Leic	do	Length of duckboards laid. Length of trench left cleared for duckboards. Length of trench to be re-cleared.	40 yds 45 yds - yds	5	Map ref. M 24 b O 5.7.
4 1+4	2	33	2/4 Leic	ADROIT C.T.	New length of trench cleared. Length of trench to be re-cleared.	154 yds	3¾	
1	1	27	2/4 Leic	ABSALOM C.T.	Carrying party.			
6 2+3	2	70	2/4 Leic	CROCODILE C.T.	New length of trench cleaned. Length of trench to be re-cleaned. Carrying party.	75 yds 120 yds -	3½	
3	3	-	-	DAYLIGHT TRACK to ABSALOM C.T.	Length of pack train (Bricks) duckboards.	23 yds - yds	4½	Map ref. M 23 b K. O.
5	1	1	-	CELLARS at APPROACH TR:	Collecting, carrying up + putting in cellars. carrying party.		7	Map ref. N 19 c 9.7.
2	1	25	2/4 Leic				4	
2 2	2	50	1	BLUELINE	Posts { 2 Gunpits + firebays &c		4	
2	1	50	1		{ 3 " " "			

Total length of trench completed:-

ABSALOM — ADROIT C.T. 1278 yds.
CROCODILE C.T. 1148 yds.

Date 3rd Nov. 1917

Basil Stacon Capt.
for O.C. 467th. Field Co. R.E.

Appendix IV

470th. Field Co. R.E.

PROGRESS REPORT - 6 a.m. 3-11-17 to 6 a.m. 4-11-17.

R.E. O.	O.R. Sect	Working Parties O.R.	Batt.	Situation	Work carried out.	Hrs	Remarks.
1	1	25	1/6	CLUCAS TRENCH W. of REDT.	Widening trench, Digging drain & temporarily relaying Duck board.	8	50 yds.
2	1	-	-	-do-	Double duck boards layed on Pulpits & transoms.	8	62 yds.
2	1	-	-	RED TRENCH N. of CLUCAS	20 yds. Duck tops made up & Revetted	8	
2	1	55	1/6	CLUCAS TRENCH W. of RED T.	Clearing trench. Firestep also clearing earth from berm thrown out by day.	6	90 yds. Night Work
1	2	50	1/6	RED TRENCH	Deepening, widening and laying duck board - Ty. 6, 5.10 to T.Y. 4, 2.9	8	All Duckboard track is now completed from CLUCAS to CENTRE TRENCH
1/4	2	-	-	-do- S.5 a 8.5	Constructing 3 firebays	6	Night Work
2	2	50	1/6	IRISH TRENCH	Converting into fire trench S.6 C.17 to S.6 a. 85. 90.	6	Night Work
5	3	50	1/6	CLUCAS TRENCH	Clearing trench and laying duck boards.	8	50 Lin yds.
5	3	5	1/6	NEW ROAD SOUCHEZ CABARET	Laying bordurs road	8	14 do
2	3	3	1/6		Laying duck board tracks from new road to CLUCAS TRENCH	8	46 do
2	3	50	1/6		Finding slag as possible and unloading at MAYSEX.	6	4 trucks Loaded & Unloaded
3	3	40	1/6		Finding slag into 6 wagons & off-loading on road	6	90 Lin yds
2	3	5	1/6		Laying bordurag road	6	10 do -
2	4	45	1/6	CLUCAS TRENCH	Clearing berm on CLUCAS trench.	6	Night Work
6	4	-	-	M23 F.5 M.	Duckboarding & cleaning out CRAZY REDOUBT	8	
1	4	100	1/6	M30 a.18	Worked TAURIDAT REDOUBT, Duckboarding, 20 yds. New track, 32 yds. grip.	6	Night Work
3		10	1/6	M.27 d 60.66	Bepping SOUCHEZ river	8	
4. 80.	9	490					

Field Salmon Capt/
O.C. 470th. Field Co. R.E.

Date 4-11-17

Appendix III

469th. Field Co. R.E.

PROGRESS REPORT – 6 a.m. 3.11.17 to 6 a.m. 4.11.17.

R.E. Sect	Working Parties O.	Working Parties O.R.	Batt.	Situation	Work carried out.	hrs.	Remarks.
1	–	10	–	La Coulette Tr.	Cutting trench under Light Railway, fixing trestles, roadway &c. N.31.c.	6	Night.
2	–	1	M.G.C.	Adept Trench	Constructing M.G. emplacement N.31.d.5.3		
	–	4	"	"	Excavating 2 fire bays. T.3.a.3.5. Revetting 2 fire bays. N.32.d.51.45.		
3	1	52	15*N.& D.	Avion Trench	Replacing sandbag revetment N.32.a.6.4. (2 places). Clearing Trench N.33.c.40.42 to N.33.c.50.42.	6	
4	1	52	17 "	Sullivan Tr.	Revetting 2 fire bays (half completed), N.32.d.9.9.		
4	–	52	15 "	Adept Trench	Carrying 14 "A" frames, 6 hurdles, 500 sandbags.		
4	–			Avion-Denver	1 roll wire, 26 pickets.		
3	–	30	"	Sullivan-Avion	duckboards etc. N.33.c.9.3. (Withdrawn owing to enemy fire)		
4	1	17	"	Sullivan Tr.	Clearing 10 yds trench. N.33.c.9.3. T.3.a.35.45 to T.3.a.30.48.	6	
3	–		"	Avion Trench	Laying 80 yds single duckboard track		
3	–	24	6 "	T.1.c.22.62	Excavating latrine (Completed) T.2.d.25.90.	8	
3	–	4	"	Adept Trench	Clearing for revetting with "A" frames. Revetting with hurdles.		
2	–	7	"	D°.	Widening & deepening 120 yds trench.		
1	–	6	"	Cucas Trench	Repairing trench boards. 32 hurdles fixed.		
1	–	42	"	La Coulotte	Filling sandbags & building up sandbag wall. 10' long, 6' high, for Town Major.		
4	1		"	Avion Trench	Sandbagging 3 fire bays (2 completed). Deepening & widening trench. Relaying 85 yds trenchboards. Berm cleared each side, 85 yds.		
4	1	60		Cucas Trench	Clearing 90 yds trench. Laying 56 yds trench boards. Clearing falls of earth in rear.		
2	–	25		Cucas – Avion	Carrying 20 trenchboards to Cucas; 15 "A" frames to Avion. Unloading at dump.	6	
	–	6		Houchin	First Army Mine School		
1	–	1		Carency	Erecting Nissen huts.		
1	–	1		Chateau de la Haie	Constructing incinerators		
2	–	6		X.10.8.8.2	Repairs to stables, Bricking horse standings &c. R.E. Camp		
	–	4			Runners.		

Date 4.11.17.

[signature] T/Lt.Col. F. Major
O.C. 469th. Field Co. R.E.

Appendix III

467th. Field Co. R.E.

PROGRESS REPORT – 6 a.m. 3rd Nov. to 6 a.m. 4th Nov. 1917.

R.E. O.i.c	Sect.	Working Parties O.	Working Parties O.R.	Batt.	Situation	Work carried out.	Hrs.	Remarks.
4	2	1	16	2/4 Leic	ADROIT C.T. (ABSALOM C.T.)	Length of Duck boards laid... Length of trench left cleared for Duckboards. Length of trench cleared. Length of trench making grip.	5	
2		1	19	2/4 Leic	do	Length of Duckboards laid. Length of trench left cleared for Duckboards. Length of trench cleared.	5	
8	4							
6	3	1	14	2/4 Leic	CROCODILE C.T.	Length of Duck boards laid. Length of trench left cleared for Duckboards. Length of trench cleared.	5	Map ref. N19c 7.5. 8.5.
7		1	20	2/4 Leic	do	Length of Duck boards laid. Length of trench left cleared for Duckboards. Length of trench cleared.	5	
3	1	2	60	2/4 Leic	ADROIT (ABSALOM C.T.)	New length of Batty. cleaned. Length of Batty. now cleaned.	3½	Map ref. M24 b.1.7.5.
4	1	2	60	2/4 Leic	CROCODILE C.T.	New length of Batty. cleaned (but tipping lip is wet from trench). Carrying party.	3	
3	3	1	-	-	DAYLIGHT TRACK. ABSALOM G.T.	Length of Bd. Path laid. (Bricks) (Clearing pile 50 yds.) – yds.	7	Map ref. M23 & 8.0.
5	1	1	12	RFA	CELLARS pt RIDE Rd.	Clearing, connecting up + installing cellars.	7	
5	8	1			CELLARS at APPROACH TR	to corner + commencing stocking cellars.	7	Map ref N19 C 9.7.
1		1	26	Co=1		Preparing fire step for firebays + keeping in firebays.	7	
1		1	28	-2		do	7	
1		1	25	-3		do	7	
1		1	25	-4		do	7	
1		1	12	ARTILLERY	ARTILLERY	No 2 Concrete Gun Emplacement.	7	

Total length of trench accepted B.L.T.

ABSALOM – ADROIT C.T. 1363 yds.
CROCODILE C.T. 1233 yds.

4th November 1917.

A. Brown Lieut.
for O.C. 467th. Field Co. R.E.

Appendix IV

490th. Field Co. R.E.

PROGRESS REPORT - 6 a.m. 4-11-17 to 6 a.m. 5-11-17.

R.E. Sect	Working Parties O.R.	Working Parties Batt.	Situation	Work carried out.	Hrs.	Remarks.
3	1	-	-	TPED TRENCH IN N/CLUCAS	Repairing & Relaying duck boards	8	
16	1	-	-	CLUCAS TRAMWAY W. of RED.T	Laying Double duck boards on Transoms & Pickets	8	1114 yds
1	1	25	196	-do-	Widening trench, digging drain & temporarily relaying duck boards	8.30	"
1	1	44	196	-do-	Clearing bach Burn over 5ft	6	125 " } Night
1	1	4	196	-do-	Unloading stores from train & assisting with above	6	} Work
20	2	55	196	IRISH TRENCH M.6.a.95.96	Excavating and constructing 16 New fire-bays	5	Working party worked 3½ hrs owing to moving on train at LENS JUNCTION
1	2	50	196	-do-	-do-	6	
1	3	50	196	CLUCAS TRENCH	Clearing trench & Laying duck boards	8	140 hrs yds
5	3	5	196	NEW ROAD	Laying & clearing road	2	16 do
5	3	5	196	NEW ROAD N CLUCAS T.	Laying duck board track	6	40 do
2	3	40	196		Loading slag into L.S. Wagons & Spreading on road	6	115 do
3	3	50	196		Loading slag at foot & and unloading at M.19.c.5.x.	6	4 trucks } Night
2	3	5	196		Laying & clearing road	6	} Work
2	3	45	196		Clearing Tack Burn.	6	12 yds }
2	4	-	-	CLUCAS TRENCH M.23.6.8.4.	Duck boarding & clearing out CRAZY REDOUBT	8	
9	4	100	196	M.30 a.1.f.	Duck boarding and road to TRIAUMONT REDOUBT	6	190 mx - Mass. 1105 lb
3		25	196	M.33.9.yo.25	Clearing SOUCHEZ River	8	

Date. 5-11-17.

[signature]
O.C. 490th. Field Co. R.E.

Appendix IV

469th Field Co. R.E.

PROGRESS REPORT – 6 a.m. 4.11.17. to 6 a.m. 5.11.17.

R.E.		Working Parties			Situation	Work carried out.	Hrs.	Remarks.
O.	Sect	O.	O.R.	Batt.				
1			16					
	2	1	4	M.G.C.	La Coulotte Tr.	Cutting Trench under Light Railway. N.31.c. (Completed.)		
		1	4		Adept Trench	Constructing M.G. emplacement. N.31.d.5.3		
		1	53	1/5.Forr	Avion Trench	2 Fire Bays ½ revetted (Cyril June) T.3.a. 25.50.		
					Dº	2 Fire Bays revetted (Beaver June) N.32.d.48.45.		
3		1	42	3rd N. & D.	Sullivan Trench	Completing revetment of 2 Fire Bays, Revetting one other. (5 complete in all)		N.32.d.95.90 to N.32 d.97.88
	4	1	50		Avion – Beaver J.	Carrying 500 sand bags & 26 pickets from La Coulotte Dump.		
	6				Avion – Cyril June	" 500 " 1 coil plain wire, 13. 7' pickets from La Coulotte.		
	2				Sullivan – Beaver	" 500 " " 18 pickets		
					Adept – Cyril Jc	20 "A" frames, & 14 hurdles, from La Coulotte.		
		1	29		Adept Trench	Filling sand bags & revetting one fire bay (completed) "A" frames. Excavating second fire bay, & clearing trench. T.2.d.25.90.		
	2		6		Adept Trench	Fixing 24 hurdles, cutting V waterway & laying trench boards		
	2		6		Dº	55yds extra waterway cut.		
	2		18		Dº	Widening & deepening 70 yds Trench		
			11		Clucas Trench	Fixing 31 "A" frames, & clearing falls.		
			2		La Coulotte	Finishing repairs to quarry, back to Red Trench.		
	4		6		Avion Trench	Reported to Town Major.		
			13		Dº	Carried 13 hurdles, 12 "A" frames, 36 pickets		
		1	45		Dº	1 Firebay completed, 2 Firebays excavated & partly sandbagged. Duckboards laid, Trench cleared of falls, 180 yds. N.32.c.60.55.		
	4	1	58	5"	Clucas Trench	Battering & deepening Trench & laying duckboards, 60 yds. N.26.d.80.05.		
			20		Dº	Carrying duckboards from Dump.		
1					Houchin.	First Army Mine School		
1		1			Carency.	Erecting Nissen Huts.		
2	1		2			Constructing incinerators.		
13		1				Forming brick horse standings, repairing stables, in R.E. Camp and constructing roadway to Transport Lines.	6	
4	4				X.10.6.8.2	Runners.		

Date 5.11.17........   for O.C. 469th Field Co. R.E.

Appendix IV

Sheet 1

457th. Field Co. R.E.

PROGRESS REPORT - 6 a.m. 4th Nov: to 6 a.m. 5th Nov. 1917.

R.E.		Working Parties		Situation	Work carried out.		Hrs.	Remarks.
O.	Sect	O.	O.R.	Batt.				
7	2	1	18	2/4 LEIC	ABSALOM-ADROIT C.T.	Length of A.P. trench cleared. Length of left trench for duckboards. Length of left trench re-cleared.	36 yds. 40 yds. 35 yds.	5
8	4	1	19	2/4 LEIC	do	Length of Aa.P. trench laid. Length of left trench left planked for duckboards. Length of trench re-cleared.	45 yds. 25 yds. — yds.	5	Map ref. N19c 75.7.5.
8	3	1	15	2/4 LEIC	CROCODILE C.T.	Length of A.P. trench laid. Length of trench left planked for duckboards. Length of trench re-cleared.	50 yds. 60 yds. 40 yds.	5
8	2	1	20	2/4 LEIC	do	Length of A.P. trench laid. Length of trench left planked for duckboards. Length of trench re-cleared.	40 yds. 50 yds. — yds.	5	Map ref. M 24 to 15.8.
6		2	74	2/4 LEIC	ABSALOM-ADROIT C.T.	New length of A.P. trench dug. Length of A.P. trench re-cleared. Trench Party.	150 yds. 15 yds.	3½
9		2	74	2/4 LEIC	CROCODILE C.T.	New length of A.P. trench planned. Length of A.P. trench to be cleared. Bandying Party.	100 yds. 58 yds.	3½
		1	2/4 25		Post 1 BLUE LINE { 2 { 3 { 4	Examining fire-steps & trench in the bays. Filling and keeping levelling. do	20	5	Working & prepared officer trial of fire in taken of M.E. type.
		1	26					
		1	26					

Total length of trench completed:
ABSALOM-ADROIT C.T. 1434 yds.
CROCODILE C.T. 1323 yds.

Date: 5th Nov. 1917.

for O.C. 457th Field Co. R.E.

Appx 2.

457th. Field Co. R.E.

PROGRESS REPORT – 6 a.m. 4th Nov. to 6 a.m. 5th Nov. 1917.

R.E.			Working Parties			Situation	Work carried out.	Hrs.	Remarks.
O.	O.R.	Sect	O.	O.R.	Batt.				
1	5	-	1	?	?	GREEN LINE	Modernisation of front line Company Commanders.		(1 man permanently attached to each officers mess)
-	1	4	1	?	?		Constructing reinforced concrete gun emplacements for 295 BDE RFA		
-	1	-	1	?	?	Bde RE DUMP	N.C.O. in charge.		
-	4	-	1	HQ	RFA	RFA Bde HQ	Carrying cement and clothing orders for RFA HQ	8	
-	1	-	1	-	-	Approx M238.2.8.	Instructing M.G.C. in sandbagging.		LANCE CORPL.
-	6	-	1	-	-	V Corps School			
-	5	-	1	-	-	470th F.C. RE HQrs	Course on Dugouts.		
-	6	-	1	-	-	M21c.7.8.	Erection of Nissen Huts.		
-	3	-	1	-	-	do	Sick.		
-	10	-	1	-	-		On guard.		
-	1	-	1	-	-	M21c.7.8.	Runner.		
-	1	-	1	-	-	do	Drawing and transporting stores.		Keeping Company Strength
-	1	-	1	-	-	do	Sanitary.		
-	7	-	1	-	-	do	Cooks.		MENS COOKHOUSES 2, OFFICERS 1, SERGTS MESS 1
-	1	-	1	-	-	do	On leave.		

Date 5th Nov: 1917.

E. Moran Lieut.
for O.C. 457th. Field Co. R.E.

Appendix V

4/10th. Field Co. R.E.

PROGRESS REPORT - 6 a.m. 5-11-14 to 6 a.m. 6-11-14.

R.E.		Working Parties			Situation	Work carried out.	Hrs.	Remarks.
O.	Sect	O.	O.R.	Batt.				
1	1	1	25	1/6	LUCAS TRENCH N. of REDT	Widening trench. Digging drain & temporarily relaying duck boards	8	35 yds
		-	10	1/6	-do-	Carrying duck boards from Dump.	8	
14	1	-	-	-	-do-	Laying Double duck boards on Pickets & Transoms	8	40 yds
3	1	1	50	1/6	-do-	-do-	6	12
20	2	2	144	1/6	IRISH TRENCH	Clearing back from Avn. 5ft	6	170 yds Night work
						Excavating 5 new fire bays and carrying wiring Material from it &c.	6	Night work
9	4	1	30	1/6	M.23 d. 2. H	Duckboarding & clearing out CRAZY REDOUBT	8	Breakdown on line Right
7	4	2	140	1/6	M.30 a.1-8	2nd Last of 200 yds of trench, & carrying wiring material	4	Rain very late. 3 working
2	3	1	4	1/6	S.8 d.	Laying duck board track to CLUCASTRENCH	3	
5	3	-	6	1/6	S.9.	Working between SOUCHEZ & GIVENCHY	3	
5	3	-	-	-		Laying & carrying -do-	3	
21	3	6	290	1/6	M.35 d	Digging cable trench laying cable and filling in.	12	Night work
21		-	-	-		-do-	12	two party consisted of Corps signallers

Date 6-11-14

[signature]
O.C. 4/10th. Field Co. R.E.

Appendix I

469th. Field Co. R.E.

PROGRESS REPORT – 6 a.m. 5.11.17. to 6 a.m. 6.11.17.

R.E.		Working Parties			Situation	Work carried out.	Hrs.	Remarks.
O.	S.R.	Sect	O.	O.R.	Batt.			
2	16	2	—	—	—	La Coulotte	Repairing dug-out to Town Major's instructions.	8	Day
—	2	2	—	21	—	Adept Trench	Wiring in front of Adept Trench, 100 yds.	6	Night
—	1	—	—	—	—	La Coulotte	Carrying party from La Coulotte R.E. Dump.	6	"
—	1	—	—	—	—	Dº	In charge of La Coulotte R.E. Dump.		
—	8	—	—	—	—	Adept Trench	Guide for material from Lens Junction to La Coulotte Dump.		
—	5	—	7	51	15th N & D	Dº	Excavating third fire bay & filling sand-bags. Second fire bay half revetted.	8	T.2.d.25.90
—	2	3	—	20	"	Adept–Cyril Jn	Completing revetment of 2 fire bays (making 3 completed), & excavating 4 others.	6	T.2.d.2.5 to T.2.d.15.32
—	1	—	—	—	"	Cyril–Irish Jn	Carrying 1000 sand bags, 16 "A" frames & 8 hurdles, from La Coulotte.	6	"
—	2	—	—	—	"	Beaver Trench	Fixing latrine seat. T.1.C.1.6.	2	
—	2	—	—	—	"	Cyril Trench	Relaying duckboards where uneven, for 100yds. at T.2.c.25.85.	3	
—	2	—	—	—	"		Repairing broken duckboards, from Ried Trench to 300 yds. S.W. of Lens-Arras Rd.	8	S.12.a.2.6 to S.6.6.95.
—	2	3	1	32	16th	Adept Trench	Deepening & widening 125 yds trench & replacing boards.		
—	3	—	—	14	"	Dº	Fixing 10 "A" frames, excavating 3 fire bays & filling 250 sandbags.		
—	1	—	—	6	"	La Coulotte	Reported to Town Major.		
—	2	4	1	—	9th	Clucas Trench	Clearing trench forward & laying duck boards. 52 yds cleared. N.26.d.95.15	6	Clucas Trench is cleared up to front line.
—	1	—	—	—	5th	Dº	Carrying 33 duckboards, & 33 transoms.		
1	5	1–4	—	—	—	Houchin	First Army Mine School.	1	
1	6	1	—	—	—	Carency	Erecting Nissen Huts.	1	
—	2	1	—	—	—	Chateau de la Haie	Constructing brick incinerators.	1	
—	13	1	—	—	—	X.10.b.8.2	Physical exercises, Box Respirator & Wiring Drill. Forming road, & doing general repairs, in R.E. Camp.	8	
—	4	1–4	—	—	—		Runners.		

Date 6.11.17.

_____ 2 Lieut.
For O.C. 469th. Field Co. R.E.

Appendix V

467th. Field Co. R.E.

PROGRESS REPORT – 6 a.m. 5th Nov. to 6 a.m. 6th Nov. 1917.

R.E.		Working Parties			Situation	Work carried out.	Hrs	Remarks
O.	Sect	O.	O.R.	Batt.				
1	2	1	20	2/4 LEIC	ABSALOM – ADROIT C.T.	Length of trench cleaned. Length of trench left cleaned for duckboards. Trench re-cleaned.	5	
6	4	1	17	2/4 LEIC	do	Length of trench cleaned. Length of trench left cleaned for duckboards. Length of trench re-cleaned.	5	Mat. of N.y.E. £75.
6	3	1	15	2/4 LEIC	CROCODILE C.T.	Length of trench cleaned. Length of trench left cleaned for duckboards. Length of trench re-cleaned.	5	
8		1	20	2/4 LEIC	do	Length of trench cleaned. Length of trench left cleaned for duckboards. Length of trench re-cleaned. For duckboards.	5	Mat. of N.y.E. £25.8.6
3	1	2	46	2/4 LEIC	ABSALOM – ADROIT C.T.	New length of trench cleaned. Length of trench re-cleaned.	4	
4	4	1	24	2/5 S.S.		Company portal.		
1	1	–	27	2/4 LEIC				
9	2+3	2	75	2/5 S.S.	CROCODILE C.T.	New length of trench cleaned. Length of trench re-cleaned. Carrying party.	3½	
		2	75	2/4 LEIC				
1		1	–		(Post H			
1		1	–		" 3			
1		1	12		" 2	Laid duckboards, fire bays &c.	4	
1		1	13		" 1	Cleaned & laid firestep &c.	4	
					BLUE LINE			

Total length of trench cleaned:
ABSALOM – ADROIT C.T. 1499 yds.
CROCODILE C.T. 1423 yds.

6th Nov. 1917. .... for O.C. 467th. Field Co. R.E.

Pkt No 2.

467th. Field Co. R.E.

PROGRESS REPORT - 6 a.m. 5th Nov. to 6 a.m. 6th Nov. '17.

R.E.		Working Parties			Situation	Work carried out.	Hrs.	Remarks.
O.i/c	Sect	O.	O.R.	Batt.				
3	-	1	1	-	DAYLIGHT TRACK to ABSALOM C.7	Road flagging	5	
5	-	1	1	-	GREEN LINE	Water accumulators of Front Line Company Commanders constructing re inforced concrete gun emplacements for 295th Bde R.F.A		
1	-	1	1	-	Bde R.E. Dump	N.C.O. in charge		
1	-	1	1	-				
3	-	1	20	R.F.A.	R.F.A. Bde H.Q.	Clearing, constructing up and erecting collars for R.F.A. H.Q.rs.	8	Day work
3	-	1	20	do	MAP REF Do	do do	6	Night work

Date 6th November 1917.

.... Lieut.
for O.C. 467th. Field Co. R.E.

Appendix V

40th. Field Co. R.E.

PROGRESS REPORT – 6 a.m. 6-11-17 to 6 a.m. 7-11-17.

R.E.		Working Parties			Situation	Work carried out.	Hrs.	Remarks.
O.	O.R.	Sect	O.	O.R. Batt.				
	8	1	-	-	RAILWAY M35 c.2.5 to road M29.d.4.4	Carrying wiring materials from Railway at M.35 c. 1.5.	4	Night
1	13	1	-	-	-do-	150 yds Single Apron Entanglement Erected 150 " Centre Fence Erected	4	Work
1	26	2	-	-	IRISH TRENCH	Erecting single Apron Fence in front of trench for a distance of 500 x. Av from junction of IRSH & C's at reserve.	9	Night-work
	8	3	-	-				
	16	4	-	-	M.30.a	350yds Double Apron from M.30.a.1.9 to M.30.a.0.4 200 " Fence erected from M.30.a.0.4 to M.30.a.0.1	6	Same had to be spent on carrying. Yk Effing did not arrive until 2 a.m. when the infantry had left
	8		-	-				
1	14	3	-	-	NEW ROAD	Laying Corduroy road	6	16 hours Night-work
	1	2				Reconnaissance of STONY CROOK		

Date ....7-11-17......

[signature] Baxter
O.C. 4/0th. Field Co. R.E.

Appendix II

469th. Field Co. R.E.

PROGRESS REPORT - 6 a.m. 6.11.17. to 6 a.m. 7.11.17.

R.E.		Working Parties		Situation	Work carried out.	Hrs	Remarks.
O.	Sect	O.R.	O.R. Batt				
1	1	6	—	La Coulotte.	Preparing wiring material ready for carrying party.	6	Night.
		8	—	Lens-Arras R⁰.	Carrying party for material for H.T.M.B. from Lens-Arras R⁰ to Saskatoon R⁰. Train did not arrive until 5.20 a.m. 7ᵗʰ.	8	Day
	2	9	—	La Coulotte.	Revetting sides of bridge at La Coulotte.	6	Night.
	2	2	—	D⁰	Repairing dug-outs at La Coulotte.	8	
		2	—	D⁰	Guides for R.E. material from Lens Station to La Coulotte Dump.		
1	4	18	—	Adept Trench	Cutting out 3 fire-bays, & sandbag revetting same.		
1	1-4	5	—	Houchin.	First Army Mine School.		
—	1	6	—	Carency.	Erecting Nissen Huts.		
—	1-4	4	—		Runners.		
1	3	31	—		Employed upon various small jobs, preparatory to being relieved by N⁰ 1 Sec.		

Date. 7-11-17.

J.R.R. Whitmore... 2ⁿᵈ Lieut:
for O.C. 469th. Field Co. R.E.

Appendix VI

447th. Field Co. R.E.

PROGRESS REPORT – 6 a.m. 6th Nov. to 6 a.m. 7th Nov. 1917.

Note:- No night work owing to operations.

R.E.		Working Parties				Situation	Work carried out.	Hrs.	Remarks.
O.	Sect	O.	O.R.	Batt.					
7	2	1	18	2/4 Leic	Absalom-Adroit C.T.	Length of Duckboards laid – 40 yds. Length of Trench left cleared for duckboards – 30 yds. Length of Trench re-cleaned.	5	
6	4	1	–	–	do	Length of Duckboards laid – 36 yds. Length of Trench left cleared for duckboards – 20 yds. Length of Trench re-cleaned.	5	Map ref. N9c 8.5, 8.5.
6	3	1	15	2/4 Leic	Crocodile C.T.	Length of Duckboards laid – 50 yds. Length of Trench left cleared for duckboards – 40 yds. Length of Trench re-cleaned – 20 yds.	5	
6	3	1	–	–	do	Length of Duckboards laid – 35 yds. Length of Trench left cleared for duckboards – 35 yds. Length of Trench re-cleaned – – yds.	5	Map ref. N124 & 4. 8.5.
6	1	–	20	–	RFA Bde H.Q.	Placing & cementing concrete reinforcements & collar for RFA H.Q.	8	Day work
3	–	–	20	–	do	do	6	Night work.
1	1	–	–	–	Bde RE Dump	Reconnaissance (reinforced concrete gun-emplacements for 295th Bde RFA)		
1	1	–	–	–	N130, 8.6	Reconnaissance in charge. Company R.E. Dug-outs; strengthening same.		
2	4	–	–	–	Fosse No 6	Collecting coal for cook-houses & billets at Forward H.Q.		

Total length of Trench completed.

Absalom-Adroit C.T. 1575 yds.
Crocodile C.T. 1508 yds.

7th Nov. 1917. for O.C. 447th. Field Co. R.E.

Appendix IV

470th Field Co. R.E.

PROGRESS REPORT - 6 a.m. 7/11/17 to 6 a.m. 8/11/17.

R.E.		Working Parties			Situation	Work carried out.	Hrs.	Remarks.
O.C.	Sect	O.	O.R.	Batt.				
1	1	1	50	178	LUCAS TRENCH W.H.GIVENCHY	Clearing back Berm over 5ft	6	120 yds
8	1	-	10	178	CITE DES GARENNES	6 lorries carrying materials from railway	4	
9	1	-	-	-	M29 d 47 to M29 d 95	150 yds Double Apron. Finished less 3 Horizontal wires. 150 " Centre Fence erected	6½	Infantry working separate } Night Work
26	2	2	200	178	PHELAN TRENCH	Finishing Apron Fence. Clearing trench & cutting O.T. from Drawn to Codger trenches for a distance of 150 yds	6	Night Work
1	3	3	-	-	LUCAS TRENCH	Duckboard track between NEWROAD & LUCAS TRENCH Cutting Berm	8	100 yds
2	3	1	50	178	NEW RD.	Loading slag into G.S. Wagons & spreading on road	6	150 "
4	3	1	35	178	do.	Laying bordure on New Road	6	24 "
8	3	-	5	178		Loading timber. Unloading at site	6	4 Loads
4	3	-	-	-		Taking notice boards to BROWN LINE & Guides.	6	
2	3	-	-	-			6	With the exception of a 50 yds gap there is some wire the entire way from M24 c.10. to M29 b.8.5.
10	4	-	-	-	M29 d	100 yds of fence improved to Double Apron M30 a 1.4. to M30 a 0.3 50 " " Double apron fence from M30 B 0.9 to M30 a 5 M29 c.10. to M29 d.8.5. 200 " " Fence from ASSIGN TRENCH TO M29 d.8.5.	8	M24 c.10. to M29 b.8.5.
1	4	1	100	178	M30.a.18.	Digging drains, improving trenches & carrying wire	4	Only 100 infantry. These arrived at 8.30 p.m.

Date 8.11.17

_____ Capt. R.E.
O.C. ....th.Field Co. R.E.

Appendix VI

469th Field Co. R.E.

PROGRESS REPORT – 6 a.m. 7.11.17. to 6 a.m. 8.11.17.

R.E.		Working Parties		Situation	Work carried out.	Hrs	Remarks.
C.R.	Sect	O.	O.R. Batt.				
2		-	-	-	La Coulotte	Preparing wiring material ready for carrying party	8	Day.
8		-	35	-	Adept Trench	Carried material for 300 yds wire, & put out 100 yds double apron wire fence	6	Night.
10	1	-	20	-	N.26.c.3.	Carrying material from La Coulotte to T.M.B. emplacement.	6	"
2		-	-	-		Making necessary improvements to billets for winter occupation	8	Day.
7		1	50	-	Adept Trench	Widening & deepening left of trench, 75 yds.	6½	Day
-		-	-	-	Cyril Junction	Cutting fire bays & altering existing bays.	6½	"
2		-	-	-	La Coulotte	Repairing trench boards	6½	"
2	2	2	50	-	Avion Trench	Dug-out repairs (for Town Major)	6½	"
3		2	50	-	Cyril-Avion Tr.	Clearing berm, widening, deepening, & clearing trench, left of Cyril.	6½	Night.
2		2	60	-	Adept-Avion	Clearing berm & bottom of trench, 150 yds, forward	6½	"
2		2	50	-	Adept Trench	Carrying materials from La Coulotte.	6½	"
						Clearing berm, widening & deepening trench, emptying sandbags		
						150 yds cleared, left of Cyril.		
13		1	24	6th N.St.	Adept Trench	Cutting firebays & revetting same. 5 bays under construction	WIRE 7	
1		-	6	-	La Coulotte	Reported to Town Major	line 5	
1		1	27	-	Columbia Tr.	Clearing 60 yds berm each side & completing sump pit. Completing latrine at N.36.a.6.0.10	4½	
1	4	1	40	-	Avion Trench	Clearing 75 yds berm each side, deepening & widening trench. Excav. 2 firebays	6	
1		1	19	-	Lucas Trench	Clearing 70 yds berm each side, battering & clearing out trench	6	
2		1	38	-	Adept Trench	" 75 " " " & clearing out falls.	6	
					Do	Carrying 15 sheets expanded metal, 70 angle iron pickets, 1 coil plain wire	6	
5	1-4	-	-	-	Houchin.	First Army Mine School		
6	3	-	-	-	Carency.	Erecting Nissen Huts.		
25	5	-	-	-	X.10.b.8.2	Baths. Kit Inspection &c.	8	
4	1-4	-	-	-		Runners		

Date. 8.11.17 ....

H.R.Barkletny .... 2nd Lieut.

for O.C.469th.Field Co. R.E.

Appendix III.

Sheet No. 1.

467th Field Coy R.E.

Progress Report – 6 am 7th Nov. to 6 am 8th Nov. 1917

R.E.			Working Parties					
O.R.	SECT.	O.	O.R.	BATT.	SITUATION.	WORK CARRIED OUT.	HRS	REMARKS.
8	1		20	2/5 LINC.	ABSALOM-ADROIT C.T.	Length of Duckboards laid. Length of Trench left cleaned for duckboards. Length of Trench re-cleaned.	5	INFANTRY PARTY ½ HOUR LATE.
8	4	1	19	2/5 LINC.	do	Length of Duckboards laid. Length of Trench left cleaned for duckboards. Length of Trench re-cleaned.	5	do do
6	3	1	20	2/5 LINC.	CROCODILE C.T.	Length of Duckboards laid. Length of Trench left cleaned for duckboards. Length of Trench re-cleaned.	5	Rey Labor
7		1	21	2/5 LINC.	do	Length of Duckboards laid. Length of Trench left cleaned for duckboards. Length of Trench re-cleaned.	5	
3	4	2	48	2/7 SHERWOOD	ABSALOM-ADROIT C.T.	New length of Bottom cleaned Trench. Length of Berm reclaimed. Carrying party.	4	Rightrate.
6		2	56	2/5 LINC.	do	New length of Berm cleaned. Length of Berm reclaimed. Carrying party.	4	
1		-	27	SHERWOODS				
3		2	61	2/5 LINC.	CROCODILE C.T.	New length of Berm cleaned Trench. Length of Berm reclaimed. Carrying party.	3½	
6		2	78	2/7 SHERWOODS	do	New length of Berm cleaned. Length of Berm reclaimed. Carrying party.	3½	

26 yds. 30 yds. – yds.
36 yds. 35 yds. – yds.
50 yds. 60 yds. 30 yds.
45 yds. 50 yds. – yds.
144 yds.
200 yds. yds.
160 yds. yds.
160 yds. yds.

Date 8th Nov. 1917.

Total length of Trench completed.

ABSALOM-ADROIT C.T. 1561 yds.
CROCODILE C.T. 1518 yds.

D. B. Irwin Major
O.C. 467th Field Coy R.E.

Appendix VII

467th Field Coy. R.E.

Sheet No. 2. Progress Report – 6 a.m. 7th Nov: to 6 a.m. 8th Nov: 1917.

RE	WORKING PARTIES			SITUATION	WORK CARRIED OUT.	HRS.	REMARKS.
O OR SECT	O	OR	BATT				
8	1	20	2/5 ABSALOM ADDITG.I.	ABSALOM ADDIT G.I.			
1 {2	1	50	2/5 LEIC	Post 1	Excavating Trench & sandbagging	4	
2	1	29	2/5 LEIC	" 2	do	4	
1 {2	1	47	2/5 LEIC	" 3	Excavating Firebay & sandbagging	4	
1	1	18	2/5 LEIC	BLUE LINE " 4	do	4	
1	6			GREEN LINE.	Under instructions of front line Company Commanders		
4				DAYLIGHT TRACK to ABSALOM C.T.	Camouflaging	5.	
1	1			RFA BDE H.Q.	Constructing reinforced concrete gun emplacements for RFA 295th BDE.		
4				do	do do for RFA H.QRS		
3				do	Clearing, Connecting up + Starting collar for RFA H.QRS	8	Day
					do do do		Night
1	1			BDE RE DUMP.	N.C.O. in charge.		

Date: 8th Nov: 1917.

† B. Jews. Major
OC. 467th Field Coy. R.E.

Appendix VII

490th. Field Co. R.E.

PROGRESS REPORT - 6 a.m. 8-11-17 to 6 a.m. 9-11-17.

R.E. O.R.	Working Parties O.	O.R.	Sect	Batt.	Situation	Work carried out.	hrs	Remarks.
1	1	40	1	1/8	CLUCAS TRENCH IN BIRTHDAY VILLAGE	Clearing Trench & digging drain & relaying Duck boards where trench was flooded.	8	
1	1	10	1	1/8	TED TRENCH N OF CLUCAS	Repairing, relaying & replacing old duck boards with new	8	1300hrs } Night
1	1	50	1	1/8	CLUCAS T ON ONENCHEN	Clearing back from over 6ft	6	} Work
1	-	-	1	-	CLUCAS RES. TRENCHES	300 yds of Route Apren fence completed	5½	
-	-	-	-	-				
1	2	10	3	1/8	CHEDDAR TRENCH	Laying duck board transport forward to CLUCAS TRENCH	9	1030hrs Night
2	2	50	3	1/8	"	Cutting Berm	6	4yds no }
2	-	35	3	1/8		Grading sides and spreading on road	5	12 Losses } Work
2	3	-	3	1/8		Laying 60 duckways	6	
3	3	5	3	1/8		Leading sundries	6	
-	-	-	-	-				
1	4	-	4	-	M 29 d	Improving length of M.L.W. commenced yesterday and completing 50 yds gap.	6	
1	4	30	4	1/8	M 30 a 1.8	Drainage Tranmont TEDIVOT.	5	}Night
4	-	53	4	1/8	M 29 B.9.H.	Digging S.T from CRAZY to CROCODILE trench & clearing out CRAZY	6	}Work
5	3	25	3	1/8	M 30 a 1.8	Digging 2nd line back and drawing same	6	
1	4	20	4	1/8	"	Barrying stores	6	
1	-	-	1	1/8		Digging drainage	6	
-	-	-	-	-				
1	20	170	2	1/8	PHELAN TRENCH	Continuing digging, deepening & clearing from DAWSON to CADGER TRENCHES.	6	}Work

Date 9-11-17

[signature]
O.C. 490th. Field Co. R.E.

Appendix VIII

469th. Field Co. R.E.

PROGRESS REPORT — 6 a.m. 8.11.17. to 6 a.m. 9.11.17.

R.E.		Working Parties			Situation	Work carried out.	Hrs	Remarks.
O.	Sect	O.	O.R.	Batt.				
5		1	-	-	Columbia & Saskatoon June	Making Heavy Trench Mortar Emplacements. N.26.c.3.	8	Day
6	1	1	-	-	S.19.d.1.8.	Improving billets for winter occupation	6	Night.
7		2	44	-	Adept Trench	150 yds double apron wire fence erected	7	Day. (Left of Cyril.)
					N.26.c.3.	Carrying material from train to T.M.B. emplact		
8		1	26	-	Adept Trench	Cutting fire bays, filling sandbags, laying trench boards, revetting worst parts. Widening 116 yds	6	Night
2		2	50	-	Avion Trench	Widening, preparing bottom, clearing berm, cutting firebays. (Left of Cyril).	6½	"
2	2	2	50	-	Cyril Trench	Clearing bottom & berm (Adept forward) 140 yds	7	"
4		2	100	-	Adept Trench	Cutting fire steps, emptying sandbags, clearing berm, preparing bottom (Left of Cyril.)		
2		-	-	18th N.Staff	La Coulotte	For trench boards, carrying materials. Repairing dug-outs for Town Major		
4		1	10	-	Adept Trench	Fixing 14 "A" frames, excavating 2 fire bays. Revetted 2 fire steps.	R.E. 8	
2	1	1	4	-	D°	Completed revetting of 3 fire bays.	INF 7	
3		1	10	-	D°	Deepened & widened 30 yds trench		
-		1	6	-	La Coulotte	Reported to Town Major	5½	(Task)
3		1	19	-	Columbia Trench	Completing sump pit & latrine. 40 yds berm cleaned	6	(Task)
3	4	1	30	-	Avion Trench	50 yds Trench deepened & duckboards temp'y relaid. One firebay completed.	6	
1		1	38	-	Lucas Trench	Clearing 130 yds Berm each side. Battering trench sides & clearing falls.	6	
2		1	57	-	Adept Trench	150 " " Backing up firebays.		
2		1	20	-	Avion Trench	Carrying 22 trench boards & 12 "A" frames		11 men reported as arranged @ 8:30 p.m.
5	1-4	-	-	-	Houchin	First Army Mine School		
4	1-4	-	-	-		Runners		
6	3	-	-	-		Erecting Nissen Huts		
20	3	-	-	-	Carency X.10.b.2	Constructing 30 S.yds Transport R., R.E. Camp, Camp Services	8	
						Lecture on Wiring Drill.		

| 93. | - | 15 | 444 | |

Date 9 Nov. 1917.

.... Lieut.
for O.C. 469th. Field Co. R.E.

Sheet No 1.   Appendix VIII

467th. Field Co. R.E.

PROGRESS REPORT – 6 a.m. 8th Nov to 6 a.m. 9th Nov. 1917.

R.E. Sect	O.R. O.	Working Parties O.R.	Batt.	Situation	Work carried out.	Hrs	Remarks.
7	1	20	2/5 Lincs.	ABSALOM–ADROIT C.T.	Length of Duckboards laid. 30 yds Length of Trench left cleared for duckboards. 35 yds Length of Trench reclaimed. 30 yds	5	⎫ ⎪ ⎪ DAY WORK. ⎬ ⎪ ⎪ ⎭
8	1	20	2/5 Lincs.	do.	Length of Duckboards laid. 20 yds Length of Trench left cleared for duckboards. 50 yds Length of Trench reclaimed. yds	5	
6	1	20	2/5 Lincs.	CROCODILE C.T.	Length of Duckboards laid. 60 yds Length of Trench left cleared for duckboards. 100 yds Length of Trench reclaimed. 40 yds	5	
6	1	20	2/5 Lincs.	do.	Length of Duckboards laid. 60 yds Length of Trench left cleared for duckboards. 100 yds Length of Trench reclaimed. yds	5	
5	2	67	7th Leic.	ABSALOM–ADROIT C.T.	New length of Berm cleared of Trench. 120 yds Length of Berm reclaimed. 20 yds Carrying Party. yds	3¾	⎫ ⎪ ⎪ NIGHT WORK. ⎬ ⎪ ⎪ ⎭
3	2	67	3/4 Leic.	do.	New length of Berm cleared of Trench. 220 yds Length of Berm reclaimed. yds Carrying Party. yds	3¾	
4	2	69	2/5 Lincs.	CROCODILE C.T.	New length of Berm cleared of Trench. 120 yds Length of Berm reclaimed. yds Carrying Party. yds	3¾	
4	1	1/4	2/5 Lincs.	do.	New length of Berm cleared of Trench. yds Length of Berm reclaimed. 110 yds Carrying Party. yds	3¾	

TOTAL LENGTH OF TRENCH COMPLETE

ABSALOM – ADROIT C.T. 1687 yds.
CROCODILE C.T. 1723 yds.

Date 9th Nov 1917.

Basil E. Sta......
O.C. th. Field Co. R.E.

Sheet No. 2

467th. Field Co. R.E.

PROGRESS REPORT - 6 a.m. 8th Nov. to 6 a.m. 9th Nov. 1917.

R.E.		Working Parties			Situation	Work carried out.	Hrs.	Remarks.
O.	Sect	O.	O.R.	Batt.				
2	4	1	14	1/5 Leic.	Post 1 ⎫	Sandbagging Excavating	4	
	1	1	36	do	" 2 ⎬ BLUE LINE	do.	4	
	1	1	27	do	" 3 ⎪	do.	4	
	1	1	40	do	" 4 ⎭	do.	4	
1	4	—	—	—	GREEN LINE	Under instructions of Front line Company Commanders.		
	4	—	—	—	Daylight track to ABALOM C.T.	Laying duckboards and making steps etc. 30 yds	5	
	1	1	—	—	R.F.A. Bde. H.Q.	Constructing reinforced concrete gun emplacements for 295th Bde. R.F.A.		
	4	1	—	—	do.	Clearing connecting up & strutting cellars for R.F.A. H.Q.	8	Day.
	3	—	—	—		do.	6	Night.

..............9th Nov 1917.....

David C. Heaven...........
O.C. ....th. Field Co. R.E.

Appendix IX

490th. Field Co. R.E.

PROGRESS REPORT — 6 a.m. 9-11-14 to 6 a.m. 10-11-14.

R.E. O.C.	C.R.	Sect	Working Parties O.	O.R.	M.G. Batt.	Situation	Work carried out	hrs	Remarks
1	1	1	1	44	198	Lucas Trench in Givenchy	Clearing out Mud, Draining & duck boarding	8	
1	1	1	1	4	198	Red Trench N of Givers	Retaping Duck boards, Digging drain, relaying duckboards	8	
1	12	1	–	–	–	Givers N.W. of Red	Single Duck board party, Piquets & forms	3	30 yds Night
1	3	1	–	–	–	do	Clearing fire road, thrown on Bern by Day party	3	8 Work
1	1	1	1	49	198	do	Clearing falls in trench	6	
							Clearing back Bern. Over 6ft	6	130 yds
1	19	2	1	80	198	C.T. between Dawson's & Deer Trenches	Deepened from 4ft to 4½ft over ½ft	1½	160 Rmo * The party started about whilst
1		2	1	67	198			6	200 yds digging wounded 4 men to
1		2		46	19D	Dawson Tr	Clearing out trench	5	taken off and put Dawson
2	3	3		10	198	new R.E. dugout	Both Mat track from new R.E. to Lucas Trench	3½	3½ yds
2	3	3	1	50	198	Olivers T.	Cutting Bern	8	
4	6	3	1	35	M.E.		Grading slag & spreading on road	6	100 tons
3	3	3	–	5	M.E.		Laying Cordwroy road	6	Night
							Loading & Unloading Timber	6	14 H Loads Work
1	10	4	1	26	148	M 30. a 1.8	Draining Triangle Redoubt	6	
1	9	4	–	30	198	M 23. b. 8H	Widening & clearing of C.T. from Crazy to Curry Crook	6	
1	5	3	–	15	198	M 38.d. 1.3	Draining & Wiring round S.P.	8	Night
1	6	4	1	110	198	do	Digging 2nd & 3rd lines	6	Work

Date ...10-11-14...

O.C. 490th Field Co. R.E.

Appendix IX

469th. Field Co. R. E.

PROGRESS REPORT - 6 a.m. 9.11.17. to 6 a.m. 10.11.17.

R.E.		Working Parties			situation	Work carried out.	Hrs	Remarks.
O.R.	Sect	O.	O.R.	Batt				
4	1	1	—	—	Columbia & Saskatoon Junc. S.16.9.1.8.	Making Heavy Trench Mortar Emplacement N.26.c.3	8	Day
3	1	1	—	—		Making necessary improvements to Billets for Winter Accommodation	8	"
10		—	30	G.N.Staff	Adept Trench	Carrying wiring material from La Coulotte, & erecting 170 yds Double Apron Fence	6	Night
7		1	50	—	Adept Trench	Revetting 30 yds "A" Frames, Widening 100 yds Trench. Revetting 4 Fire Steps	7	Day (Right of Cyril Tr.)
2	2	2	50	—	Cyril Trench	Widening & clearing trench bottom & berm, 100 yds. (Avion back)		
2		2	50	—	Cyril-Adept Tr.	Widening berm, 200 yds. (Forward)		
1		1	50	—	Adept Trench	Carrying stores from La Coulotte Dump		
3		3	100	—	— Do —	Cutting fire bays. Clearing 300 yds berm each side (Left of Cyril).	5	Night.
3		1	10	G.N.Staff	Adept Trench	Deepening & widening 30 yds Trench	6¾	
6		1	11	—	— Do —	Fixing 2) "A" Frames, & Revetting 3 Fire Steps	6	
3		1	6	—	La Coulotte Tr.	Reported to Town Major	5	
2		1	25	—	Columbia Tr.	Clearing 130 yds Berm each side		
	4	1	46	—	Avion Trench	Laid 20 yds Trench Deepened & Duckboards 30 Excavated 1 Firebay & Sump at N.32 c.55.60	6	
1		1	15	—	Clucas Trench	80 yds Berm cleared each side, & Falls cleared	9	
2		1	15	—	Adept Trench	100 " " " " " " "		
					Avion Trench	Carried 25, 2ft "A" Frames, 25 Sheets Ex.M, 12 Angle Iron Pickets, 14 Duckboards		
2		1	25	—	Clucas Trench	5 Latrine Boxes	4½	
1	1-4	—	—	—	Houchin	First Army Mine School		
4	1-4	—	—	—		Runners		
6	3	1	—	—	Carency	Erecting Nissen Huts		
20	3	1	—	—	X.10.b.8.2	Constructing 10 yds Road for Transport. R.E. Camp. Camp Services. S.B.R. Drill. Changing Containers in Box Respirators	7	

Date. 10th. Nov. 1917.

M.W. Bennett .... Capt.
For O.C. 469th. Field Co. R.E.

Appendix IX

Sheet No. 1.

___th. Field Co. R.E.

PROGRESS REPORT – 6 a.m. 9th Nov. to 6 a.m. 10th Nov. 1917

R.E.		Working Parties			Situation	Work carried out.	Hrs.	Remarks.
O.C.	Sect	O.	O.R.	Batt.				
5		1	17	1/5 Linc.	ABSALOM ADROIT C.T.	Length of Breastworks laid. Length of trench with top protection wires. Length of trench cleaned.	5	
5	4	1	20	1/5 Linc.	do.	Length of Breastworks laid. Length of trench with top protection for duckboards. Length of trench deepened.	4½	
6	3	1	20	1/5 Linc.	CROCODILE C.T.	Length of Duckboards laid. Length of trench top covered for duckboards. Length of trench deepened.	5	AT WORK
7		1	20	1/5 Linc.	do.	Length of Duckboards laid. Length of trench with clearance for duckboards. Length of trench deepened.	5	
		1	28	1/5 Linc.	ABSALOM FORRESTER	New length of Trench opened. Length of Bath reclaimed. Carrying Party.	3	
	3	2	55	1/5 Linc.	do.	New length of Trench cleaned. Length of Paths reclaimed. Carrying Party.	3	
		2	17	1/5 Manchesters	CROCODILE C.T.	New length of Trench opened. Length of Bath reclaimed. Carrying Party.	2½	WET WORK
	3	2	55	1/5 Manchesters	do.	New length of Trench opened. Length of Bath reclaimed. Carrying Party.	2½	

TOTAL LENGTH OF TRENCH COMPLETED.
ABSALOM – ADROIT C.T. 16,87 yds.
CROCODILE C.T. 17,23 yds.

Date 10th Nov. 1917.

O.C. ___th. Field Co. R.E.

Sheet No 2.

467th. Field Co. R.E.

PROGRESS REPORT – 6 a.m. 9th Nov. to 6 a.m. 10th Nov. 1917.

R.E.		Working Parties			Situation	Work carried out.	Hrs.	Remarks.
C.R.	Sect	O.	O.R.	Batt.				
1	2	1	49	2/5 Leic.	Post 1.	2 Firebays excavating sandbagging	3	
1	2	1	46	2/5 Leic.	" 2.	3 " Clearing & excavating trench.	3	
1	1	1	21	2/5 Leic.	" 3.	Excavating Trench.	4	
1	1	1	12	2/5 Leic.	" 4.	do do	4	
1	5	–	–	–	GREEN LINE. Daylight Track to Absalom C.T.	Under instructions of Front line Company Commanders. Length of Track laid { Bricks Duckboards Camouflaging etc. 30 yds	5	
1	4	–	–	–	R.F.A. Bde.HQ	Constructing reinforced concrete gun emplacements per 2/5th Bde.R.F.A.		
–	1	1	–	–				
–	3	–	–	–	467th Field Co.R.E.	Cleaning, connecting up & grouting cell ages for R.F.A. Bde. H.Q.	8	
–	6	–	–	–	Bde.R.E. Dump.	Repairing torpid Billets. do		
–	3	–	–	–		N.C.O. in charge + 2 Sappers		2 Sappers employed altering replacement spindles for strong point in front line.

Date: 10th Nov. 1917.

.... O.C. 467th. Field Co. R.E.

Appendix X

470th. Field Co. R.E.

PROGRESS REPORT – 6 a.m. 10/11/14 to 6 a.m. 11/11/14

R.E.			Working Parties				Work carried out.	hrs.	Remarks.
O.	O.R.	Sect	O.	O.R.	Batt.	Situation			
1	16	1	–	–	–	CADGER TR. W. of DAWSON	Clearing out timber etc. from bottom of trench	4	4 Hours.
1	–	1	–	22	1/8	IRISH TRENCH N. of LUCAS	Deepening firebays & traverses	6	50 " Nightwork
	2	2	1	50	1/8	LUCAS TR.	Clearing trench	8	
	24	2	–	–	–	do	do	4	
	2	3	–	–	–	YEW RD & BLUNDERT	Laying duck board walk from New rd. to LUCAS TRENCH	8	8 Hours
	9	3	–	–	–	LUCAS T	Clearing trench.	5	
	10 5 1	4 3 1	–	–	–	M.30.a.18	Draining TRAUMONT REDOUBT	8	
	2	4	–	30	1/8	M.23 & B.H.	Cleaning C.T. from CRAZY to CRONY REDOUBTS and Duck boarding in CRAZY Redoubt.	6	
	2 6	4 3	1	40	1/E	M.30.a.18	Clearing Dugn. Draining, and digging 3rd Jacks in TRAUMONT Redoubt	6	6 Nightwork

Date 11-11-14

[signature] Capt.
O.C. 470th Field Co. R.E.

Appendix X

469th Field Co. R.E.

PROGRESS REPORT – 6 a.m. 10.11.17. to 6 a.m. 11.11.17.

R.E.		Working Parties			Situation	Work carried out.	Hrs	Remarks.
O.	Sect	O.	O.R.	Batt.				
	4				Columbia & Saskatoon Junc.	Making Dug-out at N.26.c.3	8	Day
	4				D°	D°	6	Night.
1	1		20	2nd N. Staff	Saskatoon Rd.	Unloading Rails & Carrying to Saskatoon Road	8	"
	6				La Coulotte Tr.	Widening trench under bridge for 12 ft. ready to receive trestles for bridge	8	Day & Night.
	2		8	"	Clucas Trench	Erecting camouflage in Front Line, top of Clucas	8	Night.
	2				S.16.a.1-8	Improving billets for winter occupation	8	Day.
	11	2	50	2nd N. Staff	Adept Trench	Making firebays, revetting & fixing "A" frames. Making fire step. (from Cyril)	8	"
	3	1	50	"	D°	Carrying 14 hurdles from La Coulotte Dump	6	Night.
	3	1	50	"	Cyril Trench	Clearing & making 80 yds Berm both sides. 60 yds trench cleared	6	"
	5	1	4	16th N. Staff	Adept Trench	Fixing trenchboards & 11 "A" frames	6	"
	4		14	"	Clucas Tr.	Clearing falls & trench bottom	8	"
	1		6	"	La Coulotte	Reported to Town Major	6	"
	3	1	34	"	La Coulotte Tr.	Clearing 80 yds Berm each side & clearing trench bottom	6	"
	2	2	45	"	D°	" 130 "	6	"
	2	1	32	"	Clucas Trench	60 yds trench & berm cleared	6	"
	2	1	23	"	Avion Trench	Carried trench boards to Avion trench	6	"
	16	3			X.10.b.8.2	Wiring Drill & Lecture	6	"
	4	3			D°	On Camp Services		
	6	3			Cargency	Erecting Nissen Huts		
	5	1.4				On Courses of Instruction		
	4	1.4				Runners		

Date 11-.11-.17....

W.M.White Lieut.
for O.C. 469th Field Co. R.E.

Sheet. No.1.   467th Field Co. R.E.   Appendix X

PROGRESS REPORT — 6 a.m. 10th Nov. to 6 a.m. 11th Nov 1917.

R.E.		Working Parties			Situation	Work Carried Out		Hrs.	Remarks
O.R.	Sgt.	O.	O.R.	Battn.					
5	–	–	1	20	2/5 Lines.	ABSALOM – ADROIT C.T.	Length of Duckboards laid Length of Trench left cleared for duckboards Length of Trench re-cleaned	– yds. – yds. 40 yds.	5
7	4	–	1	19	2/5 Lines.	do.	Length of duckboards laid Length of Trench left cleared for duckboards Length of Trench re-cleaned	40 yds. 40 yds. – yds.	6	Trench in bad condition owing to putting in of slabs.
6	3	–	1	15	3/5 Lines.	CROCODILE C.T.	Length of Duckboards laid Length of Trench left cleared for duckboards Length of Trench re-cleaned	20 yds. 80 yds. – yds.	5
7	–	–	1	20	2/5 Lines.	do.	Length of Duckboards laid Length of Trench left cleared for duckboards Length of Trench re-cleaned	25 yds. 40 yds. 40 yds.	6	3 sappers + 7 inf. employed in repairing duckboards + clearing up in rear owing to falling in of trench sides.
7	–	–	1	25	2/5 Lines.	ABSALOM – ADROIT C.T.	New length of Berm cleared Length of Berm reclaimed Carrying Party. Desultry cutting	100 yds. 45 yds.	4
8	3	–	2	26	2/5 Lines.	CROCODILE C.T.	New length of Berm cleared Length of Berm reclaimed Carrying Party.	120 yds.	4
1	–	–	–	15					
–	–	1	1	40	–	ABSALOM – ADROIT C.T. "G" Party.	Berm reclaimed. Improving + cuttings. Carrying Party.	50 yds.	

TOTAL LENGTH OF TRENCH COMPLETE.

ABSALOM – ADROIT C.T.   1647 yds.
CROCODILE C.T.   1888 yds.

Date. 11th Nov. 1917.   O.C. 467th Field Co. R.E.

Sheet No. 2.

467th Field Co. R.E.

PROGRESS REPORT 6 a.m. 10th Nov. to 6 a.m. 11th Nov. 1917.

R.E.		Working Parties.			Situation	Work carried out.	Hrs.	Remarks.
O.	Sect.	O.	O.R.	Batln.				
-	1	1	17	25 Leic:	Post 1 } Blue Line	2 Firebays in progress.	4	
-	2	1	39	2/5 Leic:	" 2 }	3 Firebays in progress.	3½	
-	1	1	30	2/5 Leic:	" 3 }	5 Firebays in progress	4	
-	2	1	29	2/5 Leic:	" 4 }	" " "	4	
-	1	5	-	-	GREEN LINE.	Under instructions of Front line Company Commanders		
-	-	-	-	-	Daylight Track to Absalom C.T.	Length of Track laid {Bricks Duckboards — yds — yds	5	
-	-	4	-	-		Camouflaging etc.		
-	1	1	-	-	Bde. H.Q.	Constructing concrete gun emplacements for 295th Bde. R.F.A.		
-	-	4	-	-		Cleaning, connecting up & starting cellars for R.F.A. Bde. H.Q.	8	
-	1	1	-	-	Bde. R.E. Dump.	N.C.O. in charge.		
-	-	10	-	-	467 Field Co R.E.	Repairing Forward Billets etc.		

Date. 11th Nov. 1917.

O.C. 467th Field Co. R.E.

S E C R E T.   Appendix A

                                                              Copy No. 10

                    59th. Divisional R.E. Order No.4

                                 by

             Lieut.Colonel.G.B.Roberts, R.E. C.R.E.59th.Division.

                    _____

Ref. 1/40,000.
Sheets 36 b & c.   12.11.17.

1.   The 59th.Division (less Artillery) will be relieved
by the 1st Canadian Division (less Artillery).
        The relief is to be completed by 6 p.m. 18th.November.

2.   "A" and "B" Infantry Brigade Groups 1st Canadian Division
will come under the orders of G.O.C. 59th.Division on their
arrival in the forward area.

3.   "A" Canadian Brigade will relieve 177th Inf.Bde. in the
LENS Sector, and "B" Canadian Brigade will relieve the 176th
Inf.Bde. in the AVION Sector. The details of the relief to
be arranged between the Brigades concerned.

4.   The command of the LENS Sector will pass from the G.O.C.
177th.Inf.Bde. to G.O.C. "A" Canadian Brigade on completion
of relief 14/15 November.

5.   The command of the Divisional front will pass from the
G.O.C. 59th.Division to G.O.C. 1st Canadian Division at 10 a.m.
17th.November.

6.   The actual time of reliefs on the evening of the 17th
will be arranged by the O.C. Field Companies concerned.

7.   Two officers and 10 other ranks per Field Company will
remain in the forward area until 6 p.m. on the evening of
the 18th for the purpose of showing the relieving Field
Companies the work on hand in their respective sectors.

8.   The completion of relief on the night 17/18th will
be reported by O.C. Companies to C.R.E. by wire.

9.   The reliefs of Field Companies will take place in
accordance with the attached Movement Table.

10.   ACKNOWLEDGE.

                                        Captain & Adjutant for
                                        C.R.E. 59th.Division.

Issued at noon

Copy No. 1.   59th.Division G.
         2.   59th.Division Q.
         3.   176th.Inf.Bde.
         4.   C.R.E. 59th.Division.
         5.   C.R.E. 1st.Canadian Division.
         6.   O.C. 59th.Divisional Train.
         7.   O.C. 467th.Field Co. R.E.
         8.   O.C. 469th.Field Co. R.E.
         9.   O.C. 470th.Field Co. R.E.
        10.   War Diary.
        11.   "

DIVISIONAL R.E. MOVEMENT TABLE.

59th. Divisional R.E. / 1st. Canadian Divl. Engineers.

Date.	Unit.	Details.	From	To	Unit	Details	From	to	Remarks.
10 a.m. 17th.	Hd.Qtrs.	-	CHATEAU de la HAIE	Out.	Hd.Qtrs.	-	HERSIN - NOULETTE Area.	CHATEAU de la HAIE.	
10 a.m. 17th.	Divisional Dumps.	1 Officer 40 Other rks.	LENS June.R.E.Dump X.12.c.1.9.	Out.	Divl. Dumps.	1 Officer. 40 Other ranks.	do.	LENS June.R.E. DUMP.X.12.c.1.9.	
Night of 17/18th.	467th.Fld. Co.R.E.	4 sections less transpt.	Forward billets M.21.c.70.90.	Rear billets X.4.b.25.25.	1st. Fld.Co.	4 sections less transport.	HERSIN - NOULETTE Area.	Forward billets M.21.c.70.90.	
do.	469th.Fld. Co.R.E.	1 section less transpt.	Forward billets S.16.a.10.80.	Rear billets X.10.b.80.20.	2nd. Fld.Co.	1 section less transport.	do.	Forward billets S.16.a.10.80.	
do.	do.	2 sections less transpt.	Forward billets S.6.b.70.05.	Rear billets X.10.b.80.20.	do.	2 sections less transport.	do	Forward billets S.6.b.70.05.	
do.	470th.Fld. Co.R.E.	1 section less transpt.	Forward billets S.10.c.25.25.	Rear billets X.18.a.20.70.	3rd. Fld.Co.	1 section less transport.	do.	Forward billets S.10.c.25.25.	
do.	do.	1 section less transpt.	Forward billets M.29.c.7.6.	Rear billets X.18.a.20.70.	do.	1 section less transport.	do.	Forward billets M.29.c.7.6.	
17th.					Pioneer Battn.	Personnel.	do.	Billets in GIVENCHY.	These should be arranged beforehand by a representative.
17th.					do.	Transport.	do.	Transport Lines X.16.d.5.4.	
19th.	467th.Fld. Co.R.E.	Whole Coy. with transpt.	Rear billets X.4.b.25.25.	Out.	1st.Fld. Co.C.E.	Hd.Qtrs. and transport.	do.	Rear billets X.4.b.25.25.	
19th.	469th.Fld. Co.R.E.	Whole Coy. with transpt.	Rear billets X.10.b.80.20.	Out.	2nd.Fld. Co.C.E.	Hd.Qtrs. and transport.and 1 section.	do.	Rear billets X.10.b.80.20.	
19th.	470th.Fld. Co.R.E.	Whole Coy. with transpt.	Rear billets X.18.a.20.70.	Out.	3rd.Fld. Co.C.E.	Hd.Qtrs., trans pt. & 2 sectns.	do.	Rear billets X.18.a.20.70.	

Appendix XI

4/0th. Field Co. R.E.

PROGRESS REPORT – 6 a.m. 11-11-14 to 6 a.m. 12-11-14.

R.E.		Working Parties		Situation	Work carried out.	hrs	Remarks.
O.	C.R. Sect	O.	O.R. Batt.				
	2	1	35 1/8	LUCAS TR W OF RED	Clearing away earth from Berm which has been thrown up by day party	6	500 yds } Night
	1/4	1	–	BADGER TR Mr DAWSON	Trench cleared out, widened, deepened and drainage trench dug. 3 firebays cut out, ready for revetting	6	15 yds } Work
		1/9 2 } 8 3 }	30 1/8	LUCAS TR	Clearing LUCAS trench	8	
		2 3	5 1/8	NEW RD to LUCAS TR	Fixing duck boards from New rd to LUCAS trench.	8	146 yds
		10 4 } 5 1 } 1	–	M 30 a 18	Draining & Revetting TRAUMONT Redoubt	8	
		5 4 } 1 3 }	30 1/8	M 23 b 9 H	Clearing & duck boarding C.T. CRAZY to CRAZY Duckboarding CRAZY	8	Night Work
		5 4 } 5 3 } 1	35 1/8	M 30 a 18	Berm cleared and 3rd Jack on TRAUMONT Redoubt	6	Night Work
		2 4	–		Painting & erecting Notice-boards		

Date... 12/11/14 ....

J. Cameron Major.
O.C. 4/0th. Field Co. R.E.

Appendix XI

469th Field Co. R.E.

PROGRESS REPORT - 6 a.m. 11.11.17. to 6 a.m. 12.11.17.

R.E. O.	Sect	Working Parties O.	Working Parties O.R.	Working Parties Batt.	Situation	Work carried out	Hrs	Remarks
4					Columbia & Saskatoon June	Making Dug-out at N.26.c.3	8	Day
6					Dº	Dº	8	Dº
1		1	18	4th S.Sn	La Coulotte Tr.	Carrying Rails to Dº	6	Night
2	1	1	—	—	Dº	Widening trench to receive frames for bridge under La Coulotte Rd	8	Day
4		1	—	—	Dº	Dº	9	Day & Night
2		1	—	—	S.16.a.1.8.	Improvements to billets for winter occupation	8	Day
1		1	50	6th S.St	Cyril Trench	Clearing all falls for 600yds forward of Adept	8	Day
5		2	50	"	Adept Trench	Constructing firing bays & traverses	8	"
		—	30	"	—Dº—	Revetting & laying trench boards. (150 yds in progress)	8	"
2	2	1	20	"	—Dº—	Deepening & widening trench 70 yds.	8	"
2		—	—		La Coulotte	Repairing partition at Brewery H.Q.	6	Night
2		—	50	"	Adept Trench	Carrying 1000 sandbags, hurdles, & 50 'A' frames.	6	"
		3	100	"	Cyril Trench	Clearing 235 yds trench & making berm	6	"
2		1	3	6th N.St	Adept Trench	Repairing damage to trench by shell fire.	8	Day
6		—	24	"	Lucas Trench	Clearing falls from M.36.d.55.5 to N.31.d.85.60; at N.36.d.60.10. Repairing Dº	8	"
		—	6	"	La Coulotte	Reported to Town Major Capt Timms, R.A.M.C.	8	"
2	4	2	75	"	Cyril Trench	Excavating sump	6	Night
2		2	50	"	La Coulotte Tr.	Trench cleared for double duckboards 200 yds. Sump completed	6	"
1		1	28	"	Avion Trench	55 yds trench cleared, & 60 yds berm (each side) (1 completed)	6	"
2		2	34	"	Clucas Trench	100 yds berm cleared each side & falls cleared. Forming fire bays.	6	"
2		2	47	"	Adept Trench	180 yds Dº Dº	6	"
		—	—	"	La Coulotte	84 trench boards carried to La Coulotte Trench. 45 hurdles to Adept Tr.	—	
13	1-4					Detached on Courses of Instruction at Divl Dump &c.		
10	3				Carency. X.10.b.8.2	Erecting Nissen Huts.	8	
4	1-4				Dº	Wiring Drill & cleaning Cº Transport	8	
4						Camp Services		
						Runners		

Date 12.11.17.

[signature] Lieut.
for O.C. 469th Field Co. R.E.

Sheet No. 1.   467th Field Coy R.E.   Appendix X

Progress Report – from 11th to 6am 12th Nov: 1917

R.E. O	O.R. Sect	Working Parties O	O.R.	Battn	Situation	Work carried out	Hours	Remarks
1	6	1	20	2/5 LINC	Abalone – Admit C.T.	Length of duckboard laid. Length of trench left cleared for duckboards. Length of trench recleared.	50 yds 45 yds 40 yds	5
1	7	1	17	2/5 LINE	do	Length of duckboards laid. Length of trench left cleared for duckboards. Length of trench recleared.	– 35 yds 35 yds	5	Box latrine fixed.
1	6	1	18	2/4 LINE	Crocodile C.T.	Length of duckboards laid. Length of trench left cleared for duckboards. Length of trench recleared.	20 yds 30 yds 40 yds	5
1	7	1	20	2/5 LINE	do	Length of duckboards laid. Length of trench left cleared for duckboards. Length of trench recleared.	– 11 yds 350 yds	5	Box latrine fixed.
1	10	2	28 11	2/5 LINC	Abalone – Admit C.T.	New length of trench recleared. Carrying party. Reclearing trench.	100 yds 100	3½
1	6	2	39	2/5 LINE	CROCODILE C.T.	New length of trench. New length of trench relaid. Length of trench relaid. Carrying party. Reclearing trench.	200 yds 100 yds	4
	2+3	2						

Date 12th Nov: 1917.

Total length of trench complete
Abalone – Admit C.T.   1687 yds.
Crocodile C.T.   1908 yds.

B. Jenn. Major
O.C. 467th Field Coy R.E.

Sheet 2

467th Field Coy R.E.

Progress Report – 6am 11th to 6am 12th Nov: 1917.

R.E.			Working Parties		Situation	Work carried out	Hrs	Remarks
O	OR	Sect	OR	Bn				
1	2	1	40	3/5 Leic	Post 1	5 Firebays in progress. 3 complete in morning	4	
	2	1	32	2/5 Leic	" 2	" " " "	3¾	
	2	1	13	2/5 Leic	" 3	Sandbagging, Ingresses, dugouts, trench drainage, fire steps	4	
1	2	1	24	2/5 Leic	" 4	Construction of firebays proceeding	4	
	6	1	–	–	Green Line	Under instruction of Works Coy Officer		
	4	1	–	–	Daylight track to Absalom C.T.	Camouflaging	5	
	1	1	–	–		Constructing concrete gun emplacements for 275 Bde R.F.A.		
	5	1	–	–	Bde: H.Q.	Clearing, connecting up & hutting cellar for R.F.A. Bde H.Q.		
	1	1	–	–	Bde R.E. Dump	N.C.O. in charge		
	9	1	–	–	467 Field Co R.E.	Repairing forward tracks, &c.		

November 12/17.

A. B. Jones. Major
O.C. 467 Field Coy R.E.

Appendix IV

490th. Field Co. R.E.

PROGRESS REPORT - 6 a.m. 12-11-17 to 6 a.m. 13-11-17.

R.E. O.	Sect	Working Parties O.R.	Batt	Situation	Work carried out.	Hrs	Remarks.
1	1	20	1/8	CLUCAS TR W. of RFD	Clearing Berry 5ft Wide & 3ft Deep.	6	65yds Night Work
1	1	-	-	CADGER TR Nr DAWSON	Unloading "A" Frames etc from train. Trench cleared and against 3 Firebays partly Sandbagged, Revetted	6	50yds
1	2	4	1/8	Nr N.V.P to CLUCAS TR	Laying duck boards track from Newrd to CLUCAS TR	8	30 yds A Platoon should have reported.
8	3	21	1/8	CLUCAS TR.	Clearing CLUCAS trench	8	
19	2						
10	4			M30 a I.E.	Drawing & revetting TRIAUMONT Redoubt	8	
5	3						
1	4	30	1/8	M23 b.8.4.	Cleaning & duckboarding C.T. CRAZY to CRONY Cleaning out CRONY	8	Night Work
5	3						
3	4	20	1/8	M30 a I.E.	Clearing Burn Jacob to TRIAUMONT Redoubt Carrying stores	6	Night Work
5	3						

Date 13-11-17

[signature] Major.
O.C. 490th. Field Co. R.E.

Appendix XII

469th. Field Co. R.E.

PROGRESS REPORT – 6 a.m. 12.11.17. to 6 a.m. 13.11.17.

R.E.		Working Parties			Situation	Work carried out.	Hrs	Remarks.
O.	Sect	O.	O.R.	Batt.				
6	1				Columbia & Saskatoon Junc.	Making dug-out at N.26.c.3.	8	Day
6					Do	Do	8	Day & Night
4			20	10th S Staff	La Coulotte Tr.	Widening & deepening trench to receive frames. Carried corr. iron for revetting.	8	Do
2					Columbia & Sask.	Carrying rails to Dug outs. N.26.c.3.	6	Night
2					S.16.a.1.8.	Improving billets for winter occupation	8	Day
15		2	100	6th S.Staff	Adept Trench	Constructing firing bays & traverses. Revetting. Laying trench boards. 50 yds completed 150 yds in hand	8	Day
2	2	1	40		Cyril Trench	Clearing Falls for 500 yds. (Forward of Adept)	8	"
2					La Coulotte	Repairing Steps in Brewery	8	"
2		1	50		Cyril Trench	Supporting Victoria Rd Bridge over trench	8	Night
2		2	8		Adept Trench	Carrying 40 hurdles & 60 "A" frames from La Coulotte Dump	6	"
					Do	Wiring in front of Adept Tr. (50 yds completed) Materials carried up.		
2	4		4	4th N.Staffs	Clucas Trench	Widening & clearing berm. Fixing hurdles & clearing falls	8	Day
2		1	25		Adept Trench	Fixing 6 "A" frames & 30 hurdles. Widening & deepening 30 yds trench & clearing falls		
6			6		La Coulotte	Reported to Town Major. Capt Timms (R.A.M.C.)	6	Night
2		2	50		Cyril Trench			
11		2	46		Avion Trench	40 yds trench deepened. Relaying trench boards. Completed 1 Firebay 200 yds wiring, (100 yds completed)		
2		1	30		Adept Trench	200 yds berm cleared each side, & falls cleared.		
					Columbia Tr.			
15	4					Detached on courses of instruction &c Runners.		
4	4				Carency, X.10.b & 2	Erecting Nissen Huts	6	Day
6	3				Do	Clearing Co. Transport. Wiring Drill &c	6	Do
16	5					Camp Services	6	
4								

13th Novr 1917.

J.W. [signature] Lieut.
for O.C. 469 th.Field Co. R.E.

Appendix XII

Sheet No. 1. 467th Field Co. R.E.

PROGRESS REPORT – 6 a.m. 12th Nov: to 6 a.m. 13th Nov: 1917.

R.E. Sect.	Working Parties O.	Working Parties O.R.	Working Parties Battn.	Situation.	Work carried out.		Hrs.	Remarks.
7	1	19	2/5 Linc	ABSALOM – ADROIT C.T.	Length of Duckboards laid. Length of Trench left cleared for Duckboards. Length of Trench recleared.	— 50 yds. —	5	
6	1	22	2/5 Linc	do.	Length of Duckboards laid. Length of Trench left cleared for Duckboards. Length of Trench recleared.	— 40 yds. —	5	LATRINE FIXED.
6	3	20	3/4 Linc	CROCODILE C.T.	Length of Trench left cleared for Duckboards. Length of Duckboards laid. Length of Trench recleared.	10 yds. 24 yds. 80 yds.	5	
5	1	19	2/5 Linc	do.	Length of Duckboards laid. Length of Trench left cleared for Duckboards. Length of Trench recleared. See remarks.	— — —	5	THE CLEARING OF TRENCH WHERE SIDES HAD FALLEN IN COMPLETED.
6	2+3	38 70	2/5 Linc	CROCODILE C.T.	New length of length of Berm recleared. Carrying party.		4	CLEARING AND BOTTOMING TRENCH. 10 O.R. PUMPING FROM TRENCH.
	2	25	2/5 Linc	do	New length of length of Berm recleared. Carrying party.			

TOTAL LENGTH OF TRENCH COMPLETED.

ABSALOM – ADROIT C.T. 1687 yds.
CROCODILE C.T. 1932 yds.

Date 13th Nov: 1917

T. B. New. Major
O.C. 467th Field Co. R.E.

Sheet No. 2.

467th Field Co. R.E.

PROGRESS REPORT 6 a.m. 12th Nov. to 6 a.m. 13th Nov. 1917.

R.E.			Working Parties			Situation.	Work carried out.	Hrs. at Work.	Remarks.
O.	O.R.	Sect.	O.	O.R.	Batt.				
-	2	-	1	19	2/5 LEIC	(POST 1)	3 FIREBAYS IN PROGRESS	3½	left work early
-	2	-	1	31	2/5 LEIC	" 2	" " " " & sandbagging &c.	3½	moving to go
-	2	-	1	16	2/5 LEIC	" 3	SANDBAGGING FIREBAYS AND EXCAVATING TRENCH.	3½	
-	2	-	1	10	2/5 LEIC	" 4	BERM CLEARING	3½	attack
-	5	-	-	-	-	GREEN LINE	UNDER INSTRUCTIONS OF FRONT LINE COMPANY COMMANDERS.		
-	4	-	-	-	-	DAYLIGHT TRACK TO ABSALOM.C.T.	CAMOUFLAGING	5	
-	1	-	-	1	-		CONSTRUCTING CONCRETE GUN EMPLACEMENTS FOR 295 BDE R.F.A.		
-	4	2+1	-	31	R.F.A.	BDE H.Q.	CLEARING, CONNECTING UP AND STRUTTING CELLARS FOR R.F.A BDE HQ	7	
-	1	-	-	-	-	BDE RE DUMP	N.C.O. IN CHARGE.		
-	13	-	-	-	-	467 FIELD CO RE BILLETS	REPAIRING FORWARD BILLETS ETC.		

Date Nov. 13th 1917.

A. B. Irw.... Major.
O.C. 467th Field Co. R.E.

Appendix XIV

490th. Field Co. R. E.

PROGRESS REPORT - 6 a.m. 13-11-14 to 6 a.m. 14-11-14.

R.E. Sect.	Working Parties O.	O.R.	Batt.	Situation	Work carried out.	Hrs.	Remarks.
0	4	15	1	CADGER TR Mr DAWSON	Sandbagging New fire bays	6	2 Completed 1 partly completed (Night work)
1	1	15	1	DAWSON TR between PHELAN and CADGER	Deepening & widening where necessary & draining	6	
	3	8	178	CLUCAS TR	Clearing CLUCAS trench	8	
1	2	19 4	178	NEW RD & CLUCAS TR	Fixing duck boards, track from New rd. to CLUCAS trench	8	30 yds
	4 3	10 5	178	M 30 a 18	Draining & revetting PIRMONT REDOUBT	8	
1	4 3	5 1	178	M 23 b 94	Clearing & duck boarding CRONY REDOUBT	8	
	4 3	4 5		M 30 a 15	Carrying stores Painting signs	4	Night work
	4	1					

Date 14-11-14

.... Major
O.C. 490th Field Co. R.E.

Appendix XIII

469th Field Co. R.E.

PROGRESS REPORT – 6 a.m. 13.11.17. to 6 a.m. 14.11.17.

R.E.		Working Parties			Situation	Work carried out.	hrs.	Remarks.
C.R.	Sect	O.	O.R.	Batt				
5					Columbia & Saskatoon Tr.	Making dug-out at N.26.c.3	8	Day
5					Dº	Dº	8	Night
7	1				La Coulotte Tr.	Completing & fixing Bridge under La Coulotte Road	8	Day
1					S.16.a.1.8	Improving Billets for winter occupation	8	"
15		2	100	6th 5.5 Pr	Adept Trench	Constructing Firing Bays & traverses. Revetting. Laying trench-boards. (25 yds completed) (200 yds in progress)	8	Day
1	2	1	40	"	Cyril Trench	Clearing falls for 300 yds forward of Avion	8	"
2					Dº	Erecting supporting frames for Victoria Rd Bridge (Completed) Revetting in progress	8	"
3		1	48	1st N.Fr.	Adept Trench	Deepening & widening trench, clearing falls. Fixing 19 hurdles behind "A" frames		
			6	"	La Coulotte	Reported to Town Major		
2	4	1	35	"	Columbia Trench	Clearing falls & berm from M.36.d.70.25 to N.31.a.3.3. Sump cleared	8	Day
1			2	"	Dº	Fitting Latrine Box		
13	1.-4					Detached on Courses of Instruction &c.		
4	1.-4					Runners (1 per Section)		
6	3					Erecting Nissen Huts &c		
2	3				Carency	Constructing Incinerator	8	Day
18	3	1			Chateau de la Haie X.10.b.8.2	Clearing Co. Transport & preparing to relieve Nº 4 Section	6	"
10	4							

NOTE:- 10 men of Nº 4 Section were "Gassed" & Removed to Field Ambͩͤͩͤ

Date. 14th Nov. 1917.

_____ I. Lieut.
for O.C. 469th Field Co. R.E.

Appendix XIII

447th Field Co R.E.

Progress Report 6am 13th to 6am 14th November, 1917 :—

R.E. OR SECT	WORKING PARTIES O	O.R.	BATT	SITUATION	WORK CARRIED OUT		HRS AT WORK	REMARKS
6	-	1	20	2/5 LINC	ABSALOM – ADROIT C.T.	Length of Duckboards laid. Length of trench left cleared for duckboards. Length of trench recleared.	— yds. 60 yds.	5	
16	-	-	-	-	Do	Length of Duckboards laid. Length of trench left cleared for duckboards. Length of trench recleared.	24 yds. 18 yds. — yds.	3	NO WORK
6	3	1	20	2/4 LINC	ABSALOM – CROCODILE C.T.	Length of Duckboards laid. Length of trench left cleared for duckboards. Length of trench recleared.	90 yds. 40 yds. — yds.	5 DAYS	Fixing box latrine and curing buckets.
6in	-	-	-	-	Do	Length of Duckboards laid. Length of trench left cleared for duckboards. Length of trench recleared.	15 yds. — yds. 60 yds.	2	40 yards Duckboards left loose by working party.
1	-	-	-	-	GREEN LINE	Under instructions of front line Company Commanders.			
8	-	-	-	-	DAYLIGHT TRACK TO ABSALOM C.T.				
4	-	-	-	-	-	Camouflaging.		5	
1	-	-	-	-	-	Constructing concrete gun emplacements for 295 Bde RFA			
4	2+1	-	31	RFA Bde H.Q.		Collecting and breaking bricks for concrete and concreting cellars for RFA Bde H.Q.		7	
1	1	-	-	Bde R.E. Dump		N.C.O. in charge.			
3	-	-	-	Hut & Fwd Billets		Work in camp			

November 14th 1917.

† B Munr P
O.C. 447th Field Co R.E.

Appendix XII

2/1th. Field Co. R.E.

PROGRESS REPORT – 6 a.m. 14-11-15 to 6 a.m. 15-11-15.

R.E.		Working Parties			Situation	Work carried out.	Hrs	Remarks.
C.	Sect	O.	O.R.	Batt				
1	1		19	1	IRISH TRENCH N. of CLUCAS	Deepening trench over 1/2 ft	5	150 yds Night work
	2		6	2	RED TRENCH	Repairing duck-boards	8	
1	2		11	3	CLUCAS.TR	Clearing drain in CLUCAS trench	8	200 yds
	3		2	3	NEW RD to CLUCAS TR	Carrying duck-boards to track	8	
	1		11	4	M 3A a 1 8.	Draining + Revetting TRAUMONT Redoubt	8	
1	3		5	3	M 28. b & H	Clearing out CHERRY Redoubt	8	
	3		5	4	M 30 a 1 8	Carrying stores	6	Night work
	4		7	1		Painting signs		

Date 15-11-15

Roberton Major
O.C. 2/1th.Field Co. R.E.

2/1th (North Midland) Field Coy. R.E.

Appendix XII

469th. Field Co. R.E.

PROGRESS REPORT – 6 a.m. 14.11.17. to 6 a.m. 15.11.17.

R.E.		Working Parties			Situation	Work carried out.	hrs	Remarks.
O.	Sect	O.	O.R.	Batt				
6	1	-	-	-	La Coulotte Rd Clucas – Rep. Tr. Clucas – La Coulotte	Clearing trench near Bridge under La Coulotte Rd Revetting at corners of trenches	8	Day
8	1	-	-	-			8	"
1	2	2	4	16" SS Stpt	Cyril Trench	Completed revetting Victoria Rd Bridge over Cyril.	8	"
7	"	1	96	"	Adept Trench	Constructing Firing Bays & Traverses. Revetting & laying trench boards	8	"
13	"	1	25	"	Do	Double apron fence. 200 yds pickets put out. (Work interrupted by shell fire.)	6	Night
1	"	-	50	"	Do	Barbed wire & pickets carried from La Coulotte Dump		
-	"	-	75	"	Do	Hurdles & Sand bags carried "		
5	2	2	100	16"N Stpt	Adept Trench	Clearing trench left of Clucas. N 31. b.4.5 to N 31. b.5.7	8	Day
8	"	1	42	"	Do	Carrying wiring materials from La Coulotte.	6	Night
1	3	1	30	"	Do	Clearing 150 yds berm both sides trench, left of Clucas. N 31.b.25.0 to N 31.b.5.7	6	"
1	"	-	24	"	Do	Carrying Hurdles, 'A' Frames & Sand bags from La Coulotte.	6	Day
1	4	-	-	-	X.10.b.8.2	Kit Inspection, Baths, Digging & erecting new Latrine &c.		
26								
13	1-4					Detached on Courses of Instruction &c.		
4	1-4					Runners.		
6	3				Carency	Erecting Nissen Huts &c.		
2	3				Chateau de la Hae	Constructing Incinerator.		

Date. 15th. Nov. 1917.

W.W. White .... Lieut.
for O.C. 469 th. Field Co. R.E.

Appendix XIV

467th Field Co. R.E.

Sheet No. 1.

PROGRESS REPORT – 6 a.m. 14TH to 6 a.m. 15TH NOV: 1917.

R.E.			Working Parties			Situation	Work carried out.	Hrs.	Remarks.
O.R.	Sect.	O.	O.R.	Bat'n.					
6	–	–	22	3rd Gen: Infy.	ABSALOM–ADROIT C.T.	Length of Duckboards laid. — yds. Length of Trench left cleared for duckboards — yds. Length of Trench left recleared. 60 yds.	5	† INFANTRY PARTY WORKING 8 – 11 a.m., other ½ 11 – 2 p.m.
18	–	–	–	–	do	Length of Duckboards laid. 26 yds. Length of Trench left cleared for duckboards — yds. Length of Trench by Trench recleared. 30 yds.	5	Trench listioned 18 yds
6	3	–	–	–	@ CROCODILE C.T	Length of Duckboards laid. 40 yds. Length of Trench left cleared for duckboards — yds. Length of — yds.	5	3 new carrying party
16	–	–	–	–	do	Length of Duckboards laid. 42 yds. Length of Trench left cleared for duckboards — yds. Length of Trench recleared. — yds.	5	3
2	–	–	1	–	GREEN LINE	UNDER INSTRUCTIONS OF FRONT LINE COMPANY COMMANDERS		
4	–	–	1	–	DAYLIGHT TRACK	CAMOUFLAGING	5	
1	–	–	1	–		CONSTRUCTING CONCRETE GUN EMPLACEMENTS FOR 295 BDE RFA		
4	1½	–	31	RFA	Bde H.Q.	COLLECTING AND BREAKING BRICKS FOR CONCRETE AND CONCRETING CELLARS FOR RFA BDE H.Q.	7	ADDITIONAL 6 RE FIXING GAS CURTAINS 3 HOURS
1	–	–	1	–	Bde Dump	N.C.O. IN CHARGE.		

TOTAL LENGTH OF TRENCH COMPLETED
ABSALOM–ADROIT C.T. 1687 yds
CROCODILE C.T. 2119 yds

Date. Nov: 15/17.

[signature] Major
O.C. 467th Field Co. R.E.

Appendix F

1/0th. Field Co. R. E.

PROGRESS REPORT – 6 a.m. 15-11-17 to 6 a.m. 16-11-17.

R.E.		Working Parties		Situation	Work carried out.	Hrs	Remarks.
O.R.	Sect	O.	O.R.	Batt.			
19	1			173M 78TH M.T CLUIAS	Deepening trench over 1ft (Completed)	3	150 yds
5	1			do	do (Completed)	4	26 yds
14	1			do	Cutting tunnels in 6 firebays	4	
8	2			RED TRENCH	Preparing trench boards (Complete)	8	
11	2			CLUIAS TR.	Clearing drain in CLUIAS trench	8	200 yds
4	3						
2	3			NEW R.P. & CLUIAS TR.	Laying duck boards, trench from New R.P. to Cluias Tr.	8	20 tunnels
16	4						
1	3			M30 A.T.B.	Draining & Revetting BEAUMONT Redoubt	6	
10	4						
5	4			M.4 & Y.O.	Duck boarding, cleaning out CRONY CROON	9	
1	3				Painting Signs		
1	4						

Date 16-11-17

O.C. 1/0 th. Field Co. R.E.

....
O.C. 1/0 th. Field Co. R.E.

Appendix XV

469th. Field Co. R.E.

PROGRESS REPORT — 6 a.m. 15.11.17 to 6 a.m. 16.11.17.

		Working Parties					
R.E.				Situation	Work carried out.	Hrs.	Remarks.
O.	C.S.M.	Sect	O.R.	O.R. Batt.			
1			3	2 5th Staffs	Cyril - Adept Tr.	Revetting junction of trenches with "A" frames & hurdles.	8	Day.
			3	6 "	Cucas Red Tr.	Do. Do. & expanded metal.		
		1		4 "	La Coulotte Br. S.9.d.4.9.	Constructing trench board steps each side of bridge. (Completed)	8	Day.
			2			Improvements to Billets.		
			3	34 5th S.St.	Adept Trench	Constructing firing bays & traverses, revetting & laying trench boards. (25 yds completed)	8	Day.
1		2	2	75 "	Do.	Wiring materials carried from La Coulotte Dump 100 yds in progress)	6	Night.
			2	75 "	Do.	200 yds Double Apron fence completed in front of Adept.		
			1	50 5th N.St.	Adept Trench	Carried up 2000 sandbags, 20 "A" frames, 50 hurdles & 75 trench boards from La Coulotte Dump		
1		3	1	45 "	Do.	Revetting trench (Left of Cucas) 13 "A" frames & 36 hurdles fixed forward of existing work towards Columbia Tr.	8	Day.
			1	20 "	Do.	Carrying materials for & erecting 300 yds double apron fence in front of Adept trench between N.31.d.5.1 & T.1.b.8.9	6	Night.
			1	58 "	Do.	Clearing 70 yds germ each side (left of Cucas) from N.31.b.3.1 to N.31.b.3.3		
					Do.	Carrying "A" frames & hurdles from La Coulotte Dump		
1			15		X.10.b.8.2	Cleaning, Co. transport, erecting new latrine, Box Resp. Drill &c.	6	
1			26	1.4	Do.	Do.		
			13	1.4	Do.	Detached on courses of instruction &c.	8	
		4	6		Carency	Runners		
		5	2		Chateau-de-la-Haie	Erecting Nissen huts &c		
						Constructing incinerator		

Date 16th Nov. 1917.

.... Major.
O.C. 469th. Field Co. R.E.

Sheet No 1.

Appendix IV

467th Field Co. R.E.

PROGRESS REPORT – 6 a.m. 15.11.17. to 6 a.m. 16.11.17.

R.E.		Working Parties			Situation.	Work carried out.		Hrs.	Remarks.
O.	Sect:	O.	O.R.	Battn.					
6	1	1	–	1	ABSALOM–ADROIT C.T.	LENGTH OF DUCKBOARDS LAID. LENGTH OF TRENCH LEFT CLEARED FOR DUCKBOARDS. LENGTH OF TRENCH RECLEARED.	26 yds. 26 yds.	5	
6	1	1	–	1	do	LENGTH OF DUCKBOARDS LAID. LENGTH OF TRENCH LEFT CLEARED FOR DUCKBOARDS. LENGTH OF TRENCH RECLEARED.	35 yds. 40 yds.	4	
6	3	1	–	1	CROCODILE C.T.	LENGTH OF DUCKBOARDS LAID. LENGTH OF TRENCH LEFT CLEARED FOR DUCKBOARDS. LENGTH OF TRENCH RECLEARED.		5	
6	1	1	–	1	do	LENGTH OF DUCKBOARDS LAID. LENGTH OF TRENCH LEFT CLEARED FOR DUCKBOARDS. LENGTH OF TRENCH RECLEARED.	20 yds.	4½	
11	–	2	75	3rd Can	ABSALOM–ADROIT C.T.	NEW LENGTH OF BERM CLEARED LENGTH OF BERM RECLEARED CARRYING PARTY	35 yds. 153 yds.	4	6 men worked on pump. 11 men deepening trench 90s
9	2	1	26	1st Can	CROCODILE C.T.	NEW LENGTH OF BERM CLEARED LENGTH OF BERM RECLEARED. CARRYING PARTY	 250 yds.	4	
	3	1	25	Batt					
2	4	1	50	Can 1st.	BLUE LINE POST 1	5 FIREBAYS IN PROGRESS (HALF COMPLETED).		4	
2	4	1	42	"	" 2	"		4	
2	2	1	43	"	" 3	"		4	
2	–	1	50	"	" 4	"		4	

TOTAL LENGTH OF TRENCH COMPLETED.
ABSALOM–ADROIT C.T. 1713 yds.
CROCODILE C.T. 2179"

Date. Nov 16/17.

D. B. Mw. MAVOR
O.C.
467th Field Co. R.E.

Sheet. No 2.

467th. Field Co. R.E.

PROGRESS REPORT – 6 a.m. 15.11.17. to 6 a.m. 16.11.17.

R.E.		Working Parties			Situation	Work carried out.	Hrs.	Remarks.
O.	O.R.	Sect.	O.	O.R.	Bat'tn.			
1	4	-	-	-	-	GREEN LINE	UNDER INSTRUCTIONS OF FRONT LINE COMPANY COMMANDERS		
-	4	-	-	-	-	DAYLIGHT TRACK.	CAMOUFLAGING	5	
-	1	-	-	-	-		CONSTRUCTING CONCRETE GUN EMPLACEMENTS FOR 295 Bde R.F.A.		
-	10	-	-	-	-	Bde H.Q.	COLLECTING AND BREAKING BRICKS FOR CONCRETE AND CONCRETING CELLARS FOR R.F.A. BDE HQ. FIXING GAS CURTAINS TO CELLARS.	7	
-	1	-	-	-	-	Bde RE DUMP	N.C.O. IN CHARGE.		

Date. Nov 16/17.

A. B. Knox. Major
O.C. 467th. Field Co. R.E.

ORIGINAL.

Vol 10

War Diary

Thanks of ?????

Headquarters. R. Engineers

59th Division.

Volume X

From 1st Nov 1917 - to - 30th Nov 1917

[Stamp: HEADQUARTERS, R.E. 59th (NORTH MIDLAND) DIVN. No. 2 – DEC. 1917]

Army Form C. 2118

WAR DIARY
INTELLIGENCE SUMMARY

HEAD QUARTERS
59 DIVISIONAL R.E.

(Erase heading not required.)

Place	Date	Hour	Summary of Events and Information	Remarks and references to Appendices
CHATEAU DE LA HAIE	1/11/17		467 FIELD Coy RE working on Divisional Defence lines in forward area per appendix 1 attached	Sheet 36ᵇ and 3ᶜ 1/40,000
			469 " " " "	Kum
			470 " " " "	Kum
do.	2/11/17	11.30 pm	Addendum to 59 DIVISION ORDER Nº 72 Copy Nº 5 received	Kum
			Work of FIELD Coy 5 as shown in appendix II attached	
do.	3/11/17		Work of FIELD Coys as shown in appendix III "	Kum
		6.30 pm	59 DIVISION ORDER Nº 73 Copy 5 received	
do.	4/11/17		Work of FIELD Coys as shown in appendix IV attached	Kum
		1 pm	59 DIVISION ORDER Nº 74 Copy 5 received	
do.	5/11/17	10 am	Addendum to 59 DIVISION ORDER Nº 73 Copy Nº 5 received	Kum
		noon	G 301 received postponing the operations ordered in 59 DIV ORDER Nº 73	
			Work of FIELD Coys as shown in appendix V attached	
do.	6/11/17		Work of FIELD Coys as shown in appendix VI attached	Kum
do.	7/11/17	7.30 am	Addendum Nº 2 to 59 DIVISION ORDER Nº 73 Copy Nº 5 received	Kum
		7.30 pm	59 DIVISION ORDER Nº 75 Copy 5 received	
		2 pm	59 DIVISION Nº G 302 detailing parralle GERMAN Policy in this sector received	
			Work of FIELD Coys as shown in appendix VII attached	
do.	8/11/17	10 am	G 73/1 Copy 5 detailing zero hour for operations detailed in DIV ORDER Nº 73, received	Kum
		10 am	361/14 G detailing defence scheme for the Division received	
			Work of FIELD Coys as shown in appendix VIII attached	
do.	9/11/17		Work of FIELD Coys as shown in appendix IX "	Kum
do.	10/11/17		Work of FIELD Coys as shown in appendix X "	Kum

Army Form C. 2118

WAR DIARY
INTELLIGENCE SUMMARY
(Erase heading not required.)

Continued —

Place	Date	Hour	Summary of Events and Information	Remarks and references to Appendices
CHATEAU de la HAIE	11/11/17	noon	59 Division Order No 76 Copy No 6 received. Move of Division with march tables in appendix XI attached	Sheet 36.B and 36.C 1/40,000
do	12/11/17	noon	Work of Field Coys RE to shown in appendix XI attached. CRE order No 4 copy attached, marked appendix A, issued to all concerned	Khan
do	13/11/17	3.30 pm	Work of Field Coys RE to shown in appendix XII attached. 59 Division Order No 77 copy No 6 received	Khan
do	14/11/17		Work of Field Coys RE to shown in appendix XIV	Khan
do	15/11/17		Work of Field Coys RE to shown in appendix XV	Khan
do	16/11/17		Work of Field Coys RE to shown in appendix XVI	Khan
do	17/11/17	10 am	CRE hands over to CRE 1st Canadian Division as per CRE order No 7 dated 12/11/17	
		6 pm	467 Field Coy relieved in forward billets in line by 1st Canadian Field Coy RE	
		10 pm	469 and 470 Field Coys relieved in forward billets by 3rd and 2nd Canadian Field Coy RE respectively	
HERMAVILLE		2 pm	CRE opens office at HERMAVILLE	Khan
	18/11/17	6.30 am	59 Division Order No 78 Copy No 5 received	do
		1.30 pm	Addendum to 59 Division Order No 78 Copy No 5 received	do
	19/11/17	7.30 am	3 Field Coys RE move under orders of 176 Infantry Bde to GOUY-EN-ARTOIS	Khan
			59 Division Warning Order No 79 Copy No 5 received	
BASSEUX		6 pm	CRE moves office from HERMAVILLE to BASSEUX	do
	21/11/17	10 pm	CRE moves office from BASSEUX to ACHIET-LE-PETIT	Khan
			467 Field Coy RE moves to COURCELLES LE COMTE	
			469 " " " ACHIET-LE-PETIT	
			470 " " " GOMIECOURT	

Original.

Vol/11

War Diary
of
Headquarters R. Engineers.

59th Division.

Volume XI.

From 1st Dec. 1917 - to - 31st Dec. 1917.

Army Form C. 2118

WAR DIARY
or
INTELLIGENCE SUMMARY

of HEAD QUARTERS
59 DIVISIONAL R.E.

(Erase heading not required.)

Instructions regarding War Diaries and Intelligence Summaries are contained in F.S. Regs., Part II. and the Staff Manual respectively. Title Pages will be prepared in manuscript.

Place	Date	Hour	Summary of Events and Information	Remarks and references to Appendices
TRESCAULT	1/12/17		467 and 469 FIELD Coys RE employed upon defence work in front of FLESQUIERES	Sheet 57D 1/40000
			470 FIELD Coy RE moved to VALLULART WOOD	
			CRE 40 Division who asked to put his field coys to work on the HAVRINCOURT - FLESQUIERES road	
			2 Platoons 258 TUNNELLING Coy RE were ordered to start completion of dugouts in the NINE WOOD - BOURLON WOOD Switch line.	Khan
do	2/12/17 8.30 am		59 DIVISION ORDER N° 83 Copy N° 6 received	
			467 FIELD Coy RE wiring in front of Sunken road from L8 6.2.8 to L6 6 central	Khan
			469 " working on FLESQUIERES defence line	
			470 " resting in camp of VALLULART WOOD	
	3/12/17		787/14/1.G. received detailing policy of Division	
			787/14/3.G. " " " detailing work of machine guns in accordance with 787/14/1.G	
			467 FIELD Coy RE wiring in front of Hollow Road right and left of LA JUSTICE	
			469 " " " wiring and digging defences infront of FLESQUIERES	
			470 " " " marched from VALLULART WOOD to TRESCAULT. Repaired bridge over trench at Road junction with SHAFTESBURY AVENUE in Q16A.	Whm
			40 DIVISIONAL RE working on HAVRINCOURT - FLESQUIERES ROAD	
	4/12/17 2.30 pm		59 DIVISION ORDER N° 84 copy N° 5 received	
			40 DIVISIONAL RE repaired 650 yds HAVRINCOURT - FLESQUIERES road between K23 A.S.2 and K23 b.7.7. Pioneers improved HAVRINCOURT - GRAINCOURT road and all roads in HAVRINCOURT. Also infantry track to GRAINCOURT from K18 d.10.50 to K18 b.1.6.	
			467 FIELD Coy RE constructed double apron fence from FLESQUIERES defences	
			469 " " completing FLESQUIERES defences	
			470 " " clearing enemy wire in rear of HINDENBURG Support line	Khan

WAR DIARY
or
INTELLIGENCE SUMMARY
(Erase heading not required.)

Army Form C. 2118

Instructions regarding War Diaries and Intelligence Summaries are contained in F.S. Regs., Part II. and the Staff Manual respectively. Title Pages will be prepared in manuscript.

Place	Date	Hour	Summary of Events and Information	Remarks and references to Appendices
TRESCAULT	5/12/17	2 pm	CRE closed office and opened same here at LITTLE WOOD P.26.b.3.1.	SHEET 57c/140,000
LITTLE WOOD			467 FIELD Coy } employed upon defences round FLESQUIERES.	
			469 } Removing wire from many HINDENBURG Support lines and blowing	
			470 } up enemy guns that could not be removed.	K/m
	6/12/17		2 Sections 258 TUNNELLING Coy RE ordered to commence consolidation of dug-outs in HINDENBURG Support line and in FLESQUIERES.	K/m
do.	6/12/17		Continuation of work detailed above.	
do.	7/12/17		LIEUT. K.G. GRIFFITHS wounded by shrapnel in arm and forearm.	
			467 FIELD Coy RE } completed 250 yds low wire entanglement 4 yards wide from K.26.a.3.5. to K.26.a.8.3. 600 yards double concertina wire from K.19.a.5.5 to L.13.c.8.7.	Km
			469 } Erecting shelters in old British front line	
do.	8/12/17		470 CRE order round marked appendix 1. and attached hereto	
			CRE 467 FIELD Coy RE } concentrating up front line defences with 2% Division on our right. Hurrying up enemy dugouts and working on FLESQUIERES defences. Making dugouts, burying in front HINDENBURG UNSEEN SUPPORT trench by removing Knife rests from behind and putting them in front. Incorporating HINDENBURG UNSEEN SUPPORT trench right and left of Sunken Road running W. TRIANGLE WOOD Erecting shelters for infantry in old British front line.	K/m
do.	9/12/17	8 am	59 DIVISION ORDER No. 85 copy by 470 FIELD Coy RE 467 FIELD Coy RE was relieved by 470 FIELD Coy RE HEAD QUARTERS 467 moved at Q.3.d.5.3. and 470 FIELD Coy RE K.36.a.5.9. A.6.9. FIELD Coy RE working in defences in FLESQUIERES.	K/m

1875 Wt. W593/826 1,000,000 4/15 I.B.C. & A. A.D.S.S./Forms/C. 2118.

WAR DIARY
INTELLIGENCE SUMMARY — Confidential

Army Form C. 2118

(Erase heading not required.)

Instructions regarding War Diaries and Intelligence Summaries are contained in F.S. Regs., Part II. and the Staff Manual respectively. Title Pages will be prepared in manuscript.

Place	Date	Hour	Summary of Events and Information	Remarks and references to Appendices
LITTLE WOOD	10/12/17		469 FIELD Coy RE relieved by 470 FIELD Coy RE who from to day takes on the whole of the FLESQUIERES defences	Sheet 57C
do	11/12/17		467 FIELD Coy RE cleaning down and filling in trench from K 29 d.5.1 / 40.000 also filling in trench from K 29 d.5.1 / 40.000 for 50 YARDS eastwards on the SWITCH LINE	
		8 pm	59 Division N° 787/14/11.G. Stability the PROVISIONAL Defence Scheme of the Division received. Lieut F.R.B. WHITEHOUSE and H.S. COUCH-JOHNS examined Sick 470 FIELD Coy RE continued work on the FLESQUIERES defences 469 commence work on C.T.s East UNSEEN SUPPORT SWITCH Enco. 467 FIELD Coy RE working on BILHEM — CHAPEL WOOD SWITCH	Khun
do	12/12/17	5.30 pm	59 DIVISION WARNING ORDER N° 86 Copy 6 received. Work of 467, 469 and 470 FIELD Coy RE is shown in appendix III attached. 2 Sections 258 TUNNELLING Coy RE constructing dugouts at K24 u.1.5 K27 b.98.30 Q.4.c.2.6. K24 c.2.6. K24 a.8.3, K24 b.3.2 Q.4.c.3.6	Khun
do	13/12/17		Work of 467, 469 and 470 FIELD Coy RE is shown in appendix IV attached. TUNNELLING Coy RE continued their work.	Khun
do	14/12/17	1.30 pm	59 DIVISION ORDER N° 87 Copy N° 6 received Work of 467 - 469 and 470 FIELD Coy RE to shown in appendix V attached.	Khun
		11 pm	59 DIVISION N° 787/14/11.G. Copy N° 5 received	
do	15/12/17		Work of 467, 469 and 470 FIELD Coy RE to shown in appendix VI attached	Khun
		5.30 pm	59 DIV ORDER N° 88 Copy 6 received	
do	16/12/17	10 am	CRE moved Head Quarters from LITTLE WOOD to YPRES P2 G 6-25.80. Work of 467, 469 and 470 FIELD Coy RE is shown in appendix VII attached	Khun
YPRES				

Army Form C. 2118

WAR DIARY
INTELLIGENCE SUMMARY
(Erase heading not required.)

Continued

Place	Date	Hour	Summary of Events and Information	Remarks and references to Appendices
LE CAUROY	26.12.17		Field Companies resting and pulling down in billets	Sheet 57c
do.	27.12.17		"	1/40,000
do.	28.12.17		LIEUT E.E. ROUSE reported as reinforcement from BASE to 46.9 FIELD Coy R.E.	Khm
do.	29.12.17		Field companies training	Khm
do.	30.12.17		" attend church parade 46.9 FIELD Coy RE moves from SARS LES BOIS to REBREUVIETTE M.C.R.H.	Khm
do.	31.12.17		Field Companies their fortnights general training and also commence work upon the repair of billets.	Khm
ADDENDUM YPRES	21.12.17		LIEUT A.J. PARKER reported as reinforcement from BASE to 46.9 FIELD Coy RE	Khm
			" II LIEUT J. LEWIS " " " " "	

Marlow
Capt. Adjt.
59 Div. RE

SECRET.

Copy No. 7

Appendix 1

ORDERS

by

Lieut.Col.G.B.Roberts, R.E. C.R.E.59th.Divn.

---:©:©:---

On the night of the 9/10th December 1917 the 470th Field Co. R.E. will move to FLESQUIERES and will relieve the 467th Field Co. R.E. which will move to TRESCAULT.

Details of the relief as regards work, time etc. will be arranged by the O.C. 469th Field Co. R.E. in consultation with the G.O.C. 177th Infantry Brigade.

8th December 1917.

Lieut. Colonel, R.E.
C.R.E. 59th.Division.

-x-x-x-x-x-x-x-

Copy No.1. 59th Division G.
2. 59th Division.Q.
3. 177th Infantry Brigade.
4. O.C. 467th Field Co. R.E.
5. O.C. 469th Field Co. R.E.
6. O.C. 470th Field Co. R.E.
7. War Diary.
8. War Diary.
9. File.

SECRET.   Copy. No. 8

Appendix F

ORDERS
by
Lieut.Col.G.B.ROBERTS.R.E. C.R.E.59th.Div.

----:@:@:@:----

From the 10th.instant inclusive the 469th. Field Company R.E. will cease to be attached to the 177th.Infantry Brigade and will hand over work to O.C.470th.Field Company R.E. whose Company will be allotted to the 177th.Inf.Bde. for the whole of the FLESQUIERES Defence Line.

The 469th.Field Company will commence work upon the C.T. commencing at K.24.a.3.4. and finishing at K.22.d.9.2. (N.W.CHAPEL WOOD) and the C.T. commencing at L.19.a.03.40. and finishing at K.29.b.6.1. and will assist the 178th.Inf.Bde. upon work on the HINDENBERG Front Line and shelters in the Old British Front Line.

8th.December.1917.   Captain & Adjutant.
8.p.m.   59th.Divisional R.E.

x x x x x

Copy No. 1.   59th.Division.G.
         2.   59th.Division.Q.
         3.   177th.Inf.Bde.
         4.   178th.Inf.Bde.
         5.   467th.Field Co.R.E.
         6.   469th.Field Co.R.E.
         7.   470th.Field Co.R.E.
         8.   War Diary.
         9.   War Diary.
        10.   File.

Appendix L

DAILY PROGRESS REPORT.

C.R.E. 59th. DIVISION.   Date 12.12.1917.

Item.	STRENGTH OF PARTY.			Hours.	Where employed	Nature of Work.	Remarks.
	R.E.		Working Party.				
	O.	O.R.	O.	O.R.			
1		3	60	1	70	Cyclists Finland Line K35 d.1.3. Northwards.	Taking up old chevaux de frise and setting along switch. Digging firebays in switch.	
2		1	20	3	90	North Switch Notre Dame K35 d.1.3 Southwards.	Digging new part of switch 170x dug 6' wide x 1' deep	Night work.

R. Whalley 2/Lr Major
O.C. 467 Field Coy R.E.

Appendix (a)

DAILY PROGRESS REPORT.

C.R.E. 59th DIVISION.   Date .... December 1917

item	STRENGTH OF PARTY		Working Party		Hours	where employed	Nature of Work	Remarks
	R.E.							
	O.	O.R.	O.	O.R.				
1		25	8	200	3 hours	Lieut C.T.	Wiring front line & clearing wire in front	B'ns were 3 hours late on arrival.
2		32	2 a/u sergts	200	5 hours	Lt. O.T.	do	
3		11	2	180	5	Heavy Batteries K.34.6	Unloading & unloading daily to N.G. stores and from Metz dump	
		8			5			
		26			8		Improvement of M.G. & post at Q...	

W.H. James

DAILY PROGRESS REPORT.

C.R.E. 59th. DIVISION. +/C Field Coy. R.E. Date: ....

Item	STRENGTH OF PARTY.				Hours.	Where employed	Nature of Work.	Remarks.
	R.E.		Working Party.					
	O.	O.R.	O.	O.R.				
I	2	28	4	140	8	Communication Supports	from K.24 B.76 to K.24 A.92. Putting in fire steps	
II		3	4	600	5½	Front Line	from K.18 A.74 L.13 A.23 Widening trench to 6ft. Deepening 4'6" for drainage + fire steps	
III		3	2	70	4	from Reserve	Second line was worked from K.17 B.97 to K.18 A.88	{ Heavy rain stopped burrowing gap of 10 yards from ~ bus ~
IV		3	2	75	4	" Do.	Second - half of line worked from L.13 B.51 to L.13 A.55	

O.C. 4/70 Field Coy RE

Appendix IV

DAILY PROGRESS REPORT.

C.R.E. 59th. DIVISION.

Date...13...1...1917....

Item	STRENGTH OF PARTY.				Hours.	Where employed	Nature of Work.	Remarks.
	R.E.		Working Party.					
	O.	O.R.	O.	O.R.				
1	3	47	2	70	Epluith to Notre Dame Notre	Switch Line.	Clearing trench. Digging fire bay. Repair trench boards.	
	1	23	2	8	Notre Dame Notre	Switch Line.	Digging new part of switch. 100ft. long 6' wide x 2' deep	Night work.

Signed
for Major...........
467 Field Coy R.E.

Appendix IV

DAILY PROGRESS REPORT.

C.R.E. 59th. DIVISION. Date................

Item	STRENGTH OF PARTY. Working Party.		Hours.	where employed	Nature of Work.	Remarks.
	R.E. O.R.	O. O.R.				
1	25	150	8 to 5	Right C.T.	Clearing Right C.T. and laying duckboards.	
	35	140	8 to 5	Left C.T.	[illegible] Left C.T. [illegible]	
	38	60	8 to 5	Newport Support New trenches	[illegible] clothing trench [illegible]	
	10				Repairing [illegible]	
	10	8		TRESCAULT	Repairing [illegible]	

[signature]

Appendix IV
Opposite noon 13/12/17

DAILY PROGRESS REPORT.

C.R.E. 59th. DIVISION. H/Q N.W. Lua Coy R.E. Date 12th noon 12-12-17 to 12 o'c noon 13/12/17

Item	STRENGTH OF PARTY. Working Party.				Hours.	Where employed.	Nature of Work.	Remarks.
	R.E.		O.	O.R.				
	O.	O.R.						
II	2	37	3	170	5½	K17 B 86 to K18 A.55	Widening tunnel to 6'/5' & deepening to 4'6". 350 yds in length	
III		6	2	110	5	Front line	Second tier of wire coil in front Jeanne to ensure	
IV	1	35	5	160	5	K.23 B 88.	Trench dug across both roads to connect up to L/R Jeanne tunnel the logs made, widened a berm thrown back 100yds length	
						From R.23 B 89 to K24.10		
V			6	160		R.23. B.79 to K 24. A 5.	Wiring in front of support line & cutting gaps in rear.	

L. Lawrence
Major R.E.

Appendix I

DAILY PROGRESS REPORT.

C.R.E. 59th. DIVISION.   Date 14-12-17

HEADQUARTERS, R.E.
No. 59th (NORTH MIDLAND) DIVN.
14 DEC. 1917

STRENGTH OF PARTY.			Hours.	where employed		Nature of Work.	Remarks
R.E.		Working Party.					
O.	O.R.	O.	O.R.				
3	4.5	2	75	gchts	Tunnel line	Clearing trench. Digging six bays dragging low wire entanglements over position. Re-setting chevaux-de-frise	
1	23	2	82	North Trench Horse	Tunnel line	Digging new front of tunnel 160 ft dug 6' wide 9'2" deep.	Night work

Romsey Lt.

Appendix T

14/12/17

Daily Progress Report

WORKING PARTY			HOURS	WHERE EMPLOYED	NATURE OF WORK	REMARKS
O	O.R	O.R				
	6 1	30	4	C.T.	Carrying & laying Duck boards in C.T.	3/4 Leicesters
1	18 4	140	4	Unseen Support Trench	Making gaps in wire & erecting new wire entanglement	
	6	152	6	Unseen Support Trench	— do —	3/5 Sherwoods
			8	"	— do —	3/4 Lines
1	24 5	150?	4	"	Erecting Barbed Wire Entanglement	
	22		8	Tléguerie	Carrying party for duck boards & wire & acting as guides	

All Sappers work 8 hours

HEADQUARTERS R.E. No. 469 (NORTH MIDLAND) DIVN. 14 DEC. 1917

Appendix X

DAILY PROGRESS REPORT.

C.R.E. 59th. DIVISION. No. 470. Field Coy. R.E.   Date from 12 noon. 13.12.17 to 12 noon 14-12-17

Item	STRENGTH OF PARTY.			Hours.	Where employed	Nature of Work.	Remarks. R.E.
	R.E. C.	R.E. O.R.	Working Party O.	Working Party O.R.			
I	1	21			9	K.23. B.88	Putting two bridges & ft wire across roads leading to trenches.	
II	1	20			6	N.23.B.75 to N.24.A.10	New trench widened to 1ft & deepened to 4'.6".	These two parties were shelled heavily & little work could be done.
III			8.	75	4	R.23.B.79 R.23.B.95.80	Wiring commenced in front of trench.	
IV		17	3	90	5	K.317.B.85-30 to K.18.A.30-80	Trench drains ready for duck boards.	
V	1	25	3	95	5	L.13.A.42 to L.13.A.12	Trench drained ready for duck boards. Sandbags filled to barricade across road leading to L.13.A.25 & L.12.B.10.	
VI	1		1	10	3	L.19.A.	Communication trench cleared from L.19.A.15. to L.19.A.18.	

N.B. Owing to reliefs, work did not progress as well as usual.

[signature] Major O.C.

Appendix VI

DAILY PROGRESS REPORT.

C.R.E. 59th. DIVISION.   Date 16..12..1917.

Item	STRENGTH OF PARTY.		Working Party. Hours.		Where employed.	Nature of Work.	Remarks.
	R.E.		Working Party.				
	C.	O.R.	O.	O.R.			
		4	2	81	North Shaft Area	No work was done during the day is both mines + bathing huts to V camp also Baths & 467 F.S. site	
					Fawick River	Diff. work. just fawick 162×1 [illeg] Shed. + 3 [illeg] Sheds.	

A.P.Holley Lieut:
for Major R.E. 467 Field Co[illeg]

Appendix VI

DAILY PROGRESS REPORT.

C.R.E. 59th. DIVISION.   Date ....

Item	STRENGTH OF PARTY.				Hours.	Where employed.	Nature of Work.	Remarks.
	R.E.		Working Party.					
	O.	O.R.	O.	O.R.				
		18		170	8	Valley Support Trench	Cleaning up trenches, repairing trench sides, shifting Vauban Traverse and bridges North	
				250	5	Do K 35 b	Repairing and fire stepping Vauban Support Trench K 34 b	
		4		60	5	C.T.	Cleaning C.T. from R 34 b 9.7 to 41.9 a.1.5	
		4		50	5	Front C.T.	Cleaning & laying duckboards in C.T. R 28 c	
							Bringing up & carrying R.E. materials from dump	
		4		8	8	Cross Roads	Erecting Huts	

* Whole of working hours spent in working party had not arrived.

[signature]
O.C. 4th Field Co. R.E.

Appendix I
15-12-17

DAILY PROGRESS REPORT.

C.R.E. 59th. DIVISION. 470 Field Coy R.E.   Date from 12 noon 14-12-17 to 12 noon 15-12-17

Item	STRENGTH OF PARTY.			Hours.	Where employed	Nature of Work.	Remarks.
	R.E.		Working Party.				
	O.	O.R.	O.	O.R.			
I	1	18	—	—	5	K.17.B.95 to K.18.A.75	Repairing & cleaning trench	No working party reported to this office
II	1	4	3	60	4	K.17.B.45-65 to K.18.A.30/60	Strengthening wire	
III/IV	1	2½	1	30	4½	K.18.A.16 to K.18.A.40-05	Repairing trench & putting sandbag traverses across road M.18.A.45.0.5. Deepening trench	
V	1	—	—	10	3	K.18.A.92 to K.18.95.15	Cleaning heaven row windrow trench	
VI	1	—	—	—	6	K.19.A.10.45 to K.19.A.90/10	Deepening trench under bridge	
VII	1	20	4	120	4½	K.25.B.70-90 K.25.B.80.85 K.25.B.90-90	Wiring in front of trench & cutting gaps in old German wire at points	Enemy fire being in Hindenburg support line
VIII		4		4	4 platoons 4½		

W. Robins
Major O.C.

Appendix VIII

DAILY PROGRESS REPORT.

C.R.E. 59th. DIVISION.   Date .... 11.12.1917 ....

Item	STRENGTH OF PARTY.		Hours.	Where employed	Nature of Work.	Remarks.
	R.E.	Working Party				
	O.	O.R.	O.	O.R.			
1		22		75	Smith Royal	Putting new hinges strap & cross pieces on & refixing Refixing planks on floor. Placed trench for dust [illegible]	
2				400	[illegible]	Putting new lock & painted. Getting timber & [illegible]	
3				15	"	New baking materials for Hut Park [illegible]	

Appendix VI

DAILY PROGRESS REPORT.

C.R.E. 59th. DIVISION.   Date ....

Item.	STRENGTH OF PARTY. Hours.				where employed	Nature of Work.	Remarks.
	R.E.		Working Party.				
	O.	O.R.	O.	O.R.			
				65	6	Right C.T.	
				50	8	Left C.T.	
					8		
					10	Fire Trench.	

Appendix 14
2/2/17

DAILY PROGRESS REPORT.

C.R.E. 59th. DIVISION. 470th Field Coy. R.E.   Date from 12th noon 1/2/17 to 12th noon 2/2/17

Item	STRENGTH OF PARTY.				Hours.	Where employed.	Nature of Work.	Remarks.
	R.E.		Working Party.					
	C.	O.R.	O.	O.R.				
I	1	10	2	70	8	Front Line Left Section	Draining & Deepening Trench. Wiring second belt.	
II	1	6	2	90	8	— Do —		
III	1	18	3	80	8	Front Line Right Section	Draining & Deepening Trench. Wiring to road of h.15.c.77. Wiring second belt	
IV	1	3	2	50	4½	Front Line	Completing Fence	
V	1	17	1	—	5	From K.17.D.56.00 to K.24.M.25		
VI	1	—	4	120	4	Support Line	Wiring from K.17.D.46 to K.24.M.18. cutting gaps in wire	
	1	—	8	200	6		Cleaning out support line & putting in fire bays	
	1	7	1	12	6		Working on O.P. K.24.B.75.90	
	1	7	1	12	6		Working on O.P. h.19.A.20-68	

R. Robinson
Major O.C.

DAILY PROGRESS REPORT.

C.R.E. 59th. DIVISION.   Date 17.12.17

Appendix VII

HEADQUARTERS, R.E. 17 DEC 1917 59th MIDLAND DIV.

Item	STRENGTH OF PARTY. Hours.				Where employed	Nature of Work.	Remarks
	R.E.		Working Party.				
	O.	O.R.	O.	O.R.			
			2	75	Rycroft Farm	Supplying carrying parties for RE working parties. Party from Kyts & Ck Kyts at Rycroft Form	
			1	50	Kyts Farm Rycroft	Supplying working parties & fatigues	
				30	Interior Economy	Supplying working parties from billets	

Appendix VIV

DAILY PROGRESS REPORT.

C.R.E. 59th. DIVISION.   Date ....

Item	STRENGTH OF PARTY.				Hours.	Where employed	Nature of Work.	Remarks.
	R.E.		Working Party.					
	O.R.	O.	O.R.					
	11	1	30		3	Right C.T.	Clearing & Ducksboarding trenches	These Working Parties reported at 9.10 a.m. & are leaving at 1 p.m. owing to relief.
	11	1	30		3	Left C.T.	Do. Do.	
	44	(One C.of Pioneers)			½	Bihem-Chapel Wood Switch	Clearing a line stopping Switch Trench.	Company 1 Pioneers shouldn't turned up for work
	22	1	30		10	Trescault	Erecting Elephant huts for Brigade Headquarters	Working 2 shifts.
	6				8	Grand Ravine	Erecting shelters	

Sappers work 8 hours

J.B. James
Major
Offg. Hdqrs Field Coy. R.E.

Appendix VII

DAILY PROGRESS REPORT.

C.R.E. 59th. DIVISION.   4/0 Field Coy R.E.   Date from noon 14/12/17 to noon 15/12/17

Item	STRENGTH OF PARTY			Hours	Where employed	Nature of Work	Remarks
	R.E.		Working Party				
	O.	O.R.	O.	O.R.			
I	1	11	3	70	Lt Sector front line	Outposts & Incoming Trench	
II		4	2	40	K.18.A.03 R.18.B.113	Constructing 3 Posts on the line from K.18.A.05 to K.18.B.113. Sunken road	
III		4	2	60	from hut by sector	Digging 200 yds C.T. from K.18.B 90.15 to K.18.D 95.95 third tier of wire commenced	
IV		4	1	30	Southern Right Sector	Deepening & Draining front line Southern Right Sector	
V		15	2	50	L.19.A 20.85 L.13.C.31	C.T. from L.19.40.85 to L.13.C.31	
VI		12	2	70	K.17.C 40.20 K.17.C 75-10	Wiring	
VII	1	1	3	90		Work on O.P.	
	2	17					

R.R. [signature]
Major O.C.

D A I L Y   P R O G R E S S   R E P O R T.

Appendix IX

C.R.E. 59th. DIVISION.

Date ....[illegible]....

Item	STRENGTH OF PARTY. R.E. O.	R.E. O.R.	Working Party. O.	Working Party. O.R.	Hours.	Where employed	Nature of Work.	Remarks.
	[illegible]	[illegible]	2	68	[illegible]	Switch Line	Digging fire bays. Dragging [illegible] entanglement. Widening & deepening trench from K 35 c 2 [illegible] to K 35 b 3 [illegible] Laying trench boards from K 35 b 1 5 Northward.	
	1	[illegible]	2	52	[illegible]	Ditto	Digging new part of switch 106 [illegible] 8' wide at 12' deep.	
			2	300	[illegible]	Do	[illegible] of new switch [illegible] 15" x 6" [illegible]	

[illegible]
Major
RE 467 Field Coy RE

Appendix K

DAILY PROGRESS REPORT.

C.R.E. 59th. DIVISION.

Date .18th December 1917.

Item	STRENGTH OF PARTY.			Hours.	Where employed	Nature of Work.	Remarks.
	R.E.	Working Party.					
	O.R.	O.	O.R.				
	11			8	Right C.T.	Duckboarding & clearing C.T.s	No Working Parties reported.
	11			8	Left C.T.		
	44	1		8	Bihem — Chapel Wood Switch	Clearing a fire stepping Switch Trench.	Sappers have not returned for work today, after three working hard night. They will come on at 9am tomorrow.
	23	1	20	8	Trescault	Erecting Elephant Shelter for 177th Inf. Brigade H.Q.	2/5th Removed tt. (2 shifts).
	6			8	Grand Ravine	Constructing Shelters.	

M.J. Harrard Major
O/c. 469th Field Co. R.E.

Appendix IX
18/12/17

DAILY PROGRESS REPORT.

C.R.E. 59th. DIVISION. 470th Field Coy. R.E.   Date from 12c. noon 17/12/12 to 12c. noon 18/12/17.

Remarks.

HEADQUARTERS, R.E.
16 DEC. 1917
59th (NORTH MID.) DIV.

Item	STRENGTH OF PARTY.			Working Party.			Hours.	Where employed	Nature of Work
	R.E.								
	C.	O.R.	C.	O.	O.R.				
I	1	12			100		4	C.T from K.17.D.90-65 to R.17.D.90.25	Digging C.T.
II		3		2	70		4½	Support line Left Sector	Repairing trench & putting in fire bays
III		2	1	2	60		4½	Ditto —	Wiring
IV		15		3	70		4½	Front line Right Sector	Deepening fire trench & putting in fire bays
V		4		2	50		4	Ditto	Wiring Second line from hire
VI		20		3	21+5		4	C.T from K.18.D.80-70 to K.18.B.85-15	Digging C.T. 1st Task 2ft Deep
VII	1	7		1	12		8	K.24.75.-90.	Working on O.P.
VIII	1	7		1	12		8	L.19.A.20-68.	" " "

Major O.C.

DAILY PROGRESS REPORT.

C.R.E. 59th. DIVISION. Date....................

Item	STRENGTH OF PARTY.				Hours.	Where employed.	Nature of Work.	Remarks.
	R.E.		Working Party.					
	O.	O.R.	O.	O.R.				
		36	2	12			Railway Maintenance from KOYAL 2 RAILHEAD. Making embankment from INSSEA Battery Northwards	
		17	1	52			Repair new board walk to aid Traffic Board Points from sandbagging Joining with also Artillenie from 18.8.16	
				27½			Wire repair from 2.6.3.6 to from new wire Bunkers 14.3.16	

NO. 447 Railway

Appendix F

DAILY PROGRESS REPORT.

C.R.E. 59th. DIVISION.   Date ...19th December... 1917

Item	STRENGTH OF PARTY.			Hours.	Where employed.	Nature of Work.	Remarks.
	R.E.		Working Party.				
	C.	O.R.	O.	O.R.			
1	-	23	-	30	R.E. 2½ Staff 5½	LEFT C.T.	Cleaning & Duck-boarding C.T.	Half working party arrived at 10 a.m., remainder at 11 a.m. Finish work 3 p.m. R.E. departed for Barle 11 a.m.
	-	23	-	12	10	TRESCAULT	Erecting Elephant Shelter at 177th Inf. Brigade H.Q.	
1	-	44	1	25	6	BILHEM – CHAPEL WOOD SWITCH	Duck-boarding, fixing "A" frames & connecting up trench.	Pioneers reported for work. Sappers work 8 hours.
	-	8	-	-	8	GRAND RAVINE	Erecting Shelter.	

Commander Leeds
for O.C. Hdq. Field Co. R.E.

Appendix E
from 12½ noon 18/12/17 to 12½ noon 19/12/17

DAILY PROGRESS REPORT.

C.R.E. 59th. DIVISION. 470th Field Company R.E.   Date from 12½ noon 18/12/17 to 12½ noon 19/12/17

Item	STRENGTH OF PARTY.				Hours.	Where employed.	Nature of Work.	Remarks.
	R.E.		Working Party.					
	O.	O.R.	O.	O.R.				
I	1	55	3	100	5'	K.17.D.50-05 K.17.D.90-60 Left Sector	Digging C.T. Hyver Winning 2nd Belt	
II	1	2	1	2 Relieved	5'			
III	-	3	2	100	5'	from K.18.D.87 to K.18.B.85-15	Communication T. dug 3ft deep carrying Duckboards to front line.	
IV	-	1	2	100	5'			
V	-	2	1	1	5	L.13.C.80-70	Wiring in Right Sector & improving connection between Right Sector & Right Division	
VI	-	7	1	12	8	K.24.B.75-90	Completing O.P.	
-	1	7	1	12	8	K.19.H.10-68.	Working on O.P.	

P. Roberts
Major. O.C.

Appendix X.

DAILY PROGRESS REPORT.

C.R.E. 59th. DIVISION.   Date 20th Dec. 1917.

Item	STRENGTH OF PARTY.				Hours.	Where employed	Nature of Work.	Remarks.
	R.E.		Working Party.					
	O.	O.R.	O.	O.R.				
	2	27	3	150		Northumberland Hussars	Switch Line	Widening and deepening trench from K 29 to 6 1½ northwards
			1	25		R.W.F. Pioneers	do.	Wiring from K 29 to 54 northwards
		14					K 32 to 22	Setting out camp of shelters and unloading shelters & guarding same. One officer + 25 O.R. remained with horses in rear of HAVRINCOURT from 10.30 a.m. — 3 p.m.
		14					Lyhrs Dump	Loading Pontoons & Trestle on Wagons

F. B. Frew.
Major & O.C.
467 at Field Coy R.E.

DAILY PROGRESS REPORT.

C.R.E. 59th. DIVISION. Date ....

Item	STRENGTH OF PARTY.			Hours.	Where employed.	Nature of Work.	Remarks.
	R.E.		Working Party.				
	O.	O.R.	O.	O.R.			
		1		22	8	Right O.T.	Delivery & duck covering O.T.	
		1			8	Left O.T.	Do	
					5	Bligny Cavalry Road Gate	Putting up sign-posts at R.R. & I.C. Wire Screen to camouflage the Building work A Coms	
					8	Twin Camp	Completing Elephant Huts for 178 Brigade H.Q.	
		2		6	8	Grand Rosne	Erecting Huts	

Appendix to ....

Appendix I
20/12/17

DAILY PROGRESS REPORT.

C.R.E. 59th. DIVISION. 470th Field Coy. R.E.   Date from 10/12/17. 12/0 noon to 20/12/17 12/0 noon

Item	STRENGTH OF PARTY. Working Party.					Hours.	Where employed	Nature of Work.	Remarks.
	R.E.			O.R.					
	C.	O.F.	O.:	O.F.	O.R.				
I	1	18	7	2	220	4½	K.17.D.50.05 to K.18.A.26	Deepening & widening communication trench.	
II	1	2	2	2	60	4	K.18.B.1.70	Commencing third bed of wire	
III	1	2	2	2	60	4½	Front Line Left Sector.	Deepening & draining trench	
IV		13	2		75	3	K.13.C	Improving trench & wire to connect up with Right Division	
V	1	3	1	1	50	4	L.13.D.38. L.13.A.92.	Wiring third belt.	
VI	1	18	4	4	155	5	K.18.D.75.40 K.18.B.80.30	Widening & deepening C.T.	
VII	1	1	1	1	65	4	Front Line Right Sector.	Carrying Duckboards	
VIII	1	7	1	1	12	7	L.19.A.20-68	Working on O.P.	
IX	1	8	1	1	10	7	K.23.B.57.	Working on O.P.	

HEADQUARTERS, R.E. 59th (2nd N. MIDLAND) DIV.
No. 2363
20 DEC 1917

R. Common
Major. O.C.

SECRET.   Copy.No. 10

Appendix XL

SPECIAL ORDERS By

Lieut.Colonel.G.B.ROBERTS.R.E. C.R.E.59th.Division.

No. K3880
20 DEC. 1917
HEADQUARTERS, R.E.
59th (NORTH MIDLAND) DIVN.

Reference sheet.57.c.

1. In accordance with 59th.Division Order No.89. dated 19.12.17, the 59th.Division, less Artillery, will be relieved in the Line commencing 20th.December,1917.

2. The 3 Field Companies R.E.59th.Division will be relieved on the night of the 22/23rd.December,1917 and will march to their respective Brigade Group Camps as follows;-

467th.Field Co.R.E. to 176th.Bde.Group   BARASTRE.

469th.Field Co.R.E. to 177th.Bde.Group   ROCQUIGNY.

470th.Field Co.R.E. to 178th.Bde.Gropu   BEAULENCOURT.

Arrangements for accommodation will be made direct between O.C.Field Cos. and their respective Brigades.

3. The 78th.Field Co.R.E. 17th.Division (less one section) will move into billets occupied by the 467th. Field Co.R.E. at TRESCAULT and will take over the work of the 467th. and 469th.Field Cos.R.E.

The 93rd.Field Co.R.E. 17th.Division less one section) will move into billets occupied by the 469th. Field Co.R.E. and 470th.Field Co.R.E. and will take over the work of the 470th.Field Co.R.E.

Field Companies of the 17th.Division are are taking over the Horse Lines occupied by the Field Cos.R.E. of the 47th.Division.

4. Actual details of reliefs will be arranged between Units concerned.

5. Acknowledge.

Issued at 11.a.m.
20.12.1917.

Captain & Adjutant.
59th.Divisional R.E.

Copy.No.1. 59th.Div.G.
2. 59thDiv.Q.
3. 59th.Div.Train.
4. 467th.Field Co.R.E.
5. 469th.Field Co.R.E.
6. 470th.Field Co.R.E.
7. C.R.E.17th.Div.
8. Chief Engineer,Vth.Corps.
9. War Diary.
10. War Diary.
11. 176 Bde
12. 177 Bde
13. 178 Bde
14. Office copy

Appendix X¹⁴

DAILY PROGRESS REPORT.

C.R.E. 59th. DIVISION.   Date 21st Dec. 1917

[Stamp: HEADQUARTERS, R.E. 21 DEC 1917 59th (NORTH MIDLAND) DIV.]

STRENGTH OF PARTY.			Hours.	Where employed	Nature of Work.	Remarks.
R.E.			Working Party			
C.	O.R.	O.	O.R.			
2	35	3	150	Northumberland Hussars	Switch line	Widening & deepening trench from K.29 to 61½ northwards
		1	25	R.W.F. Pioneers	do	Mining switch south of Chapel Wood
		1	32		K.32.b.22	Construction of Shelter Camp

F.B. Jeans.
Major & O.C.
467 at Field Coy R.E.

Appendix XIII

DAILY PROGRESS REPORT.

C.R.E. 59th. DIVISION.

Date ...... 3rd December 1917.

Item	STRENGTH OF PARTY			Hours.	Where employed	Nature of Work.	Remarks.
	R.E.		Working Party				
	O.	O.R.	O.	O.R.			
1	-	36	-	17	5	BILHEM – CHAPEL WOOD SWITCH	200'yds. repeated with "A" Frames & Ex. Metal. (250 yds. of this length will be repaired with "A" Frames & Excielled before tomorrow)	R.N.F. Pioneers
	-	6	-	6	5	Do.	Strengthening existing wiring in front of this position. (Two belts of wire now run the whole way from Railway at K.22.a.8.9 to K.16.a.8.4)	Do.
	-	-	3	107	4	Do.	Joining British Trench from K.16.d.3.5 to HINDENBURG SUPPORT. This was dug 6 ft wide & 3'6" deep, & will be completed to 6 ft deep tonight.	Night work 3rd Corps Cyclists
	-	-	-	-	8	RIGHT C.T.	Clearing & Duck boarding E.T.	
	-	-	-	-	8	LEFT C.T.	Do. Do.	
	1	11	-	-	8	TRESCAULT.	Erecting huts for 177th Brigade H.Q.	This was not completed yesterday owing to additions being required
	-	6	-	-	8	GRAND RAVINE.	Erecting Shelters.	

W Shewan Lieut
for O/C. 467th Field Co. R.E.

Appendix XIII
2/4/17

DAILY PROGRESS REPORT.

C.R.E. 59th. DIVISION. 470th Field Coy R.E.   Date from 12 noon 20/9/17 to 12 noon 21/9/17

[Stamp: HEADQUARTERS R.E. 59TH (NORTH MIDLAND) DIVN. No. ... 21 DEC 1917]

Item	STRENGTH OF PARTY.				Hours.	Where employed	Nature of Work.	Remarks.
	R.E.			Working Party.				
	C.	O.R.	O.	O.R.				
I	1	10	3	100	4½	R.17.D.50-05	Widening & deepening C.T.	
II	1	10	2	50	4	R.18.A.88	Wiring River bed	
III	1	1	1	20	5		Deepening frontline trenches	
IV	1	13	1	40	5	L.13.C.90-65	Trench passed to wide Rfr Div trench 4'-6" deep	
V	1	2	1	28	5		Deepening frontline Rfr trench	
VI	1	2	2	50	4		Wiring third belt Reformation	
VII	1	20	4	200	5	R.18.D.85-20 R.18.A.90-30	Constructing C.T.	
VIII	1	7		12	6	R.23.B.57	Working on O.P.	
IX	1	8		12	6	L.19.A.20-68	Working on O.P.	

[signature]
Major. O.C.

Appendix XIV

470th. Field Co. R.E.

PROGRESS REPORT - 12 noon 21/12/17 to 12 noon 22/12/17.

R.E.		Working Parties			Work carried out.	Hrs.	Remarks.
O.	Sect	O.	O.R.	Batt. Situation			
1	14	2	60	K.17.D K.18.A	Widening & deepening C.T.	4½	
1	4	2	60		Wiring thro' belt of wire	4	
1	21	3	100		Improving tunnel to rifle firemen	6	
1	21	4	160	K.18.D 23 K.18.B 23	Widening & deepening C.T.	5	
1	7		12		Working on DP	7	
1	7		12		Working on DP	7	

[signature]

Major O.C. 470th. Field Co. R.E.

Date...............

WAR DIARY / INTELLIGENCE SUMMARY

Army Form C. 2118

Continued

Place	Date	Hour	Summary of Events and Information	Remarks and references to Appendices
ACHIET-LE-PETIT	22/11/17	9 p.m.	59 Division Order N° 80 Copy N° 6 received	LENS Khm 1/100,000 Khm
ETRICOURT	23/11/17	3 p.m.	CRE close office at ACHIET-LE-PETIT and opens at ETRICOURT. 467 Field Coy RE proceeded from COURCELLES to HEUDICOURT 469 " " " ACHIET-LE-PETIT to DESSART WOOD 470 " " " GOMIECOURT to EQUANCOURT	Sheet 57c 1/20000 Khm — under their respective Brigades
do.		9.50 p.m	G.13.167 received – Field days RE taken from Brigade Group for work under CRE as per instructions received from III Corps so from the 25 inst.	Khm
do.	24.11.17	11 a.m.	CRE order N° 6 issued. See appendix B attached.	
do.	25.11.17		467 Field Coy RE proceed to BEAUCAMP to erect accommodation for themselves and to continue erecting huts for battalion camps under orders from CE III Corps.	
			469 and 470 Field Coys RE proceeded to GOUZEAUCOURT to erect accommodation for themselves, the infantry companies attached to them and 2 battalions	Khm
	27.11.17	1 p.m.	59 Division Order N° 81 Copy N° 6 received	Khm
do.	28.11.17	6.30 p.m.	59 Division Order N° 82 " " 6	Khm
TRESCAULT	29.11.17	10 a.m.	CRE moved office to TRESCAULT Q10a7 – Sheet 57c 1/20000 470 Field Coy RE upon moving, no orders by CRE from EQUANCOURT to FLESQUIERES were attacked by the enemy which had broken through our line. This company held up the enemy very successfully and eventually drove them back on their own particular front. To the other side of GOUZEAUCOURT.	
	30.11.17		¶ Lieut F.G. HARNESS was taken prisoner by the enemy. He was not wounded. 3 O.R. killed 12 O.R. wounded 4 O.R. missing	Khm

Manley Lieut R.E.
Capt & Lt Col
59

ORIGINAL.

Vol 12

WAR DIARY
of
HEADQUARTERS R.E. ENGINEERS.

59th DIVISION.

VOLUME XI.

From 1st Jan/1918 — to — 31st Jan/1918.

Army Form C. 2118

WAR DIARY

HEAD QUARTERS
59TH DIVISIONAL R.E.

INTELLIGENCE SUMMARY

(Erase heading not required.)

Instructions regarding War Diaries and Intelligence Summaries are contained in F. S. Regs., Part II. and the Staff Manual respectively. Title Pages will be prepared in manuscript.

Place	Date	Hour	Summary of Events and Information	Remarks and references to Appendices
LE CAUROY BILLET #1.	1/1/18		467th Field Company R.E. } Training notes attached Programmes APPENDIX I	Sheet 51c 1/40,000 H.F.
"	2/1/18		469th " " " " " " " " " " 470th " " " " " " " " " " Received D.H.Q letter S.G. 2/7. 59th Division G.H.Q. Reserve from Reading Lt. 31.01. See - , 01 jem. 467th Field Company R.E. } Training paper attached Programmes. APPENDIX I. 469th " " " 470th " " "	H.F.
"	3/1/18		467 " " " Bunking & repairing Billets 469 " " " } in Brigade Jeen. 470 " " "	H.F.
"	4/1/18		Received Preparatory Orders for move of 59th Division by Tactical Train. 467th Field Company R.E. } Bunking & repairing Billets 469 " " " } in Brigade areas. 470 " " "	H.F.
"	5/1/18		467 " " " " 469 " " " " 470 " " " "	H.F.
"	6/1/18		467 " " " " 469 " " " " 470 " " " "	H.F.
"	7/1/18		467 " " " " 469 " " " " 470 " " " "	H.F.

Army Form C. 2118

WAR DIARY
or
INTELLIGENCE SUMMARY
(Erase heading not required.)

Instructions regarding War Diaries and Intelligence Summaries are contained in F.S. Regs., Part II and the Staff Manual respectively. Title Pages will be prepared in manuscript.

Place	Date	Hour	Summary of Events and Information	Remarks and references to Appendices
LE CAUROY	8/1/18		467th Field Company R.E. Bombing & Improving Billets in Brigade Area.	Sheet 51.C 1/40000.
	9/1/18		469th " " "	X.T.
			470th " " "	
			467th " " "	
			469th " " "	
			470th " " "	
	10/1/18		467th " " "	N.T.
			469th " " "	
			470th " " "	
	11/1/18		467th " " "	N.T.
			469th " " "	
			470th " " "	
	12/1/18		467th " " "	N.T.
			469th " " "	
			470th " " "	
	13/1/18		467th " " "	See Appendix I
			469th " " "	N.T.
			470th " " "	
	14/1/18		467th " " "	N.T.
			469th " " "	
			470th " " "	
			Received Divisional Warning Order No.972 Copy No.6 at 11 a.m.	

Army Form C. 2118

WAR DIARY
INTELLIGENCE SUMMARY Continued

(Erase heading not required.)

Instructions regarding War Diaries and Intelligence Summaries are contained in F. S. Regs., Part II. and the Staff Manual respectively. Title Pages will be prepared in manuscript.

Place	Date	Hour	Summary of Events and Information	Remarks and references to Appendices
LE CAUROY BILLET A¹	12/1/18		467th Field Company R.E. ⎫ Bending & Repairing Billets in Brigade Area	Sheet 57 C
	13/1/18		469th " " ⎬	1/40,000.
			470th " " ⎭	N.F.
	14/1/18		467th " " ⎫	
			469th " " ⎬ "	N.F.
			470th " " ⎭	
	17/1/18		467th " " ⎫	
			469th " " ⎬ "	N.F.
			470th " " ⎭	
	18/1/18		467th " " ⎫	
			469th " " ⎬ "	N.F.
			470th " " ⎭	
	19/1/18		467th " " ⎫	
			469th " " ⎬ "	N.F.
			470th " " ⎭	
	20/1/18	11 am	Addendum to 59 Division Warning Order Nº 92 copy Nº 6 received	Kuren
	22 23 24 25 26		Field Companies proceed with the repairing and breaking of Billets in their Brigade areas.	lener

Army Form C. 2118

WAR DIARY
~~or~~ INTELLIGENCE SUMMARY
Continued

(Erase heading not required.)

Instructions regarding War Diaries and Intelligence Summaries are contained in F.S. Regs., Part II. and the Staff Manual respectively. Title Pages will be prepared in manuscript.

Place	Date	Hour	Summary of Events and Information	Remarks and references to Appendices
LE CAUROY	27/11/18	6-30 pm	1156/6/3 G received and CRE letter K 4024 copy attached issued to No. two companies concerned	Khun
	29/11/18		467 and 469 FIELD Coy RE proceeded to BERLES-AU-BOIS in accordance with CRE order K 4024 issued on the 27 inst see Appendix IV	Khun
	30/11/18		467 and 469 FIELD Coy RE proceeded from BERLES-AU-BOIS to ERVILLERS and came under orders of the CRE 40 DIVISION from that date.	Khun
	31/11/18		467 and 469 FIELD Coys RE repairing billets in ERVILLERS, GOMIECOURT BEHAGNIES, HAMELINCOURT BOIRY ST MARTIN MORY and erecting cookhouses, latrines etc. Construction of a dump dug-out for R.H.Q at BEHAGNIES. 470 FIELD Coy Training. Ammunition wiring, physical and company drill musketry, bayonet fighting, machine and Lewis gun instruction, Bombing and laying out of Trenches see Appendix III	Khun

Klaville Lew
Capt and
adjt
59 Div
RE

467th. Field Coy. R.E.

PROGRAMME OF WORK.

APPENDIX 1.

Week ending Jan. 5th. 1918.

Day.	Section 1.	Section 2.	Section 3.	Section 4.	Mounted Section.
Monday.	Musketry. Knots & lashgs. Physical Tring	Squad Drill without arms. Knots & lashings. Musketry. Physical Tng.	Demolitions. Physical Tng.	Topography. Physical Tng.	Horse Management Phy:Tng.
Tuesday.	Demolitons.	Squad Drill without arms. Topography. Box Respirator Drill	Musketry.	Knots & lashings.	Horse Management
Wednesday.	Musketry.	Squad Drill without arms. Demolitions. Recreational Training.	Topography.	Theory of Bridging.	do.
Thursday.	Theory of Bridging.	Squad Drill without arms. Musketry. Physical Training.	Demolitions.	Topography.	do. Phy:Tng.
Friday.	Topography.	Squad Drill without arms. Theory of Bridging. Box respirator Drill.	Musketry.	Demolitions.	Horse Managem't
Saturday.	R O U T E M A R C H.				

Week ending Jan. 12th. 1918.

Day.	Section 1.	Section 2.	Section 3.	Section 4.	Mounted Section.
Monday.	Demolitions.	Squad Drill without arms. Topography. Physical Training	Theory of Brid'g.	Musketry.	Box Res. Drill.
Tuesday.	Box.Res.Drill.	Company Drill Wiring. Bayonet Fighting.	Field Works.	Lecture.	Musketry.
Wednesday.	Lecture.	Squad Drill with Arms. Box Res.Drill Recreational Training.	Wiring.	Field Works.	Driving.
Thursday.	Field Works.	Company Drill. Lecture. Bayonet Fighting.	Box Res.Drill.	Wiring.	Musketry. Phy'l Tng
Friday.	Wiring.	Extended Order Drill. Field Works. Physical Training.	Lecture.	Box.Res.Drill.	Driving.
Saturday.	R O U T E M A R C H .				

APPENDIX 1.

470th. Field Co. R.E.

PROGRAMME OF TRAINING - 31.12.17 to 12.1.18.

First Week.

Section.	Monday. 9-12.	Monday. 2-3.30.	Tuesday. 9-12.	Tuesday. 2-3.30.	Wednesday. 9-12.	Wednesday. 2-3.30.	Thursday. 9-12.	Thursday. 2-3.30.	Friday. 9-12.	Friday. 2-3.30.	Saturday. 9-12.30
No.1.	Physical & Section Drill. Bayonet Exercise.	Extended Order Drill.	Physical Training & Section D'l. Bayonet Fighting.	Extended Order Drill & Musketry.	Physical Training & Section D'l Bayonet Fighting.	Company Drill.	Wiring Apron.	Laying out Trenches.	Laying out & digging trenches.	Wiring apron.	Extended Order & Company Drill.
No.2.	do.	do.	do.	do.	do.	do.	Laying out & digging Trenches.	Wiring apron.	Wiring apron.	Laying out trenches.	do.
No.3.	do.	do.	do.	do.	do.	do.	Wiring High & low.	Laying out trenches.	Laying out & digging trenches.	Wiring high & low.	do.
No.4.	do.	do.	do.	do.	do.	do.	Laying out & digging trenches.	Wiring high & low.	Wiring high & low.	Laying out trenches.	do.

Second Week.

Section.	Monday. 9-12.	Monday. 2-3.30.	Tuesday. 9-12.	Tuesday. 2-3.30.	Wednesday. 9-12.	Wednesday. 2-3.30.	Thursday.	Friday.
No.1.	Wiring High & Low.	Squad Drill.	Attack on Village & Consolidation.	Field Geometry.	Attack on Position.	Shell-hole consolidation.	Instructing Brigade in Wiring and Laying out Trenches.	
No.2.	Squad Drill & Physical Train'g.	Wiring High & Low.	do.	do.	do.	do.	do.	- ditto -
No.3.	Wiring apron.	Squad Drill & physical training.	do.	do.	do.	do.	-- ditto --	
No.4.	Physical Training & squad Drill.	Wiring apron.	do.	do.	do.	do.	-- ditto --	

APPENDIX II

467th Field Co. R.E.

C.R.E. 59th Division.

    Ref. Programme of work & training for fortnight commencing January 15th. 1918.

    As it was found quite impossible to carry out the programme of work for the first fortnight ending 14th inst, owing to the amount of work required to be done to billets in this Brigade Area, it is proposed to work in last fortnight's programme if the amount of work we have on hand will permit.

    I estimate however that the Company will be entirely engaged on renovation of billets for another week.

In the Field.   (Sd) Basil C. Deacon,
Jan.15th.1918.   Capt. for O.C.
                                          467th Field Co.
                                          R.E.

Appendix II

469th Field Co. R.E.
PROGRAMME OF TRAINING for Week ending 20th Jan. 1918

Hours.	Monday.	Tuesday.	Wednesday.	Thursday.	Friday.	Saturday.	Sunday.
Morning. 9 – 12.	Parade and Inspection. Anti-gas Drill. Bayonet fighting. Extended Order Drill.	Parade and Inspection. Practical fitting of "A" Frames, and revetting.	Parade and Inspection. Lecture on Boning, grading & levelling. Practical Levelling and Grading.	Parade and Inspection. No.1 & 2 Sections - Practical Wiring. No.3 & 4 Secs. Squad Drill & Musketry.	Parade and Inspection. Squad Drill. Anti-gas Drill. Musketry Exer's. Physical	Parade and Inspection. No.3 & 4 sections Practical wiring. No.1 & 2 sections Squad Drill and Musketry.	Parade and Inspection.
Afternoon. 2 – 4.	Lecture on Revetting, fitting of "A" frames and duck-board tracks.	Practical fitting of "A" frames and revetting.	Baths. Lecture of General interest "A Workman's House" by Lieut.Parker,R.E.	Lecture on "Strength of Materials".	Lecture on "Care of Feet & bodily health, fitting of equipment, care of arms and equipment."		Church Parade.

Week ending 20th. January 1918.

| Morning. 9 – 12. | Parade and Inspection. Squad Drill. Phy'l.exerc's. | Parade and Inspection. Musketry. | Parade and Inspection. Lecture on "Explosives & demolitions." | Parade and Inspection. Lecture on "Wiring & wiring drills. | Parade and Inspection. Nos.3 & 4 Sections: Wiring Practice. No.1 & 2 Secs. Lecture on "Trench elements, revetting, etc". | Parade and Inspection. No.1 & 2 secs. Wiring practice. No.3 & 4 secs. Lecture on "Trench elements, revetting, etc". | Parade and Inspection. |
| Afternoon. 2 – 4. | Lecture on "The use of tools, packing of tool carts, use of pendant clinometer". | Musketry. | No.3 & 4 secs: "Lecture on explosives & demolitions". No.1 & 2 secs: Gas Drill & Bayonet fighting. | No.3 & 4 secs: Practice wiring. No.1 & 2 secs: Field Demolitions. | No.1 & 2 secs: Practice wiring. No.3 & 4 secs: Field Demolitions. | | Church Parade. |

APPENDIX V

470th. Field Co. R.E.

TRAINING PROGRAMME - to January 27th.1918.

First Week.

Sect.	Monday. 9 - 12.	Monday. 2 - 3.30.	Tuesday. 9 - 12.	Tuesday. 2 - 3.30.	Wednesday. 9 - 12.	Wednesday. 2 - 3.30.	Thursday. 9 - 12.	Thursday. 2 - 3.30.	Friday. 9 - 12.	Friday. 2 - 3.30.	Saturday. 9 - 12.
No.1	Physical & sectn.drill. Bayonet ex.	Wiring, high & low.	Musketry.	Extended Order Drill.	Wiring apron.	Range.	Map reading (practical)	Laying out trenches.	Wiring apron.	Lecture: Dug-out Constrn.	Company Drill & Ext'd order
No.2	do.	Ext'd Order Drill.	Wiring high & low.	Musketry.	Map read'g (practical)	Laying out trenches.	Wiring Apron.	Range.	Musketry & ex. ord drill.	do.	do.
No.3	do.	Musketry.	Map read'g (practical)	Laying out trenches.	Wiring apron.	Ex.Order Drill.	Range.	Lecture on Demolitions.	Wiring high & low.	Wiring apron.	do.
No.4	do.	do.	do.	Wiring apron.	Range.	do.	Wiring high & low.	do.	Ex. Order Drill.	Lecture: Dug-out Constrn.	do.

Second Week.

Sect.	Monday. 9 - 12.	Monday. 2 - 3.30.	Tuesday. 9 - 12.	Tuesday. 2 - 3.30.	Wednesday. 9 - 12.	Wednesday. 2 - 3.30.	Thursday. 9 - 12.	Thursday. 2 - 3.30.	Friday. 9 - 12.	Friday. 2 - 3.30.	Saturday. 9 - 12.
No.1	do.	do.	Instructing Bde. in wiring and laying out trenches.		Range.	Lecture.	Musketry.	Shell-hole consolidation	Range.	Knots & lashings.	do.
No.2	Wiring apron.	Range.	do.	do.	Laying out trenches.	do.	Range.	do.	do.	Lecture.	do.
No.3	Ex.Order Drill.	Musketry.	Range.	do.	do.	do.	Musketry.	do.	Range.	Knots & Lashings.	do.
No.4	Phy. & Sect.Drill. Bayonet ex.	do.	Range.	do.	Wiring apron.	do.	Phy. & Section Drill.	do.	Musketry & bayonet exercise.	Range.	do.

470th Field Co. R.E.

TRAINING PROGRAMME - 30.1.18 to 9.2.18.

Day.	No.1 Section.	No.2 Section.	No.3 Section.	No.4 Section.
Wednesday.	Lewis Gun Instruction.	Wiring and Demolitions. Mobile charges.	Musketry and Bayonet fighting.	Laying out Trenches.
Thursday.	Wiring and Demolitions.	Lewis Gun Instruction.	Laying out Trenches.	Musketry and Bayonet fighting.
Friday.	Laying out Trenches and	Musketry and Bayonet fighting.	Lewis Gun Instruction.	Wiring and Demolitions.
Saturday.	Physical Training and Company Drill.			
Monday.	Musketry and Demolitions.	Laying out Trenches.	Wiring and Demolitions.	Lewis Gun Instruction.
Tuesday.	Machine Gun Instruction.	Wiring.	Demolitions.	Squad Drill.
Wednesday.	Demolitions. Mobile charges.	Machine Gun Instruction.	Squad Drill.	Wiring.
Thursday.	Wiring.	Squad Drill.	Machine Gun Instruction.	Demolitions.
Friday.	Squad Drill.	Demolitions.	Wiring.	Machine Gun Instruction.
Saturday.	Bombing; Physical Training and Company Drill.			

War Diary.

APPENDIX. IV

1156/6/3.G.
27.1.18.

C.R.E. 59th Division.
'Q'.
40th Div.(for information).

1. The 467th. and 469th. Field Cos. R.E. will march on Jan. 29th to BERLES-AU-BOIS, and on Jan.30th to ERVILLERS where accommodation is being arranged for the personnel of the Companies by 40th Division.

The transport of the Coys. will remain at BERLES-AU-BOIS.

2. On arraival in the 40th Div. area, the Field Coys. R.E. will come under the orders of the C.R.E. 40th Div. They are, however, to be prepared to entrain with their present Infantry Bdes Groups at 48 hours notice.

3. Acknowledge.

27.1.18.   (Sd) R.St.G.Gorton, Colonel.
                    G.S. 59th. Division.

O.C. 467th Field Co. R.E.   C.R.E. 59th Div.No. 4024.K
O.C. 469th Field Co. R.E.
O.C. 470th Field Co. R.E.

The two Field Coys. concerned will each send forward an Officer to arrange billets at BERLES-AU-BOIS and take over accommodation at ERVILLERS.

The O.C. 470th Field Co. R.E. will take over the work now being done by the 467th Field Co. R.E. for Colonel Thorne's Battalion.

Acknowledge.

In the Field.   (Sd) K. Neville Moss.
27. 1. 18.   Captain & Adjutant,
                            59th. Divisional R.E.

Copies to:- 176th Inf. Bde.
            177th Inf. Bde.
            59th. Div. Train.

/ WAR DIARY /
INTELLIGENCE SUMMARY

HEAD QUARTERS R.E. Army Form C. 2118
5TH DIVISION
FOR FEBRUARY

Place	Date	Hour	Summary of Events and Information	Remarks and references to Appendices
LE CAUROY	1/2/18		467 Field Coy RE working under orders of CRE 40 Division repairing huts and creating an incinerator in No 8 Camp MORY. Repairing huts in GOMIECOURT. ERVILLERS. BEHAGNIES. HAMELINCOURT. ARGYLL CAMP and FERMOY CAMP. Constructing mined dugouts at DIV HEAD QRTS at BEHAGNIES.	SHEET LENS 1/100,000
			469 Field Coy RE. Working upon mess and officers accommodation in DYSART CAMP. ERVILLERS. MORY NORTH CAMP. HAMELINCOURT. DURROW CAMP. Repairing DIV BATHS and church army hut.	
			470 Field Coy RE. Training, musketry, physical and squad drill. Instruction in LEWIS and machine guns.	
		11 am	5th Div. order No 94 Copy No 5 received	Known
do	2.2.18		Companies continue the work detailed above	Known
do	3.2.18	6 pm	CRE letter K.4053 copy attached sent to all concerned	Known
			Companies continue the work detailed in report for the 1st Feb.	
do	4.2.18		T/Lt Col A.C. HOWARD M.C. RE(T) reported for duty as CRE 5th Div. authority A.G.'s Mo. Appts/2467 dated 31/1/18. Companies continued the work detailed in report for the 1st Feb.	Known
	5.2.18 6.2.18	3 pm	Companies continue the work detailed in report for the 1st Feb. CRE inspects 470 Field Coy parade, mounted and dismounted ranks, lines transport	Known

Army Form C. 2118

WAR DIARY
INTELLIGENCE SUMMARY
Continued
(Erase heading not required.)

Instructions regarding War Diaries and Intelligence Summaries are contained in F.S. Regs., Part II. and the Staff Manual respectively. Title Pages will be prepared in manuscript.

Place	Date	Hour	Summary of Events and Information	Remarks and references to Appendices
LE CAUROY	19/2/18	9pm	59 DIVISION ORDER No 95 copy No 5 received	Sheet - LENS 1/100,000
			CRE 40 DIVISION letter 194/4 dated 6/2/18 regarding relief of field Companies received.	
			59 DIVISION Administrative instructions No 13 received	Khm
	20/2/18		470 FIELD Coy RE proceed under the orders of 178 BDE by route march to GOUY-EN-ARTOIS area.	
			469 FIELD Coy RE. working upon accommodation in DYSART CAMP NORTH CAMP MORY. DURROW CAMP. MORY ABBEY CAMP. Constructing a dug out on the MORY-ECOUST RD. Erecting linen store room at DIV. BATHS.	
			467 FIELD Coy RE. working at Nº 2 Camp MORY, DIVL TRAIN Camp GOMIECOURT. FERMOY CAMP. ENNISKILLEN CAMP. ARGYLE CAMP. water point at ERVILLERS, D.A.D.O.S. Store, Monterncy in ERVILLERS. Sinking well in ARGYLE Camp, making dugouts at ANX BEHAGNIES	Khm
	21/2/18		467 and 469 FIELD Coy RE continue the work as detailed in report for yesterday	
			469 FIELD Coy RE. moved into the Camp of the 209 FIELD Coy RE B.21.d.5.8	Sheet 57c 1/40,000
			470 FIELD Coy RE moved from the GOUY-EN-ARTOIS area to MERCATEL area CRE called upper CE 7th Corps and routed 469 Fielding RE	Khm

Army Form C. 2118

WAR DIARY
or
INTELLIGENCE SUMMARY Continued

(Erase heading not required.)

Instructions regarding War Diaries and Intelligence Summaries are contained in F.S. Regs., Part II. and the Staff Manual respectively. Title Pages will be prepared in manuscript.

Place	Date	Hour	Summary of Events and Information	Remarks and references to Appendices
LE CAUROY	10/2/18	10 am	CRE office closed at LE CAUROY at 10 am and opened at the same hour at GOMIECOURT	See Sheet 57 C } 4400 5/3 }
GOMIECOURT		10 am	467 Field Coy RE taken over from the 226 Field Coy RE in the right Sector and taken over accommodation as follows. HQrs and 3 Sections in MOREUIL C10 c.6.3. Transport and 1 Section in ERVILLERS B20 a.2.3	
			469 Field Coy RE continue work upon Camps in back area	Khm
do	11/2/18		470 — do — in camp at M.23 c.25.	
			CRE went round centre sector of divisional front line.	
			469 Field Coy RE taken over from the 231 Field Coy RE in the centre sector. They are found at accommodation at C.8 a.2.3 ECOUST & 3 Sections at	Khm
do	12/2/18		CRE went round all the sectors	
			470 Field Coy RE took over from 229 Field Coy RE in the left Sector. Their own accommodation as follows. HQrs. 1 Section and Transport at ST LEGER T26 c.9.1, 3 Section at V19 a.2.3.	Khm
BEHAGNIES	13/2/18	10 am	CRE takes over from CRE 40 Division and moved Office to BEHAGNIES	
			CRE went round left sector and visited 177 and 178 Infantry Bde Head Quarters	Khm
			12 Yorkshire Regt. Pioneers come under 59 Division from 10 am to day	
do	14/2/18		CRE went round right sector	
			467 Field Coy RE repairing wells and billet in MOREUIL, constructing tramway in RAILWAY RESERVE, making dugout for Company HQ in TANK AVENUE constructing track from MOREUIL to VRAUCOURT, and sign posting to BATTLE ZONE.	

WAR DIARY
INTELLIGENCE SUMMARY — Continued

Army Form C. 2118

Place	Date	Hour	Summary of Events and Information	Remarks and references to Appendices
BEHAGNIES	14/2/18		Continued:— 46.9 FIELD Coy R.E. making dug-outs in trenches. Biggon Trenches in BATTLE ZONE. Making tramway C.T. in ECOUST. Building a trench foot treatment shelter. Clearing mud out of PELICAN AVENUE to BOVIS TRENCH, GORDON RESERVE, Extracting company stables and making earth work tramway. Protection. 470 FIELD Coy R.E. bevelling and duckboarding GOODWOOD LANE, ENFIN TRENCH. Revining and levelling parapet and parados in BORDER TRENCH, making a T.M. Emplacement in STRAY SUPPORT. Rigging ECOUST switch. PIONEERS:— Working in STAFFORD LANE, LEG LANE, QUEENS LANE, TANK AVENUE. NEW TRENCH to left of TANK AVENUE and to right of JR, SYDNEY AVENUE. Repairing Tramways, ECOUST MORY ROAD and ECOUST-SUCRERIE ROAD.	Sheet 57 B and 57 C 1/40000
do.	15/2/18		CRE and ADJT visited the centre sector with O.C. 469 Field Coy.	Kwm
do.	16/2/18		CRE visited right centre and left Brigade Headquarters. Inspected 470 Field Coy billets and Transport lines at ST LEGER	Kwm
do.	17/2/18		CRE inspected billets and Transport lines of 469 FIELD Coy R.E. at ERVILLERS in the morning and visited MORY BATHS and Personnel Rooms in the afternoon	Kwm
do	18/2/18		CRE inspected all work along the whole Divisional front. Lt. E.S. MILLARD reported for duty with 469 FIELD Coy in lieu of Lt. E.S. ROUSE to command Pinnel Light Section	Kwm
do	19/2/18		CRE visited right Artillery (cap) and Centre Road Bombs. Infantry work done by the Field Companies and 12" YORKS PIONEERS were taking over from do to Dw on Tr. 13	Appendix II Kwm
do	20/2/18	10 am	CRE visited Left Brigade front and ECOUST. 53 DIVISION WARNING ORDER No 97 copy 5 received	Kwm

WAR DIARY

INTELLIGENCE SUMMARY

Army Form C. 2118

Continued

(Erase heading not required.)

Place	Date	Hour	Summary of Events and Information	Remarks and references to Appendices
BEHAGNIES	21/2/18		CRE went round right sector of Divisional Front	K.W.M. Ord. S.P.S. & S.P. 1/40 oom
	22/2/18		CRE took the O.C. 6/7. ROYAL SCOTS PIONEERS round the work being done by the 12? YORKS PIONEERS and visited the 470 FIELD Coy REs	K.W.M.
		5pm	CRE attended a conference held by G.O.C DIVISION	
	23/2/18		CRE visited U 69 and 470 FIELD Coy., CAPT M.A. BOSWELL 469 F.Coy evacuated sick	K.W.M.
	24/2/18		CRE went round right sector and visited 176, 177 and 178 INF. BDES. Head quarters	K.W.M.
	25/2/18		CRE accompanied CE VI Corps and G.S.O.I. on a tour of inspection of the Divisional front line.	K.W.M.
	26/2/18		CRE went round left sector of Divisional front, and visited Centre Bde. Head quarters. Copy of works progress report of work carried out on 59 DIVISIONAL FRONT marked appendix III is attached hereto. 59 DIV WARNING ORDER N° 98 K.W.M. copy N°5 received	
	27/2/18	7.30 pm	CRE visited the 3 Brigade Head quarters. G.O.C in C visited Divisional Headquarters	
			CRE OPERATION ORDER N° 2 issued to all concerned see appendix IV attached hereto.	K.W.M.
	28/2/18	after 7.30pm	59 DIVISION ORDER N° 99 copy N°5 received	
			CRE went round right and centre Brigade fronts.	

K Whittleworth
Capt. & adj
59 Div. R.E.

SECRET.

C.O. 467th. Field Co. R.E.
    469th. Field Co. R.E.
    470th. Field Co. R.E.
    "G" 59th. Div. (for infmn)
    C.R.E. 40th. Div. "   "

1. Upon a date to be notified later the Field Coys of the 59th. Divl R.E. will take over from the Field Coys of the 40th. Division as follows:-

2. Right Sector.
   The 467th. Field Co. R.E. will take over from the 224 Fd. Co. 40th. Division with accommodation as follows:-
   Headquarters and 3 sections in cellars in MORCHIES C.10.c.6.3.
   Transport and 1 Section in BEUGNIERS B.20.a.2.2. (arrangements are being made to send this section forward)

3. Centre Sector.
   The 469th. Field Co. R.E. will take over from the 231 Fd. Co. 40th. Division with accommodation as follows:-
   Headquarters and 1 Section and Transport in the Tunnellers Camp MORY, B.22.b.7.7.
   Three sections at ECOUST, C.8.a.2.3.

4. Left Sector.
   The 470th. Field Co. R.E. will take over from the 229 Fd. Co. 40th. Division with accommodation as follows:-
   Headquarters, 1 Section and Transport at ST. LEGER, T.28.c.9.1.
   Three sections in Chalk Pit, at U.19.a.2.3.

5. On Wednesday next the 8th. instant, each O.C. Field Company will send an Officer to report to the O.C. of the Field Co. (40th. Division) they are relieving, in order that he may obtain as much information as possible about the Sector before the relief takes place. If two Officers can be spared it would be advantageous.

6. Until further Orders 1 Section only per Field Company will be attached to each of the Brigades in the line, the 3 remaining sections being employed upon work in the Battle Zone and elsewhere.

7. Each Field Company will run its own R.E. Dump. A reliable N.C.O. or sapper should be sent to the Dump a few days before the taking over in order to get a grip of the work.
   The Dumps are located as follows:-

   224 or 467th. Field Co. R.E.   MORCHIES.   C.10.c.6.2.
   231 or 469th. Field Co. R.E.   GUINNESS Dump.   C. 2.a.5.4.
   229 or 470th. Field Co. R.E.   ECOUST.   C. 2.b.4.9.

   These Dumps are fed from the Divisional Dump at MORY and feed the Forward Brigade Dumps by push-trucks where the Railway is beyond the jurisdiction of the L.R. Coy.

8. No.1. and No.4. Sections of the 174th. Tunnelling Coy with Head Qtrs. at H.1.b.6.1. and No.3. Section 181 Tunnelling Coy. with Hd. Qtrs. at B.10.a.4.1. are at the disposal of the Division for the construction of dug-outs and emplacements.

9. A Pioneer Battalion (weak in strength) is also at the disposal of the Division.

10. Acknowledge.

In the Field.
3rd. February. 1918.

Captain & Adjutant.
59th. Divisional R.E.

SECRET.

Chief Engineer VI. Corps.
Hd. Qtrs. 'G' 59th. Division.

Herewith Progress Report of work carried out on this Divisional Front.

During the past week the fine weather has enabled good work to be done in re-claiming and repairing the trenches which had fallen in during the recent thaw.

Particular attention has been given to constructing wide berms wherever possible.

As regards new work - the trenches started by the 40th Division in APEX have been continued, also the new Support Trench from LONDON RESERVE in a S.E. direction across TANK AVENUE. TIGER Trench is being re-dug as an additional line in Left Brigade Sector, and PONTEFRACT Trench is being re-dug for the same purpose in Right Brigade Sector, NEW PELICAN LANE is being re-claimed from U.21.d.5,0. to the Front Line and will be firestepped throughout its length to protect the Right Flank of Left Brigade.

Schedule of Work attached.

In the Field
19. 2. 1918.

Lieut. Colonel. R.E. (T).
C.R.E. 59th. Division.

Schedule of Work.

Trenches &c.

New Work. Extension of FOX TROT LANE from LONDON RESERVE S.W. 700 yds. of trench, average depth 5', 12 fire-bays, 340 yds trenchboarded.

New Support Trench in APEX. SHEFFIELD Support to TOWER Support, 180yds. dug, average depth 2'.

PONTEFRACT Trench. 400 yds dug, 7' wide, 18" deep, 300yds. double-apron fence completed.

TIGER Trench. 180yds. dug, 4'6" deep, 120 yds. double-apron fence completed.

FRONT and CLOSE Support Lines. 500 yds double-apron fence wired, 700 yds. re-claimed and cleaned.

COMMUNICATION TRENCHES. 2,600yds. trenches bermed.

Accomodation.

New dug-outs are being made for Right Bn. H.Q. Right Brigade, and for a Company H.Q. in TANK AVENUE. This work is about 75% complete.

Miscellaneous.

~~New dug-outs are being made fo~~
A new A.D.S. is being made at C.10.c.7.7. to accomodate 50 stretcher cases. The excavation is commplete and elephant shelters are being installed.

Baby-elephant shelters have been erected at No. 3. Post, Right Brigade, to accommodate the garrison.

A Trench-foot treatment shelter at ECOUST has been completed for 177th. Inf. Bde.

O.P% at ECOUST. Concrete completed to ground level, 250 c. ft. reinforced concrete made and 250 c. ft. reinforced concrete put in.

H.T.M. Emplacement at U.13.c.9,4. completed.

BATHS at ST.LEGER AND ERVILLERS ARE BEing entirely re-construct -ed- their present condition is most unsatisfactory.

Road maintenance.

ECOUST - MORY road - 120 loads hard core, 540yds. road cleaned

Schedule of work (continued)

    60 loads road metal put down.

    ECOUST - SUCERIE road - 600 yds roads cleaned.

    VAULX road -20 loads metal put down, road cleaned B.30.c.8.7. -B.30.d.7.9., three sump holes cleaned out.

    SUCERIE - VRAUCOURT road - 100 yds road scraped, 28 loads metal put down.

D.H.Q. Dug-outs.

    Dug-outs for D.H.Q. Two headings driven to a depth giving 32 ft cover.

In the Field.   Lieut. Colonel. R.E. (T).
19th. February. 1918.   C.R.E. 59th. Division.

SECRET.

Appendix II

Chief Engineer, VI.Corps.　　　　　　　　　　　　　　K.4171/1
Hd.Qtrs.'G' 59th Division.

　　　Progress Report of work carried out on 59th.Divl.Front herewith.

　　　In regard to new work PONTEFRACT and DEWSBURY Trenches have been reclaimed and partially dug as a front line of the Battle Zone of Right Brigade Sector.

　　　In the Left Brigade a new Switch has been dug from MAN Lane joining TIGER Trench at about U.26.b.o.9.

　　　TIGER Trench itself has been reclaimed from RAILWAY Reserve to KNUCKLE AVENUE as a Support Line to the First System.

　　　Wiring, both in front of New Trenches and the existing Lines, has taken precedence over other work during the past week.

　　　The Schedule of work is attached.

In the Field,
26th February 1918　　　　　(Sgd) A. C. HOWARD.
　　　　　　　　　　　　　　　　　Lt.Col.R.E.
　　　　　　　　　　　　　　　　　　C.R.E. 59th Division.

S E C R E T.   War Diary.   Appendix No.

Chief Engineer, VI.Corps.
Hd.Qtrs.G.59th.Division.

Schedule of Work.

Trenches &c.

New Work.

FOX Support has been dug to depth from LONDON Reserve to within 50 yds of the front line in U.29.a. and forestepped for 60% of its length.

New Support Trench in APEX- 50% dug 3' deep - remainder dug to depth and fire-stepped. One double-apron fence complete, second double-apron fence 75% completed.

PONTEFRACT Trench dug to depth from SYDNEY Avenue to C.10.a.cent. - 7' wide 18" deep to C.10.a.1.5.

DEWSBURY Trench- five 30' fire-bays with island traverses dug have been completed. One double-apron fence has been completed throughout DEWSBURY, one belt is complete and the second belt half complete in front of PONTEFRACT.

TIGER Trench - 420 yds double apron fence have been partially completed in front of TIGER Trench, 770 yds of new fire trench have been dug as a Switch from TIGER Trench from in U.26.b.0.9. to MAN Reserve.

COMMUNICATION Trenches, Wiring etc.- 4,000 yds trenches bermed. General wiring - 1.800 yds double-apron fence has been put up, - strengthening and repairing existing wire on Divisional Front.

MISCELLANEOUS.

    Strong Points, Nos.9.10.11 and 12 have been constructed in ECOUST - NOREUIL Trench.

    400 yds of trench have been dug for Water Supply in RAILWAY Reserve and 1½" pipes laid and jointed.

    New A.D.S. at C.10.c.7.7.- excavations completed, one and a half shelters erected.

    O.P. at ECOUST - concrete completed to 10' above ground level.

    Dug-outs at Centre Bde.H.Q. - extensions of existing dug-out accommodation have been started.

ROAD MAINTENANCE.

    ECOUST - MORY Road - 100 loads of hard core - 400 yds of road cleaned - 50 loads of road metal put down.

ECOUST - SUCRERIE Road - 300 yds cleaned - 30 loads road metal put down.

DUG-OUTS at D.H.Q.

    These have now been handed over to the 174th.Tunnelling Co.R.E.

S E C R E T.   Copy. No. 9.

OPERATION ORDER No. 2.

by

LIEUT.COL. A.C.HOWARD.D.S.O. C.R.E. 59th.Division.

Refce. 1/20.000 51.b.S.E. and 57.c.N.W.   27. 2. 1918.

1. The 34th.Division is under Warning Order from VI.Corps to take over the Centre Western Sector of the Corps on the nights March 1/2nd. and Mar.2/3rd. relieving in the Line the 178th.Inf. Bde. and the 8th.Bde. of the 3rd.Division.

2. The Boundary between the 34th. and 59th.Divisions on relief will be as follows:-
    U.15.c.7.0.- Front Line at U.21.b.2.0.- PELICAN AVENUE (inclusive to 34th.Division)- U.26.c.85.40.- T.30.d.0.0.- BALLY Copse (inclusive to 34th.Division.)

3. The 470th(North Midland)Field Co.R.E. will be relieved by the 208th.Field Co.R.E., the relief of Field Coys. to be completed by 12.Noon, March. 1st 2nd.

4. On relief the 470th.Field Co.R.E. will move to the Camp at S.21.d.5.0.

5. An advance Party of officers of the 208th.Field Co.R.E. and probably 209th.Field Co.R.E. will report at 178th.Inf.Bde.H.Q. at 9.30.a.m. 28th.Instant. They will be met by officers of the 470th(North Mid)Field Co.R.E. who will hand over all details of work in the Line, the work in hand by the 470th.Field Coy. to be handed over to a representative of 208th.Field Co.R.E.
    The work in the Sector in charge of the Pioneers, namely, maintenance of Communication Trenches, wiring of the Reserve Line of the First System and Front Line of Battle Zone to be handed over to the representative of the 209th.Field Co.R.E.

6. All Stores and Pumps now in charge of 470th.Field Co.R.E. will be handed over and a receipt obtained, the receipt to be forwarded to this Office by 6.p.m. on the 1st 2nd.March.

7. The utmost care is to be taken that all billets and horse lines are handed over in a clean and sanitary condition.
    A certificate that this has been done will be obtained from the relieving Unit and forwarded to this Office.

8. Acknowledge.

                                                    Lieut.Colonel.R.E.(T)
                                                    C.R.E. 59th.Division.

Issued at 7 p.m.

        Copy No.1. 470th.Fd.Co.R.E.   Copy No.6. 178th.Inf.Bde.
             2. 468th.Fd.Co.R.E.   7. C.R.E.34th.Div.
             3. 467th.Fd.Co.R.E.   8. File.
             4. 59th.Div.G.   9. War Diary.
             5. 59th.Div.Q.   10. "   "

ORIGINAL.

Vol 13

WAR DIARY
of
HEAD QTRS R.E. 59th DIVISION.

VOLUME XIII

From 1st Sept. 1918 – to – 28th Febr. 1918.

59th Divisional Engineers

WAR DIARY

C. R. E.

59th DIVISION

MARCH 1 9 1 8

Report on Operations - see Appx VI.

ORIGINAL

O/C 59th Div

Vol 14

WAR DIARY

of

HEADQUARTERS R. ENGINEERS.

59th DIVISION.

VOLUME XIV.

1st March 1918 to 31st March 1918

Army Form C. 2118

WAR DIARY
INTELLIGENCE SUMMARY

HEAD QUARTERS
59 DIVISIONAL ROYAL ENGINEERS
FOR MARCH 1918.

(Erase heading not required.)

Instructions regarding War Diaries and Intelligence Summaries are contained in F. S. Regs., Part II. and the Staff Manual respectively. Title Pages will be prepared in manuscript.

Place	Date	Hour	Summary of Events and Information	Remarks and references to Appendices
BEHAGNIES	1/3/18		CRE visited the Divn. Brigade Head Quarters	Sheets 57c 1/40000 57B ditto
"	2/3/18		CRE visited the RIGHT BRIGADE SECTOR. From this date the divisional front consists of the two original right and Centre Bde fronts. the Left Brigade front having been taken over by the 34 DIVISION. 470 FIELD Coy. R.E. relieved in the Left Brigade Sector by a field Coy of the 34 Divn and marched into camp at MORY	Khnn
"	3/3/18		CRE made a reconnaissance of the BATTLE ZONE on the divisional frontage. and also had round right Brigade Sector.	Khnn
"	4/3/18		CRE went round front line with GSO1 in the morning and the CE II Corps in the afternoon	Khnn
"	5/3/18		CRE inspected Camps with the AAQMG Bavacum in the morning and went round Sector in the afternoon. CRE's programme of work done during the week is attached hereto marked appendix I.	Khnn
"	6/3/18		CRE went round right sector and ECOUST SWITCH	Khnn
"	7/3/18		CRE went round right Sector and visited 176 and 177 Brigade Headquarters	Khnn
"	8/3/18	3 p.m.	CRE held a Conference of O.C. Companies and Reported CRE inspected work done on HOREUIL SWITCH and FRONT LINE of 2nd SYSTEM and had round RIGHT Sector of Divisional Front	Khnn

Army Form C. 2118

WAR DIARY
INTELLIGENCE SUMMARY

(Erase heading not required.)

Instructions regarding War Diaries and Intelligence Summaries are contained in F.S. Regs., Part II. and the Staff Manual respectively. Title Pages will be prepared in manuscript.

Place	Date	Hour	Summary of Events and Information	Remarks and references to Appendices
BEHAGNIES	9/3/18	8pm	OPERATION ORDER Nº 3 by CRE. See appendix I attached. Issued to all concerned.	Sketch 51 & 57 C
	10/3/18	8am	CRE visited right Batt. Sector. 59 Div WARNING ORDER Nº 101. Copy Nº 5 received. CRE visited BATTLE ZONE and Trenches in Right Batt. Sector	Copy 1/No ono.
		3.15	59 DIVISION ORDER Nº 100 received. CRE went to III ARMY TANK SCHOOL to witness the action of tank miniature upon tanks.	Known
	11/3/18		CRE visited right Brigade Sector in the afternoon.	Known
	12/3/18		CRE progress report to work carried out on the Divisional front during the week ending 12. is attached hereto marked appendix III. 59 DIVISION OPERATION ORDER Nº 102 Copy 5 received	Known
	13/3/18	3pm	CRE went round part of right sector and visited 470 Head Quarters at ECOUST.	Known
	14/3/18		CRE went round left sector of the Divisional front.	Known
	15/3/18		CRE went round right sector of the Divisional front in the morning and inspected the work being done by night working party on MOREUIL SWITCH.	Known
	16/3/18		CRE went round line with CE VI CORPS. 59 DIVISION ORDER Nº 103 copy 4 received	Known
	17/3/18	8pm		
	17/3/18		CRE visited both 177 and 178 Batt. Headquarters and went round a portion of the right Prelim. Also inspected 467 Field by transport. CRE OPERATION ORDER Nº 4 Copy attached marked appendix IV issued to all concerned.	Known

1875 Wt. W593/826 1,000,000 4/15 J.B.C. & A. A.D.S.S./Forms/C. 2118.

Army Form C. 2118

WAR DIARY
INTELLIGENCE SUMMARY Continued.
(Erase heading not required.)

Place	Date	Hour	Summary of Events and Information	Remarks and references to Appendices
BEHAGNIES	18/3/18		CRE went round part of right sector.	Kemp/Hulse
	19/3/18		CRE progress report upon work done on the divisional front for the week ending March 19 attached hereto marked appendix V	Kemp 57 R 51 B 1/40,000
	20/3/18		CRE went round right sector	Kemp
	21/3/18		German offensive began upon our front. Lt. W. HULSE, Lt. D.G. KEMP M.C., Lt. J.W. ENGLISH and C.S.M. BROOKS.J. Killed are missing. 2 wounded and 1 killed No. 9 FIELD Coy. 2 missing OR 467. Lt. A OF COBLEY wounded (at duty.) 4 OR wounded. 2 OR missing. Report of days work previously to OR wounded. Field Corps R.E. is attached hereto marked appendix VI	Kemp
	22/3/18	9am	Divisional Headquarters move from BEHAGNIES to BUCQUOY.	Kemp
BUCQUOY	23/3/18	9am	Divisional Head Quarters move from BUCQUOY to BOUZINCOURT.	Kemp
BOUZINCOURT	25/3/18	3 PM	Divisional Head Quarters move from BOUZINCOURT to CONTAY	Kemp
CONTAY FIENVILLERS	26/3/18	6am	Divisional Head Quarters move from CONTAY to FIENVILLERS	Kemp
VILLERS CHATEL	28/3/18		Divisional Head Quarters move from FIENVILLERS to VILLERS CHATEL by Train. Taking two days. Divisional transport proceeds by route march taking the night in the FOUFFLIN under orders of CRE Divan and halts for the night at RICAMETZ area proceeding to VILLERS	
"	29/3/18	-	CHATEL next day arriving 6 pm 29.	Kemp

WAR DIARY

INTELLIGENCE SUMMARY Continued

Army Form C. 2118

Place	Date	Hour	Summary of Events and Information	Remarks and references to Appendices
VILLERS CHATEL AREA	30/3/19		CRE Head Quarters in MINGOVAL 467 Field Coy RE in CAUCOURT 469 " " BETHENSART 470 " " HERMIN 470 Field Coy RE commanded by Major L. Robinson DSO RE was inspected by H.M. the King at HERMIN CRE order No.9 issued to all concerned for emy marked appendix VII.	KMM
LILLERS AREA	31/3/19		Transport of 59 Division (less Artillery) under Lt Col A.C. Howard M.C. CRE 59 Div. proceeded to LILLERS AREA by route march staying there the night on their way up to BELGIUM.	KMM

Khazie more Lieutenant
Capt 59 Div RE

SECRET.

Chief Engineer, VI.Corps.
Headquarters.'G' 59th.Div.

Progress Report of work carried out on the 59th. Divisional Front for the Week-ending 5th.March, herewith.

The most important new work has been the digging and wiring of the extension of NOREUIL Switch from IGARHE Corner to RAILWAY Reserve, and the joining up of PONTEFRACT Trench with the front line of the Battle Zone.

Wiring has again been given precedence over other work.

During the past week approximately 20.000 yds of double apron fence have been put up on this Divisional Front. The schedule of work is attached.

(signed) A.B.Howard

5.3.1918.

Lieut.Colonel.R.E.(T)
C.R.E. 59th.Division.

Secret.

SCHEDULE of WORK.

TRENCHES.

New work.

The extension of NOREUIL Switch has been dug from C.10.c.9.8. to RAILWAY Reserve in C.5.a.5.2. to an average depth of 1'9" and wired on the E. side to Corps standard.

TIGER Trench was dug out to STRAY Reserve before handing over to the 34th. Division.

FOX Support has been dug out to depth throughout its length and fire-stepped.

New Support trench in APEX has been dug to depth and protected by wiring to Corps standard.

PONTEFRACT Trench has been dug out to its junction with the front line of Battle Zone at C.9.b.3.6. to a depth of 3 feet.

WIRING.

The Reserve line of first System and the firing line of the Battle Zone are now wired throughout to Corps standard.

A new double apron fence has been erected in JOY RIDE Trench from PELICAN Lane to FOX TROT.

Wire in front of Close Support Line has been maintained and strengthened.

A large amount of work has been done in wiring in Gun Positions for the 59th.Divl.Artillery.

COMMUNICATION TRENCHES.

Strong maintenance parties have been employed in keeping the main communication trenches open and in good repair.

MISCELLANEOUS.

Trench shelters and Baby elephants have been installed through-out the Divisional Front to accommodate the additional Battalions moved forward under the new scheme of dispositions.

ROADS.

Permanent parties have been engaged in repairing the following roads.:-

MORT HOMME - ECOUST.   SUCRERIE- ECOUST. SUCRERIE - VRAUCOURT as far as the Right Brigade Headquarters.

5.3.1918.

(signed) A.C.Howard
Lieut.Colonel.R.E.(T)
C.R.E. 59th. Division.

SECRET.   Copy No. 7

OPERATION ORDERS
No. 3.
by C.R.E. 59th. Division.

Reference Map. 57.c.N.W.1/20.000.   9th. March. 1918.

1.   The 470th(North Midland)Field Company R.E. will relieve the 467th(North Midland)Field Company R.E. in the Right Subsector on the night 11/12th. March.

2.   The relief is to be completed by 6.a.m. March 12th. and completion to be reported to this Office by wire.

3.   The details of relief and the handing over of all work in hand by both Field Coys. will be arranged between Os.C.Coys. concerned in such a manner as to ensure that there is no break or delay in any work in consequence of the relief.

4.   Headquarters and Transport Lines of the Companies will not be exchanged on relief, but the 3 sections of the 467th.Field Co.R.E. now in advanced billets NORBUIL. will take over billets for 3 sections at ENVILLERS from the 470th.Field Co.R.E.,

5.   Copies of handing-over statements and duplicate receipts for trench and area stores and stores in Field Coy Dumps handed over will be forwarded to this Office by 6.p.m. Mar.12.

6.   Acknowledge.

Issued at 8.p.m.   Lieut.Colonel.R.E.(T)
                                                    C.R.E. 59th. Division.

Copy No.1.467th.Fd.Co.   Copy No.5.176th.Inf.Bde.
     2.469th.Fd.Co.   6.War Diary.
     3.470th.Fd.Co.   7.War Diary.
     4.176th.Inf.Bde.   8.File.

SECRET.

Chief Engineer, VI.Corps.
Headquarters.G. 59th.Division.

Progress Report of work carried out on the 59th.Divisional Front during the Week-ending 12th.March, herewith.

It will be seen from the attached Schedule that new trenches have been dug to improve the Close Support Line in JOY RIDE Support, the Reserve Line of the First System connecting STATION REDOUBT with RAILWAY Reserve and the Front Line of the Battle Zone covering the Valley behind TIGER Trench in U.26.c.and.d.

Wiring has been continued on an extensive scale - 17,000 yds of double apron fence having been erected.

In the Field.
12th.March.1918.

Lieut.Colonel.R.E.(T)
C.R.E. 59th. Division.

SECRET.

Schedule of Work.

NEW WORK.

A new traversed fire-trench has been dug in front of Railway embankment from U.26.c.3.4. to C.2.b.4.9.

A new traversed fire trench has been dug in front of Railway embankment from U.27.c.0.6. joining up RAILWAY Reserve at U.27.d.2.4.

A new traversed fire trench has been dug from JOY RIDE Support U.21.c.8.1. to PELICAN AVENUE U.21.c.7.3.

The NOREUIL Switch and its extension (STAFFORD Trench) have been dug out to an average depth of 3' from junction with Support Line Second System to RAILWAY Reserve in C.5.a.6.2.

The Support Line of the Second System has been dug to 18" throughout, except for a length of 80 yds E. of the SUCRERIE-ECOUST Road. It has been deepened in a number of places to 3 feet.

Further work has been done in deepening and fire-stepping PONTEFRACT Trench, TIGER Trench and JOY RIDE Support.

WIRING.

SYDNEY AVENUE has been wired on both sides with two double apron fences to SYDNEY end.

BULLECOURT AVENUE has been wired on S.E. side with one double apron fence from Front Line Second System to junction of ZEPHYR Trench.

A large amount of wire has been put out in front of JOY RIDE Support principally in shell-holes.

MISCELLANEOUS.

A large number of trench shelters and baby elephants have been installed to provide additional accommodation in the trenches.

The A.D.S. at IGAREE Corner has been completed.

A new Reserve Bde.H.Q. has been erected at B.28.a.0.0.

Splinter-proof shelters for Police have been erected at various Battle Posts.

Further work has been done in wiring in Artillery and Machine Gun positions.

Work as laid down in VI.Corps. G.X/599/160 dated 3.3.1918 has been carried out from

C.6.c.00.45. to C.6.a.3.8.

In the Field.
12th. March.1918.

Lieut.Colonel.R.E.(T)
C.R.E. 59th. Division.

SECRET.   Copy No. 6

OPERATION ORDER
No.4.
by C.R.E. 59th. Division.

Reference Maps.   17th.March.1918.

57.c.N.W.   1
51.b.S.W.20.000.

1.   The 467th(North Midland)Field Co.R.E. will relieve the
     469th(North Midland)Field Co.R.E. in the Left Sub-sector on
     the night March 20/21st.

2.   The relief is to be completed by 6.a.m. March 21st and
     completion reported to this Office by wire.

3.   The details of relief and the handing over of all work
     in hand by both Field Companies will be arranged between
     Os.C.Coys concerned in such a manner as to ensure that there
     is no break or delay in any work in consequence of the relief.

4.   Headquarters and Transport Lines of the Companies will
     not be exchanged on relief, but the 3 sections of the 469th
     Field Company R.E. now in advanced billets at ECOUST will
     take over billets for 3 sections at ERVILLERS from the 467th
     Field Company R.E.

5.   Copies of handing-over statements and receipts for trench
     and area stores and stores in Field Company Dumps handed over
     will be forwarded to this Office by 6.p.m. March 21st.

6.   Acknowledge.

                                            Lieut.Colonel.R.E.(T)
                                            C.R.E. 59th.Division.

Issued at 7.p.m.

          Copy No.1. 467th.Field Co.R.E.
               2. 469th.Field Co.R.E.
               3. 470th.Field Co.R.E.
               4. 177th.Inf.Bde.
               5. 176th.Inf.Bde.
               6. War Diary.
               7. War Diary.
               8. File.

S E C R E T.

Chief Engineer, VI.Corps.
Hd.Qtrs.G. 59th.Division.

Progress Report of work carried out on the 59th.Divisional Front for the Week-ending March 19th, herewith.

As will be seen from the attached Schedule the principle work during the past week has been the deepening of, and improving new trenches recently dug.

In the Field.   Lieut.Colonel.R.E.(T)
19. 3. 1918.   C.R.E. 59th. Division.

Secret.   Week-ending 19.3.1918.

SCHEDULE of WORK.

NEW WORK.

A new trench has been dug connecting DEWSBURY Trench at C.11.c.4.8. with HOBART Avenue.

A new trench has been dug continuing HORSE-SHOE Trench to HORSE-SHOE Support, U.29.c.2.4. to U.29.c.45.20.

A new trench has been begun in U.26.c. running from PELICAN AVENUE at about U.26.c.5.7. in an Easterly direction with a view to covering the dead ground in front of the new trench dug at the foot of the Railway embankment in U.26.c.

DEEPENING and
IMPROVING TRENCHES.

The NOREUIL Switch has been deepened to an average depth of 3'6" from C.14.d.6.9. to its junction with the Support Line of the Second System; and to an average depth of 3' from the junction of the Support Line, Second System forward to DEWSBURY Trench.

The new extension from DEWSBURY Trench to SYDNEY CROSS is being deepened and fire-stepped throughout its length.

PONTEFRACT Trench has been deepened and fire-stepped, and is being trench-boarded to its junction with the Firing-line, Second System.

The Support Line, Second System has now been dug to 18" throughout its length, and to a depth of 3' for 2,400 yards of its length.

The new trench in U.26.c.and C.2.b. forming part of the firing-line of the Second System, and the new Trench in U.27.c., Reserve Line, First System, have been deepened, bermed and fire-stepped.

WIRING.

5,780 yards of double-apron fence have been put up during the past week, mainly in improving the wiring of the Support Line, Second System, and in wiring the N.W. side of BULLECOURT AVENUE.

MISCELLANEOUS.

A large amount of additional accommodation has been provided in the trenches, using baby-elephant shelters and deck-troughing.

In the Field.   Lieut.Colonel.R.E.(T)
19th.March.1918.   C.R.E. 59th. Division.

Headquarters G.
59th. Division.

Reference your 1721/6.G. dated 24.3.18.

Herewith an account of the action on March 21/22nd, based on information supplied by Units under my Command.

Dispositions.

At midnight March 20/21st. the dispositions of the three Field Cos. R.E. were as follows:-

467th Field Co. R.E.

    3 Sections at ECOUST, C.8.a.2.7.

    1 Section & Transport at ERVILLERS.

469th Field Co. R.E.

    At MORY.

470th Field Co. R.E.

    3 Sections at NOREUIL, C.10.b.8.2.

    1 Section & Transport at MORY.

Bombardment.

Both forward Companies report intense shelling beginning about 5 a.m. on the 21st. and extending over a great depth, including the villages of NOREUIL and ECOUST; the bombardment consisted of both gas shells and H.E. I left my car at the SUCRERIE at 8 a.m. on the 21st. and walked over the high ground in C.13, 14 and 15 as far as the Support Line, Second System. The heavy ground mist made observation difficult but the following points were particularly noticeable:

(a) The depth of the barrage, which could not have been less than 3,000 yards.

(b) The accuracy of the shooting, particularly on the ECOUST-NOREUIL Road, the Support Line Second System, and the NOREUIL Switch, all of which were under my direct observation.

(c) The high percentage of shells of large calibre used on the trenches of the Second System and the intensity of the trench mortar bombardment on the First System.

(Continued)

Sheet 2.

Up to 10.30 a.m. the Support Line Second System was the forward edge of the enemy's barrage, but there was a great deal of promiscuous shelling of the high ground in C.13 and 14, of the MORT HOMME - ECOUST Valley and particularly of the NOREUIL Switch between the Supports and Reserve Lines Second System.

In addition there appeared to be considerable counter-battery work against our heavy guns in VAULX VRAUCOURT and on the NOREUIL - VAULX Road.

(d) The total absence of stragglers. During the 2½ hours that I was in the Second System I did not see a single straggler returning. Such men as I met were all runners carrying messages to or from Brigade Headquarters.

The Attack.

O.C. 470th Field Co. R.E., Major L. Robinson, D.S.O., reports that during the preliminary bombardment large numbers of gas shells fell in NOREUIL, the effects of which lasted until 9 a.m. He sustained no casualties from gas, but lost 3 O.R. by H.E. At 9.30 a.m. he tapped a message on the telephone to the effect that the enemy was in our front line and the position acute. In consequence of this he gave orders for his three sections to take up their battle positions in Trench E. of the village of NOREUIL in C.10.a., Lieut. W. Hulse in command, he himself reporting to Brigade Headquarters at the earliest possible moment. He visited the Battalion Headquarters of the 2/5th Sherwood Foresters in NOREUIL - LONGATTE Road on his way down to obtain the latest information for the B.G. Cmndg 178th Inf. Bde. The C.O. 2/5th Sherwood Foresters had then received news that DEWSBURY Trench and the new trench from IGARREE Corner to DEWSBURY were being accurately shelled with great intensity. At 9.45 a.m. he left Battalion Headquarters and looking back towards QUEANT saw the enemy swarming over the ridge in the 6th Division Front in C.12 and 17.

The whole of the 3 sections of the 470th Field Co. R.E. left in command of Lieut. W. Hulse are missing, with the exception

(continued)

Sheet 3.

of Lieut. F. C. B. Wills and 6 Other Ranks. From Lieut. Wills I learned that the Company, under Lieut. Hulse, took up their battle positions - Lieut. Hulse on the right, Lieut. Wills on the left, and 2nd Lieuts. Kemp and English in the centre. Almost at once the enemy advanced in mass against the trench they held. Accurate fire was opened which held up the enemy and caused him to turn towards the valley. As the party was in danger of being taken in reverse, Lieut. Hulse ordered a withdrawal to the sunken road by the A.D.S. at IGARREE Corner. On arrival here, the enemy were found to be coming up the road in both directions. Lieut. Wills led his men into NOREUIL Switch towards the LONGATTE - NOREUIL Road and opened fire on the enemy advancing from NOREUIL. He found himself cut off from his main body and withdrew with his six men, in good order, down the NOREUIL Switch, maintaining periodical fire on the enemy as far as possible, and eventually returned to his Company Headquarters at MORY.

He states that the feature of the enemy advance was the large number of light machine guns preceding the attacking troops and the persistent way the enemy bombed his way up the trenches.

He reported that the men of the 470th Field Co. R.E. fought most gallantly and did great execution during the short time they were engaged.

My casualties for this Company were :-

        1 O.R. Killed.
        2 O.R. Wounded.
        1 O.R. Wounded and missing.
3 Officers and 66 O.R. Missing.

The O.C. 467th Field Co. R.E., Major D. B. Frew, reports that at 5 a.m. an intense bombardment opened on ECOUST, in consequence of which he withdrew his men to deep dug-outs. Many direct hits were obtained on his Headquarters, but with the exception of his C.S.M. being killed during the withdrawal to the dug-outs, he escaped casualties at this period.

His telephone wire was cut at the outset, and he could not

(Continued)

Sheet 4.

get any news until at 9 a.m. an Artillery officer going forward reported that there was no attack on our Divisional Front but that the Division on our right was being attacked.

At 10 a.m. the barrage behind ECOUST increased to great intensity and a runner going back to Brigade reported enemy had penetrated RAILWAY Reserve. At 10.20 a.m. another runner reported enemy entering ECOUST and that the whole of the infantry forward of ECOUST had been cut off. Without placing undue reliance on this information O.C. 467th Field Co. R.E. from his own observation of the situation decided to withdraw his men to the First Line of the Third System. He chose this line on account of the absence of any other troops in support line of Second System. He selected the point where the battery of 4 machine guns were situated in C.13.c., placing his men E. and W. of these machine guns. He also secured a detachment of men from the Trench Mortar Battery and 2 3" Stokes Mortars, together with 2 Lewis Gunners of the Sherwood Foresters with a Lewis Gun.

The situation appeared very critical as the barrage was advancing towards this line, and in the absence of any other troops he was only able to occupy about 180 yards front. In view of the importance of supporting the battery of M.Gs. he decided to remain, and at about 1.15 p.m. parties of the 2/4th Leicesters began to arrive in the trench. On Colonel Colquhoun's arrival he reported to him and remained at his disposal until 4 a.m. on March 22nd, when he was relieved by a battalion of the Highland Light Infantry, and withdrew to his Company Headquarters at ERVILLERS.

His total casualties were :-

1 O.R. Killed.
3 O.R. Wounded.
2 O.R. Missing.
1 O.R. Wounded and missing.
2 O.R. Gassed.
1 Officer, Wounded, at duty.

He states that at 2 p.m. the enemy could be plainly seen advancing in large numbers from ECOUST and came under the

(Continued)

Sheet 5.

most destructive fire from the 4 M.Gs. in his position.

Major Robinson, Major Frew, Lieut. Wills and I are all agreed that the machine gunners of these more or less isolated batteries and guns stuck to their posts in a most courageous manner, in spite of the intensity of the bombardment, while Major Frew and Lieut. Wills are in a position to speak in the highest praise of the losses inflicted by these gunners on the advancing enemy.

The 469th Field Co. R.E. in reserve at MORY took no part in the fighting.

On the night of March 22nd/23rd. the Field Cos. were ordered to dig out the Army Line N. of MORY, but as this was not possible on account of the rapid advance of the enemy, they dug a trench in front of ERVILLERS, and then, in the absence of any other troops, withdrew to AYETTE.

The 6/7th Bn. Royal Scots Fusiliers (Pioneers) were withdrawn from my control on the morning of March 21st. to bridge a gap left by the Division on our right between VRAUCOURT and VAULX. You will doubtless receive details of their operations from this Battalion direct, including the story of their counter-attack the along the NOREUIL Switch.

In a letter dated 30th March received from a Hospital in London, Col. Hart relates the following :-

"On the night of the 21st. there was a machine gun worrying my left company, so a couple of the men went out and fetched it in together with the very small Boche soldier who was working it. The gun and the Boche were sent back and the incident is now probably lost in the hurly-burly of the great battle, but if ask you may be able to get the narrative. It was 'C' Company - I didn't hear the men's names."

I saw this Battalion in action at the SUCRERIE on March 22nd. and was particularly impressed with the high moral and the fine offensive spirit being shewn by all ranks, in spite of their having sustained heavy casualties.

(Continued).

Sheet 6.

It is difficult to obtain accurate information of what happened even to my own men on the 21st of March, but all sources of information and all stories which one hears have one outstanding point in common, viz. the total absence of anything like a disorderly retreat or rout on the part of any units of the 59th. Division in the forward systems.

In the Field.
4th April 1918.

Lieut. Colonel, R.E. (T)
C. R. E. 59th. Division.

War Diary

Copy No. 28.

OPERATION ORDER
No. 5.

by C.R.E., 59th Division.

Reference LENS 11,) 1/100,000.   27.3.18.
HAZEBROUCK 5a.)

1. The 59th Division transport (less Artillery and 177th Inf. Bde.) will proceed by march route under the orders of the C.R.E. 59th Division as follows :-

    28th March. HERLIN-le-SEC Area via HARDINVAL, HEM, BOUQUEMAISON, FREVENT and NUNCQ.

    29th March. ST. POL, PERNES and LILLERS, to BUSNES area.

2. The head of the column will pass the cross roads at the first L in LONGUEVILLETTE at 8.30 a.m.

3. Transport will march in the following order and will pass the starting point at the times named :-

59th Div. Train	8.30 a.m.
176th Inf. Bde.	8.37 a.m.
3/7th R.S.F. (Det.)	8.47 a.m.
178th Inf. Bde.	8.50 a.m.
467th Field Coy. R.E.)	
469th do.)	9.0 a.m.
470th do.)	
2/1st N.M.Field Ambulance)	
2/2nd do.)	9.7 a.m.
2/3rd do.)	
59th Bn. M.G.C.	9.15 a.m.
Div. Headquarters	9.20 a.m.
59th Div. Signals	9.25 a.m.
2/1st N.M.Mob.Vet.Section	9.30 a.m.

4. Strict march discipline will be maintained throughout the march, particular attention being paid to the following points :-

    (a) Intervals of 20 yards will be maintained between each Group of 6 vehicles.

    (b) Breaksmen are to march in rear of, and not at the side of their wagon.

    (c) All limbers, tool carts, etc. to be properly balanced.

5. The column will halt at 50 minutes past the hour resuming the march punctually at the hour.

6. Watches will be synchronised at the starting point as units pass.

7. Advance billeting parties from units will meet Capt. K.N.Moss, Adjutant 59th Div. R.Engineers at the Sub-area Commandant's office FOUFFLIN-RICAMETZ at 11.30 a.m., these parties to be provided with marching-in-states.

8. Supply wagons will be returned to Div. Train on the night of the 28th instant.

Issued at 10.30 p.m. by D.R.

P.C.Howard
Lieut.Colonel,R.E. (T).
C.R.E. 59th Division.

For Distribution P. T. O.

DISTRIBUTION :-

Copy No.		
1	-	'G' 59th Division.
2	-	'Q' 59th Division.
3 - 7		176th Inf. Bde.
8 - 12		178th " "
13	-	Det. 6/7th R.S.F.
14	-	59th Div. Signals.
15	-	59th Bn. M.G.C.
16	-	59th Div. Train.
17	-	A.D.M.S.
18	-	2/1st N.M.Fd.Ambulance.
19	-	2/2nd N.M.Fd.Ambulance.
20	-	2/3rd N.M.Fd.Ambulance.
21	-	D.A.D.V.S.
22	-	A.P.M.
23	-	Camp Comdt.
24	-	467th Field Coy. R.E.
25	-	469th do.
26	-	470th do.
27	-	Office.
28	-	War Diary.
29	-	do.
30	-	C.R.E. 59th Division.

SECRET.   Copy No. 39

OPERATION ORDER NO. 9
by
C.R.E., 59th DIVISION.

Ref.1/100,000 HAZEBROUCK 5A
& LENS 11.   30-3-18.

1. Transport of 59th Division (less Artillery) will move to the Second Army Area under orders of C.R.E. 59th Division on March 31st and following days.

2. On March 31st they will proceed by march route from the VILLERS-CHATEL Area to LILLERS via RANCHICOURT, HOUDAIN, and MARLES-lez-MINES.

3. 177th Inf. Bde. will join the column at HOUDAIN, The head of the 177th Inf. Bde. column resting on the cross roads 800 yards east of N in DIVION at 12 noon.

The head of the main column will pass the Starting Point at cross roads at first A in BARAFFLE at 11 a.m.

Units will pass the Starting Point in the following order and at the times named :-

177th Inf. Bde.   )
515 Coy. A.S.C.   ) Join South of DIVION at 12 noon.

176th Inf.Bde.   ...   11 a.m.
514 Coy.A.S.C.   ...   11.20 a.m.
516   do.   ...   11.27 a.m.
2/1 N.M.Fd.Amb.   ...   11.34 a.m.
470 Fd.Co.R.E.   ...   11.45 a.m.
467   do.   ...   11.55 a.m.
469   do.   ...   12.5 p.m.
6/7 R.Scots Fus. ...   12.15 p.m.

178th Inf.Bde.   ...   12.25 p.m.
2/3 N.M.Fd.Amb.   ...   12.45 p.m.
Div.H.Q.   ...   1.5 p.m.
Mob.Vet.Sec.   ...   1.15 p.m.
59th Bn. M.G.C.   ...   1.25 p.m.
2/2 N.M.Fd.Amb.   ...   1.40 p.m.

4. The column will halt at 10 minutes before the clock hour, resuming the march at the clock hour. Watches will be synchronised at the Starting Point at 11 a.m. March 31st.

5. Transport officers are responsible for the maintenance of the strictest march discipline, particular attention being given to the following points :-

   (a) Brakesmens' kits will be worn and not placed on the wagons.

   (b) Brakesmen will march at the rear and not at the side of their vehicles, and will not be allowed to hold on to the wagons.

   (c) Intervals of 20 yards will be maintained between every group of 6 wagons, and intervals of 100 yards will be maintained between Units.

   (d) The above intervals must be maintained and every effort made to prevent straggling. No unit will leave the column except under orders of the officer commanding the column.

   (e) All wagons must be properly packed and balanced.

6. Billeting parties will report to Captain K.N.Moss, Adjutant, 59th Div. R.E. at Town Major's Office, LILLERS tomorrow, March 31st at 11.30 a.m. They will be provided with complete marching-in-states.

7. Further orders will be issued in regard to the destination and route for April 1st, on which day the column is ordered to be clear of LILLERS by 9.30 a.m.

8. The Headquarters of O.C. Column on night March 31st/April 1st, will be at Town Major's Office, LILLERS.

Lieut.Colonel,R.E.(T),
C.R.E. 59th Division.

Issued at 11.40 p.m. by D.R.

DISTRIBUTION :-

Copy No.			Copy No.	
1	-	59th Division "G"	29	- 6/7 R.Scots Fus.
2	-	do. "O"	30	- D.A.D.V.S.
3 - 7		176th Inf. Bde.	31	- 59th Bn.M.G.C.
8 - 12		177th " "	32	- C.R.E.
13 - 17		178th " "	33	- A.P.M.
18 - 21		Div.Train.	34	- Camp Comdt.
22	-	A.D.M.S.	35	- Town Major, LILLERS.
23	-	2/1 N.M.Fd.Amb.	36	- Signals.
24	-	2/2 do.	37	- Office.
25	-	2/3 do.	38	- War Diary.
26	-	467 Fd.Co.R.E.	39	- War Diary.
27	-	469 do.		
28	-	470 do.		

59th Divisional Engineers

C. R. E.

59th DIVISION

APRIL 1918.

ORIGINAL

Army Form C. 2118

WAR DIARY
INTELLIGENCE SUMMARY of HEAD QUARTERS R.E. 59 DIVISION (APRIL)

(Erase heading not required.)

Instructions regarding War Diaries and Intelligence Summaries are contained in F.S. Regs., Part II and the Staff Manual respectively. Title Pages will be prepared in manuscript.

Place	Date	Hour	Summary of Events and Information	Remarks and references to Appendices
COUTHOVE CHATEAU	1/4/18	10 am	Head Quarters Division went from VILLERS CHATEL to COUTHOVE CHATEAU on the PROVEN – POPERINGHE ROAD (BELGIUM)	
			The Transport of the Division moved from LILLERS area to MORBECQUE by route march.	
		6 pm	59 Div. WARNING ORDER No. 120 copy No. 4 received	
"	2/4/18	6 pm	Divisional Transport (less Artillery) arrived in WATOU-PROVEN AREA	
"		11 pm	59 Div. ORDER No. 111 copy No. 4 received	
"	3/4/18		2 LT. E. H. HUMPHRYS ⎫ reported from duty with 470 Field Coy. R.E.	
			2 LT A.T OWEN ⎬	
			2 LT NEWPORT ⎭	
			CRE Operation Order No. 10 issued to all concerned per appendix 1	
	4/4/18		467 Field Coy RE relieved 11 Field Coy RE ⎫	
			469 " " 212 " " ⎬ as per CRE order No. 10	
			470 " " 222 " " ⎭	
YPRES	5/4/18	10 am	CRE Headquarters closed at COUTHOVE CHATEAU at 10 am and opened at same hour at the RAMPARTS YPRES taking over from CRE 33 Div.	
			CRE visited each Field Coy and the pioneers	
			2 LT W. H. MILLER reported for duty with 467 Field Coy RE vice 2 LT M. H. JONES evacuated sick	

1875 Wt. W593/826 1,000,000 4/15 J.B.C. & A. A.D.S.S./Forms/C. 2118.

ORIGINAL

Army Form C. 2118

WAR DIARY
or
INTELLIGENCE SUMMARY Continued
(Erase heading not required.)

Instructions regarding War Diaries and Intelligence Summaries are contained in F. S. Regs., Part II. and the Staff Manual respectively. Title Pages will be prepared in manuscript.

Place	Date	Hour	Summary of Events and Information	Remarks and references to Appendices
YPRES	6/4/18	—	CE II'd ARMY called upon CRE. 470 FIELD Coy moved up to the proximity of Eeling was on the night Brigade sector of the 29 DIVISIONAL FRONT and ordered to make a reconnaissance of the line	Sheet 28 1/40 000 1"27 Known
"	7/4/18		CRE went round Divisional line 59 DIV. ORDER No 112 copy No 5 received	Known
"	8/4/18	3pm	CRE held a conference of OC. field Companies and dept in which the policy of work was detailed by CRE.	Known
"	"	5pm	59 DIV ORDER No 113 copy No 5 received	Known
"	9/4/18		CRE went round Divisional front	Known
"	10/4/18		CRE went round Battle Zone with GSO2. 59 Bn order No 114 copy 5 received	Known
"	11/4/18	1am	CRE Head Quarters (Man HQ) except CRE moved to BRANDHOEK CAMP.	Known
"	12/4/18	2.30 am	59 DIVISION ORDER No 115 Copy 6 received Head Quarters Division move to BRANDHOEK Field Coy's join their affiliated Brigades and the 467 and 469 march into ROOK CAMP in ELAMERTINGHE. — And the 470 Field Coy, provided by route march with 178 INF BDE to DRANOUTRE.	Known
"	13/4/18	10 pm	D.H.Q move to ABEELE. Personnel of 467 and 469 FIELD Coy's RE entrain at BRANDHOEK at 5pm for GODEWAERSVELDE and finalpart proceed by route march via WATOU to the same place 59 G drew up their battle stand Quarters in WESTOUTRE. LIEUT H.L. BUTTER MC/RE reported for duty with 469 Field Coy vice LIEUT J.A. [illegible]	Known

Wt. W593/826 1,000,000 4/15 J.B.C. & A. A.D.S.S./Forms/C. 2118.

ORIGINAL

Army Form C. 2118

WAR DIARY
or
INTELLIGENCE SUMMARY   Continued

(Erase heading not required.)

Instructions regarding War Diaries and Intelligence Summaries are contained in F. S. Regs., Part II. and the Staff Manual respectively. Title Pages will be prepared in manuscript.

Place	Date	Hour	Summary of Events and Information	Remarks and references to Appendices
ABEELE	14/4/18		CRE only proceed 59 G, at battle Head Quarters in WESTOUTRE Rear BHQ ordered to move to WESTOUTRE but orders were cancelled	Sheets 27 and 28 /20 000 and HAZEBROUCK SA 1/100.000
WESTOUTRE		11 pm	467 FIELD Coy holding a portion of the line in front of BAILLEUL under the 176 INF BDE in accordance with Division Order No 120 received at 9 pm. 469 FIELD Coy working in Flying Corps Camp on Summit of MONT ROUGE 470 FIELD Coy are stationed at M 21 d 5 6 Sheet 28 and are under 178 INF BDE	Known
WESTOUTRE	15/4/18		Rear BHQ joins G, at WESTOUTRE. Reach CRE Head Quarters open up at BOESCHEPE Sheet 27 470 FIELD Coy report 1 OR wounded 467 " " report 5 OR wounded 2 OR missing	Known
"	16/4/18		469 FIELD Coy in view of DIV ORDER No 121 join the 177 Composite Brigade under B.G. 177 INF BDE and take up a position at 467 FIELD Coy are to relieved in the line and move in billets in WESTOUTRE at MISC G.S. Sheet 28. G.A. 211 received - by Sheet 176 and 177 BDEs move into CORPS RESERVE and Rendezvous 470 FIELD Coy report 2 O.R. wounded. their Head Quarters now at M 24 a 2 7 Sheet 28	Known
"	17/4/18	Noon	59 G, move to R 18 C.9.5 Sheet 27	
BOESCHEPE	"	"	CRE move to REAR HEAD QUARTS RE at BOESCHEPE R 9 d 73 Sheet 27 469 FIELD Coy report 1 OR wounded	
"	18/4/18	12.30 pm	G.C. 10 ordering 467 FIELD Coy R.E. to proceed to STEENVOORDE and to come under the orders of G.O.C. 176 INF B.O.E. Receive	Known

1875 Wt. W593/826 1,000,000 4/15 J.B.C. & A. A.D.S.S./Forms/C. 2118.

ORIGINAL Army Form C. 2118

WAR DIARY
or
INTELLIGENCE SUMMARY. Continued.

(Erase heading not required.)

Instructions regarding War Diaries and Intelligence Summaries are contained in F.S. Regs., Part II. and the Staff Manual respectively. Title Pages will be prepared in manuscript.

Place	Date	Hour	Summary of Events and Information	Remarks and references to Appendices
BOESCHEPE	18/4/18		1 O.R. of 470 Field Coy killed. 2 O.R. " " wounded.	Sent HAZEBROUCK 5th 1/100 000
	19/4/18	8.30 a.m	G.S. 12 ordering 176 Bde Group to VOX VRIE area. Arrived at 8.30 a.m.	
		2 p.m	Advanced Head Quarters close upon up at COUTHOVE CHATEAU	Known
COUTHOVE CHATEAU			467 Field Coy 3 O.R. bayonetted wounded. 469 " " " 13 O.R. of Transport " . 7 Horses wounded 4 killed.	
		4 p.m	CRE went to a conference at VIII Corps Headquarters held by Corps Commander	Known
"	20/4/18		CRE works the 3 Field Coys in the afternoon	
		11 p.m	CRE under H.M. wants to see concerned re approach II attacked	Known
"	21/4/18		467, 469, 470 Field Coys and 6/7 Royal Scot Pioneers proceeded by route march to HOUTKERQUE M.T. area in accordance with CRE order 11. Intr Head Quarters R.E. rejoined R.H.Q. at the CONVENT F.22.d. Sheet 27 owing to lack of accommodation in HOUTKERQUE AREA M.T.	
CONVENT F.22.d Sheet 27		7 p.m	467 Field Coy HQ at E.26.b.30. Sheet 27 469 " " " E.19.d.28. 470 " " " D.24.b.70. 6/7 Royal Scot Pioneers E.26.b.89. CRE went round proposed new army line with C.E. Corps and majors JAMES and ROBINSON.	Known

WAR DIARY
or
INTELLIGENCE SUMMARY

ORIGINAL Army Form C. 2118

Place	Date	Hour	Summary of Events and Information	Remarks and references to Appendices
CONVENT F22d	22/4/17		CRE out all day inspecting and arranging work upon WATOU - CAESTRE defence line Sheet 27.	
		6 pm	CRE attended a conference at CE office VIII Corps	Kern/1000000
	23/4/17		CRE went over WATOU - CAESTRE defence line with Divisional Commander.	Kern
BOMBECQUE	24/4/17		CRE moved Headquarters to BOMBECQUE Sheet 19.	
			CRE went round front line left sector of WATOU - CAESTRE LINE and all out support line of its front sector of left sector with CE VIII Corps	Kern
			CRE went round WATOU - CAESTRE LINE	Kern
"	25/4/17		CRE met G.O.C. Division at WATOU at 9.30 am	
	26/4/17		No 9 and 470 Field Coy RE and Pioneers working on WATOU LINE	
			467 Field Coy working upon HERZEELE lent Major DB Green OC 467 Field Coy RE made a reconnaissance of the POPERINGHE LINE in accordance with G.62 dated 25". 59 Division order No 123 Copy No 4 received at 6 pm	Kern
			All 3 Field Coys and 6/7 ROYAL SCOT PIONEERS employed upon Divisional Sector of WATOU - CAESTRE LINE	
	27/4/17		CRE office closed at BAMBECQUE and opened at same hour at DIV HEAD QUARTER Camp in F22 d.	
"		7 pm	3 Field Coys and Pioneers ordered to move to ST. JAN-TER BIEZEN by CRE order marked appendix III attached.	
			Earl went left details whore to head over the work on the WATOU Line to 30 Div at 12 noon Tomorrow Major M.H. JONES RE reported for duty with 467 Field Coy RE having been sick of the Boat

ORIGINAL

Army Form C. 2118

WAR DIARY
or
INTELLIGENCE SUMMARY
(Erase heading not required.)

Continued

Instructions regarding War Diaries and Intelligence Summaries are contained in F.S. Regs., Part II. and the Staff Manual respectively. Title Pages will be prepared in manuscript.

Place	Date	Hour	Summary of Events and Information	Remarks and references to Appendices
CONVENT F.2.d Sheet 27	28/4/15		CRE went round SWITCH and POPERINGHE lines of defences with a view to detailing work to Field Companies. 467 and 469 FIELD Coys RE ordered forward in order to be nearer their work on the SWITCH LINE and POPERINGHE LINE of defences. CRE went round SWITCH LINE with CE 5th Corps	Sheet 27 and 28 1/40 000
				Khan
	29/4/15	6 pm	59 DIV ORDER No. 125 Copy M/c received. 6/7 ROYAL SCOT FUSILIERS (Runners) were found under CRE instructions and commenced wiring the SWITCH LINE RE dump made at G.20.a.5.7	Khan
	30/4/15		469 and 470 Field Coys RE., 6/7 Royal Scot Fusiliers, 134 A.T. Coy the 121st and 126th Labour Companies engaged digging a line of Resistance from G.32.d Sheet 28 to the road running H and S in L.35.d Sheet 27 joining up with the 33rd DIVISION. 467 FIELD Coy Taping out and digging a support line in rear of SWITCH LINE CRE visited this work in hand and superintended the detailing of Labour for the work. 2/Lt W H MILLER transferred from 467 to 470 FIELD Coy RE	Khan

K Maillehson
Capt. Adjt
Sq Div R.E.

SECRET.   Copy No. 12.

OPERATION ORDER
No. 10
By C. R. E. 59th. Division.

Reference Sheets Nos. 27 & 28. 1:40,000.
Belgium and France.   3rd. April 1918.

1. On the night 4/5th April the 59th. Division will relieve the 33rd Division in the Right Sector of the 33rd Divisional Front.

2. On April 4th the following reliefs will take place:-

   (a) The 467th (N.Midland) Field Co. R.E. will relieve the 11th Field Co. R.E. at I.8.b.3.4. (Transport at H.18.b.6.8). and will be in support to the 177th Infantry Brigade in the Line.

   Two sections of this Company will be employed on the Battle Zone under the Chief Engineer, VIIIth. Corps.

   (b) The 469th (N.Midland) Field Co. R.E. will relieve the 212th Field Co. R.E., taking over all work in the line and billets at I.8.a.7.1. (Transport at H.18.b.6.8.) and will be support to the 177th Infantry Brigade in the Line.

   (c) The 470th (N.Midland) Field Co. R.E. will relieve the 222nd Field Co. R.E. at I.3.b.4.5. (Transport at I.1.d.2.4.) and will be in support to the 177th Infantry Brigade in the Line.

   (d) The 6/7th Bn. Royal Scots Fusiliers (Pioneers) will take over work of 18th Middlesex Regt. Pioneers, with billets at MIDDLESEX Camp.(Transport at I.3.c.0.7.) and will be in support to the 177th Infantry Brigade in the Line.

3. Advance Parties from Field Cos. R.E. and 6/7th Bn. Royal Scots Fusiliers (Pioneers) will complete the taking over of the own work and billets (detailed above) by 10 a.m. April 4th.

4. Dismounted personnel of Field Cos. R.E. of the 59th Division will entrain at 11.45 a.m. on the 4th instant at QUINTIN Station (G.7.b.7.0.) detraining at TRANSIT Dump, YPRES, I.7.c.9.7. at 1.15 p.m.

   Dismounted personnel of 6/7th Bn. Royal Scots Fusiliers (Pioneers) will entrain at 12 Noon on the 4th instant at QUINTIN Station (G.7.b.7.0.) detraining at SAVILLE Road, Stone Spur, I.3.c.1.4.

   Each Unit will send an Officer in advance to the entraining station to make the necessary arrangements as all entraining must be completed in 15 minutes.

5. Transport of Field Cos. R.E. and 6/7th Bn. Royal Scots Fusiliers (pioneers) will proceed by march route to their new transport lines on the 4th instant.
   Particular attention is directed to VIIIth Corps Standing Orders under which intervals of 25 yds. will be kept between each section of 6 vehicles and 100 yds. between Units.
   The head of the column will pass the road junction at G.3.c.7.2 (Sheet 28) as follows :-

6/7th Bn. Royal Scots Fusiliers (Pioneers)	9 a.m.
467th. Field Co. R.E.	9.30 a.m.
469th. Field Co. R.E.	9.45 a.m.
470th. Field Co. R.E.	10.0 a.m.

Continued.

Continued.

6. The 6/7th. Bn. Royal Scots Fusiliers (Pioneers) will detail 4 Lewis Gun Teams, of at least 2 men per team, to take over from the 18th Middlesex Regt. Pioneers Anti-Aircraft Guns in Battery positions.

These Teams are to report at MIDDLESEX Camp, (I.3.c.0.7) by 10 a.m. the 4th instant.

7. C. R. E. Headquarters will close at COUTHOVE Chateau at 10 a.m. on the 5th April, and will re-open at the same hour at the RAMPARTS, YPRES, I.8.a.95.25.

8. ACKNOWLEDGE.

A.C.Howard
Lieut.Colonel, R.E.(T)
C. R. E. 59th.Division.

Issued at 5 p.m.

Copy No. 1. 'G' 59th.Division.
2. 'Q' 59th.Division.
3. 177th Inf. Bde.
4. 467th Field Co. R.E.
5. 469th. Field Co. R.E.
6. 470th. Field Co. R.E.
7. 6/7th Bn. R.S.F. (Pioneers).
8. Divisional Train.
9. Chief Engineer, VIIIth.Corps.
10. C. R. E. 33rd Division.
11. Office.
12. War Diary.
13. War Diary.
14. File.

SECRET.   Copy No. 10.

ORDER No. 11.

by

C.R.E. 59th. Division.

Reference sheets:-   20th April 1918.
   BELGIUM and FRANCE.
   Sheets 27 and 28. 1/40.000

1.   The 59th Divisional R.Engineers and the 6/7th Bn.Royal Scots
        Fusiliers (Pioneers) will proceed by route march in rear of
        177th Infantry Brigade to-morrow the 21st April to No.1.
        HOUTKERQUE Area (Sheet 27. E.15. E.25. E.26. and E.27)

        The column will proceed via INTERNATIONAL CORNER (A.9.a.1.5)
        - F.10.d.9.1.- F.21.a.2.5.- F.7.d.6.6.- E.22.b.6.2.- E.22.d.6.5.

2.   Units will march in the following order;-

              469th (North Midland) Field Co.R.E.
              470th (North Midland) Field Co.R.E.
              467th (North Midland) Field Co.R.E.
              6/7th Bn.R.S.F. (Pioneers)
              Hd.Qtrs. 59th Divisional R.E.

        The head of the column will pass the starting Point (A.23.c.2.5)
        at 10.a.m. and will pass INTERNATIONAL CORNER (A.9.a.1.5) at
        11.10.a.m. The 467th Field Co.R.E. and the 6/7th Bn.R.S.F.(Pioneers)
        will join the column at INTERNATIONAL CORNER.

        Headquarters 59th Divi.R.E. will join the column at F.21.a.2.6.
        at 12.20.p.m.

3.   Strict march discipline will be maintained, particular
        attention being paid to Corps Standing Orders under which spaces
        of 100 yards will be maintained between Units and 25 yards between
        every group of 6 vehicles or 10 animals.

4.   The column will halt at 10 minutes to the clock hour, resum-
        ing the march at the clock hour.

5.   Advance billeting parties from Units will meet Captain H.N.
        Moss.R.E. at the Church, WATOU at 11.a.m. on the 21st instant.

6.   C.R.E. Headquarters will close at the Chateau COUTHOVE at
        12 Noon and open at HOUTKERQUE No.1.Area at the same hour.

7.   Acknowledge by bearer.

                                                    [signature]
Issued at 11.p.m.   Lieut.Colonel.R.E.(T)
                                                    C.R.E. 59th Division.

         Copy. No.1. 'G' 59th Div.   Copy No.6. 6/7th Bn.R.S.F.
               2. 'Q' 59th Div.   7. 59th Div.Train.
               3. 467th Field Co.R.E.   8. C.R.E.
               4. 469th Field Co.R.E.   9. Office.
               5. 470th Field Co.R.E.   10. War Diary.
                                            11. War Diary.

SECRET.
Copy No. 5.

ORDER
by
C.R.E. 59th. Division.

Ref. Sheets 27.28-29.
1:40,000.

27.4.18.

1. The 3 Field Cos. and Pioneers will move at once by route march to rejoin the Division.

2. The 469th Field Co. R.E. will detail an Officer who is conversant with the two portions of the WATOU Line and each of the 3 Field Cos. and the Pioneers will detail 2 N.C.Os. who know the portion of the WATOU Line on which their Units have been working.
   The N.C.Os. of each Unit will report to the Officer of the 469th Field Co. R.E. at Company H.Q. at E.19.d.2.8.
   These details will remain behind in order to show relieving troops all the work in hand on the Divisional Portion of the WATOU Line.

3. Units will proceed to ST.JAN TER BIEZEN and a representative of each Unit will report to 178th Brigade Headquarters at ROAD CAMP in order to get information as to billeting area.

4. C.R.E. Headquarters will close at BAMBECQUE at 7 p.m. and open at Divisional Headquarters, the CONVENT, F.22.d. Sheet 27. at the same hour.

5. ACKNOWLEDGE.

Issued at 5.30 p.m.

Captain & Adjutant for
C. R. E. 59th Division.

Copy No. 1 O.C. 467th Field Co. R.E.
        2 O.C. 469th Field Co. R.E.
        3 O.C. 470th Field Co. R.E.
        4 O.C. 6/7th. R.S.F. (Pioneers).
        5 War Diary.
        6 War Diary.
        7 File.

War Diary

of

Adv. H.Q. 59th Division

Vol. XVI

From 1st May to 31st May 1916

WAR DIARY
or
INTELLIGENCE SUMMARY.

HEAD QUARTERS
39 DIVISIONAL RE

Army Form C. 2118.

(Erase heading not required.)

Place	Date	Hour	Summary of Events and Information	Remarks and references to Appendices
CONVENT F.22.d	1.5.18		467 Field Coy RE continuing work on Support line 500 yards in rear of SWITCH LINE	Sheet 27 sheet 28
			469 Field Coy RE occupied by the 121 and 126 LABOUR Companies engaged upon	
			digging the forward line to the POPERINGHE LINE and the RESERVE LINE behind	1/40 000
			the SWITCH LINE and one Coy of RESISTANCE running from G.32.d Sheet 28	
			to near running H and 8 in L.35.d Sheet 27 which was dug yesterday	
			470 Field Coy RE employed upon improving and pushing the trench dug from	
			G.32.a.3.8 Sheet 28 to L.35.d.2.6 Sheet 27. The 134 Army Troops Coy RE employed	KWW
			running in front of the Trench	
			39 Division order Nº 126 Copy 4 received	
"	2.5.18		467 Field Coy RE continuing work on Support line 500 yds in rear of SWITCH LINE	
			469 " at the disposal of G.O.C. 177 INF BDE	
			470 " " 6/7 Bn R.S.F. (PIONEERS) employed digging a reserve	
			line to the rear of Scottish line which the 470 completed yesterday between	
			G.32.a.3.8 Sheet 28 and L.35.d.2.6 Sheet 27	
"	3.5.18		CRE visits all the work in progress and superintends the laying of new	
			defence line in process of construction.	
			467 and 469 Field Coys engaged upon the same work as yesterday	
			470 FIELD Coy RE and PIONEERS employed upon the continuation of the	
			work on the RESERVE LINE to the RENINGHELST SWITCH	

Army Form C. 2118.

WAR DIARY
or
INTELLIGENCE SUMMARY.

Continued

(Erase heading not required.)

Place	Date	Hour	Summary of Events and Information	Remarks and references to Appendices
VOGELJE CAMP	4.5.18		467 Field Coy RE. digging night flank of RESERVE LINE from G.27.d.7.9 to G.28.c.8.7 and making defended localities at G.28.b.5.2 and G.27.a.1.3	Sheet 27 & 28 1/40,000
F22 d 5 8			469 Field Coy RE working with 177 Inc BE on night subsector of the divisional front	
			From W of the POPERINGHE - REHINGHELST road to junction with the French on the EAST POPERINGHE LINE	
			470 Field Coy RE together with 6/7 R.S.F. (Pioneers) digging reserve trench of RESERVE LINE.	Kwm
"	5.6.18	8am	59 DIVISION ORDER No. 127 Copy 4 received ordering 178 RE group less 470 Field by to ST. OMER	Kwm
			" " " No. 128 " " to ST. OMER area	
		11am	G.149 dated 5" received withdrawing 176 and 177 Bde groups less 467 and 469 Field Coys	
			467 Field Coy RE digging reserve line and making it a continuous trench	
			469 Field Coy RE attached to 177 Bde.	
			470 Field Coy and Pioneers continued their work of yesterday in an westerly direction	Kwm
SHRINE CAMP	6.5.18	11am	CRE office closed at VOGELJE Camp and opened in HOUTKERQUE of the same name	
HOUTKERQUE			467 Field Coy pushed off their work upon defended localities and moved to SHRINE Camp HOUTKERQUE	
			469 Field Coy finish their work upon defended localities already commenced and marched to SHRINE CAMP HOUTKERQUE.	
			470 Field Coy in conjunction with 6/7 R.S.F. (Pioneers) completing wiring of reserve line. pushing out strong point 500 yds of trench left to join up to the WATOU CAESTRE line about I.K. 25 d 8 o. and completing the work left unfinished by the infantry the day before - afterwards marched to SHRINE CAMP HOUTKERQUE	Kwm

WAR DIARY
INTELLIGENCE SUMMARY — Continued.

Army Form C. 2118.

Place	Date	Hour	Summary of Events and Information	Remarks and references to Appendices
ST OMER	7/8/16		CRE Ch. 3 Field Coy Pioneers and M.G Battalion dismounted personnel marched from 2nd Inward from SHRINE CAMP to ST. OMER.	Sheet HAZEBROUCK
			CRE Headquarters and 467 and 469 Field Coys accommodated in CASERNE de LA SA 1/100,000 BARRE.	
			470 Field Coy accommodated in CASERNE d'ALBRET.	Khan
"	9/8/16		59 DIVISION ORDER Nº 129 Copy 4 received detailing move of Division from VIII Corps to X Corps.	
			CRE went to interview CE X Corps	Khan
"	9/8/16		467 and 470 Field Coys RE proceeded by route march with 178 Bde to MAMETZ area.	
			469 Field Coy RE proceeded by route march with 177 Bde to MAMETZ area.	
HESTRUS	10/8/16		CRE moved office from ST OMER to HESTRUS	
			Field Coy's moved forward under Brigade orders from MAMETZ area to FERMES area.	Khan
			59 Division ORDER Nº 130 received ordering works of Field Corps	
"	11/8/16		467 Field Coy RE moved into camp at J.9 Sheet 36B	
			469 " moved into camp at J.32.a.88	
			470 " " " " O.2.c.23	
			CRE received letter K4616 orders to all concerned copy attached marked Appendix II	Khan
	12/8/16		467 Field Coy RE now accommodated in 30 RUE D'AIRE AUCHEL	
			469 Field Coy RE in camp at J.32.a.88	
			470 Field Coy RE in camp at Q.7.a.8.9.	
			CRE CE X Corps came to see CRE	Khan

WAR DIARY
or
INTELLIGENCE SUMMARY. Continued.—
(Erase heading not required.)

Army Form C. 2118.

Place	Date	Hour	Summary of Events and Information	Remarks and references to Appendices
HESTRUS	13/5/18		CRE visited all three Field Companies in the morning. Klim	Sheet 36 B
"	14/5/18		CRE went to see CE 1st Army and CE I Corps. Klim	1/45000
"	16/5/18		CRE visited all 3 Field Corps and CE. R.B. Line in the evening	and Sheet
THEROUANNE	17/9/18	10 am	CRE officer stood at HESTRUS at 10 am and opened up at new H.Q. at BILLET MARIE THEROUANNE CRE saw O.C. 3 Company Commanders in the morning	36 D 1/20000
"	18/5/18		CRE inspected the FRENCH defences of the Year 1916 on the line north and south of ST OMER.	Klim
" to	19.5.18 26.5.18		107RB reconnoitring new "D'Aecks" R.B.Lewis R.H. Defences.	
"	22.5.18		259" Field Co. arrived at CLARQUES about 136 A for work on D'Aecks R.B Line	
"	25.5.18		431st Field Co. H.Q. moved to ERQUES about 131 D for work on D'Aecks R.B Line	
"	27.5.18		Work on D'Aecks R.B Lewis began between MERTHES and ERQUES	
"	28.5.18 to 21.5.18		Work on reverse line of defence D'Aecks R.B Lewis	

31. 5. 1918.

Lewis Col RE
CRE 53rd Division

Secret.

O.C. 467th Field Co.R.E.
O.C. 469th Field Co.R.E.
O.C. 470th Field Co.R.E.

Brig-Gen. C.J.Armstrong. C.M.G. R.E.) for
Headquarters G. 59th Division.) information.

Subject:- Work on 'B.B' Line.

1. The 59th Divisional R.E. will be employed on the construction of the 'B.B' Line.

2. The Technical Staff has already been formed under Brig-Gen C.J.Armstrong C.M.G. R.E. Chief Engineer of the Line.

3. This Technical Staff deals with all matters of siting and tracing-out defensive works, the supply of R.E. stores and the allotment of Labour.
    Os.C Field Coys.R.E. 59th Division are not, and will not be responsible for any of these matters. They will devote their whole energies to the control and the carrying on of the work and organization of working-parties and the carrying on of the work as laid down by the Technical Staff. There must be no misunderstanding on this point.
    The Technical Staff exists to ensure a continuity of policy and such questions as comparative seniority of officers do not arise.
    Os.C. Field Companies are personally responsible to me for the avoidance of any friction in the carrying on of the work.
    In the event of C.R.Es Sectors requiring any further technical assistance such officers as they require will be lent by the O.C. Field Company and attached to the Staff of the C.R.E. concerned.

4. For the purposes of technical organization the Line is at present divided into three sectors as under:-

Sector.	C.R.E.	Headquarters.
A.	Major Napier-Clavering.R.E.	REBREUVE.
B.	Major Reid.R.E.	CAUCHY-a-la-TOUR.
C.	Major Cheetham.R.E.	LES TOURBIERES.

5. The 467th Field Company R.E. is at the disposal of the C.R.E. 'B' Sector. The 469th and 470th Field Coys.R.E. are placed at the disposal of the C.R.E. 'A' Sector.

    As soon as possible after the receipt of these orders Os.C. Coys will report to their respective C.R.Es (Sectors) for further instructions.

6. Officers commanding Field Companies will be advised by their Sector C.R.E. if and when, it desirable for them to move their location.
    Immediately on receipt of such advice they will communicate with me as all moves must be arranged through 59th Division 'Q'.

11th May, 1918.

Lieut.Colonel R.E.(T).
C.R.E. 59th Division.

Appendix I

Secret.   Copy No. 10

O R D E R   No.13.

by C.R.E. 59th Division.

- o - o - o -

Reference sheets :-
Nos. 27 and 28.
BELGIUM and FRANCE.   5th May 1918.

1. The 59th Divisional R.Engineers and the
    6/7th Bn.Royal Scots Fusiliers Pioneers will
    withdraw from the forward area to-morrow, May 6th
    to SHRINE Camp, HOUTKERQUE. (sheet 27. E.20.b)

2. There are no restrictions as to time or route,
    but Units will complete their day's work on the
    REMINGHELST line before withdrawal.

3. Advance billeting parties will report to
    Captain K.N.Foss at the Church, HOUTKERQUE, at
    10.30.a.m. to-morrow the 6th instant.

4. C.R.E. Headquarters will close at VOULIJE
    at 11.a.m. to-morrow, and open at 11.a.m. the
    same hour at SHRINE Camp.

5. Acknowledge.

Issued at 8.30.p.m.   Lieut.Colonel R.E.(T)
                                                   C.R.E. 59th Division.

Distribution :-
                Copy No.1. 'G'59th Division.
                     2. 'Q'59th Division.
                     3. 467th Field Co.R.E.
                     4. 459th Field Co.R.E.
                     5. 470th Field Co.R.E.
                     6. 6/7th Bn.R.S.F.Pioneers.
                     7. 59th Div.Train.
                     8. C.E. VIII.Corps.
                  9 & 10. War Diary.
                    11. Office.

Original.

WAR DIARY

of

HEAD QTRS R.E. 59th DIVISION

Vol XVII.

From 1st June to 30th June
-1918-

Vol 17

Army Form C. 2118.

WAR DIARY "HEAD QUARTERS R.E. 59TH DIVISIONAL R.E.
or
INTELLIGENCE SUMMARY.
(Erase heading not required.)

JUNE 1918

Instructions regarding War Diaries and Intelligence Summaries are contained in F. S. Regs. Part II. and the Staff Manual respectively. Title pages will be prepared in manuscript.

Place	Date	Hour	Summary of Events and Information	Remarks and references to Appendices
THEROUANNE	1/6/18		467 and 470 FIELD Coys RE employed under CRE^s of B and A Sectors of BB LINE respectively.	Sketch 36 D 36 B
			469 FIELD Coy employed under CRE 59 DIV who is in charge of D SECTOR BB LINE	36 A 1/40 000
				Kum
do	4/6/18		PORTUGUESE troops arrive in area for work on D Sector and come under orders of G.O.C. Corps in whose area they are working. Strength about two thousand	Kum
do	6/6/18		PORTUGUESE troops commence work in the BILQUES subfield.	
			LT COL. A.C. HOWARD M.C. CRE 59 DIV leaves division to take up the appointment as CRE 41st DIV, A 200 g/2 G.H.Q. 1/6/18	
			MAJOR H.A.S. PRESSEY takes over D Sector BB LINE from Lt Col. HOWARD	Kum
do	13/6/18		LT COL. L.J. COUSSMAKER M.C. reported as CRE 59 DIV vice Lt Col. A.C. HOWARD M.C. Authority A.G. M^s APPTS/3795 dated 6/6/18	Kum
do	16/6/18		467, 469 and 470 FIELD Coys comes under CRE^s of B. D and A sectors respectively for discipline, interior economy and accommodation vide X Corps N°9/193/G	Kum

dated 17 June 1918.

WAR DIARY continued
INTELLIGENCE SUMMARY

Army Form C. 2118.

(Erase heading not required.)

Place	Date	Hour	Summary of Events and Information	Remarks and references to Appendices
THEROUANNE	24/6/18	10 am	CRE closed his office in THEROUANNE at 10 AM and opened up at BOMY	Sheets 36A 36B
BOMY			R 32 d 7.3. Sheet 36 D at the same hour	Sheet 36 D 1/40000
"	28/6/18		59 Div N° 546/6/3 G ordering 2 Sections of 470 FIELD Coy R.E. to reinforce Divvarmen received	Known
"	30/6/18		2 SECTIONS 470 FIELD Coy RE joined Divisional school at CREPY the remaining portion of 470 FIELD Coy 469 and 467 FIELD Coys are still engaged respectively upon A, B and D Returns BB LINE.	Known
				Known

Kraskbr?
Capt RE
19.30

ORIGINAL

Vol 18

War Diary

of

Headquarters R. Engineers.

59th Division

Vol. XVIII

1st July 1918 to 31st July 1918

Army Form C. 2118.

WAR DIARY
INTELLIGENCE SUMMARY.
(Erase heading not required.)

HEAD QUARTERS
59TH DIVISIONAL R.E

JULY

Instructions regarding War Diaries and Intelligence Summaries are contained in F.S. Regs., Part II and the Staff Manual respectively. Title pages will be prepared in manuscript.

Place	Date	Hour	Summary of Events and Information	Remarks and references to Appendices
BOMY	1/7/18		467, 469 and 470 FIELD Coys have two Sections with Divisional School continue to be employed on the BB LINE under CRE's of B, D, and A Sectors respectively.	Sheets 36 P, 36.3, 36 A, 36 1/40000
"	7/7/18		CRE order No 20 with instructions attached issued to all concerned re transfer of the two R.E Sections at Divisional School to 178 and 177 Bde areas. Six copies attached marked appendix I	
MONCHY-CAYEUX	11/7/18		CRE closed office at BOMY at 3 p.m. and opened up again at MONCHY CAYEUX Sheet 44c at the same hour.	
	11/7/18		470 FIELD sustained the following abnormal casualties as the result of enemy bombing. 3 R. F'L.D killed. 2 R. F'L.D wounded and evacuated – other sustained minor injuries which did not necessitate evacuation	
	17/7/18		Location of units is as follows :–	
			Headquarters R.E. MONCHY-CAYEUX	
			467 FIELD Coy CAUCHY-à-LA TOUR C.27.c.3.8 Sheet 44 b	
			469 " CLARQUES L.23 central " 36 d	
			470 " NEAR HOUDAIN J.26.d.32 " 44 b	

Army Form C. 2118.

WAR DIARY
INTELLIGENCE SUMMARY.   *Continued*
(Erase heading not required.)

Instructions regarding War Diaries and Intelligence Summaries are contained in F. S. Regs. Part II. and the Staff Manual respectively. Title pages will be prepared in manuscript.

Place	Date	Hour	Summary of Events and Information	Remarks and references to Appendices
MONCHY-CAYEUX	23/7/18		467, 469 and 470 FIELD Coys RE reported 59 DIVISION from BB LINE	LENS SHEET 1/10,000 Sheet 51 c 1/40,000
	24/7/18		467, 469 and 470 FIELD Coys RE took over from the 8th and 9th Battalions of the 3rd CANADIAN BDE RE in the line and opened up their Head Quarters as follows :– 467 FIELD Coy at R26 c.0.5.; 469 FIELD Coy at R31 d 5.6 470 FIELD Coy at R31 c 6.9 Sheet 51c SE. CRE moved Head Quarters from MONCHY-CAYEUX together with 59 DIVISION H.Q.	Kum
GROSVILLE	26/7/18		and took over the Head Quarters of the 3rd CANADIAN BDE RE at R26 c.F.8. The employment of RE units and pioneers is as follows :– 467 FIELD Coy RE – 2 Sections forward with BDE in the line – employed drawing and duckboarding forward system. 1 Section with PIONEERS working upon CT³. 1 Section working on the repair of their own billets. 469 FIELD Coy RE are in Reserve and are training 470 FIELD Coy RE – 2 Sections working upon M.G. dugouts in CHAT- -MAIGRE and BRICKFIELDS defended localities; 1 Section improving front line of 2ND SYSTEM (PURPLE), 1 Section on CT⁴ with PIONEERS	Kum

Army Form C. 2118.

WAR DIARY
or
INTELLIGENCE SUMMARY. Continued
(Erase heading not required.)

Instructions regarding War Diaries and Intelligence Summaries are contained in F. S. Regs., Part II. and the Staff Manual respectively. Title pages will be prepared in manuscript.

Place	Date	Hour	Summary of Events and Information	Remarks and references to Appendices
GROSVILLE	26.7.18		PIONEERS are employed as follows. 1 Coy attached to 177 TUNNELLING Coy RE for assistance with work on M.G. emplacements and dugouts and	
			2 Coys. working on CT's. The PIONEERS are the 25TH Bn. KING'S ROYAL RIFLE Corps	Known
	28.7.18		ADJT attended a conference of the Divisional Commander for the CRE absent on leave.	Known
	29.7.18		Forward pickets of each field Coy are located as follows	
			467 3 pickets at - M25 d 2.5 Sheet 51 B S.W.	
			16.9 3 " R 35 a 20 35 Sheet 51 C S.E.	
			470 2 " R 35 a 20 35	
			463 FIELD Coy RE have two sections working upon ROSS LANE the remainder of the Company doing various look out & jobs of work	Known
	30.7.18		59th Division ORDER 146 received and copies issued to FIELD Coys.	Known
	31.7.18 6 pm		463 FIELD Coy RE lost 4 Horses killed and 4 wounded by enemy shelling	Known

Mallison
Capt. R.E.
R.E.

ORDERS
No 20
by

Lieut-Colonel L.J.COUSSMAKER.M.C. R.E.

C.R.E. 59th Division.

Reference;-   7th July 1918.
    LENS & HAZEBROUCK
    1/100.000.

1.   The 2 R.E. sections under the command of
    Lieut.F.C.B.Wills.M.C. and 2nd.Lieut.F.D.C.
    Newport will, on the 8th instant be transferred
    from the Divl.School as follows.

2.   The section under the command of Lieut.
    Wills will proceed to 177th Inf.Bde area, and
    will be accommodated by the 11th Somerset Light
    Infantry at AUDINGTHUN and rationed by them
    from the 10th inst inclusive.

3.   Lieut Wills will detail 3 carpenters, one
    painter and two fitters to report to C.R.E. at
    BOMY on the 10th instant for temporary attach-
    ment to Divisional Workshops.

4.   The section under the command of 2nd.Lt.
    Newport less 6 sappers will proceed to HESTRUS
    to take down 5 Nissen huts; the work to be
    commenced and finished on the 9th inst. A party
    of 20 Infantry will report at HESTRUS on the
    9th inst for assistance.

5.   The section will be rationed by the Divl.
    School up to and including the 9th instant.

5.   On the evening of the 9th July the section,
    less 6 sappers left at Divl.School will proceed
    to PREDEFIN (178th Bde area) and will be accom-
    modated by the 36th Bn.Northumberland Fus. and
    rationed by them from the 10th inst. inclusive.

6.   The 6 sappers left at Divl.School for the
    erection of 2 Nissen huts will re-join their
    section at PREDEFIN on completion of work.

7.   O.C.Sections will, upon arrival in their
    Bde.areas report immediately to Bde.Majors to
    arrange work.

8.   Lieut.Newport will detail half his section
    for work with the 176th Bde and half with the
    178th Bde.and supervise both.

9.   Completion of these moves to be wired to
    this office.

10.   Acknowledge.
                                Captain & Adjutant.

Copy No.1.Lt.Wills.   6. 177th Inf.Bde.
        2.Lt.Newport.   7. 178th Inf.Bde.
        3.59 Div.G.   8. Cmdt.Divl.School.
        4.59 Div.Q.   9. 470th Fd.Co.
        5.176th Inf.Bde. 10. Office.
        11 & 12 War Diary.

Lieut. F.C.B. Wills. M.C. R.E.
2nd. Lieut. F.D.C. Newport. R.E.

Reference C.R.E.s. Order No.20 of even date.

You will while at AUDINCTHUN
PREFEDIN.

1. Assist Battalion Commanders in every way you can with the instruction of their men in Field works.

    (a) To ensure this being done in accordance with the Brigadier's wishes you will report daily to the Brigade Major for instructions.

    (b) It is intended as far as possible to standardise all trench work, and for this reason the methods shown on the attached drawings will be strictly adhered to.

    (c) The above, of course, refers to deliberate work when time and the enemy allow.

    (d) Short lengths of trenches showing their different stages at completion of tasks, also the various forms of revetment will be at once constructed (at sites selected by Brigades) great care being taken that these are models in every detail. The Infantry will then have them thoroughly explained to them before they are asked to carry any of them out.

2. Carry out any R.E. work in the area, such as Water Supplies, repairs to billets etc.
    (a) For instructions as to above you will report daily to the Staff Captain.
    (b) You will ask Brigades to provide you with all unskilled labour.

7th July 1918.   Lieut. Colonel R.E.
                                  C.R.E. 59th Division.

Copies to H.Q.trs. G.   Lieut. Wills. M.C. R.E.
         H.Q.trs. Q.   2nd. Lt. Newport. R.E.
         176th Inf. Bde.   War Diary.
         177th Inf. Bde.
         178th Inf. Bde.   Office Copy.

ORIGINAL

WAR DIARY
of
HEADQUARTERS R. ENGINEERS.
59th DIVISION

Vol. XVII

1st August 1918 -to- 31st August 1918

WAR DIARY
INTELLIGENCE SUMMARY.

HEAD QUARTERS
59 DIVISIONAL R.E.

Army Form C. 2118.

AUGUST

Place	Date	Hour	Summary of Events and Information	Remarks and references to Appendices
GROSVILLE	1/8/18		No.1 Field Coy RE employed as follows. 2 sections attached to B.D.E in the line to assist infantry in developing & improving for beys. 1 section on drainage and duckboarding in S.T.B.W. 1 section with pioneers working on ROSS LANE C.T. 1/20 vs. of trenches in forward system. Section back in rear billets opening Lewis gun posts in rear.	app upt to
			No.2 Field Coy RE Employed as follows. 2 Sections living forward at R.30.a.25.48 working upon ROSS LANE C.T. & jumper employed upon repairs to wooden bridge at R.27.a.57 and both points at R.30.d.45 to P.30.a.59 and P.18.b.7 and S.T.E.	
			4 No Field Coy RE 2 sections duckboarding training and repairing BOISLEUX AVENUE 1 section working on his Batt. H.Q. at R.35.a.0. Post 51.c. 1 min under C.R.E employed upon construction of demolition points & was acting dugout at A.D.S. at R.29.d.10.90. 1 was cutting a tunnel through railway embankment at M.21.a.65.15 to my positions in Tyrrels Side. 1 sub section employed as drivers about in back area.	
			PIONEERS (2.5 Bn K.R.R.) 2 companies working on ROSS LANE and 1 company attached to 177 TUNNELLING Co RE	
			CRE returned from leave	

Army Form C. 2118.

WAR DIARY
INTELLIGENCE SUMMARY.
(Erase heading not required.)

Instructions regarding War Diaries and Intelligence Summaries are contained in F.S. Regs., Part II. and the Staff Manual respectively. Title pages will be prepared in manuscript.

Continued —

Place	Date	Hour	Summary of Events and Information	Remarks and references to Appendices
GROSVILLE	4.8.18		CAPT F.C SALMON 470 FIELD Coy RE evacuated sick	Sheet 57c SE S7 B SW
do		6.8.0	FIELD Coy and PIONEERS continued the work detailed yesterday. CRE went round line with OC 467 FIELD Coy and visited all work in hand in left subsector	Kim 1/20 000 Kim Kim
do		7.8.11	CRE went round all work in hand by 470 Field Coy RE with the OC company	Kim
do		8.8.21	CRE went round right subsector of Divisional front with OC 469 FIELD Coy	do
do		12.8.18	467 FIELD Coy RE employed as follows:— Fire stepping duckboarding and draining FIFE AVENUE and fixing ladders at intervals. Continuing Coy HQ in FIFE AVENUE. Brickbanding and draining ROSS LANE and LANCS AVENUE. Jacking gas curtains to Bde HQrs. Erecting D Coy Headquarters. Repairing light railway in left Bde area from junction of PURPLE LINE & Switch Winter and CT in front area and making tram for Stand Aspersin Klin. 469 FIELD Coy RE employed as follows:— Brickbanding and draining MERCATEL SWITCH SUPPORT FIR LANE fire stepping and pulling fire bays in RED LINE FORFAR AVENUE. Making LG emplacement at CROSS ROADS in BOISLEAUX au MONT & Gorelling light Railway in right Bde area and Repairing Sime in order	

WAR DIARY
or
INTELLIGENCE SUMMARY.

Army Form C. 2118.

Place	Date	Hour	Summary of Events and Information	Remarks and references to Appendices
GRESSVILLE	12.8.18		470 Field Coy RE employed as follows:— Erecting Soup Kitchen at	Sheet 57 C SE
			S3a.75.70 and M27c.2.8. Construction of Stragglers Post at R33.a.7.3	57 B SW
			Connecting BE Rails at Buff-Red Huts. Extending BABETTE OP at S4.a.55.05.	1/20,000
			Continuing and making dugouts at S3a.3.0. S3.b.05. S2.d.6.3. R35.a.0.1.	
			R35.c.65.95. R31.c.05.95. R29.d.27. (3 galleries and 1chamber being constructed)	K.m.
			Carrying on interior work as detailed in yesterday report.	
			470 Field Coy RE move their Hq.headquarters from R31.c.8.9. to R	K.m.
"	20.8.18		467 Field Coy RE employed as follows. Inc. stepping, duckboarding and drawing FIFE AVENUE	
			duckboarding and drawing LAMES AVENUE & ROSE LANE — Renewing gas curtains	
			to dugouts at M27a.7.2 — Constructing dugouts at M29a.55.55. M17.f0.7 M27.a.5.6	
			Sinking water tanks. Cabeling light Railway — Labour material making M.G.E. at	
			M33.f.67	
			469 Field Coy RE employed as follows:— Duckboarding drawing and burying	
			BOISLEUX AVENUE RED TRENCH SUPPORT RED TRENCH SOUTH Fixing gas proof	
			protection to dugouts. Making a dugout at R30.c.13. Patrolling light	
			Railways in BOE area Making latrine trough and fixing them in the Brewery	

WAR DIARY or INTELLIGENCE SUMMARY

Army Form C. 2118.

(Erase heading not required.)

Place	Date	Hour	Summary of Events and Information	Remarks and references to Appendices
GOMIECOURT	21.8.18		470 Field Coy RE employed constructing dug-outs at R.35.c.o5.95 R.35.c.o5.95	Sheet 57 SE
			R.29.d.27. Filling timber & making camp shelters at S.3.a.75.70 & M.27.a.7.2.	57 B SW
			Creosoting roof of RE shelter at BHQ R.35.R.01. Working on Pioneer Camps	1/20,000
			at R.22.c.73. Pioneers late filling holes at BEHAGNIES & BOIRY –	
			Working have standings at BOIRY – repairing roads in the area	Kern
			On the night of the 21st/22nd – 470 Field Coy RE constructed a bridge across the	
	22.8.18		COJEUL RIVER at BOISLEUX ST MARC. In Appendix I attached hereto	Kern
	22.8.18		On the night of the 22nd/23rd the 3 Field Coys carried out work preparatory	
			to offensive operations on the Divisional front on the morning of the 23rd	
			for details of which see Appendix I attached hereto	
			59 Division ORDER No 150 copy 6 ordering relief of the Division by the	
			52nd and 56th DIVISIONS on the 23rd was received	Kern
			59 Division ORDER No 151 copy 6 issued ordering move of Divisional Transport	
BAVINCOURT	23.8.18		CRE moved office & EHQs at BAVINCOURT. 2 O.R. for Essex wounded (gas)	Kern
	24.8.18		CRE Entrained at SAULTY together with the 3 Field Coys enroute for	
			VILLERS area	

Army Form C. 2118.

WAR DIARY
INTELLIGENCE SUMMARY. *Continued*
(Erase heading not required.)

Instructions regarding War Diaries and Intelligence Summaries are contained in F. S. Regs., Part II. and the Staff Manual respectively. Title pages will be prepared in manuscript.

Place	Date	Hour	Summary of Events and Information	Remarks and references to Appendices
MORBECQ FONTES	26.9.18	10 am	CRE visited HQ 74th Div. also OPs MORBECQ FONTES	HAZEBROUCK AREA Sheet 5A A/N 36A
			467 Field Coy at BOURECQ. 469 Field Coy at ST QUENTIN. 470 Field Coy at MARINE PLE	1/40000
BUSNES	27.9.18	10 am	CRE moved his HQrs overflow to BUSNES and took over from the CRE 74 Div	
P.26.C.15.00			467 Field Coy at BUSNES. HQ 5 R.A.R.E. at P.9.a.9.8.	
			469 " " 5 R.M.R.E. at ROBECQ P.19 ε 63	
			470 " " 439 Field Coy R.E. at ROBECQ and CALONNE-SUR-LA-LYS in accordance with D.O. No. 153 Sept. 5 were on the 25th went	
			S.9 D.O. HQ 134 Coys M.S. macadam adamant. 177 Bdes with 1 Rahurm RE to form the Advance Guard of the Division and to take over from the	Ken
			229 Inf. Bde 74 Division	
	28.9.18		Field Coys carry on with work handed over to them by RE Coys of the 74 Division.	Ken
			CRE visited Field Companies	
	29.9.18		CRE visited Bde in the line and all 3 Field Coys	
			Notification received by OC 470 Field Coy RE that Lt F.C.B. WILKES has been evacuated to base wounded gas (shell). Lt F.C.B. WILKES and	

A6945 Wt.W11422/M1160 350,000 12/16 D.D.&L. Forms/C/2118/14.

WAR DIARY
INTELLIGENCE SUMMARY. Continued
(Erase heading not required.)

Army Form C. 2118.

Place	Date	Hour	Summary of Events and Information	Remarks and references to Appendices
BUSNES	29.8.15		Continued – II Lt W.H. MILLER was evacuated to Field Ambulance at O.23.c and suffering from 'flu.	Appx-36A 1/40 am
	30.8.15		CRE went forward to arrange for coordinates of bridges and reconnaissance of roads in the area needed by the gunners. 21 Field Companies are employed as follows:- 467 Field Coy RE erecting 2 nissen huts at P.7.c.o.4 making the roofs of houses in ST FLORIS in order to provide accommodation for men. Party of men patrolling demolition points in the Lark area. Erecting 2 nissen huts at P.17.b.4.3 (Coventry) Collecting blankets in Divisional Reception camp. & LINGHEM 469 Field Coy RE working on RESERVE LINE between J.13.d.0.4 and P.6.a.c.4. P.12.d.9.5.30 and D.19.d.5.0.60 and wiring at P.6.d.5.7 11b dan tr open. Area completed. Patrolling muces in area and pushing pions. Reconnaissance of forward Roads and bridges. 470 Field Coy RE. Erecting staff shelters at Q.14.6.6.3 and Q.cc.w.3 for accommodation of men and monthly improving fields in area. Wall up.	KMM

WAR DIARY
or
INTELLIGENCE SUMMARY.
(Erase heading not required.)

Army Form C. 2118.

Place	Date	Hour	Summary of Events and Information	Remarks and references to Appendices
BUSNES	30.9.18		Continued	Ref 36 A
			Reconnaissance of roads in the forward area and BRIDGES over the RIVER LAWE and making infantry bridges across River on R.P.L.3 and R.9 - Field Company moved forward to make bridges over the river	1/40,000
		11 pm	CRE issued orders to 467 and 469 FIELD Coys and to PIONEERS per	
			Appendix II attached hereto.	R.W.
	31.7.18		467 and 469 FIELD Coys RE together with the pioneers work in accordance	
			with instructions given in appendix II	
			BRIDGING returns. Pontoon C Q3 c 43 and to P11 a 05	A.A.
			470 Fd Coy RE working upon roads and Bridges in forward area	
			Lt. G.P.V. GIBBS reported for duty with 470 Fd Coy RE and was temporarily	p.w.
			attached to 469 Fd Coy RE.	

Kenelm Lee
Capt. RE
A/CRE 46

for CRE 46

Headquarters.G.
59th Division.

Reference map 51.b.S.W. 1/20.000.

The following work was been carried out on the 59th Divl. front preparatory to the attack made by the 52nd Division on the morning of the 23rd instant.

Bridge over COJEUL River.

On the evening of August 21st I gave the O.C.470th Field Company R.E. instructions to throw a trestle brdige, double-baulked and double chessed across the COJEUL River at BOISLEUX St.MARC.

A party of sappers under Lieut.Humphreys were sent ahead to prepare a site for the bridging equipment which arrived at 9.30.p.m.

Owing to a considerable amount of gas shelling the men had to be constantly withdrawn and very little progress could be made before 1.a.m.

By 3.a.m. the Bridge was completed - gas respirators having been worn continuously from 11.p.m. until 2.a.m.

During the work the O.C. was very sick and had to withdraw, and it was chiefly due to Lieut.Humphrey's determination that the Bridge was completed.

Work on night Aug.22/23rd.

On the afternoon of Aug.22nd I gave instructions as follows ;-

O.C.470th Field Co.R.E. and one Company of Pioneers,

1. To bridge the front line from M.36.a.3.5. to S.6.a.0.7. places bridges every 100 yds.

2. Cut gaps 4 yds wide opposite each Bridge.

3. Lay a jumping-off tape from M.36.a.cent to S.6.a.5.9.

The whole of this work was completed by 2.30.a.m.

O.C.467th Field Co.R.E. and one Company of Pioneers.

1. To bridge the front line every 100 yds from S.6.a.0.7. to S.6.c.15.00

2. Cut gaps 4 yds wide opposite every bridge.

3. Lay a jumping-off tape from S.6.a.5.9. to S.6.c.5.0.
   This work was completed by 1.40.a.m.

O.C.469th Field Co.R.E. and two Infantry carrying parties of 200 each.

1. To form two Dumps at M.35.d.5.7. and S.5.d.8.4. each stocked as follows;-

continued.

continued.

Barbed wire, 28 lb. coils.	400
Plain -do- coils.	6
Screw pickets, long	400
Screw pickets, medium	800
French wire, bundles	20
Sandbags,	6,000
Mauls,	20
Felling axes	5
Hand axes	5
Hand hammers	6
Sledge hammers,	12
Nails, mixed, lbs.	56
Tracing tapes, yds	1,000
Lift and Force Pumps	2
Suction hose lengths	4
Delivery hose, lengths	4
Troughing collapsible, feet	36
Wire cutters, pairs	40
Wiring gloves, pairs	30
Crowbars	4
Hand saws	2
Anti-gas frames	12
Anti-gas cloth, yards,	50
Camouflage, rolls,	4
Camouflage nets	8

2. A Tool Dump at M.35.d.0.6. stocked as follows;-

Shovels	1,300
Picks.	650

The whole of the above stores were in the Dumps by 2.30.a.m.

26th August 1918.	Lieut.Colonel R.E.
	C.R.E. 59th Divsion.

O.C. 467th Field Co. R.E.

Bridges.

You will bridge the River LAWE about LESTREM in R.2.d. and R.3.c. to-morrow.

Bridges required to take horsed transport and field guns, and should be built at the sides of existing bridges so that permanent bridges can be built beside them by Corps Troops.

The whole of your Company is available for this work.

Bridging materials will be dumped at P.11.d.0.4. and Q.3.c.4.2.

Roads.

Two Companies of Pioneers will work under you, filling in craters or making diversions round them, along the road from Q.12.c.2.0. to R.8.b.3.5. and thence to the bridges.

Road sleepers can be obtained form P.11.d.0.4.

Acknowledge.

(signed) L.J.COUSSMAKER.Lieut.Col.R.E.
C.R.E. 59th Division.

30th August 1918.

Addendum.

Infantry Bridges are to be put across the River to provide lateral communication at the points

L.32.a.9.1.
L.34.b.5.8.

With reference to the construction of bridges for horsed transport, you may use the trestles of bridging equipment on your charge for the construction of these bridges if you consider it necessary.

L.J.C.

Copies to:-
    59th Div.G.
    25th Bn.K.R.R.C.(P)
    469th Field Co.R.E.
    470th Field Co.R.E.

War Diary

O.C. 469th Field Co. R.E.

    You will bridge the River LAWE in R.21.d. and b.

    Two sections of your Company will be available for this work.

    Bridges will be built at the side of existing bridges so that the permanent bridge can be built beside this by Corps Troops.

    Bridging materials will be dumped at P.11.d.0.4. and Q.3.c.4.2.

ROADS.

    One Company of Pioneers will work under you filling in craters or making diversions round them, along the road from Q.30.b.6.9. to R.21.d.1.8.

    Road slabs can be obtained from the Dump at P.11.d.0.4.

    The remaining 2 Sections of your Company will supervise the Portuguese on the Line of Retention.

    Acknowledge.

                            (signed) L.J. COUSSMAKER. Lieut. Col. R.E.
                                          C.R.E. 59th Division.

30th August 1918.

    Copies to:- 59th Div.G.
                     25th Bn. K.R.R.C.(P)
                   467th Field Co. R.E.
                   469th Field Co. R.E.

C.O. 25th Bn. K.R.R.C. (P)

You will place two Companies of your Battalion at the disposal of O.C. 467th Field Co. R.E. for the purpose of repairing roads from Q.12.c.3.0. to R.8.b.3.5.

They should start as early as possible to-morrow morning the 31st instant., and will bivouac in the vicinity of their work until it is completed.

You will place one Company at the disposal of O.C. 469th Field Co. R.E. for work on the road from Q.30.b.6.9. to R.21.d.1.8.

This Company will also bivouac in the vicinity of their work.

The Company will proceed to Q.30.b.6.9. as early as possible to-morrow morning the 31st instant.

You will send transport to the R.E. Dump at O.6.b.8.4. to draw the necessary picks and shovels

Acknowledge.

(signed) L.J. COUSSMAKER. Lt. Col. R.E.
C.R.E. 59th Division.

30th August 1918.

Copies to :-

59th Div. G.
467th Field Co. R.E.
469th Field Co. R.E.
470th Field Co. R.E.

War Diary

O.C. 467th Field Co. R.E.
O.C. 469th Field Co. R.E.
O.C. 470th Field Co. R.E.

Subject:- Notice Boards.

Please have Notice Boards made at once for the areas in which you are working, showing:-

    ROADS for LORRIES.

    ROADS for AMBULANCE and Horsed Transport.

    ROADS BLOCKED.

    TRACKS.

    ROAD to ---------

    TRACK to --------

    ROAD to BRIDGE for Horsed Transport.

    ROAD to BRIDGE for INFANTRY

    BRIDGE for INFANTRY.

    BRIDGE for FIELD GUNS.

Too much time must not be spent on them - the great thing is to get them up.

You will please decide what lettering is most suitable for these Notice Boards and also their size.

                      (signed) L.J. COUSSMAKER. Lieut. Col. R.E.
31.8.1918.   C.R.E. 59th Division.

Copy to 59th Div. G.

WAR DIARY

HQ R.E.
59th Divn

Vol XXII

1st September 1918 to 30th September 1918

ORIGINAL

ORIGINAL

Army Form C. 2118.

WAR DIARY
or
INTELLIGENCE SUMMARY.

HEAD QUARTERS R.E.
59 DIVISION

SEPTEMBER 1918

(Erase heading not required.)

Instructions regarding War Diaries and Intelligence Summaries are contained in F. S. Regs., Part II. and the Staff Manual respectively. Title pages will be prepared in manuscript.

Place	Date	Hour	Summary of Events and Information	Remarks and references to Appendices
BUSNES	1.9.18		Field Companies R.E. are employed as follows.	Sheet. 36A /40.000
			467 FIELD Coy R.E. are employed as follows - Permanent party looking after Bridge demolitions in Vieux area - Concreting floors of ablution sheds and stores at Divisional Reception Camp - Making divisional soda water factory at LUCHEUX near DOULLENS - Clearing and filling in shell holes on road from Q.12.c.20 to Q.P.b.69. Completing bridges over LA LAWE RIVER at R.3.C.30 and over canal at about BEAUPRÉ L.32 central.	
			469 FIELD Coy R.E. - patrolling and guarding mines in Brigade area. Bridges completed for horse transport at R.21 b.4.5 and repairing roads in vicinity of Bridges.	
			470 FIELD Coy R.E. making new M.T.R. in LESTREM and repairing and making BRIDGES.	khm
	2.9.18		59th DIVISION ORDER No. 158 Copy 5 received detailing relief of 177 Bde by 178 Bde taken Advanced HQrs opened up at Q.19.a.86 at 2 pm. Int. CRE's Office.	khm
	3.9.18		Moved to BUSNES.	khm
	4.9.18		59 DIVISION OPERATION POLICY No 2 copy No 5 received	khm

A6945 Wt. W14422/M1160 350,000 12/16 D. D. & L. Forms/C/2118/14

Army Form C. 2118.

WAR DIARY
INTELLIGENCE SUMMARY. *Continued.*
(Erase heading not required.)

Instructions regarding War Diaries and Intelligence Summaries are contained in F. S. Regs., Part II. and the Staff Manual respectively. Title pages will be prepared in manuscript.

Place	Date	Hour	Summary of Events and Information	Remarks and references to Appendices
BUSNES	4.9.18		6.19/18 received orders move of 1/17 Bde	Sheet 36 A
			467 Field Coy RE employed as follows:	1/40.000
			- erecting floor of Atelier and store sheds at Divisional Reception Camp
			at LINGHEM. - making quarries for road metal, factory at LUCHEUX.
			Repair of Roads R.15.b.30 to R.23.a.2.5.; R.16.c.7.3 to R.11.c.7.5.;
			L.34.b.25 to L.35.b.15". Two mine craters filled in at R.11.c.7.5.
			1 ton traffic BRIDGE completed at R.3.c.30-8. H.T. Bridge at R.10.d.05.05.
			Reconnoitring area east of LESTREM and repairing billets for occupation.
			Examining old German HQs for booby traps - locking and fixing
			their guards.
			409 Field Coy RE filling in enemy craters at R.15.a.90.45. Repairing
			road from R.20.c.35 to R.21.c.40.55. Repairing hand rails to Bridge
			at R.21.b.4.5. Patrolling mines and demolition points in forward area
			470 Field Coy RE constructing new Bryty at LESTREM and	Kern
			finishing bridge over RIVER LAWE
	5.9.18		Received to move new Bryty from LESTREM to R.13.d.05.70.	Kern

A6945 Wt. W14422/M1160 350,000 12/16 D. D. & L. Forms/C./2118/14.

Army Form C. 2118.

WAR DIARY
or
INTELLIGENCE SUMMARY. *[Corps Troops]*
(Erase heading not required)

Place	Date	Hour	Summary of Events and Information	Remarks and references to Appendices
BUSHES	6.9.18		470 Field Coy RE moving new BHQ from LESTREM to R.13.d.45.70.	Sheet 36 A
R.13.d.45.70	7.9.18		CRE noted HQ from BUSHES to R.13.d.45.70. 469 and 470 Field Coys RE Employed Erecting new BHQ and CRE Headquarters and improving the roads in the vicinity of DHQ.	1/40 000.
ditto	8.9.18		59 Division order ER M.160 Copy 5 received attaching officers of Brigades to the various front Positions and on the Battle line. 59 Division DEFENCE INSTRUCTIONS No 1 Copy 5 received	
R.13.d.45.70	9.9.18		Field Coys RE both employed as follows:— 467 Field Coy RE — boarding floors of dilution sheds and stores at Mounted Reception camp at LINGHEM. Preparing beds into factory at VUCHERE was finished — making signal office. Bde Headquarters — 150 yards road forward in M.15.C. — pulling up and fixing nettle bonds — repairing roads, filling in road craters and making drainage round them in the forward area. Two bridges completed at G.32.c.8.9. 469 and 470 Field Coys making new DHQ at R.13.d.45.70 and repairing roads in the vicinity.	

WAR DIARY
or
INTELLIGENCE SUMMARY. Continued

Army Form C. 2118.

(Erase heading not required.)

Place	Date	Hour	Summary of Events and Information	Remarks and references to Appendices
R.13.d.65.70	10.9.18		Companies carrying on with their work as detailed in yesterdays entry.	Plist 3/A 1/40 ORO KWM
"	11.9.18		No.7 FIELD Coy R.E. Employed upon concreting floors of ablution sheds and stores at Divisional reception camp LINGHEM. Widening road diversion at G.32.a.50.35. Repairing MANOR LANE. Making Inf. Bde and Artillery Bde Headquarters at M.7.d.3.8. – Making Bn. Headquarters at M.9.d.5.3. Erecting road screens from M.17.b.5.2 to M.17.b.9.7. – Painting and fixing notice boards for roads and road diversions. No.9 FIELD Coy R.E. Erecting shelters at ORE KOPJE – making new divisional Baths at R.3.c.20.15. – Renewing roads between MILL LANE and LAW LANE making and erecting sign boards. Improving erection of woven huts for M.G. Coys at R.15.67.5. No.10 FIELD Coy R.E. Erecting Headquarters for S.9 D. Train and finishing work at others.	KWM
"	12.9.18		Work of Field Companies R.E. is a continuation of most of the work detailed in yesterdays report. S.9 Dn order No 162 copy 5 received	KWM KWM

WAR DIARY
INTELLIGENCE SUMMARY.

Army Form C. 2118.

Cover transcribed:—

Place	Date	Hour	Summary of Events and Information	Remarks and references to Appendices
R13 d & 70	12.9.18		Field Companies carry on with work as detailed in entry for 11th inst.	Sheet 36 A, 36 B 1/40,000
			Handed over M¹ to 59 Division Defence Instructions M¹, and 59 Divisions	
			Defence instructions H² 2, 3, 4 and S¹ Moenes	Ken
	13.9.18		59 Div. Defence instructions N° 6 issued	
			467 Field Coy RE employed as follows. Carrying floor of aplelum shed and stores at LINGHEM making new cookhouses and Brigade Head-Quarters at M7d 5.8 and M7d 5.7.6. Improving and clearing up road ? near Divisional at M14 b 7.7. M9a 6.1 M15 b 7.7. Repairing road Passing in M14 c. Picking and fixing R11d and M7d. Repairing road ? Scraping and clearing roads in R11c. ?tion brigade	
			409 Field Coy RE Constructing splinter proof shelters at R11C 20.95, R13 d 4.7 Making baths at R3c 3.1 and M7 b 21. Filling in craters and shell holes in road at R15 d 9.6. Preparing bridges for demolition at R21 b 35.95. Erecting iron huts at R15 b 7.5. making and erecting Sign boards. Reconnoitring forward roads	
			470 Field Coy RE. Making Brigade Headquarters with British Flat shelters	Ken

A6945   Wt. W1422/M1160   350,000   12/16   D. D. & L.   Forms/C./2118/14

WAR DIARY
INTELLIGENCE SUMMARY.

Army Form C. 2118.

Place	Date	Hour	Summary of Events and Information	Remarks and references to Appendices
R13 d.05.70.	14.9.18		contd:— making ASC Headquarters camp with woven huts and British Shelters at	Rent 36 ad
			Q.18 a.27 (Ref. 36A). Camouflaging SMQ. — Making roof of Q18 Stores at	36A 1/40,000
			R.9.A. Erecting British Shelters at R.13 a.9.1. Erecting woven huts at	
			R.20 a.27. Painting in prog. wattle hurdles.	Klm.
	15.9.18		Field companion camp on with this wk detailed in yesterday's entry	" Km.
	16.9.18		2 Lt G.E. WALKER reported for duty with 470 Field Coy RE vice LT.	
			F.C.B. WILLS wounded gen. Capt. A.G. HENDERSON RAMC MO 59 Div.R.E. ordered to report to	
			59 Div. Defence instruction No.9 received	Km
	17.9.18		467 Field Coy R.E. engaged upon Concreting floors of Ablution sheds and stores	
			at 59° Div School LINGHEM. Improvement of road diversion for ambulances	
			traffic at M.12 b.77. — Erecting new infantry and artillery Bridges. Head lets	
			at M.7 d.5.8. Repairing and cleaning roads in R.11.C.d, R.17.b, R.11.C, M.7.b.vcl	
			Clearing MASSELOT STREET C.T. for passage of troops also WINCHESTER	
			STREET. C.T. Painting wattle hurdles.	
			469 Field Coy RE. Erecting Corps C.P. at LA GORGUE. — Completing Bath at	
			R.3.C.31. Completing shelters at ORE Hdqrs. Making road diversion round	

Army Form C. 2118.

WAR DIARY
or
INTELLIGENCE SUMMARY. Continued
(Erase heading not required.)

Place	Date	Hour	Summary of Events and Information	Remarks and references to Appendices
R14c2.9	17.9.18		Contd.	Meet 35 and 36A
			469 Field Coy RE. crater at R15a9.9 and repairing road between R15a9.4 and R15b9.4. Completed 3 splinter proof shelters at R13d4.9. 1/4 road.	
			Preparing Bridge for demolition at R21b 3.5.e.5. Enemy aware into at R15 b.7.5 making and erecting sign boards.	
			470 Field Coy RE. Stabling at Bn HQ and Company Horse lines. Continuing erection of Rustal shelters at BHQ at R19a.00. Camouflaging BHQ.	
			Sidney RE actinide. Roofing Eastern Chateau, making and erecting sign boards. Enemy Rebel Shelters at R13d4.8.	k.i.m.
R14c2.9	18.9.18		Field Companys continue work on detailed in yesterdays report.	k.i.m.
	19.9.18		Field Companies continue their work.	k.i.m.
	20.9.18		59 DIVISION ORDER N° 164 Copy 5 received detailing relief of 177 Bde by 178 Bde on night of 22/23rd. 3 OR 467 field coy killed by shell fire	k.i.m.
	22.9.18		59 DIVISION operation policy N° 3. Copy 5 received	k.i.m.
	23.9.18		DRE visited 467 field coy and went round work with them.	k.i.m.
	24.9.18		CRE visited Bates and inspected Company horse lines	k.i.m.

Army Form C. 2118.

WAR DIARY
INTELLIGENCE SUMMARY.
(Erase heading not required.)

Instructions regarding War Diaries and Intelligence Summaries are contained in F. S. Regs., Part II. and the Staff Manual respectively. Title pages will be prepared in manuscript.

Continued :-

Place	Date	Hour	Summary of Events and Information	Remarks and references to Appendices
R14c29	25.9.18		467 FIELD Coy RE employed as follows :— Improvements to Bn HQ and making Tunnel foot centre at M14d.99, making shelter at A.D.S. M7b.22, at BDE HQ	Sheet 3b and 3c I/40,000
			M7c.58. Erecting Bde Transport lines at R4d.54. Repairing Roads in R10b, R11a.	
			R17d, R18c, R11d, R17c. Painting notice boards. Clearing trench and laying	
			duckboards in MASSELOT ST. C.T. from M11a to M13c making OP in LAVENTIE	
			making tunnel foot centre at M23a.2.7. Painting and erecting notice boards.	
			Salving material.	
			469 FIELD Coy RE Erecting British Shelters at HHQ R13 d 4.9; Erecting covers	
			Horse standings at R10 b 5.2, R10 b 2.5, R10 b 9.5; 20 x; Erecting Infantry Shelters	R16b.11
			at R10 b 0.3. Drainage of Roads in forward area ; Renewing O.P.; making	
			and erecting sign boards.	
			470 FIELD Coy RE Erecting Stables for Divisional HQ, Bn Train; Erecting	
			steel shelters for accommodation at No 2 Coy Bn Train No 3 Coy 17th Train	
			at ROYAL WELSH FUS. billets at R3 d 4.2. Converting G.O.C. dugout Bde HQ	
			at R11c 3.4. Salving trench and aircraft in the area.	Khan

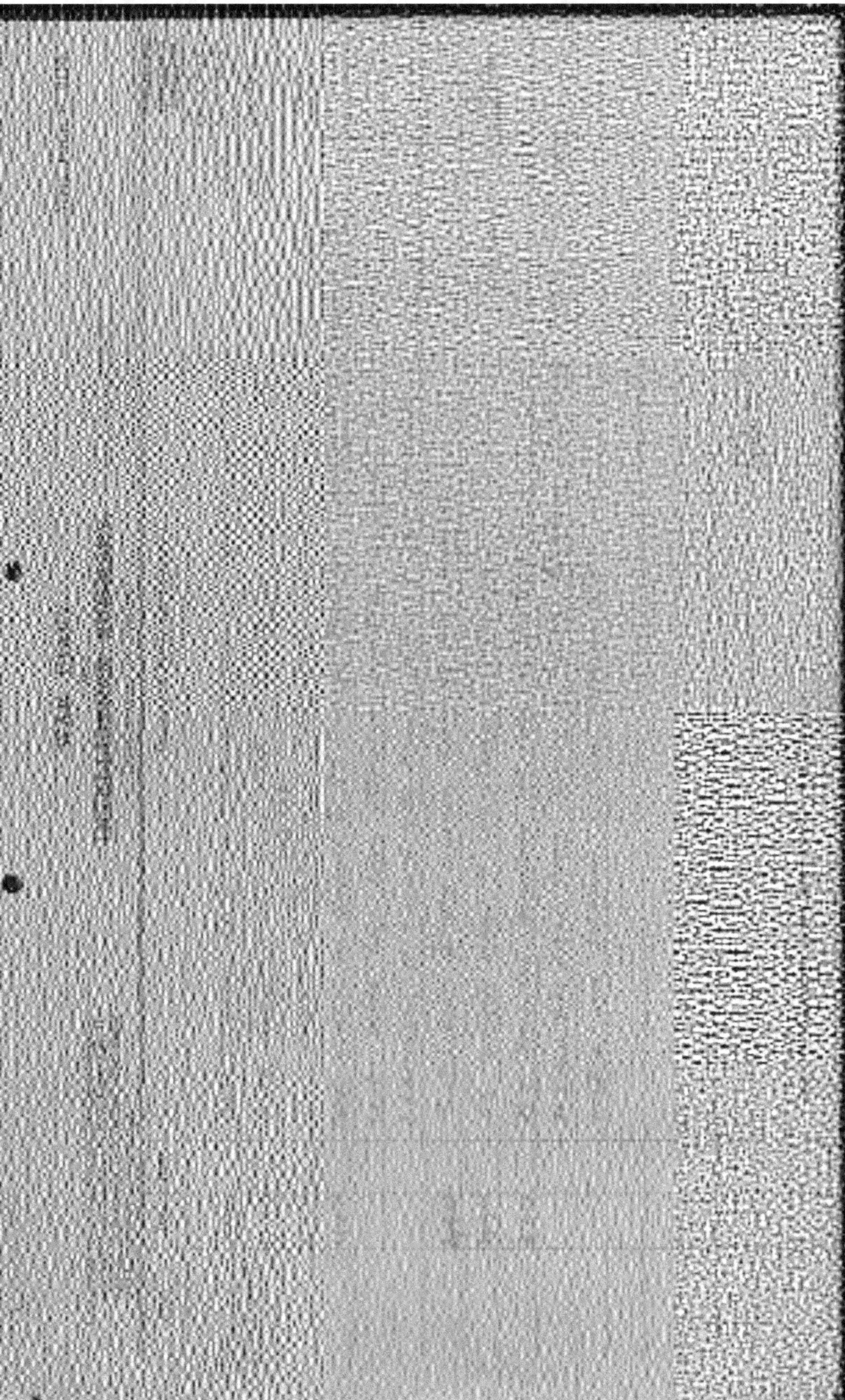

SECRET.

O.C. 467th Field Co. R.E.	Copies to 59th Divn G.
O.C. 469th Field Co. R.E.	59th Divn Q.
O.C. 470th Field Co. R.E.	176th Inf. Bde.
O.C. 25th Bn. K.R.R.C.(P).	177th Inf. Bde.
	178th Inf. Bde.

Appendix I

Reference 59th Division Operation Policy No. 4

As the Division is now to be disposed on a two-Brigade front - commencing tomorrow, the 30th instant, Field Companies will operate as follows :

467th Field Co. R.E.

Right Sub-sector (177th Infantry Brigade) until the afternoon of the 1st October, when it will be relieved by the 469th Field Co. R.E.

469th Field Co. R.E.

Divisional Reserve until the afternoon of October 1st, when it will relieve the 467th Field Co. R.E.

470th Field Co. R.E.

Left Sub-sector - 176th Infantry Brigade.

Should the Division advance, the 469th and 470th Field Coys. R.E. will be ready to move at once with the 177th and 176th Infantry Brigades respectively.

TECHNICAL CARTS AND WAGONS.

Companies will at once load and overhaul all Technical Carts and wagons, withdrawing from their present work any men required for this purpose.

Pioneers.

The 25th Bn. K.R.R.C.(P) will continue to work as at present, unless the Division advances, in which case they will be reay to move with Field Companies, R.E. as follows :-

'A' Company with 467th Field Co. R.E.
'B' Company with 469th Field Co. R.E.
'C' Company with 470th Field Co. R.E.

(SD) L.J.Coussmaker, Lt.Col.R.E.
C.R.E. 59th. Division.

29.9.18.

ORIGINAL
Vol 21

WAR DIARY
of
Headquarters RE 59th Divn.

VOLUME XXI

1st to 31st October 1918

Army Form C. 2118.

WAR DIARY
of
INTELLIGENCE SUMMARY.

HEAD QUARTERS R.E.
59 DIVISION

OCTOBER 1918

(Erase heading not required.)

Instructions regarding War Diaries and Intelligence Summaries are contained in F. S. Regs., Part II. and the Staff Manual respectively. Title pages will be prepared in manuscript.

Place	Date	Hour	Summary of Events and Information	Remarks and references to Appendices
RWC29 Sheet 36.A	1.10.19		Field Companies continued work on roads, tramways, Loop lines, standings etc.	Sheet 36 ant 36.A/1/40900
"	2.10.19		Addendum No.1 to 59 Div order No.170 issued and 59 Div order No.170 issued detailing relief of the Division by the 47 Division and taking over from 61 Div. CRE issued orders for the relief of the 61st Divisional Engineers see copy. Makes Appendix 1. attached	KW
	3.10.19		59 Division operation order No.171 issued detailing orders for the advance of the Infantry in conjunction with 47 Divisional Infantry on our divisional front.	KW
Rue Victor		10am	CRE handed over to CRE 47 Division and took over from CRE 61 Division. Field Companies relieved Field Companies of the 61st Division as per CRE order see appendix 1 attached.	
		7pm	Owing to retreat of the enemy CRE ordered Field Companies forward the work consisting of maintaining and keeping communications by roads etc. A large number of craters exceeding along the roads and at every cross roads in the forward area was required to be filled in or divertions made round them as soon	KW

A6945 Wt. W11422/M1160 350,000 12/16 D. D. & L. Forms/C,2118/14.

Army Form C. 2118.

WAR DIARY
or
INTELLIGENCE SUMMARY.
(Erase heading not required.)

Instructions regarding War Diaries and Intelligence Summaries are contained in F. S. Regs., Part II. and the Staff Manual respectively. Title pages will be prepared in manuscript.

Continued

Place	Date	Hour	Summary of Events and Information	Remarks and references to Appendices
RICE WORKS	4/10/18		467 Fld Coy RE ordered to make extension Murannel H49 c/6 H15c central/wagon	Sheet H.
LA GORGUE			467 and 470 Fld Coys were together with a company of Pioneers will.	
			Each Fld Coy having men engaged upon repair of roads, filling in craters and making road diversions round them.	
			Location of Field Companies 467 Field Coy RE H31 a.3.3. 469 FIELD Coy. H35c.9.6.	
			470 FIELD Coy H21 a 6.2.	Klein
G.2.d.30.25'	5/10/18		CRE worked two Head Quarters forward to G.2.d.30.25' into the camp	
			consisting of Armstrong huts and timber and CT shelters erected by	
			467 FIELD Coy RE. RE dump moved forward by lorry - no lorry	
			loads and 6 Quick loads to LAVENTIE G.34.d.21.	
			467 Field Coy continue work upon detailed Murannel HB and the	
			469 and 470 Field Companies continue work on roads.	Klein
	6/10/18		2nd Lt. G. E. WALKER 470 FIELD Coy RE severely wounded by shell	
			467 FIELD Coy RE continue work upon advance BHQ and CRE HQuts	
"			and amenuse erection of Murannel Park and Blanket huts at BAC ST MAUR	
			469 FIELD Coy with a company of Pioneers and a Bn of 1st Portuguese Division	

A6945 Wt. W14422/M1160 350,000 12/16 D. D. & L. Forms/C/2118/14.

WAR DIARY
or
INTELLIGENCE SUMMARY. — Continued

Army Form C. 2118.

(Erase heading not required.)

Place	Date	Hour	Summary of Events and Information	Remarks and references to Appendices
G.24.d.30.25.6.10.16			Contd —	West 36 1/40,000
			Continued work upon roads, always filled in craters and wolves	
			Observing practice of both types. Painting out front signs from Divsn.	
			tops in this forward area — Making accommodation.	
			470 Field Coy RE. Repairing roads, making roads, clearance, filling craters,	
			making mule track, found repairing billets and making and wiring	
			dug-outs — a field coy 1st PORTUGUESE Division and a company of	
			PIONEERS assisting.	KM
	7.10.11		467 Field Coy RE. Finishing work open RSF4 and ORE spring direction. Filling in road	
			craters at H.31.a.35.25" and G.36.d.50.65." Enabling buses Muirhead Ratho and Park	
			and Blacket stores at BAC ST MAUR	
			469 Field Coy RE. repairing roads in forward area, filling in craters, clearing	
			and making road Menneville. Reconnoitering ground into supply tramway	
			track. Making accommodation — Painting and fixing notice boards at cross roads	
			470 Field Coy RE. Filling in craters, repairing roads in left divisional	
			sub-sector — Painting notice boards and fixing same — repairing billets —	
			Helping small streams	J.W.

Army Form C. 2118.

WAR DIARY
or
INTELLIGENCE SUMMARY. Continued
(Erase heading not required.)

Instructions regarding War Diaries and Intelligence Summaries are contained in F. S. Regs., Part II and the Staff Manual respectively. Title pages will be prepared in manuscript.

Place	Date	Hour	Summary of Events and Information	Remarks and references to Appendices
G 3ec d 30. 25. 8.10.18			Field Companies continue the work detailed in yesterdays report	Sheet 3.6.1/450.050
		23.00	59 DIVISION ORDER No. 172. Copy S. received detailing relief of 178 Bde by 177 Bde	
		23.30	59 DIVISION ORDER No. 173. Copy S. received - notifying a verbal propostn operation on night of 30/11.	K.h.m.
"	9.10.18		59 DIVISION OPERATION POLICY No. 6. received.	K.h.m.
"	10.10.18		467 Field Coy with 1 Company Pioneers employed upon making personnel water camp for D.Hqs. Erection of Divisional Baths, Erection of shelters for Battalion accommodation.	
			469 and 470 FIELD Coy R.E. employed upon roads.	K.h.m.
	11.10.18		CRE attended a conference at 47 Div H.Q.	K.h.m.
	12.10.18		467 FIELD Coy R.E. Erecting 1.W. Divisional Baths at BAC ST MAUR. Making personnel accommodation at D.Hqs. Erecting shelters at Bde Hqrs H21a17. Erecting huts for a Bn Hqrs at H26.c.8.8. Erecting a new W.A.O.S. Stores and Armourers Shops at LAVENTIE. Erecting A type bivouac shelters at H15.d.	

A6945 Wt. W11412/M1160 350,000 12/16 D. D. & L. Forms/C./2118/14

Army Form C. 2118.

WAR DIARY
INTELLIGENCE SUMMARY. — Continued:—
(Erase heading not required.)

Instructions regarding War Diaries and Intelligence Summaries are contained in F. S. Regs., Part II. and the Staff Manual respectively. Title pages will be prepared in manuscript.

Place	Date	Hour	Summary of Events and Information	Remarks and references to Appendices
G2 ed 30.25	12.10.18		469 Field Coy. Repairing roads opening up drains and gutters and revetting sides of built up roads, making noticeboards and fixing up signs, making soup kitchen and canteen at H29.b.32. Continuing latrines and cookhouse at Batt. H.Q. at I32.d.27. Working on reinforced concrete gun emplacement and 6".	Paper 36 1/40000
			470 Field Coy. RE. Repairing roads. Opening up ditches and drains. Building bridge for HT at HNAIX. Making notice boards. Camouflaging.	Khm
			176 Rlwy. Hofdt. Repairing bombing riding course for infantry practice	Khm
			59 Division Order No 174. Copy S. received.	
"	13.10.18		Companies continue the work detailed in yesterday's report.	Khm
"	14.10.18		Lt S.S. ROWLAND reports for duty with 467 Field Coy RE vice 2/Lt G.A. PICKERING to England (duty).	
			CRE orders for Colonels of 59th Division for copy marked appendix II attached issued to all concerned.	Khm
"	15.10.18		Appendices A to 59 Division order No 174 received describing arrangements for sealing the city of Lille — work of companies the same as for 12" except	

A6945 Wt. W11422/M1160 350,000 12/16 D. D. & L. Forms/C/2118/14

WAR DIARY
or
INTELLIGENCE SUMMARY. Continued
(Erase heading not required.)

Army Form C. 2118.

Instructions regarding War Diaries and Intelligence Summaries are contained in F. S. Regs., Part II. and the Staff Manual respectively. Title pages will be prepared in manuscript.

Place	Date	Hour	Summary of Events and Information	Remarks and references to Appendices
G.34.d.30.	15		Cmdt. The 469 and 470 FIELD Coy RE who have 2 Section each producing trestles, bridging and working trestles for bridging canal at Rille	Sheet 36 1/40.000 KRM
LAVESEE	16		CRE and field Coys moved up to neighbourhood of LAVESEE post I.19.a.9.9. 469 and 470 FIELD Coy were issued with Bridging material to bridge the canal at K.20.d.4.3, K.20.d.7.4 and K.15.a.7.1. Working thereabouts.	KRM
	17			KRM
			ST. ANDRE.	
ST.ANDRE	18		CRE moves HQ to ST. ANDRE - 467 FIELD Coy move to LAMBERSART. 469 working on bridges at K.20.d.4.2 and K.20.d.7.4 470 FIELD Coy working on bridge at K.15.a.7.1	KRM
HEM	19		CRE moves HQ to HEM - 469 make their bridges at K.20.d.4.2 and K.20.d.7.4 fit to take 6 ton axle load by strengthening trestles and double closing the roadway. 470 FIELD Coy number their bridge. Detatching trestles for pontoons	
			470 FIELD Coy moves to HEMPONPONT 469 FIELD Coy RE to FLERS 469 FIELD Coy to SAILLY LEZ LANNOY	KRM
	20		470 FIELD Coy RE bridge R. MARCQ at L.29 & 6.9 to take lorries	

A6945 Wt. W11422/M1160 350,000 12/16 D. D. & L. Forms/C,/2118/14.

Army Form C. 2118.

WAR DIARY
or
INTELLIGENCE SUMMARY. Continued
(Erase heading not required.)

Instructions regarding War Diaries and Intelligence Summaries are contained in F.S. Regs., Part II. and the Staff Manual respectively. Title pages will be prepared in manuscript.

Place	Date	Hour	Summary of Events and Information	Remarks and references to Appendices
HEM	20/10/18		469 and 467 Field Coy working upon roads between HEM and TEMPLEUVE. 470 Field Coy moving to TEMPLEUVE, 467 Field Coy move to TEMPLEUVE.	Sheet 27 1/40.000 Khm
HEM	21/10/18		467 Field Coy repairing roads up to SCHELDT RIVER and prepare for bridging it. 469 Field Coy filling in road craters and repairing roads from HEM to TEMPLEUVE. 470 Field Coy RE prepare for bridging SCHELDT at I.32.a.7.4. and repair roads and fills in craters between TEMPLEUVE and the SCHELDT.	Khm
"	22/10/18		The 3 Field Coys together with Pioneers, 14th PORTUGUESE Inf Bn. 3 PORTUGUESE FIELD COY RE are all being employed upon roads from HEM to the SCHELDT. RE ordrs issued to all concerned re appendix the attached.	Khm Khm
"	23/10/18		Field Coys continue their work on roads	Khm
"	24/10/18		Field Coys continue their work on Sunday. 467 Field Coy also preparing for bridge across the SCHELDT, constructing Trestles, Launchal Rafts, or across the River. 470th Field Coy moves to FESTINGUE G.24.c.4.9.	H.P.

A6945 Wt. W14422/M1160 350,000 12/16 D. D. & L. Forms/C./2118/14.

Army Form C. 2118.

WAR DIARY
or
INTELLIGENCE SUMMARY.
(Erase heading not required.)

Instructions regarding War Diaries and Intelligence Summaries are contained in F. S. Regs., Part II. and the Staff Manual respectively. Title pages will be prepared in manuscript.

Place	Date	Hour	Summary of Events and Information	Remarks and references to Appendices
HEM	25/10/18		Field Companies continue their work on Roads & the 467th Field Coy	W.D. Sheet 37 1/40,000
"	26/10/18		on preparing for Bridge operations across the Schelot. Field Companies continue their work on Roads & the 467th Field Coy on Bridge operations.	W.D.
"	27/10/18		Field Companies continue their work on Roads & Bridge operations	W.D.
"	28/10/18		Field Companies continue their work on Roads & the 467th Field Coy on Bridge operations across the River Schelot.	W.D.
"	29/10/18		Field Companies continue their work on Roads & Bridge operations	W.D.
"	30/10/18		Field Companies continue their work on Roads & Bridge operations	W.D.
SAILLY-LEZ-LANNOY	31/10/18		C.R.E. HQrs moves to SAILLY-LEZ-LANNOY. Field Companies continue their work on Roads & Bridge operations.	W.D.

H. Taylor Lieut. R.E.
for C.R.E. 57th Division

Nov 1st 1918

O.C. 467th Field Co. R.E. O.C. 469th Field Co. R.E. O.C. 470th Field Co. R.E. O.C. 25th Bn. K.R.R.C.(P).	Copy to :- 59th Divn G. 59th Divn A & Q. 176th Inf. Bde. 177th Inf. Bde. 178th Inf. Bde. C.R.E. 47th Divn. C.R.E. 61st Divn.

Appendix I

WAR DIARY

Reference 59th Division Order No. 170. para 6.

Reliefs of 61st Divl. R.E. by 59th Divl. R.E., and of 59th Divl. R.E. by 47th Divl. R.E.

-----

1. 467th Field Co. R.E. with 'A' Company 25th Bn. K.R.R.C.(P) attached, will relieve the 476th Field Co. R.E. tomorrow morning, the 3rd inst.

2. 469th Field Co. R.E. will send two Sections tomorrow morning, the 3rd inst., to relieve the 479th Field Co. R.E.
The remaining two Sections with 'B' Company 25th Bn. K.R.R.C.(P) will continue to work in their present area until relieved by a Field Company of the 47th Divisional R.E.

3. The 470th Field Co. R.E. with 'C' Company 25th Bn. K.R.R.C.(P) attached, will relieve the 478th Field Co. R.E. tomorrow morning, the 3rd inst.

4. Details as to reliefs will be arranged between Unit Commanders concerned.

5. Completion of reliefs to be reported to this Office.

6. Work.
The 469th Field Co. R.E. and 470th Field Co. R.E. (detailed to accompany the two Forward Infantry Brigades) will be employed primarily on Communications with a view to getting forward Field Guns and First Line Transport.
Orders as to work to be issued by C.R.E.
One section per Company will always be available for inclusion in the Brigade Advanced Guard to remove obstacles, build Foot-bridges, etc.

The 467th Field Co. R.E. will follow up the 469th and 470th Field Cos. R.E. improving communications for heavier traffic and will post Notice Boards at all road junctions.
A supply of Notice Boards and large white arrows (for marking the Main Transport Route) can be drawn from the R.E. Dump.

7. Pioneers.
The Pioneer Companies will work under orders of O.C's. Field Companies to which they are temporarily attached, and will be billetted as near as possible to them.

2.10.1918.

Lieut. Colonel, R.E.
C.R.E. 59th. Division.

SECRET

Appendix

HEADQUARTERS, R.E.
No. K 1732
14 OCT. 1918
59th (NORTH MIDLAND) DIVN.

C.R.E. Orders for Advance of 59th Division.

Reference sheet 36.

In the event of the enemy making a rapid retirement East of LILLE, Companies, on receipt of the code word 'Sapper' will act as follows:

467th Field Co.R.E.

Detail two sections and two platoons of pioneers to take down 8 Armstrong huts at D.H.Q. and re-erect them with stoves and all fittings complete on a site to be notified, as follows:

G.O.C., G.S.O.1, 'G' Office., 'G' Clerks.,
Signals., A.A. & Q.M.G., G.S.O.2 & Intelligence., Mess.

One section and one platoon pioneers to take down 3 Armstrong huts at R.A. Headquarters, and re-erect with stoves and all fittings complete, on a site to be notified, as follows:

C.R.A., B.M.R.A., Signal Office.R.A.

Transport for moving above will be found by Camp Commandant and Staff Captain.R.A. respectively.

One section and one platoon pioneers to report to Adjt.R.E. at C.R.E. Headquarters. for orders.

469th Field Co.R.E.

Detail one section for work with Right Brigade. The Officer in charge of this section will keep his O.C. Coy informed of the tactical situation, and forward reports as to condition of roads, and bridges, and position of any water supplies.

One Officer and 6 intelligent N.C.O.s or men for reconnaissance of roads, bridges and water supplies.
The importance of sending back this information as it is obtained, and not waiting till the end of the day, must be impressed on this party. All sources of water supply will be reported to this office at once.

One section, half Coy pioneers, and the 14th Bn. Portuguese Infantry on repairing the road coloured red on map, from the cross roads in WEZ MACQUART to Le CARNOYE in J.35.b.3.8., removing any land mines and booby traps found.
The Officer in charge of this section with 4 intelligent sappers (preferably miners) will precede the party and search for land mines and booby traps, marking any located or suspicious places in a pre-arranged manner.

Two sections and half Coy pioneers for bridging the HAUTE DEULE Canal at the best spot between K.20.d.5.2. and K.21.a.3.8. for Field Guns and First Line Transport.

470th Field Co.R.E.

Detail one section for work with Left Brigade; The Officer in charge of this section will keep his O.C. Coy informed of the tactical situation, and forward reports as to condition of roads, and bridges, and positions of any water supplies.

One Officer and 6 intelligent N.C.Os or men for reconnaissance of roads, bridges and water supplies.
The importance of sending bak back this information as it is obtained, and not waiting till the end of the

470th Field Co. R.E. (Cntd)

day must be impressed on this party. All sources of water supply will be reported to this office at once.

One section, half Coy pioneers, and the 3rd Portuguese Field Coy on repairing the road coloured red on map from J.35.b.3.8. to K.21.a.3.8. removing any land mines and booby traps found. The Officer in charge of this section with 4 intelligent sappers (preferably miners) will precede the party and search for land mines and bb booby traps traps, marking any located or suspicious places in a pre-arranged manner.

Two sections and half Coy pioneers for bridging the HAUTE DEULE Canal at about K.15.a.75.10. for Field Guns and First Line transport.

Infantry Bridges

Infantry bridges will be thrown across as soon as the canal is reached.
If there is not sufficient debris from the destroyed bridges to carry a few planks, half pontoons would probably be the quickest method, but only rough boarding must be used for foot-way as all chesses will be required for the other bridge.

Lewis Guns.

Each section will tk take it's Lewis Gun with it, and establish posts as quickly as possible on the East side of the canal, if the enemy is still int in the neighbourhood.

ACKNOWLEDGE.

14th October, 1918.

Lieut. Colonel R.E.
C.R.E 59th Division.

Distribution.   467th Field Co. R.E.
                469th Field Co. R.E.
                470th Field Co. R.E.
Copies to: 59th Division. G.
                59th Division. Q.
                C.E. XIth Corps.
                176th Inf. Bde.
                177th Inf. Bde.
                178th Inf. Bde.
                25th Bn. K.R.R.C. (P).
                British Mission, Portuguese.
                File.
                War Diary.
                War Diary.

O.C. 467th Field Co.R.E.
O.C. 469th Field Co.R.E.
O.C. 470th Field Co.R.E.

Orders for Bridging the ESCAUT River.

As soon as the situation allows, the 467th Field Co.R.E. will bridge the ESCAUT River for Field Guns and First Line transport.

For this work, the whole of the bridging equipment of the three Field Companies will be placed, with personnel and six-horse teams complete, at the disposal of the O.C. 467th Field Co.R.E.

O.C. 470th Field Co.R.E. will give the O.C. 467th Field Co. R.E. all the assistance he can - up to the loan of two sections.

From information obtained up to date, it would appear that the best point at which to effect a crossing will be at the sluice L I.14.b.5.4. along the East bank of the river to the sluice I.8.d.8.4. and thence due East.

On receipt of the message "Bridge" the O.C. 467th Field Co. R.E. will throw bridge across at the above points as quickly as possible.

~~Int-eh~~ In the meantime, every effort will be made to get the Infantry across at ~~the above points as quickly~~ as many points as possible by light bridges, rafts and ferries.

Probably, the simplest method will be to make light rafts: secure one or two according to width of gap to cables stretched as tight as possible across the River and well secured at either end, using them as piers instead of pontoons for a light roadway of planks.

A supply of planks must be at hand for the infantry to take forward and lay across dykes and ditches.

O.C. 467th Field Co.R.E. will get his bridging equipment forward to H.23.cent. as soon as the situation allows.

Os.C. 469th and 470th Field Coys.R.E. will instruct the Officer or senior N.C.O. in charge of their respective bridging trains to report to O.C. 467th Field Co.R.E. and be ready to move at a moment's notice.

If Field Companies.R.E. receive the message 'Bridge' from DADA, they will not wait for any confirmation from C.R.E. but carry on - this will be done to save time.

Acknowledge.

22.10.1918.

Lieut.Colonel R.E.
C.R.E 59th Division.

Copies to: 59th Divn.G.
59th Divn.Q.
177th Inf. Bde.

WAR DIARY

of

HEADQUARTERS R.E.
29th Division

Vol XXII

1st Jan 1918 to 31st Jan 1918

WAR DIARY or **INTELLIGENCE SUMMARY**

Army Form C. 2118.

HEADQUARTERS R.E. 59 DIVISION

NOVEMBER 1918

Place	Date	Hour	Summary of Events and Information	Remarks and references to Appendices
SAILLY-LEZ- LANNOY	1.11.18		The 3 Field Companies 467", 469" & 470" employed upon Roads from Sailly-Lez-Lannoy to the River Schelt. 467" Field Coy also engaged on Bridging Equipt/42,000 operations across the Schelt & preparation for River Transport Bridge. Lt. G.V. Gibbs 469" Field Coy. Wounded whilst attached 467 Field Coy on Bridge operations at the Schelt. 59th Div. Order No 176 received re Portuguese 14th Batt.) transferred to 57th Division.	Sailly sheet 27 Bridging Equipt/42,000
"	2.11.18		Field Companies employed on Roads, clearing ditches & also Bridge operations on the Schelt.	H.P.
"	3.11.18		Field Companies employed on Roads, clearing ditches etc. Bridge operations on the Schelt.	H.P.
"	4.11.18		Field Companies employed on Roads, clearing ditches, also Bridge operations on the Schelt, forming Footholds on East bank of the Schelt from I.8.d.2.3. to I.14.d.1.1.	H.C.
"	5.11.18		Field Companies employed on Roads, clearing ditches. 467" Field Company & Section of 470" Field Coy. commenced Pontoon & Trestle Bridge across the SCHELDT at I.14.b.6.3. for 1st Line Transport.	H.C.

Army Form C. 2118.

WAR DIARY
or
INTELLIGENCE SUMMARY.
(Erase heading not required)

Instructions regarding War Diaries and Intelligence Summaries are contained in F. S. Regs., Part II. and the Staff Manual respectively. Title pages will be prepared in manuscript.

Place	Date	Hour	Summary of Events and Information	Remarks and references to Appendices
SAILLY-LEZ-	6.11.18		467th Field Coy Coy completed pontoon & Trestle Bridge	Apx F 37
LANNOY			across the Canal Schelolt at I.14.6.3. for 1st Line Transport	1/40,000.
			C.R.E. issues Orders for Plot of Forward Field Coy (467th) by 469th Field Coy	
			R.E. the Continuation of Bridging Operations to work during and beyond	
			advance. Apx line Nov. 1. 59th Div Warning Order to 177th received	J.T.
"	7.11.18		469th Field Coy relieve 467th Field Coy at H29.a.6.7 & 467th Field Coy move back to	
			Sinavoned Quarries at G29.a.5.b. 469th Field Coy take over all Bridging	
			Equipment, & Operations with Schelolt. Also whilst on section to advance	
			from Bruges. 470th Field Company Employed on Road. 59th Div. Order	H.T.
			No.172 Received dictating relief of 177th Brigade by 178th Brigade on 8/9th November.	
	8.11.18		Field Company employed on Roads. 469 Field Coy R.E. also on Bridging operation	
			on Schelolt. 1st Lieut. J.A. Cochran. reported for duty to 470th Field Coy R.E.	
			Authority D.A.G. C.B. 869 2/11/18.	J.T.
RAMEGNIES-	9.11.18		C.R.E. Headquarters moves to RAMEGNIES-CHIN. 469th Field Coy R.E. employed	
CHIN.			on Bridging Operations across the Schelolt. Moves to ESQUELMES I.14.c.9.4.	
			470th Field Coy R.E. Moves to OBIGIES I.21.b.3.2. Apples in Orders from River to OBIGIES H.T.	

A6945 Wt. W14422/M1160 350,000 12/16 D. D. & L. Forms/C, 2118/14.

WAR DIARY
or
INTELLIGENCE SUMMARY.

(Erase heading not required.)

Army Form C. 2118.

Instructions regarding War Diaries and Intelligence Summaries are contained in F. S. Regs., Part II. and the Staff Manual respectively. Title pages will be prepared in manuscript.

Place	Date	Hour	Summary of Events and Information	Remarks and references to Appendices
RAMEGNIES CHIN.	10.11.18		469th Field Coy R.E. employed on Pontoon Bridge Operations at I.14 & S.4. About 37 across the SCHELDT. 470th Field Coy R.E. employed in Sthrance on Roads.	1/14 a.1.6.
			Tractive East of the SCHELDT to VELAINES. 467th Field Coy R.E. moved to RAMEGNIES CHIN I.5d.2.9	H.T.
"	11.11.18		467th Field Coy R.E. moved to BRULLE J.15.a.1.6. temporarily on Roads & Craters East of the SCHELDT to VELAINES. 470th Field Coy R.E. employed on Roads & Craters East of the SCHELDT to VELAINES. 469th Field Coy R.E. employed on maintenance of Pontoon Bridge across the SCHELDT. 59th Division Order No 180 received, concentration of Division to cessation of hostilities. Hostilities ceased at 11.00. 421st Field Coy R.E. attached to C.R.E. Sparwork.	21.C.
"	12.11.18		C.R.E. moved 25th K.R.R.C.(P) to Q.34.d. to work on Railway. 470th Field Coy R.E. move to LEUZE R.35. to work on Railway under A.D.T.S. 467th Field Coy R.E. & 3 Portuguese Field Coys R.E. employed on Roads & Craters East of the SCHELDT to VELAINES. 421st Field Coy R.E. with 469th Field Coy R.E. employed on Bridge Operations & opening up of Sluices. 59th DIVISION Order No 179 received. Move of 1st, 2nd & 3rd Portuguese Batties & Portugue Div Arts E. 59th Div.	21.C.

WAR DIARY
or
INTELLIGENCE SUMMARY.

(Erase heading not required.)

Army Form C. 2118.

Instructions regarding War Diaries and Intelligence Summaries are contained in F. S. Regs., Part II. and the Staff Manual respectively. Title pages will be prepared in manuscript.

Place	Date	Hour	Summary of Events and Information	Remarks and references to Appendices
RAMEGNIES CHIN	13.11.18		470th Field Coy. R.E. employed on Railways on the area of LEUZE, 467th Field Coy employed on Roads & Culverts SCHELDT & VELAINES, also the 3rd Portugese Field Coy R.E. 469th Field Coy R.E. employed on Bridging operations & Sluices RIVER SCHELDT, note the 421st Field Coy, R.E. 59 Div. Order No 182 received. XI Corps Mounted Troops attached to Division to move to HEM.	Sheet 37 1/40,000 N.T.
"	14.11.18		467th Field Coy R.E. & 3rd Portugese Field Coy R.E. employed on Roads & Culverts East of the RIVER SCHELDT to VELAINES. 469th Field Coy R.E. & 421st Field Coy R.E. employed on Bridging operations & Sluices RIVER SCHELDT Iy & S.W. 59th Division Order No 183 received, concentration of Division in WATTIGNIES. 470th Field Coy. R.E. employed on Railways at LEUZE.	Y.
"	15.11.16		467th Field Coy R.E. moved to WILLEMS, 469th Field Coy moved to AUSTANE. 470th Field Coy R.E. employed on Railways at LEUZE. 59th Division Order 184 received. attack. Division WATTIGNIES (Apx 135)	Y
WATTIGNIES	16.11.18		C.R.E. Headquarters moved to WATTIGNIES. 467th Field Coy R.E. moved to FROIDMT 469th Field Coy. R.E. moved to SECLIN. 470th Field Coy R.E. employed on Railway at LEUZE (Apx 37)	Sheet 36 1/40,000 N.T.

Army Form C. 2118.

WAR DIARY
or
INTELLIGENCE SUMMARY.
(Erase heading not required.)

Instructions regarding War Diaries and Intelligence Summaries are contained in F. S. Regs., Part II. and the Staff Manual respectively. Title pages will be prepared in manuscript.

Place	Date	Hour	Summary of Events and Information	Remarks and references to Appendices
WAITIGNIES	17.11.18		470th Field Coy R.E employed Railway Sidings at LEUZE (Sheet 37) 467th Field Coy R.E & 469th	Sheet 36
			Field Coy repairing Billets etc	1/40,000. H.C.
"	18.11.18		470th Field Coy R.E moves to RAIN (Sheet 37) 467th Field Coy R.E. & 469th Field Coy	
			R.E. repairing Billets etc	H.C.
"	19.11.18		470th Field Coy R.E moves to TEMPLEUVE (Sheet 17) 467th Field Coy R.E employed on building	
			Group's Clerks NCO's then moves employed on LILLE. 469th Field Coy R.E.	
			employed on building Baths at SECLIN. 59th Division Order No 187 received	
			detached move up 470th Field Coy R.E into Divisional Area	H.C.
"	20.11.18		470th Field Coy R.E moves to PETIT RONCHIN. 467th Field Coy R.E employed	
			on Divisional Club LILLE. 469th Field Coy R.E employed on Baths at	
			SECLIN.	H.C.
"	21.11.18		470th Field Coy R.E employed on work for Divl. Club at LILLE. 467th Field Coy R.E.	
			employed on work at Divl Club Lille. 469th Field Coy R.E employed on Baths	
			at SECLIN	H.C.
"	22.11.18		470th Field Coy R.E. employed on work for Divl Club at LILLE. 467th Field Coy R.E.	
			employed on work at Divl Club LILLE. 469th Field Coy R.E employed on Baths at SECLIN	H.C.

A6945 Wt. W11432/M1160 350,000 12/16 D.D. & L. Forms/C/2118/14

WAR DIARY or INTELLIGENCE SUMMARY

Army Form C. 2118.

Place	Date	Hour	Summary of Events and Information	Remarks and references to Appendices
WATIGNIES	23/11/18		467th Field Coy: employed at Divisional Armourers Club LILLE. 469th Field Sheet 36	1/40,000.
			Coy: employed on Baths at WATIGNIES; completes Section Foulers 470th	
			Field Coy: R.E. employed on work for Divl. Club. Field Cos. are engaged	
			also on Education Schemes etc.	H.T.
"	24/11/18		Field Companies employed as above. 59th Division Warning Order No 166	
			received. Division to prepare to move to BARLIN, BRUAY & HOUDAIN	H.T.
			area on Nov 29th & 30th. LENS SHEET 1/100,000	
"	25/11/18		Field Companies employed as above. 59th Division Administrative Instruction	H.T.
			No 34 received. Details of preparations	
"	26/11/18		467th Field Coy. R.E. employed on work at Divisional Club. 469th Field Coy R.E.	
			employed on workshop for Club. Ballts at WATIGNIES 470th Field Coy R.E.	
			employed on work for Divl Club. Field Companies engaged on Education questions	H.T.
"	27/11/18		Field Companies employed as above and Education questions	H.T.
"	28/11/18		One section 470th Field Company moved to new area to lay out Billets 469th	
			Field Coy later to Posses BARLIN. 469th Field Coy Section to NOEUX LES MINES	
			470th Field Coy to BRUAY. Remainder of Field Companies employed as above.	H.T.

A6945 Wt. W11442/M1160 350,000 12/16 D. D. & L. Forms/C/2118/14.

Army Form C. 2118.

WAR DIARY
or
INTELLIGENCE SUMMARY.
(Erase heading not required.)

Instructions regarding War Diaries and Intelligence Summaries are contained in F. S. Regs., Part II. and the Staff Manual respectively. Title pages will be prepared in manuscript.

Place	Date	Hour	Summary of Events and Information	Remarks and references to Appendices
WATTIGNIES	29.11.18		One Section Special Field Coy R.E. employed on repairing R&RLs in own area (Bachan, Mousu, Les Mares & Cluny) areas. Sheet LENS 1/100,000	sheet 36 1/40,000
			467th Field Coy R.E. employed on work at Sivrement Church MLF. 469th	
			& 470th Field Coys R.E. employed on work for Sivrement Church 469th Field	
			Coy R.E. completed Bath at WATTIGNIES. Field Coys R.E. employed	
			on Education Question.	A.P.
	30.11.18		Three Field Coys Companies employed as above.	A.C.

A. Taylor Lieut. R.E.
for Captain & Adjutant
59th Divisional R.E.
Dec 1st 1918.

SECRET.

O.C. 467th Field Co. R.E.
O.C. 469th Field Co. R.E.
O.C. 470th Field Co. R.E.

Relief of the Forward Field Company and Orders for
the continuation of the Bridging of the ESCAUT River
and work during subsequent advance.

----

1. If the enemy is still holding the high ground in I.24 and 30 to-morrow morning, the 7th instant,

    (a) The 469th Field Co. R.E. and 'B' Coy. 25th Bn. K.R.R.C.(P). will relieve the 467th Field Co. R.E. and 'A' Coy. 25th Bn. K.R.R.C.(P).
    (b) The O.C. 469th Field Co. R.E. will at once place a section at the disposal of the G.O.C. 177th Infantry Brigade.
    (c) The pontoons in the existing bridge at I.14.b.5.4. will at once be replaced by trestles.

2. As soon as the situation allows

    (a) The culvert at I.9.c.5.2. will be bridged for 1st.Line Transport.
    (b) The O.C. 470th Field Co. R.E. will detail one section to report to G.O.C. Advanced Guard Brigade to relieve the section already supplied by the 469th Field Co. R.E.
    (c) The O.C. 470th Field Co. R.E. will detail one Officer and a few intelligent N.C.O's and Sappers (preferably miners) to go in advance and search roads and road diversions for craters and booby traps. It is thought that the level crossing at I.9.d.1.1. is mined.
    (d) The 470th Field Co. R.E. less one section, and 'C' Coy. 25th Bn. K.R.R.C. (P). will cross the ESCAUT River by the footbridges and proceed to clear the roads and fill in any craters along the Divisional Road in order that the Field Guns and 1st.Line Transport may follow as close behind the advancing infantry as possible.
    (e) As soon as the 469th Field Co. R.E. and 'B' Coy. 25th Bn. K.R.R.C (P) have completed the previously mentioned bridges they will follow the 470th Field Co. R.E. and carry out any further repairs required.

3. The 467th Field Co. R.E. and 'A'Coy. 25th Bn. K.R.R.C.(P) will be in Divisional Reserve.

4. If the enemy vacate the high ground in I.24. and 30. to-night , the 467th Field Co. R.E. will continue the bridging operations and all works detailed to the 469th Field Co. R.E., the latter being in Divisional Reserve until the relief can be carried out.

    ACKNOWLEDGE.

6th November 1918.

                                           Lieut. Colonel, R.E.
                                           C.R.E. 59th. Division.

        Copies to :-   59th. Divn G.
                        59th. Divn Q.
                        25th Bn. K.R.R.C.(P).
                        177th Infantry Brigade.
                        C.E. XI Corps.
                        War Diary (2).
                        File.

VOL: XXIII.

98/23

WAR DIARY

OF

A.H.Q 59TH Divl: R.E

FOR MONTH OF

DECEMBER,

1918.

CONFIDENTIAL.

WAR DIARY

INTELLIGENCE SUMMARY.

DECEMBER   HEAD QUARTERS R.E. 59 DIVISION

Army Form C. 2118.

Place	Date	Hour	Summary of Events and Information	Remarks and references to Appendices
WATTIGNIES	1/12/18		The field engineers continue instruction under the Educational Scheme, and the 467 Field Coy continue work on 59 Division transport park and their club for NCOs and men in LILLE	Sheet 36 1/120,000
"	2/12/18		CRE went down to visit and MOEUX-LES-MINES to arrange for repair of billets, water supply posts and housing of pumping plants. Transport of 490 Field Coy RE proceeded by route march to FOURNES	
"	3/12/18		Transport of 490 Field Coy RE proceeded by route march for BRUAY area	
		1330	59 DIVISION ORDER No. 189 Copy 5 received detailing route of Division to the HOEUX-LES-MINES - BRUAY area on 4th, 5th and 6th inst. 59 Divisional Administrative instruction No.35 copy 21 received	
"	4/12/18		490 Field Coy RE proceed by Bus to BRUAY area. The transport continuing its journey from FOURNES to BRUAY by route march	
"	5/12/18		469 Field Coy RE have dismounted personnel proceed by bus to HOEUX-LES-MINES area and transport by route march. Amendments to 59 Div order No.189 Copy 5 received CRE went by car to inspect work in new area	
"	6/12/18 11 am		CRE moved Head Quarters from WATTIGNIES to VERQUIN (south of BETHUNE) 467 Field Coy RE moved by bus and route march to BARLIN area	
VERQUIN				

Army Form C. 2118.

WAR DIARY
—of—
INTELLIGENCE SUMMARY.
(Erase heading not required.)

Instructions regarding War Diaries and Intelligence Summaries are contained in F. S. Regs., Part II. and the Staff Manual respectively. Title pages will be prepared in manuscript.

Ordnance

Place	Date	Hour	Summary of Events and Information	Remarks and references to Appendices
VERQUIN	7.12.18		467 Field Coy RE repairing huttel camps in BARLIN area occupied by 176 INF Bde and proceed with their educational schemes. 469 Field Coy RE repairing huttel Camps and billets in NOEUX-LES-MINES area occupied by 177 INF Bde, and proceed with their educational scheme. 470 Field Coy RE repairing huttel Camps in VAUDRICOURT area occupied by Divisional troops including artillery and proceed with their educational schemes. Site of Divisional RE School chosen at MINX KS P.34 - This site has numerous workshops with stoves in. A blitzer and blacksmith, tin smiths and fitters shops in good working order.	Appx 443 1/40440 Appx Appx
"	9.12.18	10am	CRE held conference of RE Field Companies, as to the education to Lewis in preparation general repairs of billets & camps	Appx
"	10.12.18		Companies continue their work as detailed in entry for the 7th	Appx
"	11.12.18		CRE held conference of OC Field Coys at 9.30. CRE attended a conference at DHQ at 11 am upon Educational Scheme.	Appx
"	12.12.18		Field Companies continue work as detailed in entry for the 7th	Appx
"	13.12.18		Field Companies continue work as detailed in entry for the 7th	Appx

Army Form C. 2118.

WAR DIARY
or
INTELLIGENCE SUMMARY.   Continued —
(Erase heading not required.)

Instructions regarding War Diaries and Intelligence Summaries are contained in F. S. Regs., Part II. and the Staff Manual respectively. Title pages will be prepared in manuscript.

Place	Date	Hour	Summary of Events and Information	Remarks and references to Appendices
VERQUIN	16.12.18		467 Field Coy RE working upon Hutment Camps at 176 Bde area & looking after waterpoints and undertaking the training of men in the Bofo in Carpentry, Asmoking and Painting. Also taking a Colonial class party in Kitchen Refuse and drawing Rats Management, storing & issue of Carpentry, Bricklaying, and general use of tools. 469 Field Coy RE proceeded line mis Reclin and HQ transport to LIGNY ST FLOCHEL to work upon the Corps Concentration Camp. Morning returns making approx huts in 173 Rds were. 470 Field Coy RE, working upon technical changes in winzing troops and running the ETS school of fr 150 students given instruction in the Joiners pattern makers Carpenters Wheelwrights Blacksmiths Tinsmiths Plumbers Glaziers Interior Decorators and Bricklayers. T/Lt READ reported for duty with 469 Field Coy RE. Companies carry on with work as detailed above. Lt H TAYLOR proceeded to England under demobilisation scheme	Kus 44/13 1/45000 Kus Kus Kus Kus Kus

WAR DIARY
INTELLIGENCE SUMMARY. Continued
(Erase heading not required.)

Army Form C. 2118.

Instructions regarding War Diaries and Intelligence Summaries are contained in F. S. Regs., Part II. and the Staff Manual respectively. Title pages will be prepared in manuscript.

Place	Date	Hour	Summary of Events and Information	Remarks and references to Appendices
VERQUIN	24/10/15		Units proceed with their work	Photo 44.B 4/10000
"	24/10/15		Lt F.S. DAPP reports to 467 FIELD Coy for duty vice 2ᴸᵀ M.H. JONES	Khun
"	25/10/15		}	Khun
"	26/10/15		} funeral holiday for the men.	Khun 1/10000
"	27/10/15		Work commenced again as per entry for the 14ᵗʰ	Khun
"	28/10/15		S9 Division under M.190 receives orders moving north of 17ᵗʰ Bde Group	
"			viz 467 FIELD Coy R.E. to HONDEGHEM (2 miles north of HAZEBROUCK)	Khun
"			467 Field Coy proceeded by route march to ST VENANT on their	
"	29/10/15		way to HONDEGHEM	Khun
"	30/10/15		469 Field Coy Then 1st Depôt & Transport at LIGNY DE ROCHER working for Corps on their concentration camp. Remaining sections working upon hutted camps in 177 Bde	
"	31/10/15		467 FIELD Coy RE moved to HONDEGHEM and	
"			470 FIELD Coy continued the work as detailed above	
"			2ᴸᵀ M.H. MILLER reported to 470 FIELD Coy	W. Hamilton? Capt. R.E. for CRE S.M.D. 31/10/15

VOL XXIV

CONFIDENTIAL

WAR DIARY

of

Headquarters

59th Divl. RE

for

January 1919

WAR DIARY or INTELLIGENCE SUMMARY

Army Form C. 2118.

Place	Date	Hour	Summary of Events and Information	Remarks and references to Appendices
VERQUIN K.5.a.6.8	1919. Jan 1st		Disposition of Field Companys as:- 467 F Coy attached for work under 19th Corps Army Hqr F Coy at LIGNY-ST-FLOCHEL building Concentration Camp (1st Army) (T.30.c) 471 F Coy Hd Qrs at VAUDRICOURT (K.4.b.5.6) working on reconstruction work. Repairs to billets & camps in 57th Divn area.	Sheet 44 B 1/40,000
	Jan 2		471 Field Coy continued work in camps - Captain K.N.MOSS (Adjutant) proceeded to ENGLAND under Demobilization Scheme - Pivotal Officer (Mining) LIEUT. A.O.F.COBLEY M.C. took over duties as Adjutant.	
	Jan 3		471 Field Coys continued work in camps.	
	Jan 4		471 F Coys continued work in camps.	
	Jan 5		471 F Coys continued work in camps - 470 F Coy moved 3 sections to OLHAIN (P.24.b.2.7) reconstructing camp huts for Horse Demobilization. Capt. B.C.DEACON R.E. struck off strength of 467 Fd Coy and posted from 29-10-18 - Authority (A.G. 65/5217 (O) 25.12.18).	
	Jan 6		471 Field Coys continued work in camps. 470 Field Coy continued work in camps — McA 59 Field Coy entrained at LIGNY STATION (T.23.d.6.0) proceeding to DUNKERQUE to join 176 Inf. Brigade.	
	Jan 8		471 Field Coys continue work in camps.	
	Jan 9		470 Field Coy working in camps. {LIEUT. A.O.F.COBLEY confirmed in appointment as from 2/1/19 as Adjutant. Authority G.O. XI Corps, A.3485, 2/1/19	
	Jan 10		470 Field Coy working in camps.	
	Jan 11		470 Field Coy working in camps.	

Army Form C. 2118.

WAR DIARY
or
INTELLIGENCE SUMMARY.
(Erase heading not required.)

Instructions regarding War Diaries and Intelligence Summaries are contained in F.S. Regs., Part II. and the Staff Manual respectively. Title pages will be prepared in manuscript.

Place	Date	Hour	Summary of Events and Information	Remarks and references to Appendices
VERQUIN K.S.a.6.8	1919			SHEET 44.13 1/40,000
	Jan 12		470 Field Coy working in Camps. AM6	
	Jan 13		470 Field Coy working in Camps - 467 Field Coy moved to DUNKIRK, Embarkation Camp, G.6.(Sheet 19.)	AM6
	Jan 14		470 Field Coy working in Camps. AM6	
	Jan 15		470 Field Coy working in Camps. AM6	
	Jan 16		Major (A/Lt Col) L.T. COUSSMAKER, M.C., R.E. awarded D.S.O.	
			Capt Lieut (A/Capt) G.L. BRONSDON, 469 Field Coy R.E. awarded M.C. } Authority
			Major (A/Lt Col.) L.T. Coussmaker. M.C., and } Div. R.O.
			Mention in Despatches: { LIEUT A.O.F. COBLEY- 467 Field Coy R.E. No 2063 dated 16/1/19
			{ No 486803, S.S. (A/Serjt) E. FRYER - 470 Field Coy R.E.} AM6
	Jan 17		470 Field Coy working in Camps - erecting hut, running Jumbos, plans, etc. } AM6
	Jan 18		Ditto. AM6. Serjt Lieut ELLIS G.H.S, 470 Field Coy proceeds to U.K. attends (STUDENT)
	Jan 19		Ditto. AM6	
	Jan 30		Ditto. AM6	
	Jan 21		Ditto. AM6	
	Jan 22		Ditto. AM6	
	Jan 23		Ditto. AM6 No 486762	
	Jan 24		Ditto. AM6	
	Jan 25		Ditto - AWARD - Driver (T/Cpl) MOSS, C, 470 Field Coy R.E. awarded Meritorious Service Medal. Authority Div. R.O. 2091 dated 25/1/19. AM6

Army Form C. 2118.

WAR DIARY
or
INTELLIGENCE SUMMARY.
(Erase heading not required.)

Instructions regarding War Diaries and Intelligence Summaries are contained in F. S. Regs., Part II. and the Staff Manual respectively. Title pages will be prepared in manuscript.

Place	Date	Hour	Summary of Events and Information	Remarks and references to Appendices
VERQUIN K.5.a.6.8	1919 JANY 26		470 Field Coy securitywork in camps. AMcK	SHEET 44B 1/40,000
	27		470 Field Coy E. ditto AMcK 2/Lt Walker G.E. returned reported in A.H.Q. still en leaving been transferred to ENGLAND date 4/1/19 Authn. 30/9H and HQ 57 Div. A 80/15/11 dated 27.1.19. AMcK	
VAUDRICOURT K.4.b.2.6	28		CRE Headquarters moved to VAUDRICOURT (K.4.b.2.6) — Field Coy (procees) with work in camps. AMcK	
	29.		Field Coy proceeding general work in camps. AMcK	
	30.		Ditto. AMcK	
	31.		470 Field Coy entrained at NOEUX-LES-MINES STATION proceeding to ETAPLES. AMcK at 16.00 hrs Authority — Movement Order. A/3364/56/30 dated 30/1/19, 57 Div.	

WAR DIARY
or
INTELLIGENCE SUMMARY.

Army Form C. 2118.

WO R8 6-9 25
V.2 25

Place	Date	Hour	Summary of Events and Information	Remarks and references to Appendices
VAUDRICOURT (K.4.b)	1919 Feb 1		Headquarters located with Bde. HdQrs. Two Field Coys (467 and 469) located at DUMKIRK) all available for employment One Field Coy (H70) located at ETAPLES } under L. of C.	SHEET 44 B 1/40,000
			LIEUT (Acting Major) W.R. JAMES. M.C commanding 469 Field Coy proceeded to U.K. under demobilization Scheme.	A/M6
	Feb 2		Battalion and work parties for Feb. 1st	A/M6
	" 3		Ditto	A/M6
	" 4		Ditto	A/M6
	" 5		Ditto	A/M6
	" 6		Ditto	A/M6
	" 7		Ditto	A/M6
	" 8		Ditto	A/M6
	" 9		Ditto	A/M6
	" 10		Ditto (of 467 (NM) Field Cm RE)	A/M6
	" 11		Ditto Lieut. P.W. FYSH } proceed to U.K. under Demob. Scheme 10/2/19.	A/M6
	" 12		Ditto	A/M6
	" 13		Ditto	A/M6
	" 14		Ditto	A/M6
	" 15		Ditto	A/M6

Army Form C. 2118.

WAR DIARY
or
INTELLIGENCE SUMMARY.
(Erase heading not required.)

Place	Date 1919	Hour	Summary of Events and Information	Remarks and references to Appendices
VAUDRICOURT	FEB 16		Location, Brunelun and work carried Feb. 16t	A.M. Sheet 44.9 40/5000
	" 17		Alto. Lt A/Major A.B. FREW. M.G. of 467 Field Coy R.E. proceeded to U.K. under Demob Scheme 17/2/19.	A.M.
	" 18		Ditto. Extract from Div. R.O. No 2155 (18/2/19) — No 488421 Cpl. HORTON. J. of the 469 Field Coy R.E. awarded the MILITARY MEDAL — Authority Third Army No 24/2629/AMS. 14.2.19.	A.M.
	" 19		Ditto	A.M.
	" 20		Ditto	A.M.
	" 21		Ditto	A.M.
	" 22		Ditto	A.M.
	" 23		Ditto	A.M.
	" 24		Ditto. The following officers are struck off strength under authority G.R.O. 5794, having appeared in WAR OFFICE LIST as LEAVE EXTENDED PENDING DEMOB. 2 Lt. JENNINGS. J. 469 Field Coy. original leave expired 25/1/19) Authority Lt. HUMPHREYS. E.H. 470 Field Coy. " " " 6/1/19) HQ 57th Div. A100/53/S9 dated 24.2.19.	A.M. A.M. A.M.
	" 25		Ditto.	A.M.
	" 26		Ditto.	A.M.
	" 27		Ditto.	A.M.
	" 28		Ditto.	A.M.

A.O.R.Colley
Captain, C.R.E.
57 Div. R.E.

Army Form C. 2118.

WAR DIARY
or
INTELLIGENCE SUMMARY.
(Erase heading not required.)

Instructions regarding War Diaries and Intelligence Summaries are contained in F. S. Regs. Part II. and the Staff Manual respectively. Title pages will be prepared in manuscript.

Place	Date	Hour	Summary of Events and Information	Remarks and references to Appendices
VAUDRICOURT (K.4.b)	1919 Mar 1st		R.E. Headquarters located with Divn. H.Qrs. 3rd Field Coys (467 and 469) located at DUNKIRK } all schools for employment. One Field Coy (470) located at ETAPLES } under G. of C. SUMMER TIME commenced force at 23.00 hours, clocks being moved forward one hour.	Sheet 44. B 1/100,000 AP16. AP16.
	Mar 2nd		Distribution of Field Coys and work, same as for March 1st — Lieut Col. L.J. Coussmaker, DSO, M.C. proceeded to DUNKIRK to take over duties of C.R.E. DUNKIRK.	AP16. AP16.
	Mar 3rd		Distribution unaltered, same as for March 1st	AP16.
	Mar 4		Ditto.	AP16.
	Mar 5		Ditto.	AP16.
	Mar 6		Ditto. R.E. Headquarters and Transport moved to BEAUMARAIS in CALAIS AREA by LORRIES.	SHEET CALAIS 15 1/100,000
BEAUMARAIS I.E.9.3.	Mar 7		Work and location of 3 Field Coys as before. Headquarter Transport left VAUDRICOURT, by road for Calais, staying for night at AIRE.	AP16.
	Mar 8		Work and location of 3 Field Coys as before. H.Qrs. Transport continued by road, staying for night at ZUDROVE near MOULLE.	AP16.
	Mar 9		Work and location of 3 Field Coys as before. H.Qrs. Transport arrived at BEAUMARAIS at 6 p.m. Capt. C. GRUMMIT, R.A.M.C. proceeded to join 73rd (N.M) Field Ambulance for duty — Casualty. A.D.M.S. 59 Div.	AP16.
	Mar 10.		Work and location of 3 Field Coys as before.	AP16.
	Mar 11.		Ditto.	AP16.
	Mar 12.		Ditto.	AP16.
	Mar 13.		Ditto.	AP16.

Army Form C. 2118.

WAR DIARY
or
INTELLIGENCE SUMMARY.
(Erase heading not required.)

Instructions regarding War Diaries and Intelligence Summaries are contained in F.S. Regs., Part II. and the Staff Manual respectively. Title pages will be prepared in manuscript.

Place	Date	Hour	Summary of Events and Information	Remarks and references to Appendices
BEAU MARAIS 1.E.9.3.	19/19 MAR 14		Work and location of Field Coys as before.	SHEET CALAIS 13. 1/100,000 A.O.K.
	MAR 15		Ditto	A.O.K.
	MAR 16		Ditto. Reinforcements 1 O.R. from 69 Field Coy reported and forwarded to 467 Field Coy at DUNKIRK	A.O.K.
	MAR 17		Ditto	A.O.K.
	MAR 18		Ditto	A.O.K.
	MAR 19		Ditto. 4 Officers Reinforcements reported to 467 Field Coy for duty: — 2nd Lt. W. PALLETT, 2nd Lt. J.B. RICHARDSON, Lt. E.M. PARKES, 2nd Lt. W.C. JOHNSTON.	A.O.K.
	MAR 20		Ditto.	A.O.K.
	MAR 21		Ditto. ORDERS by wire received from G.H.Q. 3rd ECHELON (C.W.793 dated 20/3/19) — "FIELD COYS OF 59 DIVIS. TO BE REDUCED TO CADREA".	A.O.K.
	MAR 22		Ditto.	A.O.K.
	MAR 23		Ditto. Reinforcements reported they 9.O.R. from 87th Field Coy, 8.O.R. from 69th Field Coy, and 5.O.R. from 70th Field Coy — all forwarded to 467 Field Coy at DUNKIRK.	A.O.K.
	MAR 24		Ditto.	A.O.K.
	MAR 25		Ditto. Reinforcements reported they 2.O.R. from 87th Field Coy and 1.O.R. from 70th Field Coy all forwarded to 467 Field Coy at DUNKIRK.	A.O.K.
	MAR 26		Ditto. Reinforcements reported they 2.O.R. from 70th Field Coy and 1 O.R. from 69th Field Coy all forwarded to 467 Field Coy at DUNKIRK.	A.O.K.
	MAR 27		Ditto. Reinforcements reported they 2.O.R. from 70th Field Coy and 1 O.R. from 87th Field Coy all forwarded to 467 Field Coy at DUNKIRK.	A.O.K.
	MAR 28		Ditto. Instructions received from A.D.M.S. 59 Division. (A.D.M.S. R.912/9) to hand in the various Equipment of the 59 Divis. R.E. to BASE MEDICAL STORES.	A.O.K.

Army Form C. 2118.

WAR DIARY
or
INTELLIGENCE SUMMARY.
(Erase heading not required.)

Instructions regarding War Diaries and Intelligence Summaries are contained in F. S. Regs., Part II. and the Staff Manual respectively. Title pages will be prepared in manuscript.

Place	Date	Hour	Summary of Events and Information	Remarks and references to Appendices
BEAU MARAIS 1.E.9.3.	1919 MAR 29		Work and Location of Field Coys as before.	SHEET CALAIS 13 1/100,000
	MAR 30		Nil.	Nil.
	MAR 31		Ditto. R.E. Hd Qrs Transport moved by road to FRETNUN (2.D.8.9.) Assigned 59 Div Q. 118 Letter 30/3/19.	
			officers Reinforcements reporting duty:-	
			T/Lieut. W.E. HASLOCH. R.E. } To 470 Field Coy on 22.3.19	
			T/2 Lt. C.C. TOLLIT. R.E. }	
			T/Lt A/Major R.E. FRYER. R.E.	
			Lieut. S.F. NAILER R.E. (T.F) } To 469 Field Coy on 27.3.19.	
			Lieut. R.H. SKIPPER R.E. (T.F) }	
			Lt. E.T. HART, 12th Loyal North Lancs } To 470 Field Coy on 29.3.19	
			on Probation. Authority. AG 55/7093(0)	

A.W.Stirling.
Captain R.E.
for CRE 3P.94.

WAR DIARY
INTELLIGENCE SUMMARY.
(Erase heading not required.)

Army Form C. 2118.

Place	Date	Hour	Summary of Events and Information	Remarks and references to Appendices
BEAUMARAIS I.E.9.3	1919. April 1st		R.E. Headquarters located in A 59.W1m H.Q. Gros. Two Field Coys (467 and 469) located at DUNKIRK, accepted for employment under L. of C. One Field Coy (470) located ETAPLES. LT. E.S. MILLARD (469 W. Coy) reported for duty on 31/3/19 as Actg Adjutant	SHEET CALAIS 13 1/100,000 A/616 A/616
	Ap 2		Location and work of Area. Companys as before. Reinforcements forwarded to: 4 O.R. from 87th Field Coy } account to 3 O.R. from 69th Field Coy } 469 Field Coy DUNKIRK 2 O.R. from 70th Field Coy }	A/616 GW
	Ap 3		Ditto. — CAPT. A.O.F. COBLEY. M.C., Adjutant proceeded on leave to U.K.	
	Ap 4		Ditto. — Wire from 3rd Echelon requesting numbers of Officers in Field who wish to apply to extend their service to Loughborough & Volunteers (8) more than one year, (5) more than one year & (10) less than one year. This is a priority order (CW 833). Nil return forwarded 7/4/19. Wood Field Coy.	
	Ap 5		Ditto. — H.2. O.R. from 11th Division reported at these Headquarters today	
	Ap 6		Ditto. — Reinforcements (as above) forwarded today (under 7th HAMLET. 25th K.R.R.) to C.R.E. 1st Western Division	
	Ap 7		Ditto. —	
	Ap 8		Ditto. — 2/LT W.E. HASLOCK, 470 Field Coy posted to COLOGNE R.E. Coy. Instruct Authority A.G. 10336/Compy (O) 26/3/19. Sent 5-4-19 LT. R.M. SKIPPER 469 Field Coy posted to H.Q. MENIN Sub-area. Rest. (Authority A.G. 10336/Adjts (O)) 4/Lt C.C. TOLLET 470 Field Coy posted to 353 E.&M. Co. R.E. LA FLAQUE (Rouen) — A.G. 10336/J.Cr(0) Answered to WH. C.E. Rest.	

Army Form C. 2118.

WAR DIARY
or
INTELLIGENCE SUMMARY.
(Erase heading not required.)

Instructions regarding War Diaries and Intelligence Summaries are contained in F.S. Regs., Part II. and the Staff Manual respectively. Title pages will be prepared in manuscript.

Place	Date	Hour	Summary of Events and Information	Remarks and references to Appendices
BEAU MARIAS I.E.9.3	1919 Ap 9		Work and duties of Field Coy as before. 2/Lt. H.J. HEALY, 467 F.S.Bn Co. posted to 141 Army Troops Co. R.E. (Authority A.G. 10336/14(O) of 28.3.19) Proceeded from unit on 7.4.19. Ditto 2/Lt. W. PALLETT, 467 Field Coy, posted to ROTTERDAM R.E. WORKS, 3rd Class District. (Authority, A.G. 10336/Rotterdam/(O) of 26.3.19.)	
	Ap 10		Ditto. — L/F.D.C. NEWPORT, 470 Field Coy posted to C.E. No 3 Area. (Authority A.G. 10336/3 Area/(O) are not 29/3/19) Ditto Proceeded from unit on 9.4.19.	
			2/Lt J.H. PESHEN, Ditto.	
	Ap 11		Ditto. — Mr. A. Reid, 469 Fields Coy. Proceeded from unit for demobilisation on 7.4.19.	
	Ap 12		Ditto. — Lt E.M. PARKES (S.R), 467 Field Coy, posted to C.E. No 5- Area (Authority 39 Pin. R3806/4/1 — 8 2-4-19) Proceeded from unit on 10.4.19.	
			2/Lt J.B. RICHARDSON, 467 Field Coy posted A.G.E. No. 5- Area (Authority 39 Pin. R3806/1./1. of 3-4-9) Proceeded from unit today.	
	Ap 13		Ditto. — Maj. FRYER, R.E. App. Field Coy posted to the 4th (army) Area H.Q. R.E. Staff (Authority 39 Pin. AJ784/191 of 2-4-19) Proceeded from unit on 10.4.17 L/S.C.F. NAILER, 469 Field Coy. posted to MAHIR Sub Area (Authority A.G. 10336/Mahir (O) dated 26/3/19) Ditto	
	Ap 14		Ditto. —	
	Ap 15		Ditto. —	
	Ap 16		Ditto. —	

Army Form C. 2118.

WAR DIARY
or
INTELLIGENCE SUMMARY.
(Erase heading not required.)

Instructions regarding War Diaries and Intelligence Summaries are contained in F. S. Regs., Part II. and the Staff Manual respectively. Title pages will be prepared in manuscript.

Place	Date	Hour	Summary of Events and Information	Remarks and references to Appendices
BEAU MARAIS I.E.C.9.3.	1919 Ap.17		Work & Locations of Field Coys as before. The Cos are not reduced to Cadre & not ready to embark.	Strs. CALAIS. 13. V/900 cc. Z.W.
	Ap.18.		Ditto. "Good Friday" Capt. A.O.F.COBLEY, M.C. adjutant returned from leave today 9pm	
	Ap.19		Ditto. Q/M Col. L.J. COUSSMAKER, D.S.O, M.C. (R.E.(T)) acting C.R.E. DUNKIRK proceeded to H.Q. 9th HIGHLAND DIVISION, ARMY OF THE RHINE, as C.R.E. on 9/4/19. Authority A.G. G.H.Q. Appointments 2730 dated 4/3/19.	A.W.
	Ap.20		Work and Location of Field Coys as before	A.W.
	Ap.21		Ditto	A.W.
	Ap.22		Ditto.	A.W.
	Ap.23		Ditto	A.W.
	Ap.24		Ditto	A.W.
	Ap.25		Ditto for 467th & A.B.H. Field Coys. The 470 Field Coy arrived at MARDYCK CAMP. Strs. DUNKIRK.	A.W.
	Ap.26		All three Field Coys located at DUNKIRK and Employed under L of C. DUNKIRK 26/4/19. 2nd Lt. W.C. JOHNSON proceeded to C.E. No. 5 AREA on 26/4/19. Authority:- 57 B/no. A. 3806/4/1 dated 3/4/19.	A.W.
	Ap.27.		All three Field Coys located and working L of C.	A.W.
	Ap.28.		Ditto	A.W.
	Ap.29.		Ditto.	A.W.
	Ap.30.		Ditto.	A.W.

A.W. Cobley Captain adjt.

2/357
Army Form C. 2118.

WAR DIARY
or
INTELLIGENCE SUMMARY.
(Erase heading not required.)

Place	Date	Hour	Summary of Events and Information	Remarks and references to Appendices
BEAUMARAIS J.E.9.3.	1919 May 1st		R.E. Headquarters located with 59 Div. H.Qrs. Three Field Coys located at DUNKIRK, Available for Employment under R.E. O.	SHEET CALAIS 13 1/100,000 A916
	May 2		Ditto	A916
	" 3		Ditto	A916
	" 4		Ditto. Routing from Court of Inquiry held 17/3/19 orders in F.out. Presentation charge of 59 Div. H.Qrs. R.S.M. TIDNAM, J.A. ordered to proceed to U.K. as directed by G.O.C. 59 Div. and confirmed by G.O.C. L of C. Anthority 59 Div. D.H.Q. A.355/110 A.F.W. 3067 forwarded Command Paymaster Base.	A916 A916
	" 5		Ditto. Confidential Report after 1 month probation on LIEUT. E.J. HART, 1st Lond.N.Div's forwarded to Div. H.Q. G109 13/ay.	A916
	" 6		Ditto.	A916
	" 7		Ditto.	A916
	" 8		Ditto. Instructions received to reduce all 3 field Coys labors C3/C4 to 2 on 40% Authority L of C. C.R. 3172/M.O.8 and 59 Div. M.Q. D.R. 71 22 9/519	A916 A916
	" 9		Ditto.	A916
	" 10		Ditto.	A916
	" 11		Ditto. No 27601 R.S.M. TIDNAM, J.A. proceeded to U.K. on 1115/19 as receiving orders under G.R.O. 6061.	A916
	" 12		Ditto	A916
	" 13		Ditto	A916
	" 14		Ditto	A916
	" 15		Ditto	A916

Army Form C. 2118.

WAR DIARY
or
INTELLIGENCE SUMMARY.
(Erase heading not required.)

Instructions regarding War Diaries and Intelligence Summaries are contained in F. S. Regs., Part II. and the Staff Manual respectively. Title pages will be prepared in manuscript.

Place	Date	Hour	Summary of Events and Information	Remarks and references to Appendices
BEAUMARAIS I.E.9.3	1919 May 16		R.E. Headquarters located with Hors. H.Q. Ops Mine Fields Corps (renewed below CADRE A) at DUNKIRK.	SHEET 13 CALAIS A.P.6 1/100,000
	" 17		Ditto.	A.P.6.
	" 18		Ditto. Head. M.S.C. hors and Div. M.S.C Army attached to the H.O.A.S.E. withdrawn on 17/5/19 authority 59 Div. H.Qs Q.46/105 at. 17.5.19.	A.P.6
	" 19		Ditto.	A.P.6
	" 20		Ditto.	A.P.6
	" 21		Ditto.	A.P.6
	" 22		Ditto.	A.P.6
	" 23		Ditto.	A.P.6
	" 24		Ditto. Subard a/c clash — (Balance in hand (Francs 247.90) handed over to C.M.22.59 Base Cashier CALAIS.	A.P.6
	" 25		Ditto.	A.P.6
	" 26		Ditto.	A.P.6
	" 27		Ditto. Hors. Zinebund G.S. Wagon with Services handed over to this H.Qrs. by 59 Divisional Train	A.P.6
	" 28		Ditto. Instructions rec'd for Lieut W.H. MILLER, 470 Defence Subsector, 59 Div. A.P./572 of 27/5/19 D.A.G. CR997/16/5M. (which Respecting Permission to return from, until proceeding in need CADRE	A.P.6
	" 29		Ditto. {Because this is the only officer remaining in need CADRE	A.P.6
	" 30		Ditto.	A.P.6
	" 31		Ditto.	A.P.6

Captain
't Ready, DIVN. R.E.

No. RE 59D
Army Form C. 2118.

WAR DIARY
or
INTELLIGENCE SUMMARY.
(Erase heading not required.)

Instructions regarding War Diaries and Intelligence Summaries are contained in F.S. Regs., Part II. and the Staff Manual respectively. Title pages will be prepared in manuscript.

Place	Date	Hour	Summary of Events and Information	Remarks and references to Appendices
BEAUMARAIS 1919 I.E. 9.3. JUNE 1.			R.E. Headquarters located with 59 Div. H⁰ Qrs; CROREs of 3 Field Coys located at DUNKIRK. Lieut. E.S. MILLARD, 467 Field Coy RE, proceeded to Z.I.K. Estan for DISPERSAL. A.M.	SHEET. CALAIS 13 1/100,000 A.M.
	" 2.		ditto	A.M.
	" 3.		ditto	A.M.
	" 4.		ditto	A.M.
	" 5.		ditto. Field Coys received orders from Base, Dunkirk, thro CRE DUNKIRK to reduce CADRES to EQUIPMENT GUARDS of 1 Off and 13 O/R per Coy. Capt A SWAN (467 Fd Coy) and Capt R.L. Bradon (469 F.Coy) proceeded to Z.I.K. with remainder of CADRES for DISPERSAL	A.M.
	" 6.		ditto	A.M.
	" 7.		ditto	A.M.
	" 8.		ditto	A.M.
	" 9.		ditto	A.M.
	" 10.		ditto	A.M.
	" 11.		ditto	A.M.
	" 12.		ditto	A.M.
	" 13.		R.E. H⁰ Qrs Equipment Guard and all wagons and Equipment moved to DUNKIRK on 13/6/19 arriving 5 p.m. — Located at MARDYCK CAMP, ST POL (G.6.b.5.7.) with 467 Fd Coy (Nwkrk, 59 Pin A.Q. 750 n.b./19) 7.P.M	A.M.
DUNKIRK. G.6.b.5.7.	" 14.		Equipment Guards of all 3 Field Coys and H⁰ Qrs located at DUNKIRK, awaiting Embarkation orders.	A.M.
	" 15.		ditto	A.M.
	" 16.		ditto	A.M.

Army Form C. 2118.

WAR DIARY
or
INTELLIGENCE SUMMARY.
(Erase heading not required.)

Instructions regarding War Diaries and Intelligence Summaries are contained in F. S. Regs., Part II. and the Staff Manual respectively. Title pages will be prepared in manuscript.

Place	Date	Hour	Summary of Events and Information	Remarks and references to Appendices
DUNKIRK G.6.b.5.7	JUNE 17		All 3 Field Coys and Divisional Headquarters R.E. reduced to Equipment Guard awaiting Embarkation.	Appx.
	18		Ditto	A976.
	19		Ditto	A976.
	20		Ditto	A976.
	21		Ditto	A976.
	22		Ditto	A976.
	23		Ditto	A976.
	24		Ditto	A976.
	25		Ditto	A976.
	26		Ditto	A976.
	27		Ditto	A976.
	28		Ditto	A976.
	29		Ditto	A976.
	30		Ditto	A976.

A.S.P. Adley
J. Abernethy, Lt.
59. N.M. Divisional Engineers

Army Form C. 2118.

WAR DIARY
or
INTELLIGENCE SUMMARY.
(Erase heading not required.)

Instructions regarding War Diaries and Intelligence Summaries are contained in F.S. Regs., Part II. and the Staff Manual respectively. Title pages will be prepared in manuscript.

Place	Date	Hour	Summary of Events and Information	Remarks and references to Appendices
DUNKIRK G.6.5.7.	1919. July 1st		Equipment Guards of NCOs and all 3 Field Corps located at Mardyck Camp, Dunkirk awaiting Evacuation orders.	A.M.G.
	2nd		Ditto	A.M.
	3rd		Ditto	Ditto
	4		Ditto	N.M.
	5		Ditto	do.
	6		Ditto	A.M.
	7		Orders received to proceed to England. (Authority – Base, Dunkirk. Q.2737 dated 7/7/19.)	A.M.
	8		Reported to A.M.L.O. Dunkirk and No.1 Camp. Dunkirk. in accordance with instructions from C.R.E. Dunkirk.	A.M.
	9		No.3457/9. E.C. A/Sergt A. Stevens reported from leave to U.K.	N.K.
	10		All wagons and Equipment of HQrs and 3 Field Corps transport to Docks. No.3457/7 E.C. A/Sergt A. Stevens proceeded to C.R.E. No.4 Area, Namur. Authority: {C.E. Brit. Tn. F&F E.1/49/1 – 23/5/19.}	N.K. A.M.
	11		Equipment Guard security ordrs from A.M.L.O. to load equipments to Barges.	A.M.
	12		Orders to load received – Wagons & Equipment of Kent Engineers embarked. Wagons & Equipment of 3 Field Corps not completed.	A.M.
	13		Wolfrik at Docks	A.M.
	14		Wolfrik at Docks – Rupert Roleiar	A.M.
	15		Loading of Barges completed	A.M.
	16		All remaining officers and men of Equipment Guards of HQrs and 3 Field Corps dispatched to Boulogne to Boulogne for Evacuation. Final Entry.	N.K.

A.N. Wolton Capt. R.E.
65th (North Midland) R.E.

www.ingramcontent.com/pod-product-compliance
Lightning Source LLC
Chambersburg PA
CBHW080822010526
44111CB00015B/2591